ALL THE PRAYERS OF THE BIBLE

ALL THE PRAYERS OF THE BIBLE

A Devotional and Expositional Classic

by
HERBERT LOCKYER, Litt. D., F.R.G.S.

*From the Prayers of the Bible we know God
as the One who hears and answers prayer.*

Zondervan Publishing House
Grand Rapids, Michigan

ALL THE PRAYERS OF THE BIBLE
Copyright 1959 by
Zondervan Publishing House
Grand Rapids, Michigan

Zondervan Publishing House,
1415 Lake Drive, S.E.,
Grand Rapids, Michigan 49506

ISBN 0-310-28120-2

Printed in the United States of America

87   88   89 / 29   28

DEDICATED

to

THE CHRISTIAN ENDEAVOUR SOCIETY

in which

Over Fifty Years Ago

I Learned To Pray

PUBLISHER'S FOREWORD

Exclusive of the *Psalms,* which form a prayer-book on their own, the Bible records no fewer than 650 definite prayers, of which no less than 450 have recorded answers.

There is a wealth of expository material for preachers in these Bible prayers, each of which is expounded for our instruction and spiritual benefit. Expository outlines are included with many of the prayers, and this book will unfold a treasure of spiritual enlightenment and edification.

All the Prayers of the Bible is a book not only for preachers, teachers, and Christian workers. It will also function as a rich devotional volume for family worship. The daily reading of the Bible prayer itself, then the author's exposition, will make the hour of worship a season of spiritual uplift. This unique volume should remain a spiritual classic to all saints who believe that "through prayer we grasp eternity."

Contents

and

Index of Prayers

8   CONTENTS AND INDEX OF PRAYERS

Prayers and Prayer in the
Old Testament

I

Prayers and Prayer in the Old Testament

While the full revelation concerning the foundation, form and fruits of prayer are before us in the New Testament, we have ample evidence in Old Testament Scriptures of the efficacy of intercourse with heaven. How those holy men of old could storm the battlements above! When there was no way to look but *up*, they lifted up their eyes to the God who made the hills, with unshakeable confidence. At times their approach to God was both unusually familiar and daring, but they were heard in that they feared.

Prayer, to the patriarchs and prophets, was more than the recital of well-known and well-worn phrases — it was the outpouring of the heart. Beset by perils, persecutions, pain and privations, they naturally turned to God in their need, believing that He was able to redeem them out of all their troubles. If they knew little of the philosophy of prayer, they certainly knew a great deal about its power, as our meditation upon the Word reveals.

Genesis

Man has been described as "a praying animal." When did he commence to pray? How did he originally approach God? What were the first words to be uttered by the creature in conversation with the Creator? In any phase of Bible study undertaken, attention must be given to what Dr. A. T. Pierson calls, "The Law of First Mention." The first reference of a Bible truth usually epitomizes any further development of same. This is so as we come to the subject of *prayer*.

What is prayer? Simplified, is it not the desire, opportunity and privilege of talking with God? Who could it have been, but to God Himself, that Adam as soon as Eve was created said, "This is now bone of my bones, and flesh of my flesh" (2:23, 24). Then the distressing dialogue between God and our first parents reveals how early man had learned to talk to God (3:9-13). At the outset, then, of humanity's course we find that prayer is, as Robert Burns expressed

17

it, "A correspondence fixed with heaven." Family prayer evidently began when the first family was formed.

We cannot be ignorant of the fact that the manner in which Adam addressed God (3:12), and Cain answered Him (4:9), appears to be lacking in the reverence due to Him as the thrice holy One. Sometimes as we shall see more clearly as we proceed, prayer-language is at times somewhat defiant.

Prayer History Begins (4:26)

Then began men to call upon the name of the Lord. — Genesis 4:26b

Several expositors refer to this verse as the first in the Bible in which prayer is mentioned. "Then began men to call upon the name of the Lord." But we cannot agree that it was only now in the 235th year of the world, the date of the birth of Enos, that men began for the first time since the Fall to worship God in prayer and adoration. We believe that our first parents would naturally and instinctively lift their voices to God. With the creation of man, prayer was a dictate of nature, "a constitutioned instinct, inwrought by the Maker." Learned Jews have given us the several forms of prayer, which Adam addressed to God for pardon.

John Milton introduces Adam as proposing to Eve the appropriate advice —

> What better can we do, than to the place
> Repairing, where He judged us, prostrate fall
> Before Him reverent; and there confess
> Humbly our faults, and pardon beg; with tears
> Watering the ground, and with our sighs the air
> Frequenting?

The reference in the text before us, then, cannot be the beginning of individual prayer, but of social worship. The godly heirs of Adam and Eve set out to develop "the deepest instinct of the soul of man," as Carlyle describes worship. The margin reads, "Then began men to call themselves by the name of the Lord." With the coming of Enos, men were conscious of their weakness, and, seeking refuge in God, wished to be distinguished as men who feared Him, and who desired to do His will. A sacredness, previously unknown, was now attached to the name *Jehovah*. One writer suggests that this may have given rise to the practice common to the Jews for centuries of giving names to children in which the name of God is interwoven.

Prayer and Spiritual Progress

(Genesis 5:21-24; Hebrews 11:5, 6; Jude 14, 15)

And Enoch lived sixty and five years, and begat Methuselah: And Enoch walked with God after he begat Methuselah three hundred years, and begat sons and daughters: And all the days of Enoch

were three hundred sixty and five years: And Enoch walked with
God: and he was not; for God took him.   — Genesis 5:21-24
By faith Enoch was translated that he should not see death; and was
not found, because God had translated him: for before his translation he had this testimony, that he pleased God. But without faith
it is impossible to please him: for he that cometh to God must believe that he is, and that he is a rewarder of them that diligently
seek him.   — Hebrews 11:5, 6
And Enoch also, the seventh from Adam, prophesied of these, saying, Behold, the Lord cometh with ten thousands of his saints, to
execute judgment upon all, and to convince all that are ungodly
among them of all their ungodly deeds which they have ungodly
committed, and of all their hard speeches which ungodly sinners
have spoken against him.   — Jude 14, 15

In eight verses the Holy Ghost gives us the brief yet blessed biog-
raphy of Enoch, who "walked with God." Amos asked the question,
"Can two walk together except they be agreed?" (3:3). With God
as his travelling Companion, Enoch must have maintained unbroken
communion with Him, although the Bible does not give us any of
the prayers the patriarch prayed. The same is also true of Noah,
who, like Enoch "walked with God" (6:9). In Genesis 6 to 9, God
is found doing all the talking. No reply from Noah is recorded unless
it be the curse and the benediction of chapter 9:25-27.

What a fellowship divine these two pre-Flood saints must have
experienced! The repeated statement about Enoch walking with God
suggests that he was a progressive saint, for walking implies progress
and spiritual progress is dependent upon unbroken communion with
heaven. The Hebrew word for "walking" signifies "to go on habitually." Thus progress in holiness was the habit of this ancient saint.
Amid the cares of family life and the corruptness of their time, both
Enoch and Noah pleased God. It was Andrew Bonar who suggested
that God and Enoch were in the habit of walking and talking daily
and then one day God said to His companion, "You have come so
far each day of our long pilgrimage together, now come all the way
home with Me." Thus, "he was not, for God took him."

Prayer and the Altar

(Genesis 12-13.)

Now the Lord had said unto Abram, Get thee out of thy country,
and from thy kindred, and from thy father's house, unto a land that
I will shew thee.   — Genesis 12:1
And the Lord appeared unto Abram, and said, Unto thy seed will I
give this land: and there builded he an altar unto the Lord, who
appeared unto him. And he removed from thence unto a mountain on the east of Bethel, and pitched his tent, having Bethel on
the west, and Hai on the east: and there he builded an altar unto
the Lord, and called upon the name of the Lord. — Genesis 12:7, 8
Unto the place of the altar, which he had made there at the first:
and there Abraham called on the name of the Lord. — Genesis 13:4

> Then Abram removed his tent, and came and dwelt in the plain of Mamre, which is in Hebron, and built there an altar unto the Lord.
> — Genesis 13:18

Worship, communion and promise are all bound up in God's call to Abraham, and in his calling upon the name of the Lord. How Abraham replied to the revelation he received, we are not told. Within the Covenant given to Abraham there was the underlying thought that true family life is dependent upon family recognition of God.

Abraham, "the fountain-head of Hebrew hero life," was a man of the altar, which he built before he called upon the name of the Lord (12:7; 13:8). Matthew Henry says of "the friend of God," "Wherever he had a tent, God had an altar, and an altar sanctified by prayer. He erected his own altar that he might not participate with idolaters in the worship offered upon theirs."

The word "altar" means "slaughter-place," and is typical of the fact that the way to God is sprinkled with the blood of the Redeemer. For the fulfilment of his commission, Abraham needed pardon, guidance, comfort, strength, courage and wisdom for which he would plead, knowing that the name of the Lord as a strong tower, covered the faithfulness, mercy and omnipotence he would need.

The altar also indicates that from earliest times, sacrifice accompanied prayer and worship. God had to be approached by His suppliants with gifts, as well as words. Seeking God the people had to sacrifice unto Him (Ezra 4:2). Isaac likewise recognized the same intimate relation between sacrifice and prayer (26:25). Such a combination was also characteristic of heathen religions. When the Philistines captured Samson, they accompanied their praise to Dagon with sacrifices (Judges 16:22). Sacrifice and intercessory prayer were combined by Job (42:8) and Samuel (I Samuel 7:6, 9). In this age of grace our access to God is made possible by Him who became our Altar and the Offering thereon (Hebrews 10:19; 13:10).

In the earlier books of the Bible, God appears to speak more to man, than man does to God. Commands were given and promises made, and early saints had little to do but fulfil the commands and believe the promises (12:1-3; See also 28:14-18). How impressive is the silence of Abraham when the Divine Voice commanded him to offer up his son as a sacrifice (22:2)! It may be that we do too much talking in our prayer periods. We have not developed the art of listening to God's voice speaking to our hearts through His Word. May grace be ours to cultivate the listening side of prayer!

Abraham, as God's friend, was on intimate terms with his Friend. An old divine commenting on Abraham's practice of prayer gives us these two thoughts —

1. All God's people are praying people. As soon will you find a living man without breath, as a living Christian without prayer.

2. Thousands who would approve themselves upright with God must be constant and persevering in religion. Abraham did not leave his religion behind him, as many do, when they travel.

Prayer for an Heir

(Genesis 15)

And Abram said, Lord God, what wilt thou give me, seeing I go childless, and the steward of my house is this Eliezer of Damascus? And Abram said, Behold, to me thou hast given no seed: and, lo, one born in my house is mine heir. — Genesis 15:2, 3

Abraham had to learn that God's delays were not denials. Twenty-five years ago, he received the promise, "Fear not, Abram: I am thy shield, and thy exceeding great reward." Can we wonder at him growing discouraged and questioning the validity of the promise received (12:1-3)? He desired the visible gift of a child, without which, Eliezer of Damascus, his trusted steward, would be his heir. But the promise of a son was renewed and Abraham believed God (15:6). The word for "believed" is "amended." He said "Amen" to God. A sign was asked for and given. A long forecast of four hundred years was granted to Abraham, and his faith was strengthened. The lesson we gather from his prayer is that what God has promised, He will fulfil — in His own good time. How we need the "Amen" of Faith!

> Not only wait, but watch;
> Pray at the door of hope, and sing,
> Faith's finger on the latch.

Prayer — the Language of a Cry

(Genesis 16)

And the angel of the Lord said unto her, Behold, thou art with child, and shalt bear a son, and shalt call his name Ishmael; because the Lord hath heard thy affliction. — Genesis 16:11

If it be true that "prayer knows no language but a cry" then in this sad, short yet suggestive chapter we have a chapter from life. Hagar offered a heart-felt cry in the hour of her deep need. Bitter words had been flung at her by Sarai, her mistress, and Hagar was distressed, sad and lonely, and fled into the wilderness. Then we have a somewhat unique yet assertive sentence, "The Lord hath *heard* thy affliction." We can see and feel affliction but *hearing* it is something of which only God is capable. Hagar's need was her prayer, and in her wilderness God met her. It seemed hard to return from what she had fled, but in obeying, Hagar found rest and joy. Harsh treatment gave birth to one of the loveliest sayings in the Bible, *Thou God seest me.* Possibly Hagar would never have known God, as she came to know Him, had she never felt the anguish of the iron entering her soul. The most difficult journey has a blessed climax when the goal is God. Hagar was comforted by the promise God gave her (16:10, 11).

Ishmael came, the child of a promise God had made to Hagar, who was to become the progenitor of a great multitude. Thus the wounded spirit of the lowly handmaid was comforted as she realized that God's promises are as soothing as His threatenings are alarming. The prayer of Hagar's heart, with no language but its own deep need, was answered in an abundant way. It is ever thus with ourselves. Our need is the prayer God hears and to which He responds.

Prayer and Revelation

(Genesis 17)

And Abraham said unto God, O that Ishmael might live before thee!   — Genesis 17:18

This remarkable chapter justifies the description of Abraham as "the friend of God" (James 2:23). Dr. F. B. Meyer, in his study on Abraham says, "It would almost appear as if these two chapters, 17 and 18, were written to show the familiarity and intimacy which existed between the eternal God and the man who was honoured to be called His friend."

Within the chapter, Abraham was privileged to witness some visible manifestation of the Lord's presence (v. 1) which caused him to fall on his face (v. 3). The American Indians put their ears to the ground when they want to listen for the approach of an enemy — Abraham bows his soul to the earth and listens for the voice of God (v. 17).

Peculiar features of Abraham's intercessory prayer for Ishmael can be noted —

1. It is the first recorded prayer in *form,* was a plea for a father on behalf of his child.
2. It was a prayer asking for more than God had offered to bestow.
3. It was a prayer receiving an immediate answer. The humble supplication of the believing patriarch received the prompt reply of a gracious and prayer-hearing God, "As for Ishmael, I have heard thee" (v. 20).

Abraham's example is a beacon-light, guiding parents to a God who hears prayer for children. Alas, sometimes selfish interests at the back of our prayers for our offspring make it difficult for God to answer!

Prayer for a Wicked City

(Genesis 18, 19)

And Abraham drew near, and said, Wilt thou also destroy the righteous with the wicked? Peradventure there be fifty righteous within the city: wilt thou also destroy and not spare the place for the fifty righteous that are therein? That be far from thee to do after this manner, to slay the righteous with the wicked; and that the righteous should be as the wicked, that be far from thee: Shall not the Judge of all the earth do right? And the Lord said, If I find in Sodom fifty righteous within the city, then I will spare all the place for their sakes. And Abraham answered and said, Behold now, I have taken upon me to speak unto the Lord, which am but dust and ashes: Peradventure there shall lack five of the fifty righteous: wilt thou destroy all the city for lack of five? And he said, If I find there forty and five, I will not destroy it. And he spake unto him yet again, and said, Peradventure there shall be forty found there. And he said, I will not do it for forty's sake. And he said unto him, Oh let not the Lord be angry, and I will speak: Peradventure there shall thirty be found there. And he said, I will not do it, if I find thirty there. And he said, Behold now, I have taken upon me to speak unto the Lord: Peradventure there shall be twenty found there. And he said, I will not destroy it for twenty's sake. And he said, Oh let not the Lord be angry, and I will speak yet but this once: Peradventure ten shall be found there. And he said, I will not destroy it for ten's sake. And the Lord went his way, as soon as he had left communing with Abraham: and Abraham returned unto his place. — Genesis 18:23-33

A study of Bible prayers reveals how God, acting as a human investigator, left His heavenly abode for earth to acquaint Himself with facts about those who needed either His blessing or condemnation (11:5; 18:20-22). It is encouraging to know that God never acts for good or ill towards any of His creatures without a full understanding and appreciation of all circumstances. What God saw in Sodom is all too common in the night-life of any city, namely, the noon-day of hell.

Abraham's intercessory prayer also teaches us that whenever we approach the Lord Most High, we must recognize that His throne is one of Grace (Hebrews 4:16), and that because it is a privilege to come before Him we must think of ourselves as dust and ashes in His sight (18:2). We must humble ourselves in His sight (I Peter 5:6). The only way *up* is *down*. There cannot be true prayer apart from deep humility, or lowliness of spirit. Robert Browning wrote of "that stoop of the soul which is bending up — raises it too." Humility, then, is the first essential of efficacious prayer.

Facing the desolating fury of a justly indignant God, Abraham had one resort, one privilege — he could *pray* for guilty Sodom. With his prayer commences "one of the most remarkable instances of human intercession to be met with in the whole compass of divine revelation, one in which the tender and sympathizing benevolence of Abraham, on the one hand, and the astonishing clemency and forbearance of God, on the other, are portrayed in colours such as the pencil of inspiration alone could present." Abraham's intercession for Sodom proves —

1. The benevolence of good men.
2. The importance of the righteous to a wicked world.
3. The kindness of God towards the guilty.
4. The humility which should ever characterize prayer.
5. The efficacy of intercessory prayer. Such prayer is ever costly — it is the saint's sweat of soul. Abraham carried on his heart the sins and sorrows of Sodom. He "sat where they sat."

But there came a point when his intercession ceased. Why did Abraham finish his plea at ten righteous? Matthew Henry suggests, "Either because he owned they deserved to perish, if there were not so many as ten; as the dresser of the vineyard, who consented the barren fig-tree should be cut down, if one year's trial more did not make it fruitful, Luke 13:9, or because God restrained his spirit from asking further." When God has finally determined the ruin of a place, He forbids it to be prayed for. In respect to Judah, God said to Jeremiah, "Pray not thou for this people, neither lift up cry nor prayer for them, neither make intercessions to me, for I will not hear thee" (7:16; 14:11). Jesus wept over and prayed for Jerusalem, without effect. Not all heart-cries for cities and sinners are answered.

Prayer after a Lapse

(Genesis 20)

So Abraham prayed unto God: and God healed Abimelech, and his wife, and his maidservants; and they bare children. For the Lord had fast closed up all the wombs of the house of Abimelech, because of Sarah Abraham's wife. — Genesis 20:17, 18

Abraham's intercessions for Abimelech, as well as for Sodom (18:22), emphasizes the need and value of intercession, as a phase of prayer, so conspicuous in the Bible (20:7-17). Samuel who regarded intercession as part of his official duty, the neglect of which was a sin (I Samuel 12:23), cried to God for a danger-beset people (I Samuel 7:3, 8; 12:19). Both Moses and Samuel stood before God on behalf of His people. Moses was an incomparable prophet in that nearly all his prayers were intercessions (Deuteronomy 34:10; Exodus 32:31), and his intercessory power was recognized by those for whom he prayed (Numbers 12:13; 21:7). Later on, we expect to return to this absorbing theme of Prophets as Intercessors.

Too often we fail God and man because of our lack of desire for prevailing intercession — the costliest service a Christian can render. John Knox could plead, "O God, give me Scotland, or I die." God gave him Scotland, and his fame as an intercessor was so marked that "Bloody Mary" confessed that she feared the prayers of John Knox more than an army of soldiers.

Prayer of Obedience

(Genesis 22)

And the angel of the Lord called unto him out of heaven, and said, Abraham, Abraham: and he said, Here am I. — Genesis 22:11

In this memorable chapter so illustrative of Calvary, and eloquent with the trials and triumphs of Abraham's faith, much is said of his obedience, but so little of his response to the voice of God. All we have is the brief reply, "Here am I" (22:11). Professor McFadyen calls attention to the fact "that prayers are often absent when we should naturally expect them."

On occasions, when prayers would seem most natural and appropriate, they are conspicuous by their absence. This is true of Jacob and news of his sons (37:34; 45:28), also of Joseph, who, although renowned for his godliness, must have prayed much in the crises of his life. The Bible, however, carries no record of the prayers Joseph offered.

Abraham manifested a deliberate readiness for the fulfilment of the divine command (22:9, 10). We are guilty of going so far and then stopping short (Acts 15:38), but Abraham went as far as God would have him go. The name he gave to the place where God provided a substitute for Isaac — *Jehovah-jireh* — was an expression of faith equivalent to a prayer (22:14).

Prayer for a Bride

(Genesis 24)

And he said, O Lord God of my master Abraham, I pray thee, send me good speed this day, and shew kindness unto my master Abraham. Behold, I stand here by the well of water; and the daughters of the men of the city come out to draw water: And let it come to pass, that the damsel to whom I shall say, Let down thy pitcher, I pray thee, that I may drink; and she shall say, Drink, and I will give thy camels drink also: let the same be she that thou hast appointed for thy servant Isaac; and thereby shall I know that thou hast shewed kindness unto my master.   — Genesis 24:12-14

Eliezer of Damascus, Abraham's eldest servant or steward, was commissioned to find a bride for Isaac and came, relying upon God for guidance, to the town of Nahor. On his journey the servant devoutly prayed for success and his prayer is remarkable, an eighteenth century writer tells us, for three things —

1. For the faith in which it was offered.
2. For the correct views on the character of God it expresses.
3. For the sign for which the pray-er presumed to ask.

Such a prayer offered with complete reliance upon divine faithfulness was sure to be answered, and was *directly* and immediately answered to by God. Success in quest called forth expression of gratitude. Further, the servant's prayer for guidance, beautiful in expression, indicates how the early saints seem to be on familiar terms with God. Prayers, then, were simple, direct and childlike. The servant prayed for a specific sign to guide him to the right woman for Isaac and the answer came almost at once, before he had done speaking to God. There would be fewer broken homes in the world today if only more prayer had ascended for guidance in the selection of a life-companion.

Prayer is a token of thanksgiving. With a grateful heart the servant blessed God for His guidance and goodness (24:26, 27). In passing, we can learn something about the place and posture of prayer. The *sphere* of prayer matters little — the *spirit* is all important (John 4:20-24). Alongside the kneeling camels at the well, Eliezer knelt and presented his request. Prayer in the fields and on a hillside (28:18-20), proves that God is no respector of places. As to *posture,* the servant "worshipped," or more literally, "he prostrated himself."

Prayer for a Barren Wife

(Genesis 25:19-23)

And Isaac intreated the Lord for his wife, because she was barren: and the Lord was intreated of him, and Rebekah his wife conceived. And the children struggled together within her; and she said, If it be so, why am I thus? And she went to enquire of the Lord.. And the Lord said unto her, Two nations are in thy womb, and two manner of people shall be separated from thy bowels: and the one people shall be stronger than the other people; and the elder shall serve the younger. — Genesis 25:21-23

That God hears and answers prayer is proved by Isaac's petition for his childless wife, Rebekah (25:21), and in Leah's prayer for conception (30:17). After twenty years of married life Rebekah is still childless, which condition caused her to be reproached by the daughters of Canaan, as well as a trial to Isaac's faith. In his need, Isaac turned to God and prayed, and as his prayer was in the line of God's purpose, it was sure to be answered (I John 5:14). Notice, too, that Rebekah "enquired" of the Lord. Those twenty years of waiting show that God does not hurry the fulfilment of His plan. It is interesting to note that Isaac had to wait twenty years before Jacob was born. Later on, Jacob endeavored to anticipate Providence by the practice of deceit but had to wait twenty years after he had received the blessing from Isaac before he received the blessing from the Lord (Genesis 27:23 with 32:29).

Prayer Changes Things

(Genesis 26)

And the Lord appeared unto him the same night, and said, I am the God of Abraham thy father: fear not, for I am with thee, and will bless thee, and multiply thy seed for my servant Abraham's sake. And he builded an altar there, and called upon the name of the Lord, and pitched his tent there: and there Isaac's servants digged a well. Then Abimelech went to him from Gerar, and Ahuzzath one of his friends, and Phichol the chief captain of his army. And Isaac said unto them, Wherefore come ye to me, seeing that ye hate me, and have sent me away from you? And they said, We saw certainly that the Lord was with thee: and we said, Let there be now an oath betwixt us, even betwixt us and thee, and let us make a covenant with thee; That thou wilt do us no hurt, as we have not touched thee, and as we have done unto thee nothing but good, and have sent thee away in peace: thou art now the blessed of the Lord. — Genesis 26:24-29

It is impossible to measure the changes wrought by prayer. The chapter before us covers a remarkable transformation in the life of Isaac, whose story begins with trouble and ends in triumph. The transition was the result of prayer. Burgess and Proudlove in their most helpful volume, *Watching unto Prayer,* sum up the truth of this chapter in three words — Violence, Vision, Victory.

1. Violence (17-23). Isaac's failure (7), arising out of the fear of man resulted in conflict. Despite the promises of God, we do not read of any sacrifice or prayer on Isaac's part. He failed in his witness, but God did not fail him (12-14). Isaac came to realize, however, that it was not enough to dig again his father's well: he must return to his father's God.

2. Vision (24-25). God met Isaac's fear with a "Fear not," and through a vision Isaac was transformed, so much so, that "he builded an altar and called upon the name of the Lord."

3. Victory (26-28). Philistines had troubled Isaac but not now. God was with His restored servant and his foes knew it (28). The practice of the presence of God makes possible a distinctive quality of life. Such a life of worship and holiness is in touch with their source.

Prayer As a Vow

(Genesis 28)

And Jacob vowed a vow, saying, If God will be with me, and will keep me in this way that I go, and will give me bread to eat, and raiment to put on, So that I come again to my father's house in peace; then shall the Lord be my God: And this stone, which I have set for a pillar, shall be God's house: and of all that thou shalt give me I will surely give the tenth unto thee.   — Genesis 28:20-22

Israel, being an earthly people, their prayers were more or less related to things of the earth — increase of family, tribe, nation, herds and material possessions (28:3). God-given power to multiply is equivalent to blessing (1:22; 28:3). Jacob, revealing his earnestness, vowed a vow, seemed as if he were driving a bargain with God (28:20-22). Too often, one's attitude in prayer is, "Now God, You do *this* for me, and then I'll do *that* for You."

How suggestive is the phrase, "This place is the gate of heaven" (17). *This place!* Any place where God lets down the ladder is a Bethel. The very place where you are *now* can become the gate of Heaven to your soul.

> God dwells not only where, O'er saintly dust,
>   The sweet bells greet the fairest morn of seven;
> Wherever simple folk love, pray and trust,
>   Behold the House of God, the Gate of Heaven.

Prayer about a Wronged Brother

(Genesis 32)

And Jacob said, O God of my father Abraham, and God of my father Isaac, the Lord which saidst unto me, Return unto thy country, and to thy kindred, and I will deal well with thee: I am not worthy of the least of all the mercies, and of all the truth, which thou hast shewed unto thy servant; for with my staff I passed over this Jordan; and now I am become two bands. Deliver me, I pray thee, from the hand of my brother, from the hand of Esau: for I fear him, lest he will come and smite me, and the mother with the children. And thou saidst, I will surely do thee good, and make thy seed as the sand of the sea, which cannot be numbered for multitude. . . .

And Jacob was left alone; and there wrestled a man with him until the breaking of the day. And when he saw that he prevailed not against him, he touched the hollow of his thigh; and the hollow of Jacob's thigh was out of joint, as he wrestled with him. And he said, Let me go, for the day breaketh. And he said, I will not let thee go, except thou bless me. And he said unto him, What is thy name? And he said, Jacob. And he said, Thy name shall be called no more Jacob, but Israel: for as a prince hast thou power with God and with men, and hast prevailed. And Jacob asked him, and said, Tell me, I pray thee, thy name. And he said, Wherefore is it that thou dost ask after my name? And he blessed him there.

— Genesis 32:9-12; 24-29

Here is a chapter fittingly illustrating how the intensely fervent prayer of a righteous man availeth much. Jacob's prayer is one of the most devout, fervent and successful prayers recorded in the Bible. Summarizing his prayer we note —

1. He approached God as the God of *his father* — a God in covenant. The appeal was to divine faithfulness. Elijah prayed in like manner (I Kings 18:36). This common feature speaks of the continuity of national history and of the gracious link that bound the worshipers to the saints of the past.

2. He addressed God as his *own* God. Jacob pleads God's promises to himself, as well as to his father. When Jacob met the angels of God in the way (32:1), and came to pray to the Divine Wrestler, he employed a mode of address, adding great power to Old Testament prayers.

3. He added to his prayer a deep spirit of self-abasement. He came to see how unworthy he was of divine mercy. With reverence, Jacob declared himself unfit to receive the least of God's mercies. Everything came before him — deceit towards his father: trickery of Esau and of Laban. What else could he do but plead for God to deliver him? But before God could answer Jacob's prayer, He had to deal with *Jacob*.

4. He presented his petition as a believer, deeply concerned for the manifestation of Divine Glory. Alfred Thomas in *Great Prayers of the Old Testament,* writes thus of Jacob — "Himself born in answer to

prayer, in spite of his defeats and blemishes of character, through which he leaves a less favourable impression on the mind than either of the two patriarchs with whom he is joined in equal honour in the New Testament, was himself evidently a firm believer in prayer. It is noteworthy that the example of Jacob is quoted by the first and last of the Minor Prophets (Hosea 12:3, 4, 12; Malachi 1:2)."

5. He illustrated the importance and efficacy of earnest, fervent, agonizing prayer in distressed circumstances. He was, of course, some-what negative in his request. His conscience-smitten mind led him to pray that he might be delivered from the brother he had wronged.

6. He shows that the surest way to prevail with men is to prevail with God. Jacob passes "from the boldness of self-confidence to the boldness of faith," and becomes Israel, the Prince of God. The Hand that touched Jacob's sinew, touched his soul and changed the sup-planter into a saint.

Jacob's joyful confession was that he had seen God face to face (v. 30). J. Sharp, in poetic vein, summarizes for each of us the deep experience of Jacob.

> Lord, I have wrestled through the livelong night
> > Do not depart,
> Nor leave me thus in sad and weary plight,
> > Broken in heart;
> Where shall I turn, if Thou shouldst go away,
> And leave me here in this cold world to stay?
>
> I have no other help, no food, no light,
> > No hand to guide,
> The night is dark, my home is not in sight,
> > The path untried;
> I dare not venture in the dark alone —
> I cannot find my way, if Thou be gone.
>
> I cannot yet discern Thee, as thou art;
> > More let me see,
> I cannot bear the thought that I must pass
> > Away from Thee:
> I will not let Thee go, except Thou bless.
> O, help me, Lord, in all my helplessness.

Prayer — the Motion of a Hidden Fire

(Genesis 39-41; 45:5, 7, 8; 50: 20, 24)

And they said unto him, We have dreamed a dream, and there is no interpreter of it. And Joseph said unto them, Do not interpretations belong to God? tell me them, I pray you.   — Genesis 40:8

And Joseph answered Pharaoh, saying, It is not in me: God shall give Pharaoh an answer of peace.   — Genesis 41:16

Now therefore be not grieved, nor angry with yourselves, that ye sold me hither: for God did send me before you to preserve life.
          — Genesis 45:5

> But as for you, ye thought evil against me; but God meant it unto good, to bring to pass, as it is this day, to save much people alive.
> — Genesis 50:20

The absence of all mention of prayer in the life of Joseph is impressive. "Occasions enough there were for it," says Professor McFadyen. "For long he trod the path of sorrow. He was destitute, afflicted, tormented. It was through a hard discipline of misunderstanding, persecution and imprisonment, that he reached his seat beside the king. Besides, he was a man of noble piety; yet it is never said that he prayed." Yet he must have done, long and hard.

The whole tenor of his life suggests an overwhelming sense of the presence and providence of God as a study of the following references clearly prove (40:8; 41:16, 25, 28, 32, 39; 45:5, 7, 8; 50:20, 24). "The controlling power that the thought of God exercised over him receives its most brilliant illustration in his memorable answer to the woman who tempted him (39:9)." Yet there is no record of a prayer that he offered for deliverance from such an enticing temptation. Joseph himself was a prayer. Such a God-conscious man must have lived in full harmony with God.

Prayer for Blessing upon the Tribes

(Genesis 48, 49)

> The sceptre shall not depart from Judah, nor a lawgiver from between his feet, until Shiloh come; and unto him shall the gathering of the people be. . . .
> Even by the God of thy father, who shall help thee; and by the Almighty, who shall bless thee with blessings of heaven above, blessings of the deep which lieth under, blessings of the breasts, and of the womb: The blessings of thy father have prevailed above the blessings of my progenitors unto the utmost bound of the everlasting hills: they shall be on the head of Joseph, and on the crown of him that was separate from his brethren.   — Genesis 49:10, 25, 26

The strange and many-sided life of Jacob is drawing to a close, and as it does, the patriarch turns to God, and prays for blessing upon the tribes. Such a blessing is in the form of a prayer. Jacob remembered the privilege his ancestors had in being permitted to walk through life in the enjoyment of divine favor. He remembered the mercy of God vouchsafed towards himself in the provision of temporal needs; he remembered Peniel, and wove his remembrances into a prayer, which became the expression of his love (v. 10). Love can find no better way of helping a loved one than that of earnest and believing prayer (Galatians 4:19; 6:18).

Jacob's final hours show us how to die — blessing and praying! "Israel said unto Joseph, Behold I die" (48:21), but he died with his eyes heavenward. May our end be as his! Jesus prayed as He died, not only for His friends, but foes. All who die in the Lord, should have their last hours fragrant with prayers for others.

Exodus

Exodus, from which we have the term *exit*, meaning, "a going out," is another Bible book proving how holy men of old came boldly before God believing that prayer was —

"The slender nerve that moveth the muscles of Omnipotence."

Broadly speaking, this second book of the Pentateuch teaches that Redemption is essential to any relationship with a holy God. Whether we think of worship, salvation or ultimately heaven the same truth applies — "No man cometh unto the Father *but by Me*" (John 14:6). The further truth unfolded in Exodus is that even a redeemed people cannot have fellowship with God unless constantly cleansed from the defilement of sin. Answered prayer is dependent upon purity. "If I regard iniquity in my heart, the Lord will not hear me" (Psalm 66:18).

Another feature of this dramatic book is the presentation of Moses as a mighty intercessor. He personifies the truth that James declares — "The effectual fervent prayer of a righteous man availeth much" (5:16). Powerful intercessions were more than a match for the murmurings of Israel.

Prayer Expressed As a Groan

(Exodus 1, 2)

And it came to pass in process of time, that the king of Egypt died: and the children of Israel sighed by reason of the bondage, and they cried, and their cry came up unto God by reason of the bondage.
— Exodus 2:23

The groans of the people of God in the first two chapters of Exodus were as prayers in the ears of God (2:23). And we read that "God heard their groaning, God remembered . . . God looked . . . God had respect" (2:23-25). Paul reminds us of the groanings of the Holy Spirit, in relation to His intercession on our behalf (Romans 8:27). Often prayers are too deep and too intense for words. They are rather like a sigh heaved from the heart than any formal utterances, as those of the Israelites were (2:11). Yet such inarticulate anguish, prompted by the Spirit, is understood by God and responded to by Him.

Prayer As a Dialogue

(Exodus 3, 4)

And Moses said unto God, who am I, that I should go unto Pharaoh, and that I should bring forth the children of Israel out of Egypt? And he said, Certainly I will be with thee; and this shall be a token unto thee, that I have sent thee: When thou hast brought forth the people out of Egypt, ye shall serve God upon this mountain. And Moses said unto God, Behold, when I come unto the children of Israel, and shall say unto them, The God of your fathers hath sent me unto you; and they shall say to me, What is his name? what shall I

say unto them? And God said unto Moses, I AM THAT I AM: and
he said, Thus shalt thou say unto the children of Israel, I AM hath
sent me unto you.   — Exodus 3:11-14
And Moses said unto the Lord, O my Lord, I am not eloquent,
neither heretofore, nor since thou hast spoken unto thy servant: but
I am slow of speech, and of a slow tongue. And the Lord said unto
him, Who hath made man's mouth? or who maketh the dumb, or
deaf, or the seeing, or the blind? have not I the Lord? Now therefore
go, and I will be with thy mouth, and teach thee what thou shalt
say. And he said, O my Lord, send, I pray thee, by the hand of
him whom thou wilt send.   — Exodus 4:10-13

How profitable it is to go through this remarkable chapter under-
lining the key-phrases, "Moses said unto God" and "God said unto
Moses" (3:13, 14, etc.). True prayer is a two-way channel — we speak
to God: God speaks to us. When Moses sought God about the responsibility of bringing the people out of Egypt his prayer reads like
a dialogue, full of life, in which one speaker seems to argue with the
other. How dominated the conversation was by question and answer!
The whole chapter is characterized by literary beauty (See 3:10-12;
4:10-13). A further example of the speech of God to man and *vice
versa* is to be found in the Book of Jonah (4:9-11).

When we unburden our hearts to God, we should listen for Him to
speak to us through His Word. Prayer is fruitless unless we receive
some reply from Him. Perhaps, as with Moses, it may be a word we
are unwilling to hear, or a word we may argue about and shrink
from as Moses did. A most valuable part of prayer, making it alive
and creative, is to say, as we conclude our talk with God, "Speak,
Lord, for Thy servant heareth."

Another feature of the prayers of Moses is his recognition of the
Lordship of the One approached. His oft-repeated use of the term,
Lord, based upon the commission received (3:13-15), is striking
(4:10, 13; 5:22; See Genesis 18:23-32). The Fatherhood of God was
also recognized which was natural, seeing Israel was known as Jehovah's son (4:22, 23).

Moses was 80 years of age when he was called to the greatest task
of his life and cannot therefore be condemned for his objections
(4:10-18). The three signs, "the rod," "the leprosy," and "water poured
out as blood," assured Moses that God would undertake for him.
"Send someone else," Moses replied to God's call (4:13), and so the
honors were shared with Aaron. Refusing complete reliance upon
God, Moses had to take second best. While he proved to be a help to
Moses, Aaron was also a trial and a hindrance.

Prayer As Complaint
(Exodus 5-7)

And Moses returned unto the Lord, and said, Lord, wherefore hast
thou so evil entreated this people? why is it that thou hast sent me?

For since I came to Pharaoh to speak in thy name, he hath done evil
to this people; neither hast thou delivered thy people at all.
                                                    — Exodus 5:22, 23

After his unsuccessful visit to Pharaoh, Moses appears to border on
impertinence when he addressed God (5:22, 23), which was the same
spirit he manifested when the people tired of manna, complained to
Moses, and Moses went to God somewhat peeved about the matter
(Numbers 10:11-15). God, however, met the impatience of Moses
with patience and consideration (6:1). Moses had to learn that
response to God's call is never easy or a pathway of uninterrupted
success. God did not state when He would deliver His people from
the hand of Pharaoh. He does not always answer in time-table fashion.
A renewed commission was necessary for further seeming disappoint-
ments (6:28, 30). True prayer results in obedience. "Moses and Aaron
did as the Lord commanded" (7:20).

Prayer in League with Omnipotence

(Exodus 8-10)

And Moses went out of the city from Pharaoh, and spread abroad his
hands unto the Lord: and the thunders and hail ceased, and the rain
was not poured upon the earth.   — Exodus 9:33
Then Pharaoh called for Moses and Aaron in haste; and he said, I
have sinned against the Lord your God, and against you. Now therefore forgive, I pray thee, my sin only this once, and intreat the Lord
your God, that he may take away from me this death only. And he
went out from Pharaoh, and intreated the Lord. And the Lord turned
a mighty strong west wind, which took away the locusts, and cast
them into the Red sea; there remained not one locust in all the
coasts of Egypt.   — Exodus 10:16-19

In his contests with Pharaoh, Moses leaned heavily upon God, who,
in unleashing the forces of nature, proved that all power is His, to be
used on behalf of His own.

Hands stretched out towards God, or a sacred shrine, is another of
the Bible postures of prayer (see I Kings 8:12). Open hands towards
heaven indicate human need and divine ability to meet it (9·29;
17:11). Charles Wesley caught the significance of the lifting up of the
hands when he wrote —

> Father, I stretch my hands to Thee,
> No other help I know;
> If Thou withdraw Thyself from me,
> Ah! whither shall I go?

As the time for Israel's deliverance from bondage drew near, Moses,
we read, "intreated the Lord" (10:18), and from the force of the
original it is to be at least inferred that Moses prayed with great
earnestness and intensity of spirit, if not with special energy of
utterance. Those mighty intercessions of his were not mere sets of

words, mechanically repeated, but fervent, intense supplications, pro-
ducing startling results (14:30, 31). The intercessory ministry of
Moses teaches us, at least, two important lessons —
1. We must be ready and willing to pray for all men, even wicked
   men.
2. We must endeavor to preserve and control our temper towards
   others, praying for them affectionately, whatever provocation
   they may heap upon us.

Prayer As Praise

(Exodus 15)

Then sang Moses and the children of Israel this song unto the Lord,
and spake, saying, I will sing unto the Lord, for he hath triumphed
gloriously: the horse and his rider hath he thrown into the sea. The
Lord is my strength and song, and he is become my salvation: he is
my God, and I will prepare him an habitation; my father's God, and
I will exalt him. The Lord is a man of war: the Lord is his name.
Pharaoh's chariots and his host hath he cast into the sea: his chosen
captains also are drowned in the Red sea. The depths have covered
them: they sank into the bottom as a stone. Thy right hand, O Lord,
is become glorious in power: thy right hand, O Lord, hath dashed
in pieces the enemy. And in the greatness of thine excellency thou
hast overthrown them that rose up against thee: thou sentest forth
thy wrath, which consumed them as stubble. And with the blast of
thy nostrils the waters were gathered together, the floods stood upright as an heap, and the depths were congealed in the heart of the
sea. The enemy said, I will pursue, I will overtake, I will divide the
spoil; my lust shall be satisfied upon them; I will draw my sword,
my hand shall destroy them. Thou didst blow with thy wind, the sea
covered them: they sank as lead in the mighty waters. Who is like
unto thee, O Lord, among the gods? who is like thee, glorious in
holiness, fearful in praises, doing wonders? Thou stretchedst out thy
right hand, the earth swallowed them. Thou in thy mercy hast led
forth the people which thou hast redeemed: thou hast guided them
in thy strength unto thy holy habitation. The people shall hear, and
be afraid: sorrow shall take hold on the inhabitants of Palestina.
Then the dukes of Edom shall be amazed; the mighty men of Moab,
trembling shall take hold upon them; all the inhabitants of Canaan
shall melt away. Fear and dread shall fall upon them; by the greatness of thine arm they shall be as still as a stone; till thy people pass
over, O Lord, till the people pass over, which thou hast purchased.
Thou shalt bring them in, and plant them in the mountain of thine
inheritance, in the place, O Lord, which thou hast made for thee to
dwell in, in the Sanctuary, O Lord, which thy hands have established. The Lord shall reign for ever and ever. For the horse of
Pharaoh went in with his chariots and with his horsemen into the
sea, and the Lord brought again the waters of the sea upon them;
but the children of Israel went on dry land in the midst of the sea.

— Exodus 15:1-19

The famous war-ballads of Moses, like the Song of Deborah (Judges 5), are prayers of gratitude to God for victories over Israel's enemies. Such war-poetry was a poetic tribute to Jehovah, their Great Man of War (15:3). The prayer-song of thanksgiving, it will be noted, was offered to God, not to Moses. The practical expression of the Prayer-Song was a fresh dedication to God, who had compassed His people about with a song of deliverance.

Prayer in Peril

(Exodus 17)

So Joshua did as Moses had said to him, and fought with Amalek: and Moses, Aaron, and Hur went up to the top of the hill. And it came to pass, when Moses held up his hand, that Israel prevailed: and when he let down his hand, Amalek prevailed. But Moses' hands were heavy; and they took a stone, and put it under him, and he sat thereon; and Aaron and Hur stayed up his hands, the one on the one side, and the other on the other side; and his hands were steady until the going down of the sun.   — Exodus 17:10-12

The murmurings of a God-delivered people must have been a trial to Moses who was treated by the grumblers as if he was responsible for their adversity (17:4). How he cried for protection against strife!

At Rephidim we have the place and power of prayer amid the fluctuations of battle (17:8-16). Moses, the intercessor on the mount, came to experience that the weaponless hand of prayer was more powerful than armies. While Joshua fought, Moses prayed. As the fight went on below, another fight went on on the hill top. The marvellous deliverance of Israel from Egypt drew from Jethro a heart-felt prayer (18:10). The full acknowledgment of God should ever ascend to Him, as He displays His power.

Another classic illustration of the divine response to sustained faith and intercession exhibited by Moses and Aaron and Hur was the Great War of 1939-45, when God turned the tide of battle, resulting in "The Miracle of Dunkirk."

It is easily seen that Moses' ministry as intercessor on the hill prefigures that of Christ, the Great High Priest, who in Heaven lives to plead and intercede for His own on earth (Hebrews 7:25).

Another dialogue between God and Moses can be traced when Moses spake to God and God answered him by a voice (19:19-24).

Prayer of the Needy

(Exodus 22:22-24)

Ye shall not afflict any widow, or fatherless child. If thou afflict them in any wise, and they cry at all unto me, I will surely hear their cry; And my wrath shall wax hot, and I will kill you with the sword; and your wives shall be widows, and your children fatherless.

— Exodus 22:22-24

When the widows and fatherless have no language but a cry (22:23), God registers the cry. He is not indifferent to the prayers of the afflicted when they plead for deliverance from injustice. If human tribunals fail to administer justice, God intervenes to deliver His own who cry unto Him day and night. "The Chancery Court of Heaven" is open to plead, judge and avenge the cause of the oppressed (Jeremiah 49:11, 12).

> His truth forever stands secure
> He saved the oppressed, He feeds the poor
> And none shall find His promise vain.

Prayer for Delay of Deserved Judgment

(Exodus 32)

And Moses returned unto the Lord, and said, Oh, this people have sinned a great sin, and have made them gods of gold. Yet now, if thou wilt forgive their sin —; and if not, blot me, I pray thee, out of thy book which thou hast written. — Exodus 32:31, 32

What another tribute to Moses, as the incomparable prophet-intercessor, this distressing and profoundly moving chapter affords! How he could pray for an apostate people in language reaching unparalleled heights of self-sacrificial devotion! (See also Deuteronomy 9:26-29.) On the Mount, the place of intercession, Moses pleaded for Israel. In spite of Israel's revolt against God and their disloyalty to Moses, he stepped into the breach, as God encouraged his servant to plead for others. Too few of us are willing and ready to stand in the gap (Ezekiel 22:30). With what passion Paul could plead for his kinsmen according to the flesh (Romans 10:1)!

The righteous wrath of Moses was permissible (32: 19, 20). It was righteous indignation, the anger of a good man. There was nothing mean nor petty about it. "Only he who loves much knows what it is like to feel that anger which is ennobling and godlike." The most moving prayer in the Bible is the incomplete prayer of Moses: "Yet now, if thou wilt forgive their sin — " Why the dash in this sentence? Why is it broken and incomplete? Was there a break in the voice of Moses, as his confession and intercession for a sinning people produced a momentary silence? "Here was a prayer with the *Cross* at its very heart."

First Prayer of Moses for Israel

(32:9-14)

And Moses besought the Lord his God, and said, Lord, why doth thy wrath wax hot against thy people, which thou hast brought forth out of the land of Egypt with great power, and with a mighty hand? Wherefore should the Egyptians speak, and say, For mischief did he bring them out, to slay them in the mountains, and to consume them from the face of the earth? Turn from thy fierce wrath, and repent of this evil against thy people. Remember Abraham, Isaac, and

Israel, thy servants, to whom thou swarest by thine own self, and saidst unto them, I will multiply your seed as the stars of heaven, and all this land that I have spoken of will I give unto your seed, and they shall inherit *it* for ever. And the Lord repented of the evil which he thought to do unto his people.   — Exodus 32:11-14

In their journey to Canaan, the Israelites encamped by divine direction at the base of Mount Sinai, where God proposed to enter into a sublime covenant with them. But while Moses was on the Mount receiving the Law, Israel below was guilty of an exhibition of depravity which has never been paralleled. In the very sight of the most wonderful manifestations of divine power and glory, the people, miraculously fed, clothed, and led, bowed down to a senseless idol. God's indignation was aroused. Moses interceded for the people. God's answer practically meant, "If you intercede for them, My hands are tied, and I cannot execute the deserved vengeance." What power prayer has! Old John Trapp says, "Able, after a sort, to transfuse a *palsy* into the hand of Omnipotence."

Examining the prayer of Moses, we find it made up of a three-fold plea —

1. That God would not reflect upon His own wisdom, by so soon destroying what He had employed so much power to preserve.
2. That He would not give advantage to the Egyptians to glory over the ruin of a race whom they so much hated.
3. That He would remember His covenant promises to Abraham, Isaac, and Jacob.

How efficacious prayer is! Moses prevailed (Psalm 106:23). How wonderful is the forbearance and condescension of God.

Second Prayer of Moses

(Exodus 32:30-34)

And Moses returned unto the Lord, and said, Oh, this people have sinned a great sin, and have made them gods of gold. Yet now, if thou wilt forgive their sin —; and if not, blot me, I pray thee, out of thy book which thou hast written.   — Exodus 32:31, 32

Moses, the meekest of men, was not long in having a holy anger fire his bosom. The stain cast upon the divine glory by the molten calf — monument of folly and madness — caused Moses to dash in pieces Israel's idol god. Reducing it to powder, Moses forced the people to mingle it with water and drink it.

Prostrating himself before the Mercy Seat, Moses pled for the forgiveness of the people who had given him many a heartache. He confessed their great sin, and again prayer was successful. God condescended to listen to the humble, importunate prayer of His servant, and forgave Israel.

Turn, however, to the warning of Jeremiah 15:1.

Third Prayer of Moses

(Exodus 33:12-23)

And Moses said unto the Lord, See, thou sayest unto me, Bring up this people: and thou hast not let me know whom thou wilt send with me. Yet thou hast said, I know thee by name, and thou hast also found grace in my sight. Now therefore, I pray thee, if I have found grace in thy sight, shew me now thy way, that I may know thee, that I may find grace in thy sight: and consider that this nation is thy people. And he said, My presence shall go with thee, and I will give thee rest. And he said unto him, If thy presence go not with me, carry us not up hence. For wherein shall it be known here that I and thy people have found grace in thy sight? is it not in that thou goest with us? so shall we be separated, I and thy people, from all the people that are upon the face of the earth. And the Lord said unto Moses, I will do this thing also that thou hast spoken: for thou hast found grace in my sight, and I know thee by name. And he said, I beseech thee, shew me thy glory. And he said, I will make all my goodness pass before thee, and I will proclaim the name of the Lord before thee; and will be gracious to whom I will be gracious, and will shew mercy on whom I will shew mercy. And he said, Thou canst not see my face: for there shall no man see me, and live. And the Lord said, Behold, there is a place by me, and thou shalt stand upon a rock: And it shall come to pass, while my glory passeth by, that I will put thee in a clift of the rock, and will cover thee with my hand while I pass by: And I will take away mine hand, and thou shalt see my back parts: but my face shall not be seen.

— Exodus 33:12-23

For the third time Moses is prostrate before God, with a prayer that seems to be a continuation or renewal of that he had already offered (32:31). This further fervent supplication of Moses causes us to consider the remarkable efficacy of Prayer. Moses stands forth alone and prays. He prays for a nation —

"more obnoxious at that hour,
    Than Sodom in her day had pow'r to be;"

and he prevailed. Praying, Moses secures pardon and blessing for all. God listened to *one* man, and thousands are blessed. Few have been honored as Moses, to whom was granted a full, unclouded view of the divine glory. Descending the Mount with a "joy unspeakable and full of glory," he all-unconsciously reflected the glory of the divine presence.

The key-verse of this impressive chapter is the one telling us that "the Lord spake unto Moses face to face" (33:9). It was not a one-way conversation though, for Moses talked with the Lord (33:12).

Prayer and Transfiguration

(Exodus 34)

And it came to pass, when Moses came down from Mount Sinai with the two tables of testimony in Moses' hand, when he came

down from the mount, that Moses wist not that the skin of his face
shone while he talked with him.   — Exodus 34:29

The true nature of God shines out of the mighty prayers of the
Old Testament. Divine attributes formed the basis of expression. To
saints of all ages, prayer is worth while seeing that "God is merciful
and gracious, slow to anger, and abundant in lovingkindness and
truth" (34:6; See Deuteronomy 4:31; Psalms 86:15; 105:8; 145:8;
Daniel 9:9). The central message of the Bible is the mercy of God, and
whoever comes to Him in penitence and sincerity will in no wise be
cast out.

The result of communion with God was a transfigured countenance.
But Moses wist not that the skin of his face shone (34:29). Of a
Greater than Moses it is said that, "as He prayed, the fashion of His
countenance was altered, and His raiment was white and glistering"
(Luke 9:29). Spirit-inspired prayer is ever the secret of a transfigured
life (Psalm 34:5 R.V.) .

Leviticus

It appears somewhat strange that a book dealing almost exclusively
of the way of approach to God, does not mention prayer. Even with
the presentation of the firstfruits, no prayer of gratitude was offered
(23:10). The absence of prayer is also noticeable in the consecration
of the priests (8:12, 36) and with other various offerings (Numbers
28). The ninth chapter, which describes a service of peculiar solemnity, only carries the briefest allusion to prayer (9:22). An equally
brief allusion is associated with the imposing ceremonies associated
with the Great Day of Atonement (16:12). Although not explicitly
mentioned, it is assumed that prayer and praise accompanied all the
services of the Tabernacle.

The plan and purpose of all Levitical offerings symbolize that shed
blood is the only basis of approach to God. Apart from the finished
work of the Cross, man has no access to God (John 14:6) . Boldness
to enter the holiest depends upon the blood of Jesus (Hebrews
10:19, 20). We have an Altar, even Jesus who sanctifies His people
with His own blood (Hebrews 13:10, 12). The Epistle to the Hebrews
is the New Testament counterpart and commentary of Leviticus.

As we leave this third book of the Pentateuch we deem it fitting to
draw attention to the striking fact of public acknowledgment of the
sins of the fathers, as well as those of the worshipers. The sins of the
ages are linked, age to age, by a chain of sin (26:40; Jeremiah 2:25;
14:30; Ezra 9:7; Nehemiah 9:2).

Numbers

We are accustomed to associate "murmurings" with the Book of Numbers, and rightly so, for it is a book eloquent with the sins and sorrows of grumbling. But it is also a book proving that prayer is our vital breath — our native air. Moses is the leader with a prayer-burden for his people. The first ten chapters of Numbers are dominated by the phrase, "The Lord said unto Moses." Not until we reach the eleventh chapter do we read of Moses praying unto the Lord (11:2). Yet he must have often responded to the voice of the Lord during the divine ordering of the host of Israel.

Prayer As Benediction

(Numbers 6:24-27)

The Lord bless thee, and keep thee: The Lord make his face shine upon thee, and be gracious unto thee: The Lord lift up his countenance upon thee, and give thee peace.   — Numbers 6:24-26

There is nothing loose, cheap or irreverent in Biblical prayers. Heart-felt utterances carry a solemn stateliness, as can be seen in the three-fold priestly blessing of Moses upon the people. The same is true of the three-fold invocation of Jacob (Genesis 48:15, 16. See Daniel 9:19). Godly Jews could trace the Trinity in the three-fold benediction of Moses.

Prayer for Preservation and Protection

(Numbers 10:35, 36)

And it came to pass, when the ark set forward, that Moses said, Rise up, Lord, and let thine enemies be scattered; and let them that hate thee flee before thee. And when it rested, he said, Return, O Lord, unto the many thousands of Israel.   — Numbers 10:35, 36

Ere the people of God set out upon the day's march, a brief petition, poetically expressed, was offered for protection against enemies. Before an assault the priests encouraged the soldiers by reminding them that they did not fight alone, but that their God was ever with them (Deuteronomy 20:2). The end of a conflict, as well as its beginning, was committed to God (10:36). Modern wars prove that the peace secured at a terrible price can be easily dissipated.

There is something impressive about the solemn prayer preceding the removal of the Ark and also sanctifying its resting place at night. The example of Moses in invoking the blessing of God morning and evening while on the march is worthy of emulation. As we begin each day we should retreat to our closet and commend ourselves and all we represent to God. At the close of the day, as darkness gathers, the grateful acknowledgment of the good providence and watchful care of God should also be ours.

Prayer for the Removal of Judgment
(Numbers 11:1, 2)

And when the people complained, it displeased the Lord: and the Lord heard it; and his anger was kindled; and the fire of the Lord burnt among them, and consumed them that were in the uttermost parts of the camp. And the people cried unto Moses; and when Moses prayed unto the Lord, the fire was quenched.

— Numbers 11:1, 2

How quickly a privileged people complained! Divinely led and fed, the people yet murmured. As they "journeyed unto the place the Lord had given," how soon they fell to complaining by the way. Their low murmurings, if not heard by Moses, were certainly heard of the Lord. Sudden, fiery judgment overtook the host. The people listened to Moses who, learning of the reason for such a divine visitation, again interceded. How Israel should have been grateful for having such an advocate at hand — one who was willing to step into the breach and, having power with God, prevail on their behalf. Praise God, we have a more willing, Almighty Intercessor than Moses!

Prayer of a Discouraged Heart
(Numbers 11:10-35)

And Moses said unto the Lord, Wherefore hast thou afflicted thy servant? and wherefore have I not found favour in thy sight, that thou layest the burden of all this people upon me? Have I conceived all this people? have I begotten them, that thou shouldest say unto me, Carry them in thy bosom, as a nursing father beareth the sucking child, unto the land which thou swarest unto their fathers? Whence should I have flesh to give unto all this people? for they weep unto me, saying, Give us flesh, that we may eat. I am not able to bear all this people alone, because it is too heavy for me. And if thou deal thus with me, kill me, I pray thee, out of hand, if I have found favour in thy sight; and let me not see my wretchedness.

— Numbers 11:11-15

Here we have an illustration of the petulant prayers of the Bible. Other depressed prophets prayed for death at the divine hand (Job 6:8; I Kings 19:4; Jonah 4:3). If only Moses had learned how to rest in the joy of all that God is in Himself how different his prayer would have been (11:23; Isaiah 59:1).

No wonder Moses gave way to his feelings. What a burden he carried! The unreasonable murmuring of the people got the better of him. Disgusted with the divinely-provided manna, they longed for the delicacies of Egypt, forgetting the brick-kilns, task-masters, oppressors and the sting of the whip. The accumulation of cares and trials wearied and discouraged Moses, so he cried to God, in language somewhat strange for a leader of the people.

God, however, took no notice of His servant's inconsistent and complaining prayer. Moses was burdened, and God knew it and graciously provided relief. Happy was it for Moses, that God did not "severely mark his fault." Moses prayed amiss, but God in condescension and grace knew how to respond to the prayer of a discouraged heart.

Prayer of a Meek Man

(Numbers 12)

And Moses cried unto the Lord, saying, Heal her now, O God, I beseech thee.   — Numbers 12:13

Murmuring is still before us, only this time it is limited, falling upon Moses rather than upon God. Miriam and Aaron, sister and brother of Moses, were huffed because they were not consulted in the choice of the seventy elders. Jealous and ill-tempered, these relatives became displeased with Moses, but were dealt with by God in tones of solemn and pointed censure. God highly commended Moses, the one to whom He could speak "mouth to mouth" (12:8). Miriam, who was evidently "first in the transgression" became leprous, white as snow. Says Bishop Hall, "Her foul tongue is justly punished with a foul face, and her folly, in pretending to rival Moses, is manifest to all. Moses interceded for his smitten sister. Affectionately and sincerely he pleaded for her. Moses prayed as one who, from his heart, had fully forgiven the jealousy of Miriam and Aaron."

In his intercession for the removal of Miriam's leprosy, we see Moses as a man, peculiarly efficacious in prayer. The proper approach to God was the very essence of simplicity. He came to the throne with a brief cry, "O God" (12:13).

Aaron's plea to Moses (12:11, 12) was actually a prayer to God and presents an illustration of the extreme ease and naturalness of Biblical prayer. Shimei's confession to the king he had cursed is another example of this vocabulary of religion (II Samuel 19: 19, 20).

Is there a lesson we can glean for our own hearts as we leave this chapter? Surely there is. In temper and conduct, may the example of Moses not be lost upon us. What a beautiful spirit he manifested. He had no reproaches, no angry denunciations. Revenge was not in his heart. Like Another, who was to come, Moses could pray for those despitefully using Him. May grace be ours to pray importunately for those who ill treat us!

Prayer for the Upholding of Divine Honor

(Numbers 14)

And Moses said unto the Lord, Then the Egyptians shall hear it, (for thou broughtest up this people in thy might from among them;) And they will tell it to the inhabitants of this land: for they have heard that thou Lord art among this people, that thou Lord art seen face to face, and that thy cloud standeth over them, and that thou

goest before them, by day time in a pillar of a cloud, and in a pillar
of fire by night.

Now if thou shalt kill all this people as one man, then the nations
which have heard the fame of thee will speak, saying, Because the
Lord was not able to bring this people into the land which he sware
unto them, therefore he hath slain them in the wilderness. And now,
I beseech thee, let the power of my Lord be great, according as thou
hast spoken, saying, The Lord is longsuffering, and of great mercy,
forgiving iniquity and transgression, and by no means clearing the
guilty, visiting the iniquity of the fathers upon the children unto the
third and fourth generation. Pardon, I beseech thee, the iniquity of
this people according unto the greatness of thy mercy, and as thou
hast forgiven this people, from Egypt even until now.

                                                    — Numbers 14:13-19

What intercession and what grace this chapter reveals! How Israel
provoked God! How aggravating their constant complaining must
have been! Yet in spite of Israel's ingratitude and rebellion, God
remained the same, the merciful and compassionate One. Moses
stands again in the presence of an insulted God, and throwing
himself into the breach, with tact and emphasis, pleads for a wayward
nation.

The prayer of Moses is immediately and fully answered. Israel is
pardoned and will not be cast off. What a blessing Moses was to the
nation! But for his firmness and decision — but more his prayers —
the people would never have entered the Land of Promise. A striking
proof of God's dealings with a wandering people is found in Hebrews
where the 40 years of wilderness failure is not even mentioned by
God. Israel leaves Egypt and enters Canaan (Hebrews 11:29, 30).
"Your sins and iniquities will I remember no more" (Hebrews 10:17).

Prayer for Divine Action against Rebellion

(Numbers 16)

And Moses was very wroth, and said unto the Lord, Respect not
thou their offering: I have not taken one ass from them, neither have
I hurt one of them.   — Numbers 16:15

How can we pray acceptably if angered in spirit (16:15)? Commenting on the "Korah" chapter, Professor McFadyen says, "The
primitive nature of ancient religion and the familiarity of men in
their relations to God are often quaintly illustrated by the motives
with which they urge their prayer upon Him. Sometimes the divine
justice is appealed to: "Shall one man sin and wilt thou be angry
with all the congregation (16:22)?" Or the divine mercy is besought
for a guilty people because of Jehovah's special relations with the
patriarchs (Deuteronomy 9:27), or because of the redemption which
He wrought for them in ancient times (Deuteronomy 7:29; I Kings
8:51-53), or because they are called by His name (Daniel 9:19).

But the more characteristically primitive appeal is the appeal to

Him to consider His reputation. If He fails to help Israel, what will the nations think (Joel 2:17)? They will be more inclined to say that He was unable than He was unwilling. So, to save His reputation, as it were, He is bound to interpose; otherwise not only Israel's name, but His name will be cut off (Joshua 7:9). George Müller, that mighty man of prayer, used arguments why God could not suffer His own glory to be dimmed or His promise to be dishonored.

While the name of God was deemed to be sufficient (12:13), divine attributes not fully realized in earlier prayers, became more common as the character of God unfolds (16:5). Moses spoke of God as "the God of the spirits of all flesh" (27:16). He is also addressed as the Father of Spirits (Hebrews 12:9), and as the Father of lights (James 1:17).

A typical reference to prayer can be gathered from Aaron's stand between the dead and the living (16:48). As we stand between the living God and those who are dead in sin, effectual prayer can stay the plague of iniquity.

Prayer for Relief from Death

(Numbers 21)

Therefore the people came to Moses, and said, We have sinned, for we have spoken against the Lord, and against thee; pray unto the Lord, that he take away the serpents from us. And Moses prayed for the people. And the Lord said unto Moses, Make thee a fiery serpent, and set it upon a pole: and it shall come to pass, that every one that is bitten, when he looketh upon it, shall live. And Moses made a serpent of brass, and put it upon a pole, and it came to pass, that if a serpent had bitten any man, when he beheld the serpent of brass, he lived. — Numbers 21:7-9

What a tragic chapter the previous one is! The death of Miriam, the bitter complaint of the people, the sin of Moses in smiting the rock, the death of Aaron — what a cup of anguish for Moses! Here, in the chapter before us, there is still more murmuring with consequent judgment. Complaining had become a *habit* with the children of Israel, even although they had vowed a vow unto the Lord (21:2). The fiery serpents aroused the people to their guilt. They had complained against God and Moses. Now, with becoming humility, they acknowledge their sin, and Moses undertakes to intercede for their relief. What a heart-moving phrase this is, "Moses prayed for the people" (21:7)! Prayer was answered, although not in the precise manner the people desired. Their request was for the *removal* of the serpents, and the avoidance of their evil. But God decided that the evil should be remedied, not by the removal of the serpents, but by a process which, while affording relief, secured other important ends. Here is an illustration of prayer being answered in a different way from what is expected or originally desired.

Among the lessons gathered from the powerful intercession of Moses at this time, these two can be cited —
1. His prayer suggests the use of means, directly prescribed by God.
2. Prayer should be offered, but not with neglect of means. Though Jacob passed the night in prayer, yet as morning breaks, he takes the best means to pacify his brother, Esau. Often prayer, without the use of just means, is mockery.

Prayer and Prophecy

(Numbers 23-24)

And he said unto Balak, Stand here by thy burnt offering, while I meet the Lord yonder. And the Lord met Balaam, and put a word in his mouth, and said, Go again unto Balak, and say thus.
— Numbers 23:15, 16

When man turns to God, God's answer to man is always serious and in conformity with the divine character. The theme of His answer to Balaam was the future greatness of Israel — earthly blessings for an earthly people. What a revelation of divine immutability we have in verse 19 of chapter 23!

Prayer for a New Leader

(Numbers 27)

And Moses spake unto the Lord, saying, Let the Lord, the God of the spirits of all flesh, set a man over the congregation, Which may go out before them, and which may go in before them, and which may lead them out, and which may bring them in; that the congregation of the Lord be not as sheep which have no shepherd.
— Numbers 27:15-17

As a true intercessor and mediator Moses brought the cause of the people before the Lord (27:5). In his prayer, regarding a successor, Moses indicates that although God was about to bury His workman, He would yet carry on His work through another leader. Ellicott's comment on verse sixteen is worthy of note — "We have a remarkable instance here of the greatness of Moses, as a type of Him whose words were, 'Weep not for Me, but weep for yourselves and for your children' (Luke 23:28). Instead of indulging in excessive grief, or in unavailing remorse, the mind of Moses was intently fixed upon the welfare of those for whose sake he had been willing that his name should be blotted out of the Book (Exodus 32:32): and instead of appointing one of his own family, or the man of his own choice, as his successor, he commits the matter to God, and prays that He will appoint one who would be a true shepherd to the flock." It is by prayer that we come to experience that God's choice is always *choice*.

Deuteronomy

The name of this last Pentateuchal book is taken from its opening phrase, "These be the words which Moses spake unto all Israel" (1:1). Within the book we have the repetition of the Law, and also emphasis upon the truth that faith in, and obedience to, God ever results in blessing from Him. Another notable fact of Deuteronomy, however, is the words of Moses addressed to God. Further glimpses of his prayer-ministry are recorded for our enlightenment and edification (5:4, 5).

Prayer for a Privileged Task

(Deuteronomy 3:23-29; See Numbers 20:1-13)

And I besought the Lord at that time, saying, O Lord God, thou hast begun to shew thy servant thy greatness, and thy mighty hand: for what God is there in heaven or in earth, that can do according to thy works, and according to thy might? I pray thee, let me go over, and see the good land that is beyond Jordan, that goodly mountain, and Lebanon.   — Deuteronomy 3:23-25

The combined mode of address, "Lord Jehovah" (3:24), is peculiarly impressive. *Lord* suggesting "possession" and "power"; while *Jehovah,* as Professor McFadyen reminds us, indicates "historical intimate relations with Israel, and consequently usually carries an atmosphere of grace about it."

The fervent request of Moses to cross over Jordan was not granted. Here we have one of the most moving petitions in the Bible. For losing his temper at the rock, smiting it when he should have only *spoken* to it, Moses forfeited the joy and privilege of entering Canaan. To the faithful servant of God, no penalty could have been so heavy. The lingering hope to go over and see the good land was finally quenched. The completion of his task was not that of leading the tribes into the promised land, but the charging of Joshua to perform such a task. Moses was allowed to see the land from afar and even eventually to tread its soil some fifteen hundred years later (4:21, 22; 32:48-52; 34:1-4; Matthew 17:3).

How many there are who die with the hope of years at last within their reach! A life-work is accepted as a divine appointment. Prayer ascends for the task that God will prosper and bless it, yet after all energy has been expended and in spite of prayers, plans fail. Either through misfortune, ill-health, or death the work of years is left unfinished. The call comes, "Get thee up into the top of Pisgah."

What is the answer to unanswered prayers? Is it that "No" is as truly an answer as "Yes"? Refusal may be the only answer possible in love and wisdom and truth. God never refuses requests without a reason. In the case of Moses, although his own sin was forgiven, the past may have been the reason for disqualification to enter Canaan.

He answered prayer — not in the way I sought
Nor in the way that I had thought He ought;
But in His own good way; and I could see
He answered in the fashion best for me.

Prayer to One Who Is Nigh

(Deuteronomy 4:7)

For what nation is there so great, who hath God so nigh unto them,
as the Lord our God is in all things that we call upon him for?
— Deuteronomy 4:7

We must not overlook this precept of prayer tucked away in the
lessons of Sinai Moses taught a new generation. That the ancient
Hebrews had an altogether unique sense of the near presence of God
is evident from many recorded prayers. The saints of old were
conscious that God had beset them behind and before (Psalm
139:5). Although God was invisible and absolute, yet nevertheless, as
the One gracious in all His ways, He resided with His own (4:12,
31, 35, 39).

Because of His residence among His people, they were urged
constantly to remember Him (6:2, 3). The motto of Hebrew festivals
was "Rejoice and Remember" (9:7; 10:21). The people rekindled
their faith by rehearsing God's goodness and righteous acts (16:11).
In this way gratitude was kept fresh and fragrant.

Prayer for the Stay of Judgment

(Deuteronomy 9:20, 26-29)

And the Lord was very angry with Aaron to have destroyed him:
and I prayed for Aaron also the same time. . . .
I prayed therefore unto the Lord, and said, O Lord God, destroy
not thy people and thine inheritance, which thou hast redeemed
through thy greatness, which thou hast brought forth out of Egypt
with a mighty hand. Remember thy servants, Abraham, Isaac, and
Jacob; look not unto the stubbornness of this people, nor to their
wickedness, nor to their sin: Lest the land whence thou broughtest
us out say, Because the Lord was not able to bring them into the
land which he promised them, and because he hated them, he hath
brought them out to slay them in the wilderness. Yet they are thy
people and thine inheritance, which thou broughtest out by thy
mighty power and by thy stretched out arm.
— Deuteronomy 9:20, 26-29

How full of suggestions is the phrase, "I prayed for Aaron"! Such
mighty intercession stayed the judgment Aaron truly deserved. Jewish
commentators ascribe the loss of Aaron's two sons (Leviticus 10:1, 2)
partly to God's anger at this time.

Another pregnant phrase is, "I prayed therefore unto the Lord"
(9:26). Here Moses pleads for a privileged people (14:1, 2) whose
rebelliousness merited divine judgment. Moses doubtless alluded to

his first intercession, before he descended from Sinai for the first time (Exodus 32:11-13). What intensity such intercession reveals! The original reads, "I fell down before Jehovah forty days and forty nights, as I had fallen down when the Lord said He would destroy you."

God's disclosure to His friend of the molten calf shook him and led to passionate entreaty for a guilty people. Are we so moved as we think of our own sins, or the sins of the Church, or the sins of the world?

Later on in Deuteronomy we discover that priestly ministry included the exercise of judicial functions, in which the people were taught the virtual distinction between "the clean and the unclean" (17:8-13; 21:5; 23:14; Ezekiel 44:14). Priests were raised up to convey the prophetic interpretation of the divine will. This is why prophecy is singled out as that which is distinctive of and essential to Israel's religion (18:5, 15-22; Amos 3:7). When priest and prayer failed Saul, in his tragic flight, he was forced to pierce the secrets of the future by the aid of necromancy (I Samuel 28:9; Isaiah 8:19, 20).

Prayer As a Blessing

(Deuteronomy 21:6-9)

And all the elders of that city, that are next unto the slain man, shall wash their hands over the heifer that is beheaded in the valley: And they shall answer and say, Our hands have not shed this blood, neither have our eyes seen it. Be merciful, O Lord, unto thy people Israel, whom thou hast redeemed, and lay not innocent blood unto thy people of Israel's charge. And the blood shall be forgiven them. So shalt thou put away the guilt of innocent blood from among you, when thou shalt do that which is right in the sight of the Lord.

— Deuteronomy 21:6-9

It is somewhat unusual that we do not have any of the intercessory prayers the ordinary priests prayed. Blessing in the name of Jehovah seems to have been one of their conspicuous functions (I Chronicles 23:20; II Chronicles 30:37). Yet public leaders were among the intercessors of old. Elders of a city would pray, as did those who implored divine forgiveness upon the people. Because righteousness exalteth a nation, how commendable it would be to find City Fathers gathered together in prayer for the well-being of the community they represent.

Prayer As Thanksgiving

(Deuteronomy 26)

And thou shalt speak and say before the Lord thy God, A Syrian ready to perish was my father, and he went down into Egypt, and sojourned there with a few, and became there a nation, great, mighty, and populous: And the Egyptians evil entreated us, and afflicted us, and laid upon us hard bondage: And when we cried unto the Lord God of our fathers, the Lord heard our voice, and looked on our affliction, and our labour, and our oppression: And the Lord brought us forth out of Egypt with a mighty hand, and with an outstretched arm, and with great terribleness, and with signs, and with wonders: And he hath brought us into this place, and hath given us this land, even a land that floweth with milk and honey. And now, behold, I have brought the firstfruits of the land, which thou, O Lord, hast given me. And thou shalt set it before the Lord thy God, and worship before the Lord thy God: And thou shalt rejoice in every good thing which the Lord thy God hath given unto thee, and unto thine house, thou, and the Levite, and the stranger that is among you. When thou hast made an end of tithing all the tithes of thine increase the third year, which is the year of tithing, and hast given it unto the Levite, the stranger, the fatherless, and the widow, that they may eat within thy gates, and be filled; Then thou shalt say before the Lord thy God, I have brought away the hallowed things out of mine house, and also have given them unto the Levite, and unto the stranger, to the fatherless, and to the widow, according to all thy commandments which thou hast commanded me: I have not transgressed thy commandments, neither have I forgotten them: I have not eaten thereof in my mourning, neither have I taken away ought thereof for any unclean use, nor given ought thereof for the dead: but I have hearkened to the voice of the Lord my God, and have done according to all that thou hast commanded me. Look down from thy holy habitation, from heaven, and bless thy people Israel, and the land which thou hast given us, as thou swarest unto our fathers, a land that floweth with milk and honey.

— Deuteronomy 26:5-15

Prayers of Thanksgiving, so common in the Old Testament, included gratitude for material things like land and food (8:10; 26:4, 10). Prayers of thanksgiving were offered by the worshipers after the basket of the first-fruits had been placed before the Altar (26:6-10). The benediction of heaven was sought only after the tithes had been reserved for the fatherless and the widows (26:12-15). Is there not a lesson for our hearts here? Obeying God's commands, the people would be blessed. Disobeying them, they would be cursed and forced to pray a heart-rending prayer for death to deliver them from "a trembling heart, failing eyes, and sorrow of mind" (28:65-68).

Prayer As a Song

(Deuteronomy 32-33)

Because I will publish the name of the Lord: ascribe ye greatness unto our God. He is the Rock, his work is perfect: for all his ways are judgment: a God of truth and without iniquity, just and right is he. . . .

Of the Rock that begat thee thou art unmindful, and hast forgotten God that formed thee. . . .

For the Lord shall judge his people, and repent himself for his servants, when he seeth that their power is gone, and there is none shut up, or left. And he shall say, Where are their gods, their rock in whom they trusted. Which did eat the fat of their sacrifices, and drank the wine of their drink offerings? let them rise up and help you, and be your protection. See now that I, even I, am he, and there is no god with me: I kill, and I make alive; I wound, and I heal: neither is there any that can deliver out of my hand. For I lift up my hand to heaven, and say, I live for ever. If I whet my glittering sword, and mine hand take hold on judgment; I will render vengeance to mine enemies, and will reward them that hate me. I will make mine arrows drunk with blood, and my sword shall devour flesh; and that with the blood of the slain and of the captives, from the beginning of revenges upon the enemy. Rejoice, O ye nations, with his people: for he will avenge the blood of his servants, and will render vengeance to his adversaries, and will be merciful unto his land, and to his people.

And Moses came and spake all the words of this song in the ears of the people, he, and Hoshea the son of Nun.

— Deuteronomy 32:3, 4, 18, 36-44

This remarkable outburst of praise was addressed to heaven as well as earth (32:1). The marvellous words forming this song were for the ears of God, as well as for the ears of the people (32:44), as was the blessing of the tribes (33). It is but fitting that the Books of Moses should close with a tribute, probably by Joshua to Moses, the incomparable prophet as an efficacious intercessor. "There arose not a prophet since Israel like unto Moses whom the Lord knew face to face" (34:10; Numbers 12:7, 8). May we leave behind us the reputation of being as mighty and constant in intercession as Moses, who was on such intimate terms with God!

> Lord, till I reach yon blissful shore,
> No privilege so dear shall be
> And thus my inmost soul to pour
> In prayer to Thee!

Joshua

Watching Moses at prayer and witnessing the results of his prevailing intercessions must have left a deep impression upon the mind of Joshua, son of Nun, successor to "the friend of God." Among the many things Joshua must have learned from his predecessor was how to betake himself to a Throne of Grace in time of need. And his was the assurance that as the Lord had been with Moses, so would He undertake for him (3:7).

In such a stirring experience as that of crossing Jordan we could have expected an outburst of praise to God, but the absence of recorded prayer where it is looked for is impressive. When Israel crosses Jordan, memorial stones were erected (4:8, 9), but no prayer of thanksgiving was expressed. Yet the determination to perpetuate the memory of the loving God, was, in itself, a tribute of praise to Him.

Prayer As a Challenge
(Joshua 5:13-15)

And it came to pass, when Joshua was by Jericho, that he lifted up his eyes and looked, and, behold, there stood a man over against him with his sword drawn in his hand: and Joshua went unto him, and said unto him, Art thou for us, or for our adversaries? And he said, Nay; but as captain of the host of the Lord am I now come. And Joshua fell on his face to the earth, and did worship, and said unto him, What saith my Lord unto his servant? And the captain of the Lord's host said unto Joshua, Loose thy shoe from off thy foot; for the place whereon thou standest is holy. And Joshua did so.
— Joshua 5:13-15

We have no doubt as to the identification of the man with his drawn sword whom Joshua encountered by Jericho, and whom the valiant soldier challenged — "Art thou for us, or for our adversaries?" We believe Him to have been the Lord Himself in one of His theophanic appearances. He could not have been an angel, for angels discount any claim to worship (Hebrews 1:5, 6, 13, 14; Revelation 19:10; 22:8, 9). The Captain of the host of the Lord was the thrice-holy One with every claim to submission and worship.

Joshua came to learn that the responsibility of the host of the Lord was not his, but the Lord's. He was but the servant commissioned to carry out divine orders (Luke 17:10). May ours be the reply as the Lord confronts us with His challenge, "What saith my Lord unto His servant?"

Prayer God Does Not Answer
(Joshua 7)

And Joshua rent his clothes, and fell to the earth upon his face before the ark of the Lord until the eventide, he and the elders of Israel, and put dust upon their heads. And Joshua said, Alas, O Lord God, wherefore hast thou at all brought this people over Jordan, to deliver us into the hand of the Amorites, to destroy us? would to God we had been content, and dwelt on the other side Jordan! O Lord, what shall I say, when Israel turneth their backs before their enemies! For the Canaanites and all the inhabitants of the land shall hear of it, and shall environ us round, and cut off our name from the earth: and what wilt thou do unto thy great name? — Joshua 7:6-9

Defeated at Ai because of Achan's covetousness, Joshua humbled himself before the Lord and until even-tide remained before His footstool. Calling upon God when in distress may not be the loftiest motive of prayer, but it is the most natural and elementary. The tragedy is that this is the only time some people pray.

> When the devil was sick,
> The devil, a saint was he.

Facing the inexplicable defeat at Ai, Joshua poured out his disappointment to God in a prayer of anguish (7:7-9).

To save His reputation, God was bound to interpose, otherwise not only Israel's name but His own name would be cut off. So Joshua pleads the name of *Jehovah* (7:26). When the Elders threw dust upon their heads, after the complete and dismal failure at Ai, they were expressing their sorrow, sincerity and earnestness. Falling to the earth upon the face (7:6) was a phase of posture expressing the reverence of an earthly superior in his approach to God.

Joshua learned by bitter experience that disaster came not as he had imagined, because God had failed the people (7:8), but because they had failed God (7:11, 12). There are times when prayer is out of order and God will not respond to it (7:10, 11; 8:1). Sin had to be put away (7:12; Psalm 66:8), and then a purged people must engage in whole-hearted effort as well as in whole-hearted prayer if victory was to be theirs. Joshua is reassured with the promise of victory (8:1; 10:8; 11:6), and with the guarantee of inward peace (8:1-6).

Leaving this chapter, we carry with us the thought that need can call us *from* a throne of grace, just as it directs us *to* it. We are not only to pray for sinners — we must arise and go out to labor for them. Prayer without purity and performance is futile.

Prayer Neglected with Dire Results
(Joshua 9:14)

And the men took of their victuals, and asked not counsel at the mouth of the Lord.   — Joshua 9:14

Because Joshua acted on his own initiative without first asking counsel at the mouth of the Lord, there came about the unfortunate alliance of Israel with Gibeon. How soon Joshua forgot to consult the Divine Captain he declared his willingness to obey (5:24)! What mistakes are prevented in any aspect of life, if only we acknowledge the counsel of the Lord, ere setting out on an undertaking! "In *all* thy ways acknowledge Him, and He shall direct thy paths" (Proverbs 3:6).

Prayer That Produced a Miracle
(Joshua 10)

Then spake Joshua to the Lord in the day when the Lord delivered up the Amorites before the children of Israel, Sun stand thou still upon Gibeon; and thou, Moon, in the valley of Ajalon.
                                                        — Joshua 10:12

Deliverance was sought, not only from sin, but from enemies of a tangible sort, and so one of the oldest prayers — a prayer of vengeance — was offered. It was a plea to God to arrest the natural order of the sun and moon during the battle of Gibeon.

Sin having been removed from the camp, Joshua renewed his

attack upon Ai. As the day declined, the enemies of God were not entirely destroyed. More light was necessary to achieve a victory, and Joshua prayed to the God who made the heavens. As he prayed, —

> Lo! the moon sits motionless, and earth
> Stands on her axis, indolent. The sun
> Pours the unmoving column of his rays
> In undiminish'd heat: the hours stand still;
> The shade hath stopped upon the dial's face.
>
> *   *   *
>
> On with thy armies, Joshua! The Lord
> God of Sabaoth is the avenger now:
>
> *   *   *
>
> On! till the avenging swords have drunk the blood
> Of all Jehovah's enemies, and till
> Thy banners in returning triumph wave.

The Lord hearkened unto the voice of *man* and altered so signally the course of nature. Joshua prayed that sun and moon might stand still, that he might fight in God's cause and for God's glory, and his prayer was magnificently answered. How true it is that —

> More things are wrought by prayer
> Than this world dreams of.

History is studded with the stories of fighting men, who, like Joshua, the war-hero, recognized the Lord as their Divine Captain, and who were first of all, His obedient soldiers. When the men of General Gordon saw his white handkerchief outside the tent, they knew it as the sign that the gallant warrior was having a season of interrupted prayer.

Judges

Sinning and repenting go to make up the record of this book, so named after those raised up to deliver Israel. The unvarying story of Judges is — the people sinned, became captives, cried unto the Lord, were delivered. Sin, Suffering, Sorrow, Salvation summarize the book.

Prayer for Direction

(Judges 1)

Now after the death of Joshua it came to pass, that the children of Israel asked the Lord, saying, Who shall go up for us against the Canaanites first, to fight against them?   — Judges 1:1

By what means the children of Israel asked the Lord for direction, we are not told, nor are we told what words they used (3:9, 15; 4:3). It is evident that the priest controlled the *oracle* by which the divine will was ascertained. This was consulted before the assault of Israel upon Canaan. The supernatural voice of God is sometimes represented as an angel's voice (13:3).

Prayer in Time of War

(Judges 4-5)

Then sang Deborah and Barak the son of Abinoam on that day, saying, Praise ye the Lord for the avenging of Israel, when the people willingly offered themselves. Hear, O ye kings; give ear, O ye princes; I, even I, will sing unto the Lord; I will sing praise to the Lord God of Israel. . . .

Blessed above women shall Jael the wife of Heber the Kenite be, blessed shall she be above women in the tent. He asked water, and she gave him milk; she brought forth butter in a lordly dish. She put her hand to the nail, and her right hand to the workmen's hammer; and with the hammer she smote Sisera, she smote off his head, when she had pierced and stricken through his temples. At her feet he bowed, he fell, he lay down: at her feet he bowed, he fell: where he bowed, there he fell down dead. The mother of Sisera looked out at a window, and cried through the lattice, Why is his chariot so long in coming? why tarry the wheels of his chariots? Her wise ladies answered her, yea, she returned answer to herself, Have they not sped? have they not divided the prey; to every man a damsel or two; to Sisera a prey of divers colours, a prey of divers colours of needlework, of divers colours of needlework on both sides, meet for the necks of them that take the spoil? So let all thine enemies perish, O Lord: but let them that love him be as the sun when he goeth forth in his might. And the land had rest forty years.

— Judges 5:1-3; 24-31

Feeding upon the Bible prayers of gratitude inspires personal praise to God. The Song of Deborah was a prayer of gratitude for victory. Such a prayer shows how the people rekindled their faith in God by rehearsing His righteous acts (5:11). Among the Jews, prophetesses were the exception. Deborah is the only judge to whom the title "prophet" is given (4:4). This noble woman possessed prophetic and poetic gifts (Exodus 15:20). Her predictions (4:9), lofty courage (5:7), the splendor of her inspired song (5), make her conspicuous. Her name means "bee." The names of Jewish women were often derived from natural objects. Deborah had "a sting for foes, and honey for friends."

Prayer for Signs

(Judges 6)

And the angel of the Lord appeared unto him, and said unto him, The Lord is with thee, thou mighty man of valour. And Gideon said unto him, Oh my Lord, if the Lord be with us, why then is all this befallen us? and where *be* all his miracles which our fathers told us of, saying, Did not the Lord bring us up from Egypt? but now the Lord hath forsaken us, and delivered us into the hands of the Midianites. And the Lord looked upon him, and said, Go in this thy might, and thou shalt save Israel from the hand of the Midianites: have not I sent thee? . . .

And Gideon said unto God, If thou wilt save Israel by mine hand, as thou hast said, Behold, I will put a fleece of wool in the floor; and if the dew be on the fleece only, and it be dry upon all the earth beside, then shall I know that thou wilt save Israel by mine hand, as thou hast said. And it was so: for he rose up early on the morrow, and thrust the fleece together, and wringed the dew out of the fleece, a bowl full of water. And Gideon said unto God, Let not thine anger be hot against me, and I will speak but this once: let me prove, I pray thee, but this once with the fleece; let it now be dry only upon the fleece, and upon all the ground let there be dew. And God did so that night: for it was dry upon the fleece only, and there was dew on all the ground.   — Judges 6:12-14; 36-40

Israel was in danger of being subjugated by Midian. Even Gideon threshed his wheat in hiding, but as he brooded over Israel's sad state, God spoke to him, so we have the call to action (6:12-16). Burgess and Proudlove tell us that the converse between God and Gideon teaches us that true prayer should be —

1. The realization of God's presence (6:12).
2. The bringing of all our troubles and perplexities to God (6:13).
3. The consciousness of God's gaze, and the assurance of God's strength (6:14).
4. The recognition of our own insufficiency (6:15).

Gideon received divine cheer as he faced his patriotic task. Somewhat skeptical, Gideon, after putting God to the test, the result of which should have satisfied his misgiving, immediately proceeded to demand another test. Some timid hearts have to be reassured by signs. "The best need no sign, and the bad need look for none" (Matthew 12:39). We are thrice blessed when, by faith, we take God at His word.

Prayer in Calamity

(Judges 10:10-16)

And the children of Israel cried unto the Lord, saying, We have sinned against thee, both because we have forsaken our God, and also served Baalim. And the Lord said unto the children of Israel, Did not I deliver you from the Egyptians, and from the Amorites, from the children of Ammon, and from the Philistines? The Zidonians also, and the Amalekites, and the Maonites, did oppress you; and ye cried to me, and I delivered you out of their hand. Yet ye have forsaken me, and served other gods: wherefore I will deliver you no more. Go and cry unto the gods which ye have chosen; let them deliver you in the time of your tribulation.

And the children of Israel said unto the Lord, We have sinned: do thou unto us whatsoever seemeth good unto thee; deliver us only, we pray thee, this day. And they put away the strange gods from among them, and served the Lord: and his soul was grieved for the misery of Israel.   — Judges 10:10-16

The constant refrain of Judges is, "Israel cried unto the Lord" (3:9; 4:3; 6:7; 10:10). But the Lord, weary of their cries, told them to go and cry unto the heathen gods they had chosen to help them (10:14).

So often in the Bible, confession is connected with calamity. Suffering is the impulse to self-examination. Sins confessed, however, were usually general rather than specific. How we need to drag out *the sin* easily besetting and naming it, seek purging from it (Hebrews 12:1; Isaiah 6:7) !

Prayer As a Bargain

(Judges 11:30-40)

And Jephthah vowed a vow unto the Lord, and said, If thou shalt without fail deliver the children of Ammon into mine hands, Then it shall be, that whatsoever cometh forth of the doors of my house to meet me, when I return in peace from the children of Ammon, shall surely be the Lord's, and I will offer it up for a burnt offering.

— Judges 11:30, 31

Jephthah's prayer of thanksgiving was accompanied by the fulfilment of a vow, and the offering of a sacrifice for his victory over the Ammonites. As some hearts feel, Jephthah's fulfilled vow seems to be inhuman and some cannot understand why God should be pleased with it. For that reason, perhaps we should consider it briefly. Jephthah was a worshiper of the God of Israel and one of the heroes of faith (Hebrews 11:32). Heathen nations of Palestine did offer human sacrifices to their false gods; but Jehovah repeatedly warned Israel not to engage in such sacrifices. Seeing Jephthah was a God-fearing judge, and knowing that human sacrifices were an abomination to God, He would not be likely to countenance them.

It is therefore possible, as Fausset suggests, that Jephthah offered his beloved daughter as a *spiritual* burnt offering unto the Lord, in the sense that she was set apart for His service, forever as a virgin (11:37-40). God's approval, which Jephthah evidently received, could not have been given for any other kind of offering. While zealous to express his faith in God's ability to deliver him from his foes, we feel that Jephthah's vow was a foolish one to make.

Prayer for an Unborn Child

(Judges 13)

And Manoah said, Now let thy words come to pass. How shall we order the child, and how shall we do unto him?   — Judges 13:12

This chapter presents a beautiful prayer of a father asking guidance in the training of his yet unborn child (13:14-18). After the visit of the heavenly messenger, with his announcement of the annunciation, Manoah betakes himself to prayer. Believing all his wife related, he asked for no signs, but took for granted that God would fulfil His promises and grant a son.

In due course Samson was born and entered upon a strange and eventful life as the deliverer of Israel from oppression. In her booklet,

Types of Prayer in the Bible, Mrs. A. T. Robertson writes of Samson —

The promised child grows up strong and obstinate, with a rough wit, and even a certain rude poetry in him, quite an earth-giant. He makes no move against the Philistines till he has a personal grudge, and this comes in a way very trying to his parents. He must needs go and fall in love with a Philistine woman, and when they protest (as well they might, under the circumstances) he repeats stubbornly, "Get her for me." The betrothal occurs, and in due time the wedding, with the riddle of the honey out of the lion. Samson's prodigious strength is not shown more plainly in rending the lion than his moral weakness in the matter of the riddle. A rather dangerous jest it is, and the secret foolishly given away to a woman's tears. Precisely so does he behave with Delilah, except that he teases her and plays with the secret. But this time it is not to play with, but a trust from God, even as his strength was, and he throws both away.

Prayer in the Face of Death

(Judges 16:28-31)

And Samson called unto the Lord, and said, O Lord God, remember me, I pray thee, and strengthen me, I pray thee, only this once, O God, that I may be at once avenged of the Philistines for my two eyes. And Samson took hold of the two middle pillars upon which the house stood, and on which it was borne up, of the one with his right hand, and of the other with his left. And Samson said, Let me die with the Philistines. And he bowed himself with all his might; and the house fell upon the lords, and upon all the people that were therein. So the dead which he slew at his death were more than they which he slew in his life. — Judges 16:28-31

Although a Nazarite unto God, we have little record of Samson's intercourse with heaven. His character is inexplicable, yet he is enrolled in the list of ancient worthies renowned for their faith (Hebrews 11:32). What a series of degradations were his! How pitiable this strong man must have looked in the prison-house of Gaza, blind and fettered! Sightless, and grinding in his bondage, he seems a sorry hero. The heathen pray and praise, and it is thus that the Philistines blessed *Dagon* for their victory over Samson. Their song of praise was accompanied by sacrifice (16:23).

> Ask for the great deliv'rer now: and find him
> Eyeless at Gaza, at the mill with slaves.

But prayer and repentance were his, and reconciled to God, he is re-invested with unusual power. "His hair grew, together with his repentance, and his strength with his hair." His prayer was holy, devout and intense. The Spirit of God moves within him, and grasping the pillars of the idol temple, Samson triumphs in his death, becoming more terrible to the Philistines than he had ever been in his life. Although his was a personal desire for vengeance, Samson went out in a blaze of glory.

"Samson made many mistakes," Burgess and Proudlove write, "but in the end he came to realize wherein lay the source and secret of his strength. At the end he was his best. It is true that thoughts of vengeance were in his heart. But the Philistines had destroyed his sight: they now regarded him as a comedian to give them sport. No wonder that a terrible wrath fell upon him, and with it a sense of his need of *God* and God-given strength."

Among the recorded prayers of the Bible, that of the dying Samson is most heart-moving. He used the name of *Jehovah* as he prays for the destruction of God's foes, who were also his foes. The Song of Lamech (Genesis 4:23), one of the oldest of Biblical poems, was a song in glorification of revenge and similar in tone to Samson's last prayer.

Prayer Directly Answered
(Judges 20:23-28)

(And the children of Israel went up and wept before the Lord until even, and asked counsel of the Lord, saying, Shall I go up again to battle against the children of Benjamin my brother? And the Lord said, Go up against him.) And the children of Israel came near against the children of Benjamin the second day. And Benjamin went forth against them out of Gibeah the second day, and destroyed down to the ground of the children of Israel again eighteen thousand men; all these drew the sword.

Then all the children of Israel, and all the people, went up, and came unto the house of God, and wept, and sat there before the Lord, and fasted that day until even, and offered burnt offerings and peace offerings before the Lord. And the children of Israel enquired of the Lord, (for the ark of the covenant of God was there in those days, And Phinehas, the son of Eleazar, the son of Aaron, stood before it in those days,) saying, Shall I yet again go out to battle against the children of Benjamin my brother, or shall I cease? And the Lord said, Go up; for tomorrow I will deliver them into thine hand.   — Judges 20:23-28

No wonder the prayers of the children of Israel were saturated with tears (20:23, 26). War is terrible at any time, but surely there is no phase of war so tragic as civil war, when citizens of a country fight against each other, with relatives on both sides. The children of Benjamin slew eighteen thousand Israelites who drew the sword. Israel, however, fought back slaying twenty and five thousand and an hundred men of valor (20:25). In times of national crisis, the courts of the most High, largely deserted in more peaceful times, are visited. If only people, as a whole, would frequent the Temple of God at all times, civil strife would not arise.

Prayer for a Lost Tribe

(Judges 21:2, 3)

And the people came to the house of God, and abode there till even before God, and lifted up their voices, and wept sore; And said, O Lord God of Israel, why is this come to pass in Israel, that there should be today one tribe lacking in Israel? — Judges 21:2, 3

There is no phase of war so tragic as that of Civil War. Here the men of Israel mourned over the separation of Benjamin from the rest of the Tribes. Separations and divisions among God's people are to be deplored and should constrain us to weep and pray even as Christ prayed for the unity of His church (John 17:21-23).

Ruth

Although there are no actually recorded prayers in this beautiful and charming picture of domestic life in a period of anarchy, the atmosphere of prayer pervades its several impressive benedictions. Godly souls like Elimelech, (whose name means, *My God Is King*), Naomi, Ruth and Boaz must have had constant traffic with heaven.

In the vocabulary of religion words like "grace" and "blessing" were equally applicable to God and man. Old, widowed and childless, Naomi nobly intercedes for her daughters-in-law. "The Lord deal kindly with you, as ye have dealt with the dead, and me. . . . The Lord grant you that ye may find rest" (1:8, 9).

The benediction of Boaz (2:4), reveals how the common pursuits of life were hallowed by a vivid sense of God. "The simple greetings on the harvest field between the master and his men take the form of short prayers." Ruth was also the recipient of another lovely benediction from Boaz (2:12). Then we have the benediction of the Elders (4:11) and of Naomi (4:14, 15). Prayers for children are frequent in the Bible. They were offered by men (Genesis 25:21), by women (Genesis 30:7; I Samuel 1:11), and invariably, as here in Ruth, by those who wish a family well.

At last Naomi's complaint, "The Almighty hath dealt bitterly with me" (1:20), is transformed into a certainty of faith and her story ends happily. In her sorrow, she prayed for a blessing upon Ruth, little expecting blessing for herself. But blessing came in full measure for Naomi and Ruth, for we journey from the Book of Ruth through the dim and distant to the coming of Christ from the line of Boaz and Ruth the Moabitess (Matthew 1:5).

I Samuel

The two Books of Samuel add several great pages to the Biblical history of prayer. What striking prayers they record for our edification! This first book begins with Hannah's voiceless prayer (1:13) and ends with a more than vocal prayer of praise on the part of the Philistines in the house of their idols over the death of Saul.

Prayer without Words

(I Samuel 1)

So Hannah rose up after they had eaten in Shiloh, and after they had drunk. Now Eli the priest sat upon a seat by a post of the temple of the Lord. And she was in bitterness of soul, and prayed unto the Lord, and wept sore. And she vowed a vow, and said, O Lord of hosts, if thou wilt indeed look on the affliction of thine handmaid, and remember me, and not forget thine handmaid, but wilt give unto thine handmaid a man child, then I will give him unto the Lord all the days of his life, and there shall no razor come upon his head. And it came to pass, as she continued praying before the Lord, that Eli marked her mouth. Now Hannah, she spake in her heart; only her lips moved, but her voice was not heard: therefore Eli thought she had been drunken.   I Samuel 1:9-13

While thousands of women prayed before Hannah's day, hers is the first recorded instance of a woman at prayer. There are relatively few illustrations of women praying, because women appear in the Bible, as in all ancient literature, less frequently than men. If only we had the story of devout women from Eve down to Hannah, what prayer-watchers we would see them to be. Certainly the world owes more to the prayers of women than it realizes. If it be true that "there are more daughters than sons in Zion, who spend more time in prayer than men, whose supplications are more fervent, whose faith is more confiding, and whose love is more pure and constant," how grateful we should be for such mothers in Israel.

Hannah's prayer at Shiloh indicates that in early times women had the right to pray in the sanctuary. In this story of rare delicacy and power the threefold use of the phrase, "thy handmaid," is an acknowledgment of unworthiness of divine blessings. Like others who sought divine aid, Hannah supported her prayer for a child by a vow. Hannah stood as she silently prayed (1:26). Of her heart-felt prayer we read, "Only her lips moved, but her voice was not heard." Words are not essential to the offering of true prayer, though they often help in the expression of our thoughts and desires. At times, however, the heart is too full for utterance, or the presence of others, as in Hannah's case, make articulate prayer impossible (Nehemiah 2:4). Prayer is the soul's sincere desire whether it is uttered or unexpressed.

Hannah's prayer is the first instance in the Bible of silent or mental prayer. Hers was a groaning that could not be uttered.

Hannah was a wife, but not a mother. Into some private corner she went and poured out her heart's desire to God. Her prayer, purely personal, carried within it the thrill of self-sacrifice. Confident that her prayer had been heard, she "did eat and her countenance was no more sad." She committed her case to God and her cry was graciously answered. Her reproach was taken away. God gave her Samuel.

The prayer and vow of Hannah teach us these five lessons:

1. The true resort for help, in the hour of need, is the Throne of Grace.
2. The deeper our trouble, the sorer we weep, the more fervently we should pray.
3. It is right to vow unto the Lord — it consecrates the blessing sought to His glory.
4. Parents should remember that children are God's gift, and should prepare them for His service and glory.
5. We should never forget our vows, but be careful to perform them.
6. When God answers us favorably, we should be mindful to praise Him.

Prayer Prophetic in Outlook

(I Samuel 2:1-10)

And Hannah prayed, and said, My heart rejoiceth in the Lord, mine horn is exalted in the Lord: my mouth is enlarged over mine enemies; because I rejoice in thy salvation. There is none holy as the Lord: for there is none beside thee: neither is there any rock like unto our God. Talk no more so exceeding proudly; let not arrogancy come out of your mouth: for the Lord is a God of knowledge, and by him actions are weighed. The bows of the mighty men are broken, and they that stumbled are girded with strength. They that were full have hired out themselves for bread; and they that were hungry ceased: so that the barren hath born seven; and she that hath many children is waxed feeble. The Lord killeth, and maketh alive: he bringeth down to the grave, and bringeth up. The Lord maketh poor, and maketh rich: he bringeth low, and lifteth up. He raiseth up the poor out of the dust, and lifteth up the beggar from the dunghill, to set them among princes, and to make them inherit the throne of glory: for the pillars of the earth are the Lord's, and he hath set the world upon them. He will keep the feet of his saints, and the wicked shall be silent in darkness; for by strength shall no man prevail. The adversaries of the Lord shall be broken to pieces; out of heaven shall he thunder upon them: the Lord shall judge the ends of the earth; and he shall give strength unto his king, and exalt the horn of his anointed.   — I Samuel 2:1-10

Prayers of thanksgiving were no doubt customarily offered for the birth of a child, as well as for recovery from sickness (Isaiah 38:10-20).

Hannah prays again but is silent no longer. Her lips are now vocal with praise over the gift of the child she had prayed for and which she had lent to the Lord (1:27, 28). Samuel came to her from God, and she recognized God's right to her boy and solemnly dedicated him to the Lord, "As long as he liveth he shall be lent to the Lord." But while her prayer-song contained a confession of faith, it was also prophetic, for her mind soared beyond her own personal joy and reached out to larger issues. What a prophecy of Christ she was inspired to utter (2:10; Psalm 2:1-9)!

Prayer in the Sanctuary
(I Samuel 3)

And the Lord called Samuel again the third time. And he arose and went to Eli, and said, Here am I; for thou didst call me. And Eli perceived that the Lord had called the child. Therefore Eli said unto Samuel, Go, lie down: and it shall be, if he call thee, that thou shalt say, Speak, Lord; for thy servant heareth. So Samuel went and lay down in his place. And the Lord came, and stood, and called as at other times, Samuel, Samuel. Then Samuel answered, Speak; for thy servant heareth.   —I Samuel 3:8-10

Called to prominent service among the people of Israel, Samuel had to learn how to detect the voice of God in the sanctuary. It was thus that the boy prayer-watcher became a leader and judge in Israel. In the temple God spoke to the lad, until his soul heard and understood. Heaven was about him in his infancy. We must not think it strange for a child to hear and respond to the voice of God. What is hid from the wise and prudent is revealed unto babes (Matthew 11:25).

At first Samuel *heard* the voice, but mistook it for Eli's, as we can well understand. Do you think God intended this, so that the boy would not be frightened as he was being initiated into the secrets of converse with God?

Alas, Eli was old and weary and the quality of his service had deteriorated! God had some heart-searching things to say to Eli and Israel and he uttered them through the lips of a child. Samuel's call must have convicted Eli of his insensitiveness to the divine voice and ineffectiveness of his ministry.

Prayer for National Trouble
(I Samuel 7)

And Samuel took a sucking lamb, and offered it for a burnt offering wholly unto the Lord: and Samuel cried unto the Lord for Israel; and the Lord heard him.   —I Samuel 7:9

What a chapter of action this is! It begins with defeat and ends with deliverance! Its key-phrase is, "I will pray for you unto the Lord" (7:5). The need of divine help felt in time of personal and national danger, and more especially in war time, drives men to God. Battlefield prayers are common to Israel's early history. So Samuel prays before the battle of Ebenezer.

Hannah's child, whose name means "Asked of God," was established to be a prophet. When war broke out between the Israelites and the Philistines, and Israel was defeated, Samuel knew what to do in such an emergency. The people besought him to pray for them (7:8), and with confidence Samuel drew nigh unto God. With the sacrifice of a lamb was the fervent prayer that Israel must be preserved from the power of her enemies. God heard and thundered His reply from which we learn:

1. God is more ready to hear the prayers of His people, when repentant, than when they remain proud and disobedient. The poured-out water was symbolic of penitence (7:5, 6). In their humiliation the people own themselves as spilt water which cannot be gathered up again. With a full confession of their sin, there came the restoration of divine favor.

2. God's ministers can pray with far more comfort and confidence for a repentant than for an impenitent people. With prayer and penitence there is fasting (7:6). A nation depended upon the prayers of a man of God, and was not disappointed.

Samuel regarded intercession as part of his official duty (10:22; 12:19). Not to pray was deemed a sin (12:23). Do we treat prayerlessness as a sin against those who need to be prayed for?

Prayer for a King

(I Samuel 8)

But the thing displeased Samuel, when they said, Give us a king to judge us. And Samuel prayed unto the Lord.   — I Samuel 8:6

Tired of being a *theocracy,* or directly governed by God, Israel yearned for a king like surrounding Gentile nations. This was the bitterest moment in Samuel's honored career. Such a nation must have soured him and led to his retiring, but on he went in quiet confidence. Fascinated by the glitter of an earthly throne, Israel was promised by God through Samuel that they would become a *monarchy.* It must have been with sad heart, however, that Samuel prayed unto the Lord (8:6). But how precious is the tribute of God's confidence in His servant (9:15). Upon what intimate terms the Lord and Samuel must have lived! (See also 10:22 for a further example in this instance.)

Prayer As Vindication

(I Samuel 12)

So Samuel called unto the Lord; and the Lord sent thunder and rain that day: and all the people greatly feared the Lord and Samuel.
— I Samuel 12:18

Saul is now king of Israel, and as Samuel resigns the government of the nation into Saul's hands, he prays that a sign might be given, ratifying displeasure of the rejection of divine government. Samuel spreads forth his hands in the sight of heaven, and thunder and rain, seldom experienced, came in the time of wheat harvest.

Samuel's attitude, benevolent and forgiving, is worthy of note. "Pray for you? Yes, to my latest breath. God forbid that I should sin against the Lord in ceasing to pray for you." May each of us be saved from the sin of prayerlessness! Virtually ejected from office, Samuel acted like a true prophet of God. Feeling the unkindness and ingratitude of those around, he could still pray for them. Of Israel, Samuel could say —

> For her, my tears shall fall;
> For her, my prayers ascend,
> To her, my cares and toils be given,
> Till toils and cares shall end.

Prayer of a Distressed King

(I Samuel 14)

And Saul built an altar unto the Lord: the same was the first altar that he built unto the Lord. . . .
And Saul asked counsel of God, Shall I go down after the Philistines? wilt thou deliver them into the hand of Israel? But he answered him not that day.   — I Samuel 14:35, 37

Jonathan had no fear of battle with the Philistines. He reminded his own heart and his armour-bearer that God was able to save by few as by many (14:6). What a senseless curse Saul pronounced (14:24) ! Saul's tragic dilemma brought him to his first altar (14:35). Some prayers are delayed (14:37) . There are some pleas God finds it hard to answer. Of old, questions were put and the answer determined by lot. In our Christian age such a method is no longer worthy or compatible with absolute reliance upon the Holy Spirit.

Prayer of a Grieved Heart

(I Samuel 15:11)

It repented me that I have set up Saul to be king: for he is turned back from following me, and hath not performed my commandments. And it grieved Samuel; and he cried unto the Lord all night.
— I Samuel 15:11

It is possible for kindness to become a sin and result in compromise (15:9). Saul's disobedience to God's commands brought about his rejection. How deeply grieved Samuel must have been over the whole situation! What a night of heartbroken intercession the prophet must have spent (15:11)! Saul was to hear his doom from Samuel the next day, and the prophet himself would have to complete Saul's work (15:32, 33). Saul's action also resulted in loss of fellowship for "Samuel came no more to see Saul until the day of his death" (15:35). No wonder Samuel cried all night unto the Lord. What a solemn task awaited him!

Prayer As a Still Small Voice

(I Samuel 16:1-12)

And the Lord said unto Samuel, How long wilt thou mourn for Saul, seeing I have rejected him from reigning over Israel? fill thine horn with oil, and go, I will send thee to Jesse the Bethlehemite: for I have provided me a king among his sons. And Samuel said, How can I go? if Saul hear it, he will kill me. And the Lord said, Take an heifer with thee, and say, I am come to sacrifice to the Lord. . . .
And he sent, and brought him in. Now he was ruddy, and withal of a beautiful countenance, and goodly to look to. And the Lord said, Arise, anoint him: for this is he.   — I Samuel 16:1, 2, 12

How precious are the phrases "Samuel said" — "The Lord said"! A peculiar feature of God's reply to the prayers of Old Testament saints is that His voice, as a still small voice, fell upon the inward ear like the voice of a man. Is this not evident in the dialogue between God and Samuel in the choice of David, and the rejection of his brethren, for the kingship? Within Samuel there was that spiritual fitness making possible the discernment of the divine will and word.

Prayer As the Secret of Courage

(I Samuel 17)

Then said David to the Philistine, Thou comest to me with a sword, and with a spear, and with a shield: but I come to thee in the name of the Lord of hosts, the God of the armies of Israel, whom thou hast defied.   — I Samuel 17:45

While no actual prayer of David is recorded in this chapter, the godly stripling must have prayed much before his courageous defiance of Goliath. David approached the boastful giant in a thoroughly religious mood. The young challenger was in no way guilty of braggadocio. Resting in past experiences of God's protecting mercy (17:34-37), he manifested a steady confidence in God's ability to undertake for him again. He believed God to be the same yesterday, today and forever, and the people came to know that the Lord saveth not with sword and spear (17:47).

Prayer As Enquiry

(I Samuel 23)

Therefore David enquired of the Lord, saying, Shall I go and smite these Philistines? And the Lord said unto David, Go, and smite the Philistines, and save Keilah. . . .
Then said David, O Lord God of Israel, thy servant hath certainly heard that Saul seeketh to come to Keilah, to destroy the city for my sake. Will the men of Keilah deliver me up into his hand? will Saul

come down, as thy servant hath heard? O Lord God of Israel, I
beseech thee, tell thy servant. And the Lord said, He will come
down. Then said David, Will the men of Keilah deliver me and my
men into the hand of Saul? And the Lord said, They will deliver
thee up.   — I Samuel 23:2, 10-12

Abimelech enquired of the Lord for David (22:10), now David
enquires of the Lord for himself (23:2, 5). Professor McFadyen remarks that, "So practical is the spirit of Biblical prayer that proper
names, elaborate descriptions of the speaker's situation, and historical
and geographical allusions are of frequent occurrence (23:11)."

In accordance with the rough spirit of a primitive time, David
blessed God when death removed his enemies (25:39). Prayer brought
the revelation of the enemies' designs (23:10-12).

Prayer for Deaf Ears

(I Samuel 28:7)

And when Saul enquired of the Lord, the Lord answered him not,
neither by dreams, nor by Urim, nor by prophets.   — I Samuel 28:6

What a pathetic chapter this is! Samuel was dead. Saul had abandoned all forms of necromancy (28:3). The methods of ascertaining
God's will are summarized in Saul's sad story (28:6, 9, 15). He prayed
unto the Lord, but the heavens were as brass — "The Lord answered
him not" (28:6). In his desperation, Saul goes back to the familiar
spirits he had put away (28:7). Mystery shrouds the reappearance of
the departed prophet, who had no new message of hope to give to
rejected Saul (28:17). God had departed from him and his doom was
sealed. How tragic is the lot of a person when he prays and is not
answered (28:6, 15) and ultimately finds himself God-forsaken!

Although there were energetic attempts to remove enchanters,
sorcerers and necromancers from Israel, they continued to flourish,
more or less through the centuries (Isaiah 8:19; Deuteronomy 18).

Prayer for Restoration of War-Spoil

(I Samuel 30)

And David enquired at the Lord, saying, Shall I pursue after this
troop? shall I overtake them? And he answered him, Pursue: for
thou shalt surely overtake them, and without fail recover all.
                                                      — I Samuel 30:8

The prophetic interpretation of the divine will was a distinct
aspect of the ministry of priest and prophet. Hezekiah, distressed by
the blasphemous insolence of the Assyrians and their menace of
Jerusalem, appealed to Isaiah and received a clear answer through
him. David, although a king as he came to avenge the destruction of
Ziklag, ascertained God's will by enquiring directly of Him (30:8).
What a world of meaning is in the phrase, *"But* David encouraged

himself in the Lord his God" (30:6)! Amid the crises of life, it is so blessed to rest in the joy of all God is in Himself.

II Samuel

Although this book, which is a continuation of the first, bears the name of Samuel, the prophet himself has no place in the book, which covers some forty years of the reign of David — the hero of the book. The influence of the great prophet Samuel, however, abides. David's association with Samuel remained vividly in his memory. The godly and intercessory life of the prophet and his wise counsel influenced David's life and government.

Prayer As to Possession

(II Samuel 2:1)

And it came to pass after this, that David enquired of the Lord, saying, Shall I go up into any of the cities of Judah? And the Lord said unto him, Go up. And David said, Whither shall I go up? And he said, Unto Hebron.   — II Samuel 2:1

At this important junction of affairs, David's first care was to know the will of God. A wrong step at the outset of his reign would have been disastrous. Possibly David's enquiry was made through the high priest Abiathar (I Samuel 20:20; 23:1, 4, 9, 10). Heaven responded to David's enquiry and up he went to Hebron. Sometimes decisions were made by lot. Such a method, however, was not satisfactory, seeing it left too much to chance. That God over-ruled in the method of the *lot* is seen in the choice of a successor to Judas Iscariot (Acts 1:24-26).

Prayer for Victory Signs

(II Samuel 5:19-25)

And David enquired of the Lord, saying, Shall I go up to the Philistines? wilt thou deliver them into mine hand? And the Lord said unto David, Go up: for I will doubtless deliver the Philistines into thine hand.

And when David enquired of the Lord, he said, Thou shalt not go up; but fetch a compass behind them, and come upon them over against the mulberry trees. And let it be, when thou hearest the sound of a going in the tops of the mulberry trees, that then thou shalt bestir thyself: for then shall the Lord go out before thee, to smite the host of the Philistines.   — II Samuel 5:19, 23, 24

Glimpses of David's increasing greatness are before us in this chapter. He went on going and growing, for God was with him (5:9). David perceived that God had established his kingdom (5:12). Twice we are told that "David enquired of the Lord" (5:19, 23), and both times he received favorable answers. His first attack upon the foe was like the bursting of a dam. David carried everything before him. This victory (5:20, 21) was so signal as to give a new name to the locality and was remembered centuries after as a memorable instance of divine aid in response to prayer (Isaiah 28:21).

David's second enquiry of the Lord resulted in another victory over the Philistines. A divine signal was given him in "the sound of a going" (5:24). David had to "bestir" himself, which means he had to be sharp, or act quickly and vigorously — and he did (5:25)! It was worthy of David that after each victory he gave glory to God (5:20, 21; 6:1, 2, 18). He destroyed the false gods and restored the worship of the true God. But David knew what it was to pray a prayer of fear (6:9).

Prayer for Blessing upon House and Kingdom
(II Samuel 7:18-29)

Then went king David in, and sat before the Lord, and he said, Who am I, O Lord God? and what is my house, that thou hast brought me hitherto? And this was yet a small thing in thy sight, O Lord God; but thou hast spoken also of thy servant's house for a great while to come. And is this the manner of man, O Lord God? And what can David say more unto thee? for thou, Lord God, knowest thy servant. For thy word's sake, and according to thine own heart, hast thou done all these great things, to make thy servant know them. Wherefore thou art great, O Lord God: for there is none like thee, neither is there any God beside thee, according to all that we have heard with our ears. And what one nation in the earth is like thy people, even like Israel, whom God went to redeem for a people to himself, and to make him a name, and to do for you great things and terrible, for thy land, before thy people, which thou redeemedst to thee from Egypt, from the nations and their gods? For thou hast confirmed to thyself thy people Israel to be a people unto thee for ever: and thou, Lord, art become their God. And now, O Lord God, the word that thou hast spoken concerning thy servant, and concerning his house, establish it for ever, and do as thou hast said. And let thy name be magnified for ever, saying, The Lord of hosts is the God over Israel: and let the house of thy servant David be established before thee. For thou, O Lord of hosts, God of Israel, hast revealed to thy servant, saying, I will build thee an house: therefore hath thy servant found in his heart to pray this prayer unto thee. And now, O Lord God, thou art that God, and thy words be true, and thou hast promised this goodness unto thy servant: Therefore now let it please thee to bless the house of thy servant, that it may continue for ever before thee: for thou, O Lord God, hast spoken it: and with thy blessing let the house of thy servant be blessed for ever.   — II Samuel 7:18-29

David sat to meditate in God's presence upon Nathan's communication to him, and to offer his praise (7:18-24), and to pray (7:25-29). The combined title he employed, "O Lord Jehovah," indicates that

David's prayer of gratitude burst forth with joy as he heard Nathan's prophecy of the brilliant future of Israel.

While sitting was not an altogether natural attitude in prayer, David "sat" as he offered his prayer (7:18), as did all Israel in a day of sorrow (Judges 20:26). Then note the repetition of the phrase, "Thy servant" (7:25, 26, etc.). Another remarkable feature of this chapter is the prominence of history, as well as of repentance and gratitude in prayer. David's prayer recalled the goodness of God in His deliverance of Israel from Egypt. God is ever the same (Psalm 44). It was in David's heart to honor God by building Him a house but his dream was realized by another. "The essence of a thing is more than its consequences or rewards," says Phillips Brooks. "If the withholding of these can drive us deeper down into the essence, is it not a blessing?"

Prayer for a Sick Child

(II Samuel 12)

David therefore besought God for the child; and David fasted, and went in, and lay all night upon the earth.   — II Samuel 12:16

Here is another instance of a prayer denied in wisdom. David's request for the child of his shame was denied in mercy as well as judgment, for the child would have been a perpetual reminder of his sin. Another son came in whose birth there was no taint of shame (See Deuteronomy 3:23-27; I Kings 19:4-18; Mark 5:20; 7:31-37).

While David's deep love for his child must not be overlooked, Ellicott, quoting Keil, says of David's prayer —

> In the case of a man whose penitence was so earnest and so deep, the prayer for the preservation of his child must have sprung from some other source than excessive love of any created object. His great desire was to avert the stroke as a sign of the wrath of God, in the hope that he might be able to discern, in the preservation of the child, a proof of divine favour consequent upon the restoration of his fellowship with God. But when the child was dead, he humbled himself under the mighty hand of God, and rested satisfied with His grace, without giving himself up to fruitless pain.

Prayer As Pretense

(II Samuel 15:7-9)

And it came to pass after forty years, that Absalom said unto the king, I pray thee, let me go and pay my vow, which I have vowed unto the Lord, in Hebron. For thy servant vowed a vow while I abode at Geshur in Syria, saying, If the Lord shall bring me again indeed to Jerusalem, then I will serve the Lord. — II Samuel 15:7, 8

Although this is another prayer supported by a vow, we have no means of knowing whether the vow was real or fictitious. It is clearly evident that Absalom here uses it as a pretext, as his heartless rebellion against his father proves. Absalom veiled his crime under the cloak of religion. He received the blessing of David at the very moment he was striking at his father's crown and life.

What bitter experiences David had to face! Following Absalom's revolt were the curses of Shimei. While no prayer was offered by David at Bahurim, his wish was the equivalent of a prayer (16:12). This confession is also striking because it shows how a man can refer to himself in the same sentence in the third person and in the first, "*Thy* servant doth know that *I* have sinned."

See also II Samuel 15:31 for an example of sincere petition in a time of crisis.

Prayer for Understanding of Affliction
(II Samuel 21:1-12)

Then there was a famine in the days of David three years, year after year; and David enquired of the Lord. And the Lord answered, It is for Saul, and for his bloody house, because he slew the Gibeonites.   — II Samuel 21:1

The Hebrew meaning of "enquired of the Lord" is "sought the face of the Lord." David turned to the true source for a knowledge of the meaning of the unusual affliction of a three-year famine and immediately received the divine reason for the nation's drought. It was because of Saul's sin in which pride, arrogance and self-will were cloaked under a zeal for God's honor and His people's welfare.

Prayer As a Psalm
(II Samuel 22)

And David spake unto the Lord the words of this song in the day that the Lord had delivered him out of the hand of all his enemies, and out of the hand of Saul: And he said, The Lord is my rock, and my fortress, and my deliverer; The God of my rock; in him will I trust: he is my shield, and the horn of my salvation, my high tower, and my refuge, my saviour; thou savest me from violence. I will call on the Lord, who is worthy to be praised: so shall I be saved from mine enemies. When the waves of death compassed me, the floods of ungodly men made me afraid; The sorrows of hell compassed me about; the snares of death prevented me; In my distress I called upon the Lord, and cried to my God: and he did hear my voice out of his temple, and my cry did enter into his ears. . . .

For thou art my lamp, O Lord: and the Lord will lighten my darkness. For by thee I have run through a troop: by my God have I leaped over a wall. As for God, his way is perfect; the word of the Lord is tried: he is a buckler to all them that trust in him. For who is God, save the Lord? and who is a rock, save our God? . . .

Therefore I will give thanks unto thee, O Lord, among the heathen, and I will sing praises unto thy name. He is the tower of salvation for his king: and sheweth mercy to his anointed, unto David, and to his seed for evermore.   — II Samuel 22:1-7, 29-32, 50, 51

With slight variations, David's song of praise to God for all He is in Himself and for all He had accomplished reappears as Psalm 18. In his old age, David grew more humble. He came to rest in God's sufficiency and to love Him more ardently (22:28-34). The favorite description of God in David's victory-song of his youth, "God is a refuge for us," of which Alexander Maclaren said, "The flight of the soul conscious of its nakedness to the safe shelter of God's breast, is a wonderful description of faith." David's last words breathe the same spirit (23:1-7).

Prayer As a Confession of Pride

(II Samuel 24:10-17)

And David's heart smote him after that he had numbered the people. And David said unto the Lord, I have sinned greatly in that I have done: and now, I beseech thee, O Lord, take away the iniquity of thy servant; for I have done very foolishly.   — II Samuel 24:10

The numbering of the people indicated that rising of spiritual pride and reliance on earthly strength which led to sin. A conspicuous fact is that David prays that punishment for numbering the people may fall, not upon innocent people, but upon himself and his father's house! David's shepherd-heart is seen in his plea for the preservation of innocent sheep (24:17). Although David's conscience was awakened and he confessed his sin and prayed for pardon, ten months elapsed before he saw his sin (24:8).

I Kings

The contribution of the two Books of Kings to the subject of prayer is somewhat impressive, seeing that some of the dynamic prayers recorded therein are used by New Testament writers to urge the saints of God to pray without ceasing. The mighty, daring prayer of Elijah reminds us that there is "Power Through Prayer," as E. M. Bounds put it. The prayers of these Books of Kings prove what Adolph Monod wrote about "Prayer setting in motion the whole power of God."

Prayer for a Wise Heart

(I Kings 3)

In Gibeon the Lord appeared to Solomon in a dream by night: and God said, Ask what I shall give thee. And Solomon said, Thou hast shewed unto thy servant David my father great mercy, according as he walked before thee in truth, and in righteousness, and in upright-ness of heart with thee; and thou hast kept for him this great kind-ness, that thou hast given him a son to sit on his throne, as it is this day. And now, O Lord my God, thou hast made thy servant king instead of David my father: and I am but a little child: I know not how to go out or come in. And thy servant is in the midst of thy people which thou hast chosen, a great people, that cannot be numbered nor counted for multitude. Give therefore thy servant an understanding heart to judge thy people, that I may discern between good and bad: for who is able to judge this thy so great a people?

— I Kings 3:5-9

The only thing Solomon wanted from God was wisdom (II Chronicles 1:7-12; James 1:5). Such a noble prayer touches unusual heights in its deliberate rejection of riches and honor. Wrapped up in many prayers are all kinds of petitions — for health, long life, destruction of one's enemies — but all Solomon desired was a wise heart to serve God who had called him to such prominent service (I Kings 4:29-34).

In the great prayers of the Bible, direct addresses are few. Looking at Solomon's prayer we find that 25 verses of it carry no direct approach at all. The basis of the plea and mode of address are mentioned for our guidance (3:5, 27). What a different ending Solomon's career would have had if only he had maintained the level of his great and lofty prayer! Somehow he forgot his request for an understanding heart and a right discernment for the fulfilment of his God-given task (11:1-43).

Prayer of Dedication

(I Kings 8:12-61)

And Solomon stood before the altar of the Lord in the presence of all the congregation of Israel, and spread forth his hands toward heaven; And he said, Lord God of Israel, there is no God like thee, in heaven above, or on earth beneath, who keepest covenant and mercy with thy servants that walk before thee with all their heart: Who hast kept with thy servant David my father that thou promisedst him: thou spakest also with thy mouth, and hast fulfilled it with thine hand, as it is this day. Therefore now, Lord God of Israel, keep with thy servant David my father that thou promisedst him, saying, There shall not fail thee a man in my sight to sit on the throne of Israel; so that thy children take heed to their way, that they walk before me as thou hast walked before me. And now, O God of Israel, let thy word, I pray thee, be verified, which thou spakest unto thy servant David my father. But will God indeed dwell on the earth? behold, the heaven and heaven of heavens cannot contain thee; how much less this house that I have builded? Yet have thou respect unto the prayer of thy servant, and to his supplication, O Lord my God, to hearken unto the cry and to the prayer, which thy servant prayeth before thee to day: That thine eyes may be open toward this house night and day, even toward the place of which thou hast said, My name shall be there: that thou mayest hearken unto the prayer which thy servant shall make toward this place. And hearken thou to the supplication of thy servant, and of thy people Israel, when they shall pray toward this place: and hear thou in heaven thy dwelling place: and when thou hearest, forgive. . . .

If thy people go out to battle against their enemy, whithersoever thou shalt send them, and shall pray unto the Lord toward the city which thou hast chosen, and toward the house that I have built for thy name: Then hear thou in heaven their prayer and their supplication, and maintain their cause. . . .

And it was so, that when Solomon had made an end of praying all this prayer and supplication unto the Lord, he arose from before the altar of the Lord, from kneeling on his knees with his hands spread up to heaven. And he stood, and blessed all the congregation of Israel with a loud voice, saying, Blessed be the Lord, that hath given rest unto his people Israel, according to all that he promised: there hath not failed one word of all his good promise, which he promised by the hand of Moses his servant. The Lord our God be with us, as he was with our fathers: let him not leave us, nor forsake us: That he may incline our hearts unto him, to walk in all his ways, and to keep his commandments, and his statutes, and his judgments, which he commanded our fathers. And let these my words, wherewith I have made supplication before the Lord, be nigh unto the Lord our God day and night, that he maintain the cause of his servant, and the cause of his people Israel at all times, as the matter shall require: That all the people of the earth may know that the Lord is God, and that there is none else. Let your heart therefore be perfect with the Lord our God, to walk in his statutes, and to keep his commandments, as at this day.

— I Kings 8:22-30, 44, 45, 54-61

Solomon's prayer for divine approval is one of the longest recorded prayers in the Bible (II Chronicles 6:12-42). This lofty prayer of Solomon's teaches us many things. First of all, divine mercy is besought for the guilty because of God's special relations with the patriarchs (8:51-53; Deuteronomy 9:29). Then hands outstretched toward the Temple or toward heaven, God's dwelling place, is a common gesture in prayer (8:22, 54; Psalm 5:7). If the worshiper was out of Jerusalem he turned toward it when praying (8:38; Daniel 6:10). People responded with "Amen" (Nehemiah 8:6). Some preachers would die of fright if they heard a congregation uttering a fervent "Amen" to earnest pulpit prayers. Solomon knelt to pray (8:54) and stood to bless the people (8:14, 22, 54). A peculiar posture in prayer is that of the head between the knees (18:42). Nearly all Bible prayers were spoken in a loud voice. Praying before a large assembly one had to raise the voice (8:55). The priests of Baal cried out aloud (8:28).

Other features of Solomon's notable prayer and blessing might be mentioned. Constant confession of sin in Israel's prayers is an eloquent proof of the seriousness of her religion. Confession had to be full for God knows the hearts of all (8:39, 46) and such confession had to be offered with all the heart (8:43). Further, in the house of prayer national or social distinctions do not count (8:41). When we pray it must be with large hearts for God desires to save all nations (II Kings 19:16-19). God hears and honors sincere prayers (9:3).

Summarizing Solomon's prayer of dedication of the Temple we note the following petitions —

1. That God would hear him and that His name should be in the house (I Kings 9:3).
2. That God would condemn the wicked and justify the righteous (Isaiah 3:10, 11).
3. That Israel, if smitten before their enemies, repented or confessed their sins, they should be restored (II Chronicles 33:11-13; Nehemiah 1:4-11). To be perfectly fulfilled hereafter (Romans 11:26).
4. That if there should be no rain because of the sins of the people, on their confession it should be sent (I Kings 28:39-41).
5. That if there should be famine, pestilence, or a foreign invasion, they should be relieved on confession (II Kings 19; Isaiah 37).
6. That if a stranger should come and pray toward the Temple, he should be heard (Acts 8:27-40).
7. That if the people went to battle, God would maintain their cause if they looked to Him (II Chronicles 14:11; 20:20).
8. That if they were carried away captive and confessed their sins and returned to Him, He would cause their captors to be merciful unto them — fulfilled in the days of Ezra and Nehemiah.

Prayer for a Withered Hand

(I Kings 13:6)

And the king answered and said unto the man of God, Intreat now the face of the Lord thy God, and pray for me, that my hand may be restored me again. And the man of God besought the Lord, and the king's hand was restored him again, and became as it was before.
— I Kings 13:6

How conspicuous the prophets are in the role of intercessors! And how effective were their intercessions. Jeroboam entreats the prophet to pray for the restoration of his withered hand and healing was granted. Elijah also interceded efficaciously for the widow's son (17:21). But not all such prayers were answered as Paul's cry for the removal of his thorn clearly proves (II Corinthians 12:8).

Prayer for Closed Skies

(I Kings 17)

And Elijah the Tishbite, who was of the inhabitants of Gilead, said unto Ahab, As the Lord God of Israel liveth, before whom I stand, there shall not be dew nor rain these years, but according to my word.   — I Kings 17:1

More is recorded of Ahab than of any other king of Israel, and he, more than any other, provoked the Lord to anger (16:30). One old writer remarks, "Never was Israel so blind with a good prophet, as when so plagued with a bad king. Never was a king so bold to sin as Ahab. Never was a prophet so bold to reprove and threaten as Elijah."
The worship of Baal threatened to eliminate the worship of God.

Elijah, "a man of like passions with ourselves," enters the presence of the tyrant and announces the judgment of God. Elijah kneels and prays a prayer of faith, which seemed to strike like a fever into the heart of the earth. A man in communion and accord with the Almighty caused the rain to cease for three and a half years. No wonder James cites this as an example of efficacious prayer (5:16-18)! Think of it! The laws of nature were suspended year after year because a God-fearing man prayed.

Because God is the great Law-Giver and Lord of Nature He can alter or suspend the working of His own laws. To someone who wrote him upon the subject of prayer for rain, Professor Huxley replied: "If the whole universe is ruled by fixed laws, it is just as logically absurd for you to ask me to answer this letter as to ask the Almighty to alter the weather! The belief in the efficacy of prayer depends upon the assumption that there is Somebody somewhere who is strong enough to modify and control the earth and its contents."

Alfred Thomas comments, "It is pre-eminently in the matter of prayer that Elijah is proposed to us as an example in the New Testament." From the long list of Hebrew saints and worthies he had been selected by James, to prove and illustrate the proposition that "the prayer of a righteous man availeth much in its working" (5:16-18 R.V.). His prayers for drought are not mentioned by our historians, but his prayer for rain may not unreasonably be supposed to be referred to in the account of I Kings 18:42-45.

Prayer for Resurrection of Dead Son

(I Kings 17:20-24)

And he cried unto the Lord, and said, O Lord my God, hast thou also brought evil upon the widow with whom I sojourn, by slaying her son? And he stretched himself upon the child three times, and cried unto the Lord, and said, O Lord my God, I pray thee, let this child's soul come into him again.   — I Kings 17:20, 21

The widow who comforted Elijah under her poor but hospitable roof, and in whose house he often prayed, now stands in need of prayer. Her son is dead and the grief of the bereaved mother affected the heart of Elijah. Flinging himself upon the dead lad, the prophet prays, and what a prayer he poured forth. He supplicated God as his heart directed. To us, his prayer may seem too familiar, but that prayer was accepted of the Lord. Such a prayer may not agree with our notions and maxims concerning acceptable prayer, but as Krummacher expresses it in his remarkable volume on *Elijah the Tishbite,* "Here we have an unconditional prayer; a prayer, too, for something temporal; a prayer for a miracle; a prayer without limitations; and yet the Lord heard and answered it. Our gracious God does not bind Himself to our maxims, nor suffer Himself to be limited by our rules."

Prayer for Divine Honor

(I Kings 18:36-41)

And it came to pass at the time of the offering of the evening sacrifice, that Elijah the prophet came near, and said, Lord God of Abraham, Isaac, and of Israel, let it be known this day that thou art God in Israel, and that I am thy servant, and that I have done all these things at thy word. Hear me, O Lord, hear me, that this people may know that thou art the Lord God, and that thou hast turned their heart back again.   — I Kings 18:36, 37

Concealed for the duration of the three and a half years of famine, it is now time for a change of operation, so the command came to Elijah, "Go, show thyself to Ahab." Why, that was like asking a man to go into a lion's den! If Ahab was arrogant enough before the famine, its long duration had not helped his spirit.

Fearlessly, however, Elijah met Ahab and faithfully condemned him for his wickedness. The imperious tones of God's voice rang in Elijah's ear impelling him to face the king (18:2, 33). Then came the test. The altars were prepared and a secret awe pervaded the multitude. The honor of God is at stake. Baal's prophets pray — nothing happens. Elijah prays at night (18:36; Ezra 9:5; Luke 1:9) — and the fire of heaven descends. His prayer reveals sublime confidence in God (18:31). Here is another prayer linked with the past (18:36). God and His people are vindicated. Elijah's brief prayer was effective (18:36, 37; 17:21). Upon the priests of Baal, the signs and wonders of the day were lost. Elijah demanded their slaughter, which was accomplished.

Would that we could know more of the power of faith and the efficacy of prayer, Carmel proclaims! Elijah, at a critical moment addresses God three times in two verses, and God heard and answered. How dramatic and exciting some of the prayer scenes of the Bible are (18:26, 28). In the crises of life men turn to God (22:5-7).

Prayer and Perseverance

(I Kings 18:45)

So Ahab went up to eat and to drink. And Elijah went up to the top of Carmel; and he cast himself down upon the earth, and put his face between his knees, And said to his servant, Go up now, look toward the sea. And he went up, and looked, and said, There is nothing. And he said, Go again seven times.   — I Kings 18:42, 43

How persevering was Elijah! The fact that there was no sign of rain did not daunt him. "Go again seven times," he said to his servant. Pray we must, but that is not enough. "Pray and not faint" is the exhortation of the New Testament (Luke 18:1; Ephesians 5:18; Colossians 4:2). The Lord must be diligently sought (Hebrews 11:6). The "seven times" of Elijah signified that he prayed on until the covenant God answered (Leviticus 4:5, 17; 8:11; 14:16). Elijah was not discouraged even by the sixth repetition of the despairing phrase of his servant, "There is no rain." The prophet knew that God had not forgotten to be gracious. Elijah persisted in prayer until the great rain came. Alas, we soon tire if answers are delayed. We must learn what it is to "give Him no rest" (Isaiah 62:7) .

Prayer for Death

(I Kings 19)

> But he himself went a day's journey into the wilderness, and came and sat down under a juniper tree: and he requested for himself that he might die; and said, It is enough; now, O Lord, take away my life; for I am not better than my fathers.   —I Kings 19:4

This is a somewhat pitiful chapter. After his victorious stand against Baal, Elijah fled from the wrath of Jezebel, and as an over-wrought prophet, wanted to die. But in God's wisdom Elijah's petulant request was refused. Had God granted the prophet's desire to die, his earthly ministry would have missed its crowning and unique glory (II Kings 2:11). Along with Moses and Jonah who presented similar requests, Elijah's unanswered prayer reminds us that we are not always fit for heaven when we are most weary of earth (Numbers 11:15; Jonah 4:1-9).

Worn in body and brain, Elijah became a prey to fear. The prophet had worn himself for God. His ministry had been a costly and exhausting one. Loneliness also was another explanation of his sense of being forsaken. "I, even I only." But how tender and understanding God was — and ever is!

II Kings

Elijah, the prophet of fire (1:10), whose remarkable power in prayer became famous in his day, must have exercised a tremendous influence over young Elisha, his successor. Elisha's prophetic prayers were efficacious as can be proven in his curse in the name of Jehovah upon the youths who mocked him (2:24); also in his prayer for the dead son of the Shunamite (4:35); in the prayer for the opening of his servant's eyes (6:17); in his petition that the foes of Israel might be smitten with blindness (6:18); in the prayer for recovery of their sight (6:26).

The mighty, prevailing prayers of the prophet prove that intercession can cover a wide area. Hezekiah prayed for recovery from illness (20:5) and for deliverance from Sennacherib (19:20). Prayers for the restoration of the dead are few and far between, but Elijah, Elisha and Peter prayed effectively in this realm (I Kings 7:21; II Kings 4:3; Acts 9:46) . Gideon's fleece and the sundial are further evidences of the variety of prayer (Judges 6:36; II Kings 20:11).

Prayer for a Dead Child

(II Kings 4:32-37)

He went in therefore, and shut the door upon them twain, and prayed unto the Lord. And he went up, and lay upon the child, and put his mouth upon his mouth, and his eyes upon his eyes, and his hands upon his hands: and he stretched himself upon the child; and the flesh of the child waxed warm. Then he returned, and walked in the house to and fro; and went up, and stretched himself upon him: and the child sneezed seven times, and the child opened his eyes.

— II Kings 4:33-35

The mantle of Elijah fell upon Elisha, who in turn knew how to find his way into the bosom of the Eternal. In his frequent journeys between Carmel and Samaria, Elisha was often entertained by the pious woman of Shunem and her husband. As a reward for her kindness to Elisha, God made her the happy mother of a son. Alas, one day he fell sick, and —

They bore him to his mother, and he lay
Upon her knees till noon — and then he died.

Elisha was sought. His staff in Gehazi's hand was not sufficient. Elisha hastened to the death-chamber, stretched himself upon the corpse, prayed to God, the Author of life, and the child lived again.

Our prayers cannot raise the physically dead, but they can prevail on behalf of those who are dead in trespasses and sins. Have you experienced the thrill of seeing the spiritually dead raised to life through your prayers?

Of the two miracles (I Kings 17; II Kings 4), Mrs. A. T. Robertson says:

"These two supreme miracles are much alike. There were many mothers in those days who lost their children, but only these two received them again from the dead. In both cases, the child has been laid upon the prophet's bed. The prophet first prays, then stretches himself upon the child, repeatedly, and life is restored. Both men had grown strong in faith by prayer and a study of God's providence. Both were deeply moved, as Jesus was in the presence of death. No doubt 'virtue went out of them' in that energetic prayer. We cannot raise the dead, but if we have a living faith we shall be able, even when suddenly called upon, to comfort others 'through the comfort wherewith we ourselves are comforted of God.' Perfunctory sympathy, like perfunctory piety, is dead."

While the Temple of old was the place of prayer in a very peculiar sense (19:14; John 4:20), yet God could be approached anywhere but not *anyhow* (John 4:24). Elisha prayed in a death chamber: Jonah in the belly of a whale (Jonah 2). The shut door is essential (Matthew 6:6).

Prayer for Vision

(II Kings 6:13-20)

And Elisha prayed, and said, Lord, I pray thee, open his eyes, that he may see. And the Lord opened the eyes of the young man; and he saw: and, behold, the mountain was full of horses and chariots of fire round about Elisha.   — II Kings 6:17

With the city encompassed by an enemy we can understand the anxiety of Elisha's servant, "Alas, what shall we do?" To him, there seemed no way out. Elisha, however, viewed the situation differently. Strong confidence was his. "Fear not, for they that be with us are more than they that be with them." Elisha knew all about the unseen resources, of which his mystified servant was ignorant. So the prophet prays that the servant's eyes may be opened, until with his inner vision he could see the vast host of unseen allies.

The narrative has its humorous side. The whole army of the Syrians was hoodwinked and led into a trap. Once in it, Elisha, the prophet of grace, quietly asked that they should be fed, treated kindly and then sent home. Here we have a practical illustration of feeding a hungry enemy (Romans 12:20, 21).

Prayer for Deliverance from Defiant Foes

(II Kings 19)

And Hezekiah prayed before the Lord, and said, O Lord God of Israel, which dwellest between the cherubims, thou art the God, even thou alone, of all the kingdoms of the earth; thou hast made heaven and earth. Lord, bow down thine ear, and hear: open, Lord, thine eyes, and see: and hear the words of Sennacherib, which hath sent him to reproach the living God. Of a truth, Lord, the kings of Assyria have destroyed the nations and their lands, And have cast their gods into the fire: for they were no gods, but the work of men's hands, wood and stone: therefore they have destroyed them. Now therefore, O Lord our God, I beseech thee, save thou us out of his hand, that all the kingdoms of the earth may know that thou art the Lord God, even thou only.   — II Kings 19:15-19

Crises drove Israel's leaders to God. Beset by foes, Jehoahaz besought the Lord (II Kings 13:4).

While the previous few chapters contain no recorded prayers, heart-felt prayers must have been offered by Elisha as he faced the enemies of God. As all true revival is born in prayer, the revival through Jehoiada must have come that way (11:17-21). Jotham also must have been a man of prayer (15:34, 35). The same factor is associated with revival under Hezekiah (18:3-7).

Good King Hezekiah, the reformer, confronted by the insults of Rabshakeh, like the prudent man he was, did not depend upon human wisdom or resort to human expedients. He went to the house of the Lord, there to pray in his day of trouble, of rebuke, and of blasphemy. Divine guidance and protection were sought, and God granted them. God's honor had been insulted. He who dwells between the Cherubim had been defied, and Hezekiah pleads with God to vindicate Himself. What an answer to his prayer the king received! God sent an angel to deal with the arrogant Assyrians and by the morning light, 185,000 of their corpses lay scattered over the field.

It is ever fearful for the enemies of the saints of God to force them to the throne of grace. Hezekiah, it must be noted, pleads the sovereignty of God. "Thou art God alone." "If God be for us, who can be against us?" One solitary saint retires to pray — one solitary angel, by the order of the Lord, destroys a vast host. The efficacy of prayer is seen in that Hezekiah through his dependence upon God had more power than the armies of Judah and the hosts of Sennacherib. Long prayers have little Biblical sanction. The earnest prayer of Hezekiah for deliverance from his foes was uttered in about a minute. Thanks introduces his brief but dynamic prayer (19:15).

Sir Winston Churchill, in his account of the First World War, refers to the Battle of the Marne and expresses his conviction that a power beyond the human was present for the Allies' deliverance. This was the confidence of Hezekiah (19:32-35). On American coins is stamped the phrase *In God We Trust*. Such a testimony is the national recognition of God in human affairs.

Prayer for Longer Life

(II Kings 20:1-11. See II Chronicles 32:20-26; Isaiah 37:14-20; 38:1-8)

In those days was Hezekiah sick unto death. And the prophet Isaiah the son of Amoz came to him, and said unto him, Thus saith the Lord, Set thine house in order; for thou shalt die, and not live. Then he turned his face to the wall, and prayed unto the Lord, saying, I beseech thee, O Lord, remember now how I have walked before thee in truth and with a perfect heart, and have done that which is good in thy sight. And Hezekiah wept sore.

— II Kings 20:1-3

In sickness men turn to God as the Lord of life with confidence that He is able to heal (Exodus 15:26). Hezekiah pleads his own integrity of heart. He also "wept sore" (20:3). We have frequent references to tears accompanying prayers.

Hezekiah was told that he must die, but for some reason or other the thought of death was unwelcome to the king, so he prayed that God would prolong his days. His prayer was heard and his tears seen. God added fifteen years to Hezekiah's life, during which time a son was born to him, Manasseh, who became an abomination unto the Lord. It might have been better for Hezekiah had he died when the divine announcement reached him. There are occasions when God grants our request, but with it comes leanness of soul.

Although Manasseh was a wicked man nothing is said in this

history of the king about his prayer of penitence (21:11-16; II Chronicles 33:12). Hezekiah had every confidence in Isaiah as a man who lived near to God. Character gives power in prayer. If we expect answered prayer we must seek habitually to live near to God.

I Chronicles

Although the two Books of Chronicles, like the two Books of Kings, are but one book in the Jewish Canon, we take them separately, sifting what each has to say concerning the practices and precept of prayer. As we read *The Chronicles* we sometimes have the feeling that there are parts worthy of omission from the Bible. How weary it becomes reading through a record of names and a catalogue of genealogies! Yet the same prove how particular the Jews were in the preservation of their heritage. Here and there we light upon a verdant spot in the desert of dry facts — a spring at which we can slake our thirst.

Prayer for Spiritual Prosperity
(I Chronicles 4:9, 10)

And Jabez called on the God of Israel, saying, Oh that thou wouldest bless me indeed, and enlarge my coast, and that thine hand might be with me, and that thou wouldest keep me from evil, that it may not grieve me! And God granted him that which he requested.
— I Chronicles 4:10

The brief but blessed prayer of Jabez is a refreshing spring. What was the nature of his prayer? This child of sorrow prayed for spiritual prosperity, the enlargement of his coast and deliverance from evil, and his request was readily granted. Jabez showed great spiritual discernment in casting his prayer in the form that he did. He prayed, not to be kept from evil, but kept from being *grieved* by evil. While God does not provide temptation, He yet permits it as He did in Christ's experience, for the strengthening of character (James 1:12-14).

How we need to make this Old Testament saint's prayer our own! Each of us is in deep need of fuller blessing, widening horizons of faith and a more constant emancipation from sin's dominion. Jabez prayed as an heir of a temporal Canaan. Ours is a great and more enduring heritage.

Prayer As Trust
(I Chronicles 5:20)

And they were helped against them, and the Hagarites were delivered into their hand, and all that were with them: for they cried to God in the battle, and he was intreated of them; because they put their trust in him.
— I Chronicles 5:20

The Reubenites, Gadites and some of the tribe of Manasseh "cried unto the Lord in battle." Here is another of those battle-prayers of the Bible (21:17). Not all such prayers were responded to. This one, however, against the Hagarites was because those who prayed "put their trust in God." Trust in God's ability to undertake if the prayer offered is in accordance with His will, is one of the basic conditions of prayer. Prayer and faith are bound together (Psalm 2:12; Matthew 9:28). How differently Saul's life would have ended if only he had sought and obeyed the Lord (10:13, 14).

Prayer of Fear
(I Chronicles 13:12)

And David was afraid of God that day, saying, How shall I bring the ark of God home to me?   — I Chronicles 13:12

David knew how to *pray*, as well as *play*, before God with all his might (13:8). There was no need of David's displeasure at God's action in smiting Uzza for touching the Ark. He surely knew the law — the Ark had to be borne without being touched (Numbers 4:15). But afraid he cried, "How shall I bring the Ark of God home?" He learned that it could be only brought home, as it was twenty years later, in God's way as the next chapter clearly shows.

Fragments of, and the Psalm of I Chronicles 16, are to be found in Psalms 96, 105, 106, all of which celebrate God's goodness to Israel and His right to praise from all the earth. How earth-bound we are when we fail to bless God from whom all blessings flow!

We further notice that it was the custom in the formal worship of a congregation of worshipers to say "Amen" (16:36). The Levites must have offered many a prayer as they lodged round about the house of God (9:27). What a blessed ministry these choristers exercised (16:4)! Incense and offering of burnt-sacrifices accompanied prayer and praise (16:1-4; 28:13, 30; II Chronicles 29:11; 31:2).

Prayer for Establishment of Covenant
(I Chronicles 17:16-27)

And David the king came and sat before the Lord. . . .
                              — I Chronicles 17:16a

As attention has already been given to this prayer (II Samuel 7:18-29), we simply pause to elaborate upon the posture adopted by David who *sat* before the Lord (17:16). While, perhaps, this posture should not be taken as a precedent, prolonged periods of prayer on the knees might cause weariness of the flesh hindering devotion of spirit.

> 'Tis not to those who stand erect,
>   Or those who bend the knee,
> It is to those who bow the heart
>   The Lord will gracious be;
> It is the posture of the soul
>   That pleases or offends;
> If it be not in God's sight right
>   Naught else can make amends.

Prayer Answered by Fire

(I Chronicles 21)

And David built there an altar unto the Lord, and offered burnt offerings and peace offerings, and called upon the Lord; and he answered him from heaven by fire upon the altar of burnt offering.
— I Chronicles 21:26

Having previously dealt with David's prayer in the choice of his punishment for numbering the people (II Samuel 24) we feel a further word is in order concerning the way God answered David's prayer and his altar-offerings. "God answered him by fire" (21:26; II Chronicles 7:1). It is somewhat impressive to turn to the Book of Acts and read of the early saints praying (1:14), then of the Holy Spirit coming upon them as fire (2:1-4).

Prayer As a Sentinel

(I Chronicles 23:30)

And to stand every morning to thank and praise the Lord, and likewise at even.   — I Chronicles 23:30

We do not have many prayers of priests. They blessed in the name of Jehovah. One of their principal functions was to "thank and praise the Lord." Yet gratitude is an inescapable aspect of prayer. There is the characteristic feature of a tribute of thanksgiving at the beginning of prayer (29:11). Is it not suggestive to read that part of the office of the sons of Aaron was to stand "every morning" and "at even" to "thank and praise the Lord" (II Chronicles 13:10, 11)? Beginning the day they would bless the Lord for the gift of sleep received and for the assurance that He is the same today as yesterday. At night, praises would ascend for all the manifold tokens of divine favor vouchsafed through the day and for His guardian care through another night. The unchanging nature and being of God is a theme for praise in prayer (I Chronicles 28:9, 10).

Prayer and Giving

(I Chronicles 29:10-19)

Wherefore David blessed the Lord before all the congregation: and David said, Blessed be thou, Lord God of Israel our father, for ever and ever. Thine, O Lord, is the greatness, and the power, and the glory, and the victory, and the majesty: for all that is in the heaven and in the earth is thine; thine is the kingdom, O Lord, and thou art exalted as head above all. Both riches and honour come of thee, and thou reignest over all; and in thine hand is power and might; and in thine hand it is to make great, and to give strength unto all. Now therefore, our God, we thank thee, and praise thy glorious name. But who am I, and what is my people, that we should be able to offer so willingly after this sort? for all things come of thee, and of thine own have we given thee. For we are strangers before thee, and sojourners, as were all our fathers: our days on the earth are as a shadow, and there is none abiding. O Lord our God, all this store that we have prepared to build thee an house for thine holy name cometh of thine hand, and is all thine own. I know also, my God, that thou triest the heart, and hast pleasure in uprightness. As for me, in the uprightness of mine heart I have willingly offered all these things: and now I have seen with joy thy people, which are present here, to offer willingly unto thee. O Lord God of Abraham, Isaac, and of Israel, our fathers, keep this for ever in the imagination of the thoughts of the heart of thy people, and prepare their heart unto thee: And give unto Solomon my son a perfect heart, to keep thy commandments, thy testimonies, and thy statutes, and to do all these things, and to build the palace, for the which I have made provision.   — I Chronicles 29:10-19

The golden verse in this magnificent chapter, with its beautiful prayer for free-will offerings for the Temple, is the ninth where we read of the people offering themselves and their gifts "willingly." What a spontaneous outburst of joy and thanksgiving there was on the part of all the people! No wonder the tongue of David was loosened to bless God as he did! There is little freedom in prayer unless offered to God out of a generous heart. With the offerings of the willing heart there naturally flows the surrender of the offerer himself (29:18). Both gifts and the giver must be placed on the altar. David is an illustration of the truth that "God loveth a cheerful giver" (II Corinthians 9:7).

The national aspect of prayer appears in the expression, *"Our* God" (20:16). Happy are the people whose God is the Lord. Bowing of the head is another posture of prayer common to the Bible (29:20; Nehemiah 8:6).

II Chronicles

In this further historical book we have much prayer material already considered. For Solomon's prayer for wisdom, 1:7-10, see I Kings 3:5-15. For the tribute of praise to God and a confession of Israel's faith, 5:13, see I Kings 8:1-11. For Solomon's prayer of dedication, offered with the spreading forth of hands, 6:12-42, see I Kings 8:22-53. The repeated cry, "Forgive," must always be our foundation petition (Matthew 6:14, 15).

> Saviour breathe forgiveness o'er us
> All our weakness Thou dost know.

Also in Solomon's moving prayer we have the recurring *IF.* Great promises are uttered by Solomon but they are all conditional. Obedience to God's Word is a vital qualification in answered prayer (John 13:17).

Prayer in National Danger

(II Chronicles 14:11)

And Asa cried unto the Lord his God, and said, Lord, it is nothing with thee to help, whether with many, or with them that have no power: help us, O Lord our God; for we rest on thee, and in thy name we go against this multitude. O Lord, thou art our God; let not man prevail against thee.   — II Chronicles 14:11

Here is another instance of prayer before battle (II Chronicles 13:4-13; 14:10, 11). Occasionally such prayers are not very real or deep. God, in answer to the cry of need, intervenes and delivers, but those who pray thereafter forget their divine deliverer (II Chronicles 16:7-9).

While King Asa's prayer only occupies one verse, his whole reign harmonized with the prayer and explains his prosperity (14:7, 8, 11). Asa prayed, planned (14:2-6), prospered and prevailed (14:12, 13). Asa was one of the few monarchs on the Throne of David whose life seemed to be guided by the influence of the man after God's own heart. Early in life, Asa set about reforming the manners and morals of the people. During his reign, Zerah of Ethiopia marched against him with an army of a million men and three hundred chariots of war. Greatly outnumbered, Asa was not perturbed, for his cause was the cause of God. Not only so, but he knew that God is not always on the side of big battalions. Asa turned to the Lord and happily his fervent, appropriate prayer has been preserved.

Asa appealed to God as *his* God, and the God of his people, and his prayer was graciously answered. God gave Asa's troops the advantages of the enemy, so much so, that confused and dismayed, they were overtaken in defeat and despoiled of vast treasures.

How different our civilization would be if we had Christian nations ruled over by men of prayer! God grant us leaders who seek divine guidance in the management of the nation's foreign relations, as well as in home affairs.

Prayer and Reform

(II Chronicles 15)

So they gathered themselves together at Jerusalem in the third month, in the fifteenth year of the reign of Asa. And they offered unto the Lord the same time, of the spoil which they had brought, seven hundred oxen and seven thousand sheep. And they entered into a covenant to seek the Lord God of their fathers with all their heart and with all their soul; That whosoever would not seek the Lord God of Israel should be put to death, whether small or great, whether man or woman. And they sware unto the Lord with a loud voice, and with shouting, and with trumpets, and with cornets. And all Judah rejoiced at the oath: for they had sworn with all their heart, and sought him with their whole desire; and he was found of them: and the Lord gave them rest round about.

— II Chronicles 15:10-15

God was found of those who diligently sought him (15:4). True reformation followed and God gave victory (15:8-19). How sad it is that such a godly king, who proved how God answers prayer, put the King of Syria and his physicians before the Lord (15:7, 10, 12)!

Jehoshaphat was another whose heart was lifted up to the ways of the Lord (17:6), but who ultimately came to depend upon the arm of flesh (18:1). Although Jehoshaphat committed his cause to God, his prayer seems a trifle superfluous, seeing he had almost a million and a quarter fighting men. Yet the Lord helped him (18:31).

Prayer and Appeal to History
(II Chronicles 20:3-13)

And Jehoshaphat stood in the congregation of Judah and Jerusalem, in the house of the Lord, before the new court, And said, O Lord God of our fathers, art not thou God in heaven? and rulest not thou over all the kingdoms of the heathen? and in thine hand is there not power and might, so that none is able to withstand thee? Art not thou our God, who didst drive out the inhabitants of this land before thy people Israel, and gavest it to the seed of Abraham thy friend for ever? And they dwelt therein, and have built thee a sanctuary therein for thy name, saying, If, when evil cometh upon us, as the sword, judgment, or pestilence, or famine, we stand before this house, and in thy presence, (for thy name is in this house,) and cry unto thee in our affliction, then thou wilt hear and help. And now, behold, the children of Ammon and Moab and mount Seir, whom thou wouldest not let Israel invade, when they came out of the land of Egypt, but they turned from them, and destroyed them not; Behold, I say, how they reward us, to come to cast us out of thy possession, which thou hast given us to inherit. O our God, wilt thou not judge them? for we have no might against this great company that cometh against us; neither know we what to do: but our eyes are upon thee.   — II Chronicles 20:5-12

Not only is this another battle-prayer (20:12), but another instance in which history is linked to prayer (20:7, 8). Further, deity is addressed three times (20:6, 7, 12). The free use of divine titles is very common in Old Testament prayers. In the answer to prayer Jehoshaphat received, the *standing still* does not mean inactivity (20:16, 17). Because of the power of prayer, we can face any issue with confidence (20:20). As we pray and believe we are established.

While we have no recorded prayers of godly Joash (24:2), he must have lived near to God. It is profitable to gather together the prayers of the dying. Life's great farewell is often fragrant when reached with a single prayer. How sad when it is a farewell prayer of vengeance (20:27)!

For Uzziah's communication with God (26:5) see II Kings 14. For the experience of Hezekiah in prayer (30:18-20; 31:21; 32:8) go back to II Kings 18. How the king met the defiance of Sennacherib (32:20, 24) has been indicated in a previous comment (II Kings 19, 20:1-11).

Men of doubt had to be assured by a sign (32:24). In response to the pleas and prayers of Hezekiah, God sent an angel to destroy the host of Sennacherib.

Prayer of Penitence

(II Chronicles 33:13)

And he prayed unto him: and he was intreated of him, and heard his supplication, and brought him again to Jerusalem into his kingdom. Then Manasseh knew that the Lord he was God.

— II Chronicles 33:13

What a manifestation of grace we have in God's reply to the prayer of Manasseh! God had previously spoken to the heart of this wicked king (33:10; II Kings 21), but he would not hearken to the divine voice. It took captivity and affliction to bring him to a realization of his need of God, and as is often the case, out of anguish of soul, God was sought (33:12). In spite of evil ways, his sincere prayer was answered (33:13, 19), and knowing that "the Lord was God," he ended his reign basking in divine favor. How willing God is to blot out the past transgressions of those who, in true penitence, seek His face!

There is no need to linger over Josiah's contribution to the prayers of the Bible (34:3), seeing these have been dealt with in II Kings 22.

Ezra

As we have learned from previous historical books, sin brought Israel into captivity. With the end of seventy years of bondage, a portion of the nation returned to Jerusalem to rebuild the Temple and renew the worship of God. While prayers are not frequent in this post-captivity book, Ezra, the ardent reformer, must have waited much upon the God he feared.

When the ancient worship had been re-established, we have a prayer of gratitude (3:11). The intimate relation between sacrifice and supplication which is of very ancient origin, is also emphasized (4:2; 6:21, 22). Personal and intercessory prayer, the latter often offered for strangers and for those who were bent on destroying the Temple of God, also find a place in Ezra (6:10, 11).

Prayer of Thanksgiving

(Ezra 7:27, 28)

Blessed be the Lord God of our fathers, which hath put such a thing as this in the king's heart, to beautify the house of the Lord which is in Jerusalem: And hath extended mercy unto me before the king, and his counselors, and before all the king's mighty princes. And I was strengthened as the hand of the Lord my God was upon me, and I gathered together out of Israel chief men to go up with me.

— Ezra 7:27, 28

In these days when many reject the substance of the unsaved for the Lord's work, it is interesting to note that gratitude was expressed for *heathen* help received. Ezra the scribe breaks out in an enthusiastic prayer of praise to Jehovah for the goodness of Artaxerxes.

Prayer and Fasting

(Ezra 8:21-23)

Then I proclaimed a fast there, at the river of Ahava, that we might afflict ourselves before our God, to seek of him a right way for us, and for our little ones, and for all our substance. For I was ashamed to require of the king a band of soldiers and horsemen to help us against the enemy in the way: because we had spoken unto the king, saying, The hand of our God is upon all them for good that seek him; but his power and his wrath is against all them that forsake him. So we fasted and besought our God for this: and he was intreated of us.   — Ezra 8:21-23

How Ezra entreated God for a safe and prosperous journey to the home-land (8:22) and for protection from perils by the way! He also prayed for the vindication of God's honor and glory (8:21, 23). True humiliation and fasting accompanied prayer (8:21, 23). Although the form of prayer used by Ezra on this occasion is not recorded, there can be no doubt that it had its foundation in the heart and was prompted by a sense of dependence upon, and confidence in, the God who answers prayer.

Prayer and Confession

(Ezra 9:5 — 10:4)

And said, O my God, I am ashamed and blush to lift up my face to thee, my God: for our iniquities are increased over our head, and our trespass is grown up unto the heavens. Since the days of our fathers have we been in a great trespass unto this day; and for our iniquities have we, our kings, and our priests, been delivered into the hand of the kings of the lands, to the sword, to captivity, and to a spoil, and to confusion of face, as it is this day. And now for a little space grace hath been shewed from the Lord our God, to leave us a remnant to escape, and to give us a nail in his holy place, that our God may lighten our eyes, and give us a little reviving in our bondage. For we were bondmen; yet our God hath not forsaken us in our bondage, but hath extended mercy unto us in the sight of the kings of Persia, to give us a reviving, to set up the house of our God, and to repair the desolations thereof, and to give us a wall in Judah and in Jerusalem. And now, O our God, what shall we say after this? for we have forsaken thy commandments, Which thou hast commanded by thy servants the prophets, saying, The land, unto which ye go to possess it, is an unclean land with the filthiness of the people of the lands, with their abominations, which have filled it from one end to another with their uncleanness. Now therefore give not your daughters unto their sons, neither take their daughters unto your sons, nor seek their peace or their wealth for ever: that ye may be strong, and eat the good of the land, and leave it for an inheritance to your children for ever. And after all that is come upon us for our evil deeds, and for our great trespass, seeing that thou our God hast punished us less than our iniquities deserve, and hast given us such deliverance as this; Should we again break thy commandments, and join in affinity with the people of these abominations? wouldest not thou be angry with us till thou hadst consumed us, so that there should be no remnant nor escaping? O Lord God of Israel, thou art righteous: for we remain yet escaped, as it is this day: behold, we are before thee in our trespasses: for we cannot stand before thee because of this.   — Ezra 9:6-15

Several features stand out prominently in this great prayer expressing confidence in God to undertake for His people. There was public confession of guilt (9:11). Particular sin, like forbidden intermarriage, had to be repented of and dealt with (9:12). Covenant relationship with God was emphasized (9:8, 13). Demonstrating genuine penitence, Ezra rent his garments, plucked off his hair, and sat confounded till the time of the evening oblation.

Ezra knew how to pray and plead (9:6) — he knew history (9:7) — he knew how to read the need of his own times (9:8, 9). He pleaded for the preservation of the nation (9:14) and for God's help (9:15). Can we wonder at such a prayer being saturated with tears (10:1)? The weeping revealed true sorrow of heart: Penitence and prayer led to performance, seeing guilt was removed (9:15). The prayer was offered before the Temple "between the porch and the altar" which, in a unique sense, was the house of prayer (Joel 2:17; Luke 19:46).

Nehemiah

Ezra's duty was the repairing of the Temple. To Nehemiah fell the task of repairing the walls and the gates. As the cup-bearer of the Persian monarch, Artaxerxes, Nehemiah was in a position to ask favors, as he did, for his sacred task. As a child of God, he knew how to present his requests and receive striking answers.

Pastor Harms of Hermannsburg, when faced with a crisis in his life, said, "I prayed fervently unto the Lord. I laid the matter in His hands, and as I rose at midnight from my knees, I said, with a voice that almost startled me, *Forward now in God's name!*" It was so with Nehemiah who prayed and built.

Nehemiah was as truly a man of prayer as Elijah but he wrought no miracles. A need and an opportunity called him and that was enough. The ruins of the city filled his soul with grief, and he prayed till his heart was near the breaking point. But nothing extraordinary happened, nothing save performance born of prayer. What pregnant sayings these are and how they summarize Nehemiah's noble work —

So I prayed.
So we built.

As we shall discover, prayer was the maintained attitude and constant habit of Nehemiah. He prayed all the time, all the way through and about everything, and he prospered because he prayed. Nehemiah prayed and used his wits. He knew God would protect him but he was careful to add a sword to the equipment used to build the wall. He trusted God but kept his powder dry.

Prayer Born of Distress

(Nehemiah 1:4-11)

And it came to pass, when I heard these words, that I sat down and wept, and mourned certain days, and fasted, and prayed before the God of heaven, And said, I beseech thee, O Lord God of heaven, the great and terrible God, that keepeth covenant and mercy for them that love him and observe his commandments: Let thine ear now be attentive, and thine eyes open, that thou mayest hear the prayer of thy servant, which I pray before thee now, day and night, for the children of Israel thy servants, and confess the sins of the children of Israel, which we have sinned against thee: both I and my father's house have sinned. We have dealt very corruptly against thee, and have not kept the commandments, nor the statutes, nor the judgments, which thou commandedst thy servant Moses. Remember, I beseech thee, the word that thou commandedst thy servant Moses, saying, If ye transgress, I will scatter you abroad among the nations: But if ye turn unto me, and keep my commandments, and do them; though there were of you cast out unto the uttermost part of the heaven, yet will I gather them from thence, and will bring them unto the place that I have chosen to set my name there. Now these are thy servants and thy people, whom thou hast redeemed by thy great power, and by thy strong hand. O Lord, I beseech thee, let now thine ear be attentive to the prayer of thy servant, and to the prayer of thy servants, who desire to fear thy name: and prosper, I pray thee, thy servant this day, and grant him mercy in the sight of this man. For I was the king's cupbearer.

— Nehemiah 1:4-11

This great prayer is impressive in that it is a declaration of divine faith. All through it Nehemiah rests his plan upon the attributes of God. In a footnote to the prayer before us Professor McFadyen remarks, "The private prayers of Nehemiah are usually addressed to 'my God' without any specific allusion to the God of Israel. Compare, even in the narrative, 'my God' (7:5). But his work was essentially a national work, and he would naturally commit it and himself to the tutelage of the national God; compare *our* God (4:4, 9; 6:16); and the long opening prayer of the book is addressed substantially, though not formally, to the God of Israel (1:5-11)."

Nehemiah proclaimed a fast before prayer (1:4) and wept as he prayed (1:4) and offered both personal and general confession of sin (1:6, 7), and called upon God to answer because of His Word (1:8). It was the prayer he prayed "day and night" (1:6). The conclusion of this great prayer reveals that Nehemiah had conceived a plan whereby he could contribute to the answering of his prayer. What else could God do but hear and answer this prayer of a patriot — a statesman's prayer in time of national defection?

Prayer in a Tight Corner

(Nehemiah 2:4)

Then the king said unto me, For what dost thou make request? So I prayed to the God of heaven. — Nehemiah 2:4

Nehemiah had no time to shut his eyes and bend his knees to spend a prolonged season of prayer. There was only time for a tight-corner prayer. His countenance was sad, whether designed to attract notice or to mirror his burdened soul, we are not told. Anyhow, the king observed Nehemiah's countenance and enquired as to its sadness. Up went a sentence prayer to God for direction, which was rewarded with a bountiful answer. God impressed the heart of the heathen king to grant Nehemiah leave of absence to repair the damaged gates and forth he went certain that God would prosper him (2:20).

In the habit of regular prayer, Nehemiah found it only natural to adopt this method of emergency prayer — a sky-telegram — "a way to escape" (I Corinthians 10:13). Silent prayers are offered when a spoken one would have been impossible. Doubtless Nehemiah had sent up many a swift and silent prayer to God, seeing prayer was the God-ward aspect of his life. Nehemiah lifted up his heart in a secret ejaculation to the God who understands the language of the heart-prayer. What a vivid view of Nehemiah's inner life do we get from his brief prayer. What an illustration of that presence of mind which may be described as the sense and practice of the Presence of. God.

We, too, should make frequent use of ejaculatory prayer, which, although it is no sufficient substitute for regular seasons of prayer, yet fills the gap between. *Ejaculatory* comes from a Latin word for the swift darts used in ancient warfare. The best way to counteract "the fiery darts" of the enemy is by the fervent darts of secret prayer (Ephesians 6:16-18). Sincere ejaculation should be cultivated, not only on particular occasions, but at all times. Wherever we are, we have a way opened towards heaven. Active in business or home, traveling here and there, or taken up with a hundred and one things, we can silently express our needs and desires a thousand times a day. The apostles made use of the "dart-prayer" in times of physical danger (Matthew 8:25; 14:30), and so did those who came to Christ in need and distress (Matthew 9:27; 15:25; John 4:49).

> The silent pleading
> Of thy spirit raised above
> Will reach His Throne of Glory,
> Who is mercy, truth and love.

Prayer for Deliverance from Reproach

(Nehemiah 4:1-6)

Hear, O our God; for we are despised: and turn their reproach upon their own head, and give them for a prey in the land of captivity: and cover not their iniquity, and let not their sin be blotted out from before thee: for they have provoked thee to anger before the builders.   — Nehemiah 4:4, 5

Sanballat tried to dissuade Nehemiah from his great task by heaping ridicule upon his efforts, but he prayed for the frustration of the plans of his foes. Nehemiah frequently broke into a paragraph or ends it with a prayer (4:4; 5:19; 13:4, 22, 29, 31). It needs close attention to discern the difference between narration and prayer. This is what Professor McFadyen calls "the phenomenon of interpolated prayer."

Prayer Triumphing over Anger

(Nehemiah 4:7-9)

Nevertheless we made our prayer unto our God, and set a watch against them day and night, because of them.   — Nehemiah 4:9

Sanballat, joined by Tobiah along with many other discouragers, came against Nehemiah again (4:7). This time through anger and conspiracy they sought to hinder Nehemiah, but his resource was prayer, so on he went with the work. Our Lord urges us to "watch and pray." Nehemiah not only made prayer unto God, but also set a watch against his angry hinderers day and night (4:9, 21).

> Gird thy heavenly armour on,
> Wear it ever night and day,
> Ambushed lies the evil one,
> Watch and pray.

Prayer and Restitution

(Nehemiah 5)

Also I shook my lap, and said, So God shake out every man from his house, and from his labour, that performeth not this promise, even thus be he shaken out, and emptied. And all the congregation said, Amen, and praised the Lord. And the people did according to this promise.   — Nehemiah 5:13

The noble patriot also faced severe heartlessness as he labored to restore the gates, but the fear of God preserved him from taking any dishonorable advantage of his official position. What a striking action that was accompanying Nehemiah's prayer (5:13)! No wonder the people said, "Amen and praised the Lord." What a touching prayer concludes this chapter (5:19; 6:14)! In Nehemiah we see the union of the two essential characteristics of all effective service — activity and prayer. All of his prayers were those of a willing and obedient worker.

Prayer against Craft

(Nehemiah 6:9-14)

For they all made us afraid, saying, Their hands shall be weakened from the work, that it be not done. Now therefore, O God, strengthen my hands. . . .
My God, think thou upon Tobiah and Sanballat according to these their works, and on the prophetess Noadiah, and the rest of the prophets, that would have put me in fear.   — Nehemiah 6:9, 14

How personal Nehemiah was in his prayers "My God" (6:14)! This was his favorite prayer-expression. Of course, he used other forms of address (1:5; 9:32). This petition against intriguers reveals the manly courage of Nehemiah, who saw through the crafty intentions of his enemies. He was doing a great work and had no time for a conference in one of the villages (6:2, 3). How often serious work for God is side-tracked by too much talk in endless conferences!

Prayer and the Word

(Nehemiah 8:1-13)

And Ezra blessed the Lord, the great God. And all the people answered, Amen, Amen, with lifting up their hands: and they bowed their heads, and worshipped the Lord with their faces to the ground.
                                                              — Nehemiah 8:6

Prostration with face to the ground preceded the bowing of the head (8:6). What a warmth of feeling must have permeated the double "Amen" of the people (8:6)! The "lifting up of their hands" was a token of their assent, while "faces bowed to the ground" expressed their adoration. The reading and sensible exposition of the Word ever inspires fervent prayer. The Scriptures add fuel to the fire of the heart's devotion.

Prayer and God's Goodness

(Nehemiah 9)

And the seed of Israel separated themselves from all strangers, and stood and confessed their sins, and the iniquities of their fathers. And they stood up in their place, and read in the book of the law of the Lord their God one fourth part of the day; and another fourth part they confessed, and worshipped the Lord their God. . . .
But they and our fathers dealt proudly, and hardened their necks, and hearkened not to thy commandments, And refused to obey, neither were mindful of thy wonders that thou didst among them; but hardened their necks, and in their rebellion appointed a captain to return to their bondage: but thou art a God ready to pardon, gracious and merciful, slow to anger, and of great kindness, and forsookest them not. Yea, when they had made them a molten calf, and said, This is thy god that brought thee up out of Egypt, and had wrought great provocations; Yet thou in thy manifold mercies forsookest them not in the wilderness: the pillar of the cloud departed

not from them by day, to lead them in the way; neither the pillar of fire by night, to shew them light, and the way wherein they should go. So the children went in and possessed the land, and thou subduedst before them the inhabitants of the land, the Canaanites, and gavest them into their hands, with their kings, and the people of the land, that they might do with them as they would. And they took strong cities, and a fat land, and possessed houses full of all goods, wells digged, vineyards, and oliveyards, and fruit trees in abundance: so they did eat, and were filled, and became fat, and delighted themselves in thy great goodness. Nevertheless they were disobedient, and rebelled against thee, and cast thy law behind their backs, and slew thy prophets which testified against them to turn them to thee, and they wrought great provocations. Therefore thou deliveredst them into the hand of their enemies, who vexed them: and in the time of their trouble, when they cried unto thee, thou heardest them from heaven; and according to thy manifold mercies thou gavest them saviours, who saved them out of the hand of their enemies. . . .

Now therefore, our God, the great, the mighty, and the terrible God, who keepest covenant and mercy, let not all the trouble seem little before thee, that hath come upon us, on our kings, on our princes, and on our priests, and on our prophets, and on our fathers, and on all thy people, since the time of the kings of Assyria unto this day. Howbeit thou art just in all that is brought upon us; for thou hast done right, but we have done wickedly: Neither have our kings, our princes, our priests, nor our fathers, kept thy law, nor hearkened unto thy commandments and thy testimonies, wherewith thou didst testify against them. For they have not served thee in their kingdom, and in thy great goodness that thou gavest them, and in the large and fat land which thou gavest before them, neither turned they from their wicked works. Behold, we are servants this day, and for the land that thou gavest unto our fathers to eat the fruit thereof and the good thereof, behold, we are servants in it: And it yieldeth much increase unto the kings whom thou hast set over us because of our sins: also they have dominion over our bodies, and over our cattle, at their pleasure, and we are in great distress. And because of all this we make a sure covenant, and write it; and our princes, Levites, and priests, seal unto it.

— Nehemiah 9:2, 3, 16-19, 24-27, 32-38

There are several features of this mighty prayer worthy of mention. Sins of the past, as well as the present, were confessed (9:2). All classes of the community are expressly mentioned in the national confession, which lasted for three hours (9:3). The goodness of God and His justice and mercy formed the basis of appeal (9:17, 19, 25, 27, 32). There is also the recognition of the ministry of the Holy Spirit in the experiences of the people (9:20). The prayer likewise has a homiletic tendency — half-narrative and half-sermon. It was a prayer prompted by a particular situation (9:22).

Prayer for Remembrance
(Nehemiah 13:14, 22, 29, 31)

Remember me, O my God, concerning this, and wipe not out my good deeds that I have done for the house of my God, and for the offices thereof. . . .

And I commanded the Levites that they should cleanse themselves, and that they should come and keep the gates, to sanctify the sabbath day. Remember me, O my God, concerning this also, and spare me according to the greatness of thy mercy. . . .

Remember them, O my God, because they have defiled the priesthood, and the covenant of the priesthood, and of the Levites. . . .

And for the wood offering, at times appointed, and for the firstfruits. Remember me, O my God, for good. — Nehemiah 13:14, 22, 29, 31

The faithful servant of God begs a merciful remembrance of what he had done for the honor of God in the observances of His Temple. In the repeated "Remember me," Nehemiah commits his fidelity to the merciful estimate of God. Something with the Sabbath, or with his retrospect of his own conduct, gives the passing prayer a peculiar pathos of humility. Of the concluding prayer of the book, "Remember me, O God, for good" (13:31), Ellicott comments that, "With these words Nehemiah leaves the scene, committing himself and his discharge of duty to the Righteous Judge. His conscientious fidelity had brought him into collision not only with external enemies but with many of his own brethren. His rigorous reformation has been assailed by many moralists and commentators in every age. But in these words he commits all to God, as it were by anticipation. It may be added that with these words end the annals of Old Testament history."

Esther

Here is another prayerless book of the Bible. Not only so, but the name of God does not occur in its ten chapters. It is for this reason that objection has been raised to its inclusion in Holy Writ. Yet, as Dr. W. Graham Scroggie has expressed it, "God is here in mystery, though not in manifestation." Along with Dr. E. Bullinger and Dr. A. T. Pierson, Dr. Scroggie believes that "the uncommunicable Name, or Tetragrammaton, Y.H.V.H., which stand in the Hebrew for Yahweh (Jehovah), occurs in this narrative four times in acrostic form, and at the critical points in the story (1:20; 5:4-13; 7:7), a fact which cannot possibly be of chance, but of divine design, and which demonstrates, as hardly anything else could, the outstanding truth of divine providence."

As a whole, *Esther* testifies to the secret watch-care of God over His faithful remnant. His providence is conspicuous in the unique way He preserved His people from extermination. It is inconceivable that saintly Jews like Mordecai, Esther and others did not pray (4:14).

Believing, as they did, in the over-ruling providence of God, they must have leaned heavily upon Him in days of crisis (4:16). Compare, too, their period of fasting before God for His intervention.

An illustration of prayer can be gathered from the invitation of the king to Esther to present her request, which she did with great success (5:23). We have not to wait, however, for our King to hold out His golden sceptre. At all times and in all places the way is open to the mercy seat where Jesus answers prayer.

> His promise is our only plea,
> With this we venture nigh.

Job

It is said of the patriarch that he was "perfect and upright . . . feared God . . . eschewed evil . . . greatest of all the men of the east" (1:1, 3). Surely it was impossible for Job to have such a character, without being a man of prayer.

Prayer of Resignation
(Job 1:20-22)

Then Job arose, and rent his mantle, and shaved his head, and fell down upon the ground, and worshipped, And said, Naked came I out of my mother's womb, and naked shall I return thither: the Lord gave, and the Lord hath taken away; blessed be the name of the Lord. In all this Job sinned not, nor charged God foolishly.
— Job 1:20-22

A godly man, Job yet witnessed the destruction of much that was dear to his heart and was mystified over the undeserved pain and suffering he was called upon to endure. His mind was baffled by the mystery of his misery. But nobly Job worshiped the Lord, whose actions were incomprehensible. Prostrate upon the ground, he uttered unresentful words of resignation. His rent robe and shaven head testified to the sincerity of his grief. He did not charge God foolishly, as alas we do when we face sorrows we cannot fathom (Ruth 1:20, 21). In his anguish, Job could yet bless the name of the Lord. Evil, as well as good, must be unmurmuringly received at the hand of the Lord.

The same spirit of resignation characterized Job's reply to his wife's question. Job had grace to bow before the will and wisdom of God (2:9, 10).

Prayer for Pity
(Job 6:8, 9; 7:17-21)

Oh that I might have my request; and that God would grant me the thing that I long for! Even that it would please God to destroy me; that he would let loose his hand, and cut me off!

What is man, that thou shouldest magnify him? and that thou

shouldest set thine heart upon him? And that thou shouldest visit
him every morning, and try him every moment? How long wilt thou
not depart from me, nor let me alone till I swallow down my spittle?
I have sinned; what shall I do unto thee, O thou preserver of men?
why hast thou set me as a mark against thee, so that I am a burden
to myself? And why dost thou not pardon my transgression, and
take away mine iniquity? for now shall I sleep in the dust; and thou
shalt seek me in the morning, but I shall not be.

— Job 6:8, 9; 7:17-21

At times, Old Testament saints in prayer manifested the spirit of
men trying to drive a hard bargain with God. But God does not
answer prayer that way. He is ever willing to grant the thing we
long for (6:8), if such a request is in accordance with His will for
our life (I John 5:14, 15). Why does God visit man, every morning,
only to torment him (7:17; Psalm 8)? Job wondered why, if he had
sinned, God did not forgive him (7:12, 20).

Sometimes, as in Job's case, "men might be tempted to address God
in words of bitter and almost irreverent audacity," says Professor
McFadyen. "But it must not be forgotten that the daring and awful
speeches of Job are spoken 'in the anguish of his spirit and in the
bitterness of his soul' (7:11; 10:1). Such prayers may be models of
intensity, but not of devotion."

Prayer for Justification
(Job 9)

Now my days are swifter than a post: they flee away, they see no
good. They are passed away as the swift ships: as the eagle that
hasteth to the prey. If I say, I will forget my complaint, I will leave
off my heaviness, and comfort myself: I am afraid of all my sorrows,
I know that thou wilt not hold me innocent. If I be wicked, why
then labour I in vain? If I wash myself with snow water, and
make my hands never so clean; Yet shalt thou plunge me in the
ditch, and mine own clothes shall abhor me. For he is not a man,
as I am, that I should answer him, and we should come together in
judgment. Neither is there any daysman betwixt us, that might lay
his hand upon us both. Let him take his rod away from me, and let
not his fear terrify me: Then would I speak, and not fear him; but
it is not so with me.   — Job 9:25-35

The God and Father of our Lord Jesus Christ, is not the God Job
imagined Him to be. Extreme sorrow somewhat beclouded the vision
of Job, who, in his despair thought of God as being devastating and
unscrupulous in His omnipotence. Once Job's anguish was past he
came to see God as One whose tender mercies are over all His works.

In a calmer frame of mind, Job was certain of vindication. His was
the inner assurance of innocence of the charges levelled against him.
"My witness is in Heaven and my Sponsor is on high" (16:19). By the
Holy Spirit, Job was inspired to give us a picture of Christ as the
Mediator between God and men (I Timothy 2:5). He is the Daysman

betwixt God and ourselves (9:33), laying His hand upon both, and through His death and resurrection, reconciling us to God (19:25-27; 33:24).

Job's Prayer against Injustice

(Job 10)

My soul is weary of my life; I will leave my complaint upon myself; I will speak in the bitterness of my soul. I will say unto God, Do not condemn me; shew me wherefore thou contendest with me. Is it good unto thee that thou shouldest oppress, that thou shouldest despise the work of thine hands, and shine upon the counsel of the wicked? Hast thou eyes of flesh? or seest thou as man seeth? Are thy days as the days of man? are thy years as man's days, That thou enquirest after mine iniquity, and searchest after my sin? Thou knowest that I am not wicked; and there is none that can deliver out of thine hand. Thine hands have made me and fashioned me together round about; yet thou dost destroy me. Remember, I beseech thee, that thou hast made me as the clay; and wilt thou bring me into dust again? Hast thou not poured me out as milk, and curdled me like cheese? Thou hast clothed me with skin and flesh, and hast fenced me with bones and sinews. Thou hast granted me life and favour, and thy visitation hath preserved my spirit. And these things hast thou hid in thine heart: I know that this is with thee. If I sin, then thou markest me, and thou wilt not acquit me from mine iniquity. If I be wicked, woe unto me; and if I be right-eous, yet will I not lift up my head. I am full of confusion; therefore see thou mine affliction; For it increaseth. Thou huntest me as a fierce lion: and again thou shewest thyself marvellous upon me. Thou renewest thy witnesses against me, and increasest thine indignation upon me; changes and war are against me. Wherefore then hast thou brought me forth out of the womb? Oh that I had given up the ghost, and no eye had seen me! I should have been as though I had not been; I should have been carried from the womb to the grave. Are not my days few? cease then, and let me alone, that I may take comfort a little. Before I go whence I shall not return, even to the land of darkness and the shadow of death; A land of darkness, as darkness itself; and of the shadow of death, without any order, and where the light is as darkness.   — Job 10

Job prayed a practical prayer. "Teach me, and I will hold my tongue" (8:24). A study of his prayers reveal, however, a multiplicity of words. Certainly we are to "take with us words," when we come before God (Hosea 14:14), but they must be "few" (Ecclesiaste 5:2) and "acceptable" (Ecclesiastes 12:10; Proverbs 15:11). We are not heard for our much speaking (Matthew 6:7).

Job refused to be condemned unjustly and demands that God will show him why he stands condemned (10:2, 7). He pertinently asks God what He expects to gain by crushing him (10:3). In a terrible moment, overwhelmed by his grief, Job uttered the audacious thought that God had created him only to destroy him (10:7-13). How violently he rejected his protestation of innocence (10:7; 13:23). In this prayer, delivered at white heat, Job does not mention the name of God (10:2-22). Although slain, Job is determined to maintain his *own* way before God (13:15).

Prayer for Light on Immortality
(Job 14:13-22)

O that thou wouldest hide me in the grave, that thou wouldest keep me secret, until thy wrath be past, that thou wouldest appoint me a set time, and remember me! If a man die, shall he live again? all the days of my appointed time will I wait, till my change come. Thou shalt call, and I will answer thee: thou wilt have a desire to the work of thine hands. For now thou numberest my steps: dost thou not watch over my sin? My transgression is sealed up in a bag, and thou sewest up mine iniquity. And surely the mountain falling cometh to nought, and the rock is removed out of his place. The waters wear the stones: thou washest away the things which grow out of the dust of the earth; and thou destroyest the hope of man. Thou prevailest for ever against him, and he passeth: thou changest his countenance, and sendest him away. His sons come to honour, and he knoweth it not; and they are brought low, but he perceiveth it not of them. But his flesh upon him shall have pain, and his soul within him shall mourn.   — Job 14:13-22

Addressing God, Job's language was free and daring. Until he was "humbled by the marvelous panorama of God's mighty window and love" (38). Job's appeals were fearless and somewhat blasphemous, shocking the oldest of his conventional friends (15:4). Yet such a boldness of approach to God was "the boldness of conscious integrity, intensified a thousandfold by his intolerable and unmerited suffering."

Job never stopped to couch his requests in stiff and ordered words. In this outburst of his, Job asks two questions, haunting many as death is faced.

"Man giveth up the ghost, and where is he" (14:10)?

"If a man die, shall he live again" (14:14)?
Desperate words are sobbed out. "How can God expect us to keep on like this? If we only *knew*. If certain of the after-life, we would gladly go when death calls (14:15). But the King of Terrors takes us away with confidence — sweeps us away like the tide — cuts us down as a tree" (10:7-9, 11, 15, 18).

Happily Job's dim light has become a full revelation, for Christ brought life and immortality to light through His Gospel (II Timothy 1:10). Through grace we have the assurance of the Father's home, beyond the separations of this life (John 14:2). In spite of his questions as to the continuity of life beyond the grave, Job asserted that he would have a new body after death, and see and acknowledge his Redeemer (19:25, 27).

Prayer and Profit

(Job 21:14-34)

Therefore they say unto God, Depart from us; for we desire not the knowledge of thy ways. What is the Almighty, that we should serve him? and what profit should we have, if we pray unto him? Lo, their good is not in their hand: the counsel of the wicked is far from me. How oft is the candle of the wicked put out! and how oft cometh their destruction upon them! God distributeth sorrows in his anger. They are as stubble before the wind, and as chaff that the storm carrieth away. God layeth up his iniquity for his children: he rewardeth him, and he shall know it. His eyes shall see his destruction, and he shall drink of the wrath of the Almighty. For what pleasure hath he in his house after him, when the number of his months is cut off in the midst? Shall any teach God knowledge? seeing he judgeth those that are high. One dieth in his full strength, being wholly at ease and quiet. His breasts are full of milk, and his bones are moistened with marrow. And another dieth in the bitterness of his soul, and never eateth with pleasure. They shall lie down alike in the dust, and the worms shall cover them. Behold, I know your thoughts, and the devices which ye wrongfully imagine against me. For ye say, Where is the house of the prince? and where are the dwelling places of the wicked? Have ye not asked them that go by the way? and do ye not know their tokens, That the wicked is reserved to the day of destruction? they shall be brought forth to the day of wrath. Who shall declare his way to his face? and who shall repay him what he hath done? Yet shall he be brought to the grave, and shall remain in the tomb. The clods of the valley shall be sweet unto him, and every man shall draw after him, as there are innumerable before him. How then comfort ye me in vain, seeing in your answers there remaineth falsehood?   — Job 21:14-34

Spirit-inspired prayer is always profitable. The witness of Bible prayers as a whole, coupled with our own experience, proves this. As uttered by Job the question seems to suggest scepticism. Hardship and sorrow often breed doubt as to the value and efficacy of prayer. The cold and calculating enquiry, "What profit should we have, if we pray unto Him?" still expresses the cynical attitude of many regarding the benefit of prayer. Tennyson has reminded us that true prayer "opens the sluice gates between our thirsty souls and the waters of eternal life." Prayer changes things, and people. It is ever true that "More things are wrought by prayer, than this world dreams of."

Prayer and Reason

(Job 23)

Oh that I knew where I might find him! that I might come even to his seat! I would order my cause before him, and fill my mouth with arguments. I would know the words which he would answer me, and understand what he would say unto me.   — Job 23:3-5

Job asked for an opportunity to reason and plead his cause (23:3-5). Evidently he did not fully appreciate the simplicity of prayer. The man at midnight entreated with importunity, till his request was granted (Luke 11:5-10). But prayer to a heavenly Father is of a different order. Prayer with importunity prevails, but God is not the unjust Judge. He invites us to reason, and prayer is given the right to plead, but if God is our Father, knowing what we need, waiting to be asked, why should there be too much pleading?

Many of the answers of Job to his friends are actually prayers cast in argumentative form (24:26-30). He declares his willingness to go before God if He is just, not as a coward with hanging head, nor yet as a penitent suppliant, but with head erect "as a prince would I go near unto him" (31:37). If we know God as He is revealed by Christ, and have experienced His saving grace and mercy, ours will never be the loud declaration of innocence, nor the proud bearing of a prince Job manifested. We will approach God reverently and humbly, yet unafraid.

Prayer Answered by Whirlwind

(Job 38)

Then the Lord answered Job out of the whirlwind. . . .   — Job 38:1

Attentive ears can detect the Divine Voice no matter how it answers. Many heard it in the processes of nature like the Psalmist in the roar of thunder (Psalm 29), or Job in the whirlwind (38, 39) who found himself overwhelmed by God's terrible majesty. "There is so much in nature that man knows not and cannot understand," comments Ellicott, "that it is absurd for him to suppose that he can judge aright in matters touching God's moral government of the world." Though Job is afterwards justified by God (42:8), yet the tone of all that God says to him is more or less mingled with reproach.

Prayer As Confession

(Job 40:3-5; 42:1-6)

Then Job answered the Lord, and said, Behold I am vile; what shall I answer thee? I will lay mine hand upon my mouth. Once have I spoken; but I will not answer: yea, twice; but I will proceed no further. . . .
Then Job answered the Lord, and said, I know that thou canst do every thing, and that no thought can be withholden from thee. Who is he that hideth counsel without knowledge? therefore have I uttered that I understood not; things too wonderful for me, which I knew not. Hear, I beseech thee, and I will speak: I will demand of thee, and declare thou unto me. I have heard of thee by the hearing of the ear: but now mine eye seeth thee. Wherefore I abhor myself, and repent in dust and ashes.   — Job 40:3-5; 42:1-6

How suggestive is the combination of these phrases — "The Lord answered Job" — "Job answered the Lord." In God's answer there was rebuke for Job for daring to reprove Him. In Job's answer there was confession not only of his vileness but of looseness of speech in addressing God. "I will lay mine hand upon my mouth" (see Isaiah 6:5, 7). In the dialogue between God and Job it is evident that Job came to know God in a new way (42:5). Much of our knowledge of God is merely hearsay. We suffer from an inadequate vision of Him. It is not until the Holy Spirit reveals all that God is in Himself to our inner consciences that we can say with Job, "Wherefore I abhor myself, and repent in dust and ashes (42:6)." Such is the confession of those who come to know that there is not His like upon the earth (41:33).

Prayer As Intercession
(Job 42:7-10)

And it was so, that after the Lord had spoken these words unto Job, the Lord said to Eliphaz the Temanite, My wrath is kindled against thee, and against thy two friends: for ye have not spoken of me the thing that is right, as my servant Job hath. Therefore take unto you now seven bullocks and seven rams, and go to my servant Job, and offer up for yourselves a burnt offering; and my servant Job shall pray for you: for him will I accept: lest I deal with you after your folly, in that ye have not spoken of me the thing which is right, like my servant Job. So Eliphaz the Temanite and Bildad the Shuhite and Zophar the Naamathite went, and did according as the Lord commanded them: the Lord also accepted Job. And the Lord turned the captivity of Job, when he prayed for his friends: also the Lord gave Job twice as much as he had before.   — Job 42:7-10

The controversy between Job and his friends forms the burden of this most ancient book. Poor Job! He was at the mercy of friends, each of whom had his peculiar views, maintained with great pertinacity, of Job's right to suffer. When at last God intervened and terminated the controversy, the friends asked Job to pray for them. They humbled themselves and solicited the prayers of the one they had unjustly condemned.

Honorable Job did not indulge in reproaches. He prayed for his friends. He is one of the noble army of intercessors. What a moment it must have been when they all knelt together, seeking forgiveness one of another, and a purer love for each other (42:7-10). How do you act toward those who wrongfully oppose you? Do you pray for them and patiently await the moment when they will turn to you as the friends of Job did toward that patriarch?

Job had been sorely tried, but his personal discipline was not complete till he journeyed from his own sorrows to the ministry of intercession for those who had misunderstood him. When Job prayed for his friends, the Lord turned his own captivity: that is, restored and reinstated him in prosperity even greater than before.

The intercession of Job is typical of Christ who became a sufferer and a mediator on behalf of man, but who is now the Intercessor on high, whose "five bleeding wounds" were "effectual prayers" for those redeemed by His blood.

The intimate relation between sacrifice and supplication, a combination of ancient origin, reappears in Job's intercession for his friends who had not been very friendly toward him (42:8).

Psalms

It is impossible within the compass of this book to enumerate all the prayers in the Book of Psalms, which is pre-eminently the prayer-praise book of the Bible and a treasury of spiritual devotion. While we have few instances of prayers in the rest of the Old Testament books which do not seem to have, as their exclusive object, some *temporal benefit,* the Psalms contain the outpouring of hearts for *spiritual blessings.*

Within these majestic Psalms, prayer and praise are woven together.

> Prayers and praises go in pairs,
> He hath praises who hath prayers.

How the Psalms which is pre-eminently a book of prayer and praise have become part and parcel of our life! Their appropriate and expressive language is ever on our lips. When the soul longs for God, what better expression could we find than, "As the hart panteth after the water brooks, so panteth my soul after Thee, O God!" When oppressed with a sense of sin and demerit, where have we a more heart-felt appeal than David's in Psalm 51, "Have mercy upon me, O God, according to Thy loving kindness; according unto the multitude of Thy tender mercies, blot out my transgressions?"

Yes, it would take a volume in itself to show how the Psalms aid us greatly in the spiritual exercises of the heart. As to the imprecatory prayers in the Psalms, which some writers deem to be unChristian in spirit, suffice it to say that they do not belong to a Christian age. Many of the Psalms have a prophetic aspect, like Psalm 2, and are related to the judgment period of the Great Tribulation.

For command of appropriate language, the standard of excellence of the prayer-expression of the Psalms cannot be superceded. Within them we have "the very thesaurus of devotional terms." Their grace and elegance of expression provide us with a rich vocabulary for use as we draw nigh to God. It is always profitable to take the sayings of psalmists and turn them into prayer. The majestic prayers of the Psalter closely follow one another. We, herewith, draw attention to a few precious samples. For further expressive prayers see Psalms 6, 10, 13, 17, 20, 28, 38, 54, 56, 58, 59, 60, 64, 69, 70, 79, 80, 83, 85, 86, 88, 94, 108, 109, 120, 123, 129, 132, 140-144.

Prayer Born of Rebellion

(Psalm 3)

Lord, how are they increased that trouble me! many are they that rise up against me. Many there be which say of my soul, There is no help for him in God. Selah. But thou, O Lord, art a shield for me; my glory, and the lifter up of mine head. I cried unto the Lord with my voice, and he heard me out of his holy hill. Selah. I laid me down and slept; I awaked; for the Lord sustained me. I will not be afraid of ten thousands of people, that have set themselves against me round about. Arise, O Lord; save me, O my God: for thou hast smitten all mine enemies upon the cheek bone; thou hast broken the teeth of the ungodly. Salvation belongeth unto the Lord: thy blessing is upon thy people. Selah.   — Psalm 3

The titles of many of the Psalms tell their story. This psalm, or prayer, of David, was offered when he fled from his rebellious son, Absalom. In the previous psalm, David wrote, "Ask of me" (2:8), and he was forever asking of God. Among the Old Testament saints, no one can tell us so much about prayer as the sweet psalmist of Israel who spent much time in "the prayer laboratory." Burgess and Proudlove analyze this third Psalm in the following helpful way —

1. David's Complaint to God (1:2). Foes surrounded him and discouragers said there was no aid from God.
2. David's Consciousness of God (3). From encompassing enemies, he lifted up his eyes to the encircling God.
3. David's Cry to God (4-5). The tenses used express an habitual act and a constant result.
4. David's Confidence in God (6). Faith banishes all fear and doubt.
5. David's Call upon God (7). Courage is not enough. God's help is necessary.
6. David's Confession about God (8). Salvation is not something but *Someone,* even the Lord Himself.

Follow the allusions to the gift and blessing of sleep in the Psalms (3:5; 4:4, 8; 5:3; 6:6, etc.).

Prayer of Holiness

(Psalm 4)

Hear me when I call, O God of my righteousness: thou hast enlarged me when I was in distress; have mercy upon me, and hear my prayer. O ye sons of men, how long will ye turn my glory into shame? how long will ye love vanity, and seek after leasing? Selah. But know that the Lord hath set apart him that is godly for himself: the Lord will hear when I call unto him. Stand in awe, and sin not: commune with your own heart upon your bed, and be still. Selah. Offer the sacrifices of righteousness, and put your trust in the Lord. There be many that say, Who will shew us any good? Lord, lift thou up the light of thy countenance upon us. Thou hast put gladness in my heart, more than in the time that their corn and their wine increased. I will both lay me down in peace, and sleep: for thou, Lord, only makest me dwell in safety. — Psalm 4

The key-phrase of this precious Psalm is surely, "Stand in awe, and sin not" (4:4). The godly are separated ones (4:3), enjoy God's smile (4:6), have a gladness not of this world (4:7), and a peace nothing can disturb (4:8). When we close our eyes in sleep, it is consoling to know that we are cared for by One whose eyes never close (Psalm 121:3, 4).

Prayer As a Morning Watch

(Psalm 5)

Give ear to my words, O Lord, consider my meditation. Hearken unto the voice of my cry, my King, and my God: for unto thee will I pray. My voice shalt thou hear in the morning, O Lord; in the morning will I direct my prayer unto thee, and will look up. For thou art not a God that hath pleasure in wickedness: neither shall evil dwell with thee. The foolish shall not stand in thy sight: thou hatest all workers of iniquity. Thou shalt destroy them that speak leasing: the Lord will abhor the bloody and deceitful man. But as for me, I will come into thy house in the multitude of thy mercy: and in thy fear will I worship toward thy holy temple. Lead me, O Lord, in thy righteousness because of mine enemies; make thy way straight before my face. For there is no faithfulness in their mouth; their inward part is very wickedness; their throat is an open sepulchre; they flatter with their tongue. Destroy thou them, O God; let them fall by their own counsels; cast them out in the multitude of their transgressions; for they have rebelled against thee. But let all those that put their trust in thee rejoice: let them ever shout for joy, because thou defendest them: let them also that love thy name be joyful in thee. For thou, Lord, wilt bless the righteous; with favour wilt thou compass him as with a shield. — Psalm 5

No day can carry the benediction of God unless it is commenced by prayer (5:3). The title of this Psalm is *Nehiloth,* meaning, "inheritance" and indicates the character of David's prayer. The righteous are the Lord's inheritance (5:8) and He will compass them about with songs of deliverance (5:12). Many aspects of this prayer can be traced in the "Inheritance Prayer." "My meditation" (5:1). "Unto *Thee* will I pray" (5:2). "In the morning will I direct my prayer unto Thee" (5:3). Prayer was offered three times a day — evening, morning and noonday (Psalm 55:17; Daniel 6:10). "I will *order* my prayer" suggests that prayer should be systematic. "I will worship towards thy holy temple" (5:7). Only men of unimpeachable reverence can experience the blessedness of sincere devotion.

Prayer for Divine Action

(Psalm 7)

O Lord my God, in thee do I put my trust: save me from all them that persecute me, and deliver me: Lest he tear my soul like a lion, rending it in pieces, while there is none to deliver. O Lord my God, if I have done this; if there be iniquity in my hands; If I have rewarded evil unto him that was at peace with me; (yea, I have delivered him that without cause is mine enemy:) Let the enemy persecute my soul, and take it; yea, let him tread down my life upon the earth, and lay mine honour in the dust. Selah. Arise, O Lord, in thine anger, lift up thyself because of the rage of mine enemies: and awake for me to the judgment that thou hast commanded. So shall the congregation of the people compass thee about: for their sakes therefore return thou on high. The Lord shall judge the people: judge me, O Lord, according to my righteousness, and according to mine integrity that is in me. Oh let the wickedness of the wicked come to an end; but establish the just; for the righteous God trieth the hearts and reins. My defence is of God, which saveth the upright in heart. God judgeth the righteous, and God is angry with the wicked every day. If he turn not, he will whet his sword; he hath bent his bow, and made it ready. He hath also prepared for him the instruments of death; he ordaineth his arrows against the persecutors. Behold, he travaileth with iniquity, and hath conceived mischief, and brought forth falsehood. He made a pit, and digged it, and is fallen into the ditch which he made. His mischief shall return upon his own head, and his violent dealing shall come down upon his own pate. I will praise the Lord according to his righteousness: and will sing praise to the name of the Lord most high.   — Psalm 7

It is somewhat bold for a mortal man to call upon God to arise and protect him from persistent foes (7:6). How this prayer vibrates with courage and confidence in the face of fierce enemies! Two things contributed to David's fearlessness — God's justice and the pleader's own integrity. Three suggested points of the prayer are —

1. David's Plea for God's Vindication (1-5). "Thrice armed is he that hath a quarrel just."
2. David's Prayer for God's Verdict (6-10). God may seem long in punishing iniquity but at last He acts.
3. David's Proclamation of God's Victory (11-17). Prayer turns to prophecy. The prophetic aspects of many of the Psalms must not be neglected (Matthew 26:54, 56; Luke 24:27, 44).

Prayer of Praise for Creation
(Psalm 8)

O Lord our Lord, how excellent is thy name in all the earth! who hast set thy glory above the heavens. Out of the mouth of babes and sucklings hast thou ordained strength because of thine enemies, that thou mightest still the enemy and the avenger. When I consider thy heavens, the work of thy fingers, the moon and the stars, which thou hast ordained; What is man, that thou art mindful of him? and the son of man, that thou visitest him? For thou hast made him a little lower than the angels, and hast crowned him with glory and honour. Thou madest him to have dominion over the works of thy hands; thou hast put all things under his feet: All sheep and oxen, yea, and the beasts of the field; The fowl of the air; and the fish of the sea, and whatsoever passeth through the paths of the seas. O Lord our Lord, how excellent is thy name in all the earth! — Psalm 8

This is one of the judgment Psalms, as the title *Gittith,* meaning "winepress," suggests. Characteristic features of the Psalm are clearly evident. Its first and last phrases are exactly alike (8:1, 9). God condescends to use the lowliest (8:2) ; is magnified as the Creator (8:3) ; is the Controller of all His creation (8:4-8). The whole Psalm is, of course, prophetic of Christ (I Corinthians 15:27; Hebrews 2:6-8).

Prayer for Preservation Here and Hereafter

(Psalm 16)

Preserve me, O God: for in thee do I put my trust. O my soul, thou hast said unto the Lord, Thou art my Lord: my goodness extendeth not to thee; But to the saints that are in the earth, and to the excellent, in whom is all my delight. Their sorrows shall be multiplied that hasten after another god: their drink offerings of blood will I not offer, nor take up their names into my lips. The Lord is the portion of mine inheritance and of my cup: thou maintainest my lot. The lines are fallen unto me in pleasant places; yea, I have a goodly heritage. I will bless the Lord, who hath given me counsel: my reins also instruct me in the night seasons. I have set the Lord always before me: because he is at my right hand, I shall not be moved. Therefore my heart is glad, and my glory rejoiceth: my flesh also shall rest in hope. For thou wilt not leave my soul in hell; neither wilt thou suffer thine Holy One to see corruption. Thou wilt shew me the path of life: in thy presence is fulness of joy; at thy right hand there are pleasures for evermore.   — Psalm 16

Here is another Psalm receiving its full and final fulfilment in Christ (Acts 2:25-28). A study of many of the great prayers of the Bible reveals an effort for those who uttered them to end on a note of single trust and gratitude, which double note ought to be dominant in our lives. Times of sorrow and perplexity, of fear and doubt, of danger and persecution may be ours but confidence in God's care in hours of special need safeguard us against despair. "A calm heart is the heritage of him who has God at his side."

The greater part of life, however, is spent in a reasonable measure of security and happiness. "The lines have fallen unto me in pleasant places" (16:6). What a blessed hope ours is (16:9-11)! May ours be the present enjoyment of all God has for us (16:11).

Prayer of the Cross

(Psalm 22)

My God, my God, why hast thou forsaken me? why art thou so far from helping me, and from the words of my roaring? O my God, I cry in the daytime, but thou hearest not; and in the night season, and am not silent. . . .

But I am a worm, and no man; a reproach of men, and despised of the people. All they that see me laugh me to scorn: they shoot out the lip, they shake the head, saying, He trusted on the Lord that he would deliver him: let him deliver him, seeing he delighted in him. . . .

They gaped upon me with their mouths, as a ravening and a roaring lion. I am poured out like water, and all my bones are out of joint: my heart is like wax; it is melted in the midst of my bowels. My strength is dried up like a potsherd; and my tongue cleaveth to my jaws; and thou hast brought me into the dust of death. For dogs have compassed me: the assembly of the wicked have inclosed me: they pierced my hands and my feet. I may tell all my bones: they look and stare upon me. They part my garments among them, and cast lots upon my vesture. But be not thou far from me, O Lord: O my strength, haste thee to help me. . . .

All the ends of the world shall remember and turn unto the Lord: and all the kindreds of the nations shall worship before thee. For the kingdom is the Lord's: and he is the governor among the nations. All they that be fat upon earth shall eat and worship: all they that go down to the dust shall bow before him: and none can keep alive his own soul. A seed shall serve him; it shall be accounted to the Lord for a generation. They shall come, and shall declare his righteousness unto a people that shall be born, that he hath done this.
— Psalm 22:1, 2, 6-8, 13-19, 27-31

What a poignant Psalm this is! It is one of the most precious of the Psalms, seeing Jesus quoted from it, as He died upon the Cross. Death (22:1-21) and Resurrection (22:22-31) are before us, seeing both are necessary for our salvation (Romans 10:9). As Christ died in agony, His mind fell back upon the old familiar words of this Calvary Psalm, in which David must have seen His day and rejoiced.

Prayer for Shepherd Care

(Psalm 23)

The Lord is my shepherd; I shall not want. He maketh me to lie down in green pastures: he leadeth me beside the still waters. He restoreth my soul: he leadeth me in the paths of righteousness for his name's sake. Yea, though I walk through the valley of the shadow of death, I will fear no evil: for thou art with me; thy rod and thy staff they comfort me. Thou preparest a table before me in the presence of mine enemies: thou anointest my head with oil; my cup runneth over. Surely goodness and mercy shall follow me all the days of my life: and I will dwell in the house of the Lord for ever.   — Psalm 23

Millions of words have been written on this incomparable prayer, pleading as it does for the provision and protection of the Divine Shepherd. Actually, the Psalm is not so much a prayer as a confession of faith. God was real to David and he knew that all he had been to his sheep when a shepherd-lad, God would be to him. This Shepherd

Psalm is a tribute to God's unfailing providence. Dr. Alexander Maclaren wrote of the Psalm, "The world could spare many a large book better than this sunny Psalm."

Prayer for the Manifestation of Divine Glory

(Psalm 24)

The earth is the Lord's, and the fulness thereof; the world, and they that dwell therein. For he hath founded it upon the seas, and established it upon the floods. Who shall ascend into the hill of the Lord? or who shall stand in his holy place? He that hath clean hands, and a pure heart; who hath not lifted up his soul unto vanity, nor sworn deceitfully. He shall receive the blessing from the Lord, and righteousness from the God of his salvation. This is the generation of them that seek him, that seek thy face, O Jacob. Selah. Lift up your heads, O ye gates; and be ye lift up, ye everlasting doors; and the King of glory shall come in. Who is this King of glory? The Lord strong and mighty, the Lord mighty in battle. Lift up your heads, O ye gates; even lift them up, ye everlasting doors; and the King of glory shall come in. Who is this King of glory? The Lord of hosts, he is the King of glory. Selah.　　　　— Psalm 24

Professor McFadyen remarks that the rapid transition of many of the Psalms from the second person to the third person and *vice versa,* make it difficult to use them in their entirety as prayers. He admits that these Psalm-Prayers powerfully suggest the reality and naturalness of the communion the writers had with God. "Meditation is on the threshold of prayer: Hebrew meditation has crossed the border."

Psalms 22, 23, 24 form a perfect triad of truth. Christ is before us as Saviour (22) — Shepherd (23) — Sovereign (24). They also suggest a progressive spiritual experience.

Prayer As Ascent to God

(Psalm 25)

Unto thee, O Lord, do I lift up my soul. O my God, I trust in thee: let me not be ashamed, let not mine enemies triumph over me. Yea, let none that wait on thee be ashamed: let them be ashamed which transgress without cause. Shew me thy ways, O Lord; teach me thy paths. Lead me in thy truth, and teach me: for thou art the God of my salvation; on thee do I wait all the day. Remember, O Lord, thy tender mercies and thy lovingkindnesses; for they have been ever of old. Remember not the sins of my youth, nor my transgressions: according to thy mercy remember thou me for thy goodness' sake, O Lord. Good and upright is the Lord: therefore will he teach sinners in the way. The meek will he guide in judgment: and the meek will he teach his way. All the paths of the Lord are mercy and truth unto such as keep his covenant and his testimonies. For thy name's sake, O Lord, pardon mine iniquity; for it is great. What man is he that feareth the Lord? him shall he teach in the way that he shall choose. His soul shall dwell at ease; and his seed shall inherit the earth. The secret of the Lord is with them that fear him; and he will shew them his covenant. Mine eyes are ever toward the Lord; for he shall pluck my feet out of the net.   — Psalm 25:1-15

To David, prayer was the ascent of his soul to God (25:1). This Psalm reveals that we can go no further in the way to heaven, than God is pleased to lead us and hold us up (25:4, 5). In his prayer, David moves from the outward and passing need of protection to the inner and permanent need of pardon (25:6, 7). Forgiven, David can claim all God has for him (25:8-15).

Prayer of a Believing Heart

(Psalm 27)

The Lord is my light and my salvation; whom shall I fear? the Lord is the strength of my life; of whom shall I be afraid? When the wicked, even mine enemies and my foes, came upon me to eat up my flesh, they stumbled and fell. Though an host should encamp against me, my heart shall not fear: though war should rise against me, in this will I be confident. One thing have I desired of the Lord, that will I seek after; that I may dwell in the house of the Lord all the days of my life, to behold the beauty of the Lord, and to enquire in his temple. For in the time of trouble he shall hide me in his pavilion: in the secret of his tabernacle shall he hide me; he shall set me up upon a rock. And now shall mine head be lifted up above mine enemies round about me: therefore will I offer in his tabernacle sacrifices of joy; I will sing, yea, I will sing praises unto the Lord. Hear, O Lord, when I cry with my voice: have mercy also upon me, and answer me. When thou saidst, Seek ye my face; my heart said unto thee, Thy face, Lord, will I seek. Hide not thy face far from me; put not thy servant away in anger: thou hast been my help; leave me not, neither forsake me, O God of my salvation. When my father and my mother forsake me, then the Lord will take me up. Teach me thy way, O Lord, and lead me in a plain path, because of mine enemies. Deliver me not over unto the will of mine enemies: for false witnesses are risen up against me, and such as breathe out cruelty. I had fainted, unless I had believed to see the goodness of the Lord in the land of the living. Wait on the Lord: be of good courage, and he shall strengthen thine heart: wait, I say, on the Lord.   — Psalm 27

What consolation this precious Psalm has brought to myriads of God's children! It is one of those songs we can sing in the night. Conscious of danger, David is more conscious of God. His confidence rests on three firm pillars —

1. His dependence upon God (27:1). He appropriates Divine guarantees against darkness, danger and defeat.
2. His deliverance in the past (27:2, 3, 12). David could sing his "Ebenezer."
3. His determination to dwell under the divine shadow (27:4-6, 12-14).

Prayer As a Cameo of Christ

(Psalm 31)

In thee, O Lord, do I put my trust; let me never be ashamed: deliver me in thy righteousness. Bow down thine ear to me; deliver me speedily: be thou my strong rock, for an house of defence to save me. For thou art my rock and my fortress; therefore for thy name's sake lead me, and guide me. Pull me out of the net that they have laid privily for me: for thou art my strength. Into thine hand I commit my spirit: thou hast redeemed me, O Lord God of truth. . . .

My times are in thy hand: deliver me from the hand of mine enemies, and from them that persecute me. . . .

O love the Lord, all ye his saints: for the Lord preserveth the faithful, and plentifully rewardeth the proud doer. Be of good courage, and he shall strengthen your heart, all ye that hope in the Lord.   — Psalm 31:1-5, 15, 23, 24

It is not difficult to trace the reproach and shame of Christ endured in this prophetic Psalm (31:5, 15 with Luke 23:4, 6). The comforting phrase, "My times are in Thy hands," suggests that prayer is an attitude as well as an act. The recorded prayers of the Bible are eloquent with that steadfastness with which the true Hebrew life was rooted and grounded in God. No wonder saints are called upon to love the Lord and to hope in Him (31:23, 24)!

Prayer of a Tragic Soul

(Psalm 32)

Blessed is he whose transgression is forgiven, whose sin is covered. Blessed is the man unto whom the Lord imputeth not iniquity, and in whose spirit there is no guile. When I kept silence, my bones waxed old through my roaring all the day long. For day and night thy hand was heavy upon me: my moisture is turned into the drought of summer. Selah. I acknowledged my sin unto thee, and mine iniquity have I not hid. I said, I will confess my transgressions unto the Lord; and thou forgavest the iniquity of my sin. Selah. For this shall every one that is godly pray unto thee in a time when thou mayest be found: surely in the floods of great waters they shall not come nigh unto him. Thou art my hiding place; thou shalt preserve me from trouble; thou shalt compass me about with songs of deliverance. Selah. I will instruct thee and teach thee in the way which thou shalt go: I will guide thee with mine eye. Be ye not as the horse, or as the mule, which have no understanding: whose mouth must be held in with bit and bridle, lest they come near unto thee. Many sorrows shall be to the wicked: but he that trusteth in the Lord, mercy shall compass him about. Be glad in the Lord, and rejoice, ye righteous: and shout for joy, all ye that are upright in heart.   — Psalm 32

Here is a prayer drenched with the penitential tears of David. Along with Psalm 51 it is associated with his dark sin. Evidently Paul was familiar with this Psalm (Romans 4:8). David was a student in God's school (32:10). Fully forgiven for his sin, David ends his prayer with an outburst of joy (32:11). Examination of this prayer of penitence reveals the following elements —

1. Sin and Silence (32:1-3)
2. Contrition and Confession (32:4-6)
3. Pardon and Peace (32:7-11)

Prayer for Protection against Enemies
(Psalm 35)

Plead my cause, O Lord, with them that strive with me: fight against them that fight against me. Take hold of shield and buckler, and stand up for mine help. Draw out also the spear, and stop the way against them that persecute me: say unto my soul, I am thy salvation. Let them be confounded and put to shame that seek after my soul: let them be turned back and brought to confusion that devise my hurt. Let them be as chaff before the wind: and let the angel of the Lord chase them. Let their way be dark and slippery: and let the angel of the Lord persecute them. For without cause have they hid for me their net in a pit, which without cause they have digged for my soul. Let destruction come upon him at unawares; and let his net that he hath hid catch himself: into that very destruction let him fall. And my soul shall be joyful in the Lord: it shall rejoice in his salvation. All my bones shall say, Lord, who is like unto thee, which deliverest the poor from him that is too strong for him, yea, the poor and the needy from him that spoileth him? . . .
Let them shout for joy, and be glad, that favour my righteous cause: yea, let them say continually, Let the Lord be magnified, which hath pleasure in the prosperity of his servant. And my tongue shall speak of thy righteousness and of thy praise all the day long.

— Psalm 35:1-10, 27, 28

The life and labors of David are reflected in his Psalms. He knew what it was to be hated and plotted against by friend and foe alike. Here he prays for deliverance from the evil schemes of both. As a Messianic Psalm, it is easy to find Christ in many of its verses (35:7, 11, 17).

The outline, elaborated by Burgess and Proudlove, carries four conspicuous sections —

1. David petitions for divine assistance (35:1-3).
2. David prays for the defeat of the aggressor (35:4-8).
3. David points to a double argument (35:1, 7).
4. David praises God for anticipated deliverance (35:9, 10).

Matthew Henry says of the divine deliverance, "No such Patron of oppressed innocency: no such Punisher of triumphant tyranny."

Prayer in Praise of Lovingkindness

(Psalm 36)

The transgression of the wicked saith within my heart, that there is no fear of God before his eyes. For he flattereth himself in his own eyes, until his iniquity be found to be hateful. The words of his mouth are iniquity and deceit: he hath left off to be wise, and to do good. He deviseth mischief upon his bed; he setteth himself in a way that is not good; he abhorreth not evil. Thy mercy, O Lord, is in the heavens; and thy faithfulness reacheth unto the clouds. Thy righteousness is like the great mountains; thy judgments are a great deep: O Lord, thou preservest man and beast. How excellent is thy lovingkindness, O God! therefore the children of men put their trust under the shadow of thy wings. They shall be abundantly satisfied with the fatness of thy house; and thou shalt make them drink of the river of thy pleasures. For with thee is the fountain of life: in thy light shall we see light. O continue thy lovingkindness unto them that know thee; and thy righteousness to the upright in heart. Let not the foot of pride come against me, and let not the hand of the wicked remove me. There are the workers of iniquity fallen: they are cast down, and shall not be able to rise.   — Psalm 36

A prayer like this one, especially verses 5 to 9, reveals how simple the language of the Bible is. Sincere prayer must be simple, not only in the sense that it is plain and intelligible, but also in that it is free from exaggeration. The publican expresses his sinnership and penitence in half a dozen words. The most impressive prayers are those expressing one's needs with fidelity, simplicity and beauty. How the heart warms to the simple words set forth in this Psalm (36:5-9)!

Prayer of a Pilgrim

(Psalm 39)

I said, I will take heed to my ways, that I sin not with my tongue: I will keep my mouth with a bridle, while the wicked is before me. I was dumb with silence, I held my peace, even from good; and my sorrow was stirred. My heart was hot within me, while I was musing the fire burned: then spake I with my tongue, Lord, make me to know mine end, and the measure of my days, what it is; that I may know how frail I am. Behold, thou hast made my days as an handbreadth; and mine age is as nothing before thee: verily every man at his best state is altogether vanity. Selah. Surely every man walketh in a vain shew: surely they are disquieted in vain: he heapeth up riches, and knoweth not who shall gather them. And now, Lord, what wait I for? my hope is in thee. Deliver me from all my transgressions: make me not the reproach of the foolish. I was dumb, I opened not my mouth; because thou didst it. Remove thy stroke away from me: I am consumed by the blow of thine hand. When thou with rebukes dost correct man for iniquity, thou makest his beauty to consume away like a moth: surely every man is vanity. Selah. Hear my prayer, O Lord, and give ear unto my cry; hold not thy peace at my tears: for I am a stranger with thee, and a sojourner, as all my fathers were. O spare me, that I may recover strength, before I go hence, and be no more.   — Psalm 39

In spite of his faith in God, there were times when David seemed to sink in the sea of despair. His more intimate grief was fear of himself. Life did not seem worth living. He knew God was dealing with him, but he would not rebel (39:9). When the stroke fell, he did not cry out, "Oh, God spare me!" He is lonely, and out of harmony with his true self, but he takes refuge in God, who would not hold peace at his tears (39:12).

Prayer and Its Accomplishment

(Psalm 40)

I waited patiently for the Lord; and he inclined unto me, and heard my cry. He brought me up also out of an horrible pit, out of the miry clay, and set my feet upon a rock, and established my goings. And he hath put a new song in my mouth, even praise unto our God: many shall see it, and fear, and shall trust in the Lord. . . .
Withhold not thou thy tender mercies from me, O Lord: let thy lovingkindness and thy truth continually preserve me. For innumerable evils have compassed me about: mine iniquities have taken hold upon me, so that I am not able to look up; they are more than the hairs of mine head: therefore my heart faileth me. Be pleased, O Lord, to deliver me: O Lord, make haste to help me. Let them be ashamed and confounded together that seek after my soul to destroy it; let them be driven backward and put to shame that wish me evil. Let them be desolate for a reward of their shame that say unto me, Aha, aha. Let all those that seek thee rejoice and be glad in thee: let such as love thy salvation say continually, The Lord be magnified. But I am poor and needy; yet the Lord thinketh upon me: thou art my help and my deliverer; make no tarrying, O my God.
                    — Psalm 40:1-3, 11-17

How dear to the Scotch is this Psalm when sung in metrical form! In it, David testifies to the fact of answered prayer (40:1-10). God has loaded His servant with benefits and he was not ashamed to express his heartfelt praise for same. The Psalm also offers a study in conflicting emotions within the soul (40:11-17). Is it not blessed to realize that prayer is never dependent on our worthiness, but on the worthiness of Him to whom we come in our need?

Prayer in Deep Distress

(Psalm 41)

Blessed is he that considereth the poor: the Lord will deliver him in time of trouble. The Lord will preserve him, and keep him alive; and he shall be blessed upon the earth: and thou wilt not deliver him unto the will of his enemies. The Lord will strengthen him upon the bed of languishing: thou wilt make all his bed in his sickness. I said, Lord, be merciful unto me: heal my soul; for I have sinned against thee. Mine enemies speak evil of me, When shall he die, and his

name perish? And if he come to see me, he speaketh vanity: his
heart gathereth iniquity to itself; when he goeth abroad, he telleth it.
All that hate me whisper together against me: against me do they
devise my hurt. An evil disease, say they, cleaveth fast unto him:
and now that he lieth he shall rise up no more. Yea, mine own familiar friend, in whom I trusted, which did eat of my bread, hath
lifted up his heel against me. But thou, O Lord, be merciful unto
me, and raise me up, that I may requite them. By this I know that
thou favourest me, because mine enemy doth not triumph over me.
And as for me, thou upholdest me in mine integrity, and settest me
before thy face for ever. Blessed be the Lord God of Israel from everlasting, and to everlasting. Amen, and Amen.   — Psalm 41

Within this Psalm we have the foreshadowing of the betrayal of
Jesus by Judas (41:9 with John 13:18, 19). Applied to David, we see
him burdened with mental and physical suffering. Body and heart
were sick. David, however, sees God as a tender Nurse (41:3). "Thou
wilt turn his bed," as the margin puts it, meaning, turning it so that
no part is uneasy. How graciously God deals with His distressed and
weary children!

Prayer As a Door of Hope

(Psalms 42, 43)

As the hart panteth after the water brooks, so panteth my soul after
thee, O God. My soul thirsteth for God, for the living God: when
shall I come and appear before God? My tears have been my meat
day and night, while they continually say unto me, Where is thy
God? When I remember these things, I pour out my soul in me: for
I had gone with the multitude, I went with them to the house of God,
with the voice of joy and praise, with a mulititude that kept holyday.
Why art thou cast down, O my soul? and why art thou disquieted in
me? hope thou in God: for I shall yet praise him for the help of his
countenance. O my God, my soul is cast down within me: therefore
will I remember thee from the land of Jordan, and of the Hermonites,
from the hill Mizar. Deep calleth unto deep at the noise of thy
waterspouts: all thy waves and thy billows are gone over me. Yet the
Lord will command his lovingkindness in the daytime, and in the
night his song shall be with me, and my prayer unto the God of my
life. I will say unto God my rock, Why hast thou forgotten me? why
go I mourning because of the oppression of the enemy? As with a
sword in my bones, mine enemies reproach me; while they say daily
unto me, Where is thy God? Why art thou cast down, O my soul?
and why art thou disquieted within me? hope thou in God: for I
shall yet praise him, who is the health of my countenance, and my
God.   — Psalm 42

Judge me, O God, and plead my cause against an ungodly nation:
O deliver me from the deceitful and unjust man. For thou art the
God of my strength: why dost thou cast me off? why go I mourning
because of the oppression of the enemy? O send out thy light and
thy truth: let them lead me; let them bring me unto thy holy hill,
and to thy tabernacles. Then will I go unto the altar of God, unto

God my exceeding joy: yea, upon the harp will I praise thee, O
God my God. Why art thou cast down, O my soul? and why art
thou disquieted within me? hope in God: for I shall yet praise him,
who is the health of my countenance, and my God.   — Psalm 43

As these two Psalms run into one another and carry the same theme
we here deal with them as one. They might have been one in the
beginning. They both deal with the journey from despair to hope
and are prayers of longing and for deliverance. Evidently, their writer
was in exile, far from the familiar scenes of his old home and his
much-loved forms of worship. He was also among enemies who added
insult to bodily injury with the repeated taunt, "Where is thy God?"
But the Psalms strike the triumphant note. "Hope thou in God; for
I shall yet praise Him." We should set our worries in the light of
these Psalms.

Prayer for Divine Assistance

(Psalm 44)

We have heard with our ears, O God, our fathers have told us, what
work thou didst in their days, in the times of old. How thou didst
drive out the heathen with thy hand, and plantedst them; how thou
didst afflict the people, and cast them out. For they got not the land
in possession by their own sword, neither did their own arm save
them: but thy right hand, and thine arm, and the light of thy
countenance, because thou hadst a favour unto them. Thou art my
King, O God: command deliverances for Jacob. Through thee will we
push down our enemies: through thy name will we tread them under
that rise up against us. For I will not trust in my bow, neither shall
my sword save me. But thou hast saved us from our enemies, and
hast put them to shame that hated us. In God we boast all the day
long, and praise thy name for ever. Selah. . . .
Yea, for thy sake are we killed all the day long; we are counted as
sheep for the slaughter. Awake, why sleepest thou, O Lord? arise,
cast us not off for ever. Wherefore hidest thou thy face, and for-
gettest our affliction and our oppression? For our soul is bowed down
to the dust: our belly cleaveth unto the earth. Arise for our help,
and redeem us for thy mercies' sake.   — Psalm 44:1-8, 22-26

As we consider Biblical prayers we must not lose sight of the
personal touch many of them manifest. "My God," as we have already
seen, was Nehemiah's favorite mode of address. Here the "my" (44:4)
may be collective rather than individual. The sovereignty of Jehovah
is recognized. As "King" He can enable His servants to push down
their enemies (44:5).

The Psalmist reveals a passionate readiness to reason with God, and
challenges Him to display His power (44:23, 26). The saints of old
were never weary of reminding themselves of the gracious purpose of
God throughout the centuries, and all He had been was a spur alike
to gratitude, penitence and confidence (44:1-5). Because God is ever
the same (Malachi 3:6), all He has accomplished, He is still able
to perform.

Prayer for a Refuge

(Psalm 46)

God is our refuge and strength, a very present help in trouble. Therefore will not we fear, though the earth be removed, and though the mountains be carried into the midst of the sea; Though the waters thereof roar and be troubled, though the mountains shake with the swelling thereof. Selah. There is a river, the streams whereof shall make glad the city of God, the holy place of the tabernacles of the most High. God is in the midst of her; she shall not be moved: God shall help her, and that right early. The heathen raged, the kingdoms were moved: he uttered his voice, the earth melted. The Lord of hosts is with us; the God of Jacob is our refuge. Selah. Come, behold the works of the Lord, what desolations he hath made in the earth. He maketh wars to cease unto the end of the earth; he breaketh the bow, and cutteth the spear in sunder; he burneth the chariot in the fire. Be still, and know that I am God: I will be exalted among the heathen, I will be exalted in the earth. The Lord of hosts is with us; the God of Jacob is our refuge. Selah. — Psalm 46

This was Martin Luther's favorite prayer, inspiring him to compose that famous battle-hymn of his — "A Mighty Fortress is our God." Three times over He is presented as a *Refuge* (46:1, 8, 11). What a sanctuary in perils in which we are utterly helpless, God is! What can we do against a changing earth, hurtling mountains, and raging storms? When sudden calamity comes, and the foundations slip from under our feet, the eternal God is there with His embracing arms. Always underneath and lower than our lowest depths.

The thrice repeated term, "Selah," gives us the natural division of the Psalm, possibly set to music and sung by the Temple choir —

1. The Power of God the Father (1-3)
2. The Presence of God the Spirit (4-7)
3. The Peace of God the Son (8-11)

Prayer of a Broken Heart

(Psalm 51)

Have mercy upon me, O God, according to thy lovingkindness: according unto the multitude of thy tender mercies blot out my transgressions. Wash me throughly from mine iniquity, and cleanse me from my sin. For I acknowledge my transgressions: and my sin is ever before me. Against thee, thee only, have I sinned, and done this evil in thy sight: that thou mightest be justified when thou speakest, and be clear when thou judgest. Behold, I was shapen in iniquity; and in sin did my mother conceive me. Behold, thou desirest truth in the inward parts: and in the hidden part thou shalt make me to know wisdom. Purge me with hyssop, and I shall be clean: wash me, and I shall be whiter than snow. Make me to hear joy and gladness; that the bones which thou hast broken may rejoice. Hide thy face from my sins, and blot out all mine iniquities. Create in me a clean heart, O God; and renew a right spirit within me. Cast me not away from thy presence; and take not thy holy spirit from me. Restore unto me the joy of thy salvation; and uphold me with thy free spirit. Then will I teach transgressors thy ways; and sinners shall be converted unto thee. Deliver me from bloodguiltiness, O God, thou God of my salvation: and my tongue shall sing aloud of thy righteousness. O Lord, open thou my lips; and my mouth shall shew forth thy praise. For thou desirest not sacrifice; else would I give it: thou delightest not in burnt offering. The sacrifices of God are a broken spirit: a broken and a contrite heart, O God, thou wilt not despise. Do good in thy good pleasure unto Zion: build thou the walls of Jerusalem. Then shalt thou be pleased with the sacrifices of righteousness, with burnt offering and whole burnt offering: then shall they offer bullocks upon thine altar.   —Psalm 51

In this prayer, drenched with David's penitential tears, we have one of the most fervent cries in the Bible for the cleansing and renewing of the heart. What a cry of a broken and contrite spirit it is! Where else can we find such profound depth and tenderness of contrition, joined with such childlike faith in God's pardoning mercy?

Alfred Thomas says that "we may call this psalm the penitent's prayer-book. The spectacle of a good man falling into open sin is a sight to make angels weep, especially that of a man so distinguished as David falling into sins so gross and flagrant." Analyzing the Psalm we have —

1. A Prayer for Forgiveness for Particular Sins and a Sinful Disposition (1-9). Root and fruit must be dealt with.
2. A Prayer for Renewal (10-12). The whole man must come under the sway of the free Spirit.
3. A Prayer and an Offering for Service Cleansed Hearts Alone Can Render (13-17).

Prayer at All Times

(Psalm 55)

Give ear to my prayer, O God; and hide not thyself from my supplication. Attend unto me, and hear me: I mourn in my complaint, and make a noise. Because of the voice of the enemy, because of the oppression of the wicked: for they cast iniquity upon me, and in wrath they hate me. My heart is sore pained within me: and the terrors of death are fallen upon me. Fearfulness and trembling are come upon me, and horror hath overwhelmed me. And I said, Oh that I had wings like a dove! for then would I fly away, and be at rest. . . .

For it was not an enemy that reproached me; then I could have borne it: neither was it he that hated me that did magnify himself against me; then I would have hid myself from him: But it was thou, a man mine equal, my guide, and mine acquaintance. We took sweet counsel together, and walked unto the house of God in company. . . .

The words of his mouth were smoother than butter, but war was in his heart: his words were softer than oil, yet were they drawn swords. Cast thy burden upon the Lord, and he shall sustain thee: he shall never suffer the righteous to be moved. But thou, O God, shalt bring them down into the pit of destruction: bloody and deceitful men shall not live out half their days; but I will trust in thee.

—Psalm 55:1-6, 12-14, 21-23

What a vivid portrayal of the treachery of Judas this Psalm affords (55:12-14)! David wrestled with despair as he thought of Ahithophel's dark crime, but he knew how to cast his burden upon the Lord (55:22). When we find ourselves surrounded with the deceit and failure of our friends, do we not sigh for the wings of a dove that we might fly away and be at rest (55:6)? Cramped hearts long for flight. Let us guard against the perils of monotony (55:19).

Prayer of Distress

(Psalm 57)

Be merciful unto me, O God, be merciful unto me: for my soul trusteth in thee: yea, in the shadow of thy wings will I make my refuge, until these calamities be overpast. I will cry unto God most high; unto God that performeth all things for me. He shall send from heaven, and save me from the reproach of him that would swallow me up. Selah. God shall send forth his mercy and his truth. My soul is among lions: and I lie even among them that are set on fire, even the sons of men, whose teeth are spears and arrows, and their tongue a sharp sword. Be thou exalted, O God, above the heavens; let thy glory be above all the earth. They have prepared a net for my steps; my soul is bowed down: they have digged a pit before me, into the midst whereof they are fallen themselves. Selah. My heart is fixed, O God, my heart is fixed: I will sing and give praise. Awake up, my glory; awake, psaltery and harp: I myself will awake early. I will praise thee, O Lord, among the people: I will sing unto thee among the nations. For thy mercy is great unto the heavens, and thy truth unto the clouds. Be thou exalted, O God, above the heavens: let thy glory be above all the earth. — Psalm 57

Here is the cry wrung from the heart of David, as he fled from Saul (see title of Psalm). This was his S.O.S. to the merciful God who knew that His servant was innocent of Saul's hatred. His soul was among the lions, but the sweet singer of Israel knew that the God who made the lions, was his safe and blessed shelter. He could say with George Whitefield, "I have thrown myself blindfolded into the Hands of God." David's heart was fixed. The tragedy with many is that their heart is mixed (James 1:8).

A true prayer is the outpouring of the heart. Then its language, especially when the pleader is a poet, is figurative and expressive (62:7). The times of devotion find a large place in the Psalms (63:1, 6; 65:8). All who are conscious of their weakness and need can call upon God (65:2). Prayers for vengeance are common to Jewish history

(69:22; 109). Communing with one's own heart is frequently alluded to (63:6; 77:6; 119:55). The Psalmist knew a great deal about soul soliloquy.

Prayer of Trust

(Psalm 71)

Deliver me, O my God, out of the hand of the wicked, out of the hand of the unrighteous and cruel man. For thou art my hope, O Lord God: thou art my trust from my youth. By thee have I been holden up from the womb: thou art he that took me out of my mother's bowels: my praise shall be continually of thee. I am as a wonder unto many; but thou art my strong refuge. Let my mouth be filled with thy praise and with thy honour all the day. Cast me not off in the time of old age; forsake me not when my strength faileth. For mine enemies speak against me; and they that lay wait for my soul take counsel together, Saying, God hath forsaken him: persecute and take him; for there is none to deliver him. O God, be not far from me: O my God, make haste for my help. Let them be confounded and consumed that are adversaries to my soul; let them be covered with reproach and dishonour that seek my hurt. But I will hope continually, and will yet praise thee more and more. My mouth shall shew forth thy righteousness and thy salvation all the day; for I know not the numbers thereof.   — Psalm 71:4-15

We here learn the secret of overcoming our troubles and our fears (71:14). Here is a Psalm full of gratitude to God for His unfailing Providence. Whoever wrote this Psalm suffered the bitterness of loneliness and separation from his friends and the hatred of enemies (71:4). But God's past deliverances were the guarantee of present and future deliverances (71:6). In his anguish, the Psalmist felt himself God-forsaken (71:11), but at the other end of the tunnel there was sunshine (71:14ff.).

Prayer for God Himself

(Psalm 73)

And they say, How doth God know? and is there knowledge in the most High? Behold, these are the ungodly, who prosper in the world; they increase in riches. Verily I have cleansed my heart in vain, and washed my hands in innocency. For all the day long have I been plagued, and chastened every morning. If I say, I will speak thus; behold, I should offend against the generation of thy children. When I thought to know this, it was too painful for me; Until I went into the sanctuary of God; then understood I their end. Surely thou didst set them in slippery places: thou castedst them down into destruction. How are they brought into desolation, as in a moment! they are utterly consumed with terrors. As a dream when one awaketh; so, O Lord, when thou awakest, thou shalt despise their image. Thus my heart was grieved, and I was pricked in my reins. So foolish was I, and ignorant: I was as a beast before thee. Nevertheless I am continually with thee: thou hast holden me by my right hand. Thou shalt guide me with thy counsel, and afterward receive me to glory.

Whom have I in heaven but thee? and there is none upon earth that I desire beside thee. My flesh and my heart faileth: but God is the strength of my heart, and my portion for ever. For, lo, they that are far from thee shall perish: thou hast destroyed all them that go a whoring from thee. But it is good for me to draw near to God: I have put my trust in the Lord God, that I may declare all thy works.

— Psalm 73:11-28

"The supreme longing of the profounder souls of Israel was for God, not His gifts but Himself" (73:25-28). Their goal was God Himself and consequently they felt God held them by the hand and guided them from earth to heaven (73:24). Having God, they asked for nothing else in heaven or earth (73:25). In the presence of God, the ultimate destinies of the good and the bad are understood (73:16).

Knowing God as the One men could draw near to (73:28), Old Testament saints never allowed the great terms goodness and loving-kindness to degenerate into empty phrases. They were always "filled with radiant and indisputable historical fact . . . The past was ever with them: it was kept alive not only in history, but in prayer" (Psalms 78, 105, 106). Because of all God is in Himself, prayer is always worthwhile (85:8; 86:5, 15; 94:1).

Prayer of a Pilgrim

(Psalms 90, 91)

Lord, thou hast been our dwelling place in all generations. Before the mountains were brought forth, or ever thou hadst formed the earth and the world, even from everlasting to everlasting, thou art God. Thou turnest man to destruction; and sayest, Return, ye children of men. For a thousand years in thy sight are but as yesterday when it is past, and as a watch in the night. . . .

So teach us to number our days, that we may apply our hearts unto wisdom. Return, O Lord, how long? and let it repent thee concerning thy servants. O satisfy us early with thy mercy; that we may rejoice and be glad all our days. Make us glad according to the days wherein thou hast afflicted us, and the years wherein we have seen evil. Let thy work appear unto thy servants, and thy glory unto their children. And let the beauty of the Lord our God be upon us: and establish thou the work of our hands upon us; yea, the work of our hands establish thou it.   — Psalm 90:1-4, 12-17

He that dwelleth in the secret place of the most High shall abide under the shadow of the Almighty. I will say of the Lord, He is my refuge and my fortress: my God; in him will I trust. Surely he shall deliver thee from the snare of the fowler, and from the noisome pestilence. He shall cover thee with his feathers, and under his wings shalt thou trust: his truth shall be thy shield and buckler. Thou shalt not be afraid for the terror by night; nor for the arrow that flieth by day; Nor for the pestilence that walketh in darkness; nor for the destruction that wasteth at noonday. A thousand shall fall at thy side, and ten thousand at thy right hand; but it shall not come nigh thee. Only with thine eyes shalt thou behold and see the reward of the wicked. Because thou hast made the Lord, which is my refuge, even the most High, thy habitation; There shall be no evil befall thee, neither shall any plague come nigh thy dwelling. For he shall give his angels charge over thee, to keep thee in all thy ways. They shall bear thee up in their hands, lest thou dash thy foot against a stone. Thou shalt tread upon the lion and adder: the young lion and the dragon shalt thou trample under feet. Because he hath set his love upon me, therefore will I deliver him: I will set him on high, because he hath known my name. He shall call upon me, and I will answer him: I will be with him in trouble; I will deliver him, and honour him. With long life will I satisfy him, and shew him my salvation.   —Psalm 91

Bible scholars feel that these two Psalms should be treated as one, and that they both cover the pilgrimage of God's ancient people through the wilderness. Yet the saints of every age have made these prayers their very own. During the First World War, Psalm 91 was known as "The Trench Psalm" because the men in France found all their experiences in it — wire entanglements, poison-gas, bombs, shells by night, trench fever, destruction by thousands. But God was ever their Defense. We have all read of the Angels at Mons. Different speakers give dramatic quality to this Psalm, often called "The Traveler's Psalm" —

> The Prelude (91:1)
> A Solo (91:2)
> A Chorus Replying (91:3-8)
> A Solo (91:9)
> A Chorus Responding (91:9-13)
> God Speaks (91:14-16)

Usually the enemies denounced are enemies of the moral order (94:5, 6), whom the God who judges righteously, is able to deal with (94:1). Prayer was offered kneeling (95:6).

Prayer As Praise for God's Greatness

(Psalm 96)

O sing unto the Lord a new song: sing unto the Lord, all the earth. Sing unto the Lord, bless his name; shew forth his salvation from day to day. Declare his glory among the heathen, his wonders among all people. For the Lord is great, and greatly to be praised: he is to be feared above all gods. For all the gods of the nations are idols: but the Lord made the heavens. Honour and majesty are before him: strength and beauty are in his sanctuary. Give unto the Lord, O ye kindreds of the people, give unto the Lord glory and strength. Give unto the Lord the glory due unto his name: bring an offering, and come into his courts. O worship the Lord in the beauty of holiness: fear before him, all the earth. Say among the heathen that the Lord reigneth: the world also shall be established that it shall not be moved: he shall judge the people righteously. Let the heavens rejoice, and let the earth be glad; let the sea roar, and the fulness thereof.

Let the field be joyful, and all that is therein: then shall all the trees of the wood rejoice Before the Lord: for he cometh, for he cometh to judge the earth: he shall judge the world with righteousness, and the people with his truth.   — Psalm 96

Although Hebrew worship was solemn, it was happy (Psalm 100). God's greatness was magnified with glad hearts. The theme of the Psalm before us is, "Crown Him Lord of All." Its four strophes are four "concentric circles round that central throne."

1. Israel, knowing God, calls other nations to worship Him (1-3)
2. As Creator, God is above all man-made gods (4-6)
3. All who worship Him are priests (7-9)
4. Divine justice and judgment are the spring of joy (10-13)

Prayers for Escape from Trials

(Psalms 102, 103, 105)

Hear my prayer, O Lord, and let my cry come unto thee. Hide not thy face from me in the day when I am in trouble; incline thine ear unto me: in the day when I call answer me speedily. For my days are consumed like smoke, and my bones are burned as an hearth. My heart is smitten, and withered like grass; so that I forget to eat my bread. By reason of the voice of my groaning my bones cleave to my skin. I am like a pelican of the wilderness: I am like an owl of the desert. I watch, and am as a sparrow alone upon the house top. Mine enemies reproach me all the day; and they that are mad against me are sworn against me. For I have eaten ashes like bread, and mingled my drink with weeping, Because of thine indignation and thy wrath: for thou hast lifted me up, and cast me down. My days are like a shadow that declineth; and I am withered like grass. But thou, O Lord, shalt endure for ever; and thy remembrance unto all generations. Thou shalt arise, and have mercy upon Zion: for the time to favour her, yea, the set time, is come. For thy servants take pleasure in her stones, and favour the dust thereof. So the heathen shall fear the name of the Lord, and all the kings of the earth thy glory. When the Lord shall build up Zion, he shall appear in his glory. He will regard the prayer of the destitute, and not despise their prayer. This shall be written for the generation to come: and the people which shall be created shall praise the Lord. For he hath looked down from the height of his sanctuary; from heaven did the Lord behold the earth; To hear the groaning of the prisoner; to loose those that are appointed to death; To declare the name of the Lord in Zion, and his praise in Jerusalem; When the people are gathered together, and the kingdoms, to serve the Lord.

— Psalm 102:1-22

Bless the Lord, O my soul: and all that is within me, bless his holy name. Bless the Lord, O my soul, and forget not all his benefits: Who forgiveth all thine iniquities; who healeth all thy diseases; Who redeemeth thy life from destruction: who crowneth thee with loving-kindness and tender mercies; Who satisfieth thy mouth with good things; so that thy youth is renewed like the eagle's. . . .

Like as a father pitieth his children, so the Lord pitieth them that
fear him.   — Psalm 103:1-5, 13
O give thanks unto the Lord; call upon his name: make known his
deeds among the people. Sing unto him, sing psalms unto him: talk
ye of all his wondrous works. Glory ye in his holy name: let the
heart of them rejoice that seek the Lord. Seek the Lord, and his
strength: seek his face evermore. Remember his marvelous works
that he hath done; his wonders, and the judgments of his mouth; O
ye seed of Abraham his servant, ye children of Jacob his chosen. He
is the Lord our God: his judgments are in all the earth.
                                                    — Psalm 105:1-7

The Lord sits above the centuries (103:13; Deuteronomy 1:31),
and has a kingdom in which there must be no restraint (103:20). He
knows how to punish those who are antagonistic to His rule (109:20).
Prayer for the Temple forms the burden of one of the most beautiful
petitions (107; see 145-150). Sometimes prayers were granted in mouth
and denied in wisdom (106:15; Mark 5:18, 19). Every answered
prayer is not necessarily for our benefit.

> That Power above, who makes mankind His care,
> May bless us most when He rejects our prayer.

Prayer of Remembrance

(Psalm 106)

They angered him also at the waters of strife, so that it went ill
with Moses for their sakes: Because they provoked his spirit, so that
he spake unadvisedly with his lips. They did not destroy the nations,
concerning whom the Lord commanded them: But were mingled
among the heathen, and learned their works. And they served their
idols: which were a snare unto them. . . .
Therefore was the wrath of the Lord kindled against his people,
insomuch that he abhorred his own inheritance. And he gave them
into the hand of the heathen; and they that hated them ruled over
them. Their enemies also oppressed them, and they were brought
into subjection under their hand. Many times did he deliver them;
but they provoked him with their counsel, and were brought low
for their iniquity. Nevertheless he regarded their affliction, when he
heard their cry: And he remembered for them his covenant, and
repented according to the multitude of his mercies. He made them
also to be pitied of all those that carried them captives. Save us, O
Lord our God, and gather us from among the heathen, to give
thanks unto thy holy name, and to triumph in thy praise. Blessed
be the Lord God of Israel from everlasting to everlasting: and let
all the people say, Amen. Praise ye the Lord.
                                            — Psalm 106:32-36, 40-48

Because there is a personal pronoun in almost every verse of this
prayer, each of us can make it our own. Have you ever prayed your
way through this great Psalm? Note the alternating surge of a sorrow
escaped and the triumphant note of thanksgiving, and linger over
the vows of a redeemed soul. Loss of faith in God and in man darkens

the Psalm, but deliverances came for the tried one when he prayed. May the Lord mercifully deliver us from speaking unadvisably with our lips (106:33)! How dependent we are upon God's unfailing mercy (106:44, 45).

Prayer for Those in Perils on Sea
(Psalm 107)

They that go down to the sea in ships, that do business in great waters; These see the works of the Lord, and his wonders in the deep. For he commandeth, and raiseth the stormy wind, which lifteth up the waves thereof. They mount up to the heaven, they go down again to the depths: their soul is melted because of trouble. They reel to and fro, and stagger like a drunken man, and are at their wit's end. Then they cry unto the Lord in their trouble, and he bringeth them out of their distresses. He maketh the storm a calm, so that the waves thereof are still. Then are they glad because they be quiet; so he bringeth them unto their desired haven. Oh that men would praise the Lord for his goodness, and for his wonderful works to the children of men!   — Psalm 107:23-31

The Sea-Prayers of the Bible deserve a section by themselves (Exodus 15:1-11; Jonah 1:4-15; 2:5-7; Psalm 107:23-31; Mark 4:35-41; Acts 27:9-25). Of Psalm 107, Burgess and Proudlove comment that it is a storm piece set to majestic music. For sheer sublimity of description it can hardly be surpassed. As we read it — especially when we live by the side of the sea — we can hear the roar of the wind and note the waves of the sea as they are lashed into fury. We can see the ship as it tosses to and fro on the great waters. Do you pray when at wit's end corner (107:27)? Believing prayer drives away all fear (Psalm 118:6). It is encouraging to know that amid the storms of life we have One who guides our barque.

> My barque is wafted by the strand, by breath Divine,
> And on the helm I feel a Hand, Other than mine.

Prayer and Affinity to Scripture
(Psalms 19, 119)

The heavens declare the glory of God; and the firmament sheweth his handywork. Day unto day uttereth speech, and night unto night sheweth knowledge. There is no speech nor language, where their voice is not heard. Their line is gone out through all the earth, and their words to the end of the world. In them hath he set a tabernacle for the sun, which is as a bridegroom coming out of his chamber, and rejoiceth as a strong man to run a race. His going forth is from the end of the heaven, and his circuit unto the ends of it: and there is nothing hid from the heat thereof. The law of the Lord is perfect, converting the soul: the testimony of the Lord is sure, making wise the simple. The statutes of the Lord are right, rejoicing the heart: the commandment of the Lord is pure, enlightening the eyes. The fear of the Lord is clean, enduring for ever: the judgments of the Lord are true and righteous altogether. More to be desired are they than gold, yea, than much fine gold: sweeter also than honey and the honeycomb. Moreover by them is thy servant warned: and in keeping of them there is great reward. Who can understand his errors? cleanse thou me from secret faults. Keep back thy servant also from presumptuous sins: let them not have dominion over me: then shall I be upright, and I shall be innocent from the great transgression. Let the words of my mouth, and the meditation of my heart, be acceptable in thy sight, O Lord, my strength, and my redeemer.   — Psalm 19

Seven times a day do I praise thee because of thy righteous judgments.   — Psalm 119:164

We combine these two Psalms, seeing that both of them extol the Word of God. The division of Psalm 19 is clear —

> God and the Sky (1-6)
> God and the Scriptures (7-11)
> God and the Soul (12-14)

For it, the Psalmist could praise God seven times a day (119:164). Of this latter wonderful Psalm, in which almost every verse extols the Word in some way or another, Ruskin says that it cost him tears to learn by heart in his childhood. Yet it became precious to him in after life. From both Psalms we learn of the greatness of God's Word and the blessedness of obeying it.

Prayer for Searching of Heart

(Psalm 139)

O Lord, thou hast searched me, and known me. Thou knowest my downsitting and mine uprising, thou understandest my thought afar off. Thou compassest my path and my lying down, and art acquainted with all my ways. For there is not a word in my tongue, but lo, O Lord, thou knowest it altogether. Thou hast beset me behind and before, and laid thine hand upon me. Such knowledge is too wonderful for me; it is high, I cannot attain unto it. Whither shall I go from thy spirit? or whither shall I flee from thy presence? If I ascend up into heaven, thou art there: if I make my bed in hell, behold, thou art there. If I take the wings of the morning, and dwell in the uttermost parts of the sea; Even there shall thy hand lead me, and thy right hand shall hold me. If I say, Surely the darkness shall cover me; even the night shall be light about me. Yea, the darkness hideth not from thee; but the night shineth as the day: the darkness and the light are both alike to thee. For thou hast possessed my reins; thou hast covered me in my mother's womb. I will praise thee; for I am fearfully and wonderfully made: marvelous are thy works, and that my soul knoweth right well. My substance was not hid from thee, when I was made in secret, and curiously wrought in the lowest parts of the earth. Thine eyes did see my substance, yet being unperfect; and in thy book all my members were written, which in continuance were fashioned, when as yet there was none of them. How precious also are thy thoughts unto me, O God! how great is the sum of them! If I should count them, they are more in number than the sand: when I awake, I am still with thee. Surely thou wilt slay the wicked, O God: depart from me therefore, ye bloody men. For they speak against thee wickedly, and thine enemies take thy name in vain. Do not I hate them, O Lord, that hate thee? and am not I grieved with those that rise up against thee? I hate them with perfect hatred: I count them mine enemies. Search me, O God, and know my heart: try me, and know my thoughts: And see if there be any wicked way in me, and lead me in the way everlasting.

— Psalm 139

No one but David, who claimed divine inspiration for his writings (II Samuel 23:1, 2) could have written a magnificent Psalm like this with its cry for deliverance from every crooked way (139:24). Professor MacFadyen writes that it is "remarkable that some of the tenderest and most beautiful voices in the Psalter break into imprecation. The man who expressed in language of unapproachable simplicity and beauty his sense of the mysterious omnipresence of God, confesses to hating his enemies with implacable hatred and prays for their destruction (137; 139:19-22)."

Among the great prayers of the Bible this one of David's is conspicuous for its expression of intimate spiritual communion with God. The Psalmist rejoiced in a three-fold security. God beset him behind [past] and before [future] and had His hand upon him [present] (139:5). The Psalm which can be divided into four strophes of six verses each is an eloquent tribute to God's omniscience, omnipresence and omnipotence.

There is no contradiction between the beginning and ending of the prayer. It starts out by saying that the intercessor had been searched (139:1) and ends by asking to be searched (139:23). In the opening part of the prayer, David is taken up with his outer life which he felt had been searched, but as he journeyed on with God he was made conscious of a world of undiscovered sin within, so prayed to be searched in the depths of his innermost being. "Any wicked way *in* me" (139:23, 24).

What a cry was wrung from David's heart, "Search me!" Can we make it our own? Other brief but suggestive cries are "Show me" (Exodus 33:13). "Strengthen me" (Judges 16:28). "Stay me" (Song of Solomon 2:5). "Send me" (Isaiah 6:8). "Save me" (Matthew 14:30). "Suffer me" (Luke 9:59).

We only wish it had been practicable to deal with all the 150 Psalms forming the Prayer and Praise Book of Israel. We trust, however, the selection given will prove what a spiritual classic we possess within the Psalms. Hosea urges us to take with us words when we turn to the Lord (14:2). There are times, of course, when we must be silent before Him (Zechariah 2:13). But when prayer is vocal what better words can we use than those found in the beautiful, expressive devotional phraseology of the incomparable Psalms?

> That implicit word of Thine, O sovereign Lord
> In all too pure, too high, too deep, for me.
> Weary of striving and with longing faint,
> *I breathe it back again in prayer to Thee.*

As we leave the prayers of the Psalms, there are several features of prayer we can weave together for our enlightenment. Psalms 116, 117, and 118 were the Psalms Jesus and His disciples sang on the way to the Cross (Mark 14:26). Humility should ever robe our prayers (Psalm 131). God knows how to circumvent the schemes of evil men (137:7). In exile, when sacrifice was not possible, the lifting up of hands in prayer could be as "the evening sacrifice" (141:2). The lifting up of the hands was a feature of Christian prayer (I Timothy 2:8). In Psalm 143 we have a three-fold prayer, "To hear . . . To know . . . To do" (8-10), and a three-fold reason, "In Thee we trust . . . Lift up the soul . . . Thou art my God" (8-10). Private prayer of special import was naturally enough often associated with the night (119:62). Many of the judgment Psalms are not for a Christian age (149:6, 7).

Proverbs

It is somewhat surprising that in a book made up of divine wisdom applied to the earthly conditions of the people of God, we have only a few isolated references to prayer. *Proverbs* contains no recorded prayers. Among the prayer-pointers of the book mention can be made of the following —

Prayer is the acknowledgment of God as the Director of our paths (3:5).

Prayer is the guarantee of inward peace and outward prosperity (3:24-26).

Prayer is the channel through which divine wisdom becomes ours (4:7; 9:10; with I Corinthians 1:2; James 1:5, 6).

Prayer is the secret of mutual delight and of a God-blessed life (8:30-34).

Prayer is a delight to God and beneficial only when offered by righteous lips (15:8, 29; see 16:1).

Prayer results in the divine vindication of the Lord's own (20:22; 23:11).

Prayer, when uttered by unholy lips, is an abomination in God's sight (28:9).

Prayer as confession for discovered sin results in the acceptance of divine mercy (28:13).

Ecclesiastes

The key-phrase of this revealing book is "Under the sun" (1:3). Solomon sought for supreme satisfaction in everything "under the sun" and came to the conclusion that all was vanity or empty. A fully satisfied life can only come from the One above the sun (Colossians 3:1-3), and prayer alone can take us up to the divine Satisfier above. Communion with God and not with our own heart is the only avenue of contentment (1:16).

What place is there for prayer in those baffled hearts who regard history as an endless and inexorable cycle in which "that which hath been is that which shall be" (1:9)? Prayer has no meaning at all to those who are fatalists (2:14; 9:2; 12:7, 8). God is not far away from any one of us (Psalm 145:18). Although God is in heaven and man is upon the earth, prayer can bring about a blessed contact between both worlds. Whether spoken to God or men, words should be few (5:2).

Song of Solomon

"Nowhere in Scripture does the unspiritual mind tread upon ground so mysterious and incomprehensible as in this book," says Dr. C. I. Scofield. "Yet the saintliest men and women of the ages have found it a source of pure and exquisite delight." The Song of Songs, which is Solomon's (1:1), shares with Esther the distinction of being a book without any reference to God or to any spiritual truth. It is without any religious sentiment or devout utterance of any kind.

Yet because it is a book symbolizing the truth of union and communion existing between Christ and His own, in the outpouring of the heart of the Bride for her Beloved we have language we can make our own (1:4). It is to be hoped that we know "the secret of the stairs" (2:14). Referring to this suggestive phrase as he applies it to prayer, Guy H. King says that the secret implies several things —

The stairs are mounted by the people with a secret name — mounted to the position in a secret refuge — mounted for the purpose of a secret interview — mounted in the prospect of a secret exhilaration.

Isaiah

Not only is Isaiah prominent as Judah's greatest orator and poet, one in whose works Jewish literature reaches its highest perfection, he is also conspicuous for the spiritual element in his writings. Isaiah stands out as the evangelical prophet who knew how to pray.

Prayer God Does Not Hear

(Isaiah 1:15; 16:12)

And when ye spread forth your hands, I will hide mine eyes from
you: yea, when ye make many prayers, I will not hear: your hands
are full of blood.
And it shall come to pass, when it is seen that Moab is weary on the
high place, that he shall come to his sanctuary to pray; but he shall
not prevail.   — Isaiah 1:15; 16:12

Despised and unprevailing prayer finds a place in this great book.
Although the lifting up of the hands is the recognized gesture in
prayer (1:15), and the sanctuary the recognized house of prayer, yet
because of the abominable lives of those assuming the attitude of
prayer, God hid His eyes from them and turned a deaf ear to their
entreaties. Mere lip homage is not sufficient. A basic condition of
prayer is sincerity (29:13). When there is a sincere desire for cleansing
of heart and a true yearning for God, then He is willing and ready
to reason with us (1:18; 2:3). God speaks of Himself as spreading
forth His merciful hands to a rebellious people (65:2; see 5:25; 8:17).
Even the pious are not content unless they can see tangible answers
to prayer. Faith must have sight (5:19).

Prayer and Cleansing

(Isaiah 6)

Then said I, Woe is me! for I am undone; because I am a man of
unclean lips, and I dwell in the midst of a people of unclean lips:
for mine eyes have seen the King, the Lord of hosts.   — Isaiah 6:5

As we read the record of Isaiah's transforming vision we are impressed with the prophet's reticence regarding his inaugural vision.
His replies to the majestic Lord are brief. In the presence of such an
August One as Isaiah saw, silence is wisdom. A three-fold vision was
granted to the prophet. Following upon the revelation of the glory
of the Lord there came confession, cleansing and commission.

1. A Vision of a Throne (1-4).

The emphasis is upon reverence in the presence of God. Of the six
wings only two were used for service (6:2).

2. A Vision of a Heart (5-6).

After pronouncing six woes upon others (Isaiah 5), Isaiah ha: one
for his own heart. "Woe is *me*" (6:5). Cleansing quickly followed
confession (6:5,7).

3. A Vision of a Sphere (8-13).

The prophet needed such a vision for the hard and unresponsive
task he was called to face. God's hard places are difficult to fill. They
need men and women who share Isaiah's soul-absorbing vision of the
sovereign Lord.

Prayer for a Sign

(Isaiah 7:11)

Ask thee a sign of the Lord thy God; ask it either in the depth,
or in the height above.   — Isaiah 7:11

Amid life's uncertainties we have God's glorious certainty. A
daring, reckless faith always meets with reward (7:9-14). What a
prophecy, this was addressed, not to faithless Ahaz, but to the whole
house of David! Mary gave her instant assent to this prayer-sign
(Luke 1:38). How descriptive is the prophecy of the plainness and
simplicity of our Lord's childhood years (7:15, 16)! God forbids the
piercing of the future secrets by the aid of necromancy (8:19). He
not only provided a sanctuary for His people but is Himself a
Sanctuary, the One from whom all revelation comes (8:14; Ezekiel
11:16). Prayer, like prophecy, has a historical context. Many Biblical
prayers were prompted by particular occasions (24:14).

Prayer of Exaltation

(Isaiah 12)

And in that day thou shalt say, O Lord, I will praise thee: though
thou wast angry with me, thine anger is turned away, and thou
comfortedst me. Behold, God is my salvation; I will trust, and not be
afraid: for the Lord Jehovah is my strength and my song; he also
is become my salvation. Therefore with joy shall ye draw water out
of the wells of salvation. And in that day shall ye say, Praise the
Lord, call upon his name, declare his doings among the people, make
mention that his name is exalted. Sing unto the Lord; for he hath
done excellent things: this is known in all the earth. Cry out and
shout, thou inhabitant of Zion: for great is the Holy One of Israel
in the midst of thee.   — Isaiah 12

What a precious prose-prayer-poem this is! The song Isaiah sang is
ever new — *God* is our Salvation. Salvation, then, is not a mere
possession but a Person. Is this not a theme for praise at all times?
Within the prayer-song we have —

> A call to trust our Divine Deliverer.
> A call to witness to His doings.
> A call to praise Him for all He is in Himself.

Prayer of Praise for Triumphs

(Isaiah 25)

O Lord, thou art my God; I will exalt thee, I will praise thy name;
for thou hast done wonderful things; thy counsels of old are faithfulness and truth. For thou hast made of a city an heap; of a defenced
city a ruin: a palace of strangers to be no city; it shall never be
built. Therefore shall the strong people glorify thee, the city of the
terrible nations shall fear thee. . . .
He will swallow up death in victory; and the Lord God will wipe

away tears from off all faces; and the rebuke of his people shall he take away from off the earth: for the Lord hath spoken it.

And it shall be said in that day, Lo, this is our God; we have waited for him, and he will save us: this is the Lord; we have waited for him, we will be glad and rejoice in his salvation. — Isaiah 25:1-3, 8, 9

This great prayer looks beyond any historical connection to the glorious triumphs of the kingdom-age when the knowledge of the Lord is to cover the earth, as the waters cover the sea. Both Paul and John dwell upon a world without tears and grave, which Isaiah predicted (25:8; I Corinthians 15:55; Revelation 21:4). All who live in eager anticipation of the Lord's return to the air for His own (I Thessalonians 4:17) may lay hold of verse 9 and apply it to the Rapture.

Prayer for Peace

(Isaiah 26)

Thou wilt keep him in perfect peace, whose mind is stayed on thee: because he trusteth in thee. Trust ye in the Lord for ever: for in the Lord Jehovah is everlasting strength:

For he bringeth down them that dwell on high; the lofty city, he layeth it low; he layeth it low, even to the ground; he bringeth it even to the dust. The foot shall tread it down, even the feet of the poor, and the steps of the needy. The way of the just is uprightness: thou, most upright, dost weigh the path of the just. Yea, in the way of thy judgments, O Lord, have we waited for thee; the desire of our soul is to thy name, and to the remembrance of thee. With my soul have I desired thee in the night; yea, with my spirit within me will I seek thee early: for when thy judgments are in the earth, the inhabitants of the world will learn righteousness. Let favour be shewed to the wicked, yet will he not learn righteousness; in the land of uprightness will he deal unjustly, and will not behold the majesty of the Lord. Lord, when thy hand is lifted up, they will not see: but they shall see, and be ashamed for their envy at the people; yea, the fire of thine enemies shall devour them.

Lord, thou wilt ordain peace for us: for thou also hast wrought all our works in us. . . .

Come, my people, enter thou into thy chambers, and shut thy doors about thee: hide thyself as it were for a little moment, until the indignation be overpast. For, behold, the Lord cometh out of his place to punish the inhabitants of the earth for their iniquity: the earth also shall disclose her blood, and shall no more cover her slain.

— Isaiah 26:3-12, 20, 21

The prophet seemed to delight in ringing the changes on "Salvation" and "Peace." His constant use of these terms has earned him the title of "The Evangelical Prophet." Without a definite experience of God's saving grace and power there can never be true peace within (Ephesians 2:14-17). Peace and joy can only come through believing (Romans 15:13). In his prayer Isaiah reminds us that God's peace is "perfect" and "ordained" (26:5, 12). Too often the chasten-

ing of the Lord closes our lips. It was the reverse with those described
by the prophet. Can we not see in the call to hide in the chambers,
a type of what will happen to the true Church ere the Great Tribulation overtakes a guilty earth (26:20, 21)? At Christ's return all who
died in Him are to arise (26:19; I Corinthians 15:1; I Thessalonians
4:16).

It is no vain or empty thing to wait upon the Lord. Note the
double waiting (30:18). Martin Luther once said, "If I should
neglect prayer but a single day, I should lose a great deal of the fire
of faith." How wonderful it is to have the Divine Arm to lean our
weight upon as we face the daily journey (33:2; see 40:29-31). For
God's response to Hezekiah's willingness to wait upon the Lord
(37:14-20) see II Kings 20. Compare Isaiah 38 with II Kings 20:1-11.

Prayer and Confidence

(Isaiah 41)

Fear thou not; for I am with thee: be not dismayed; for I am thy
God: I will strengthen thee; yea, I will help thee; yea, I will uphold
thee with the right hand of my righteousness. . . .
For I the Lord thy God will hold thy right hand, saying unto thee,
Fear not; I will help thee. Fear not, thou worm Jacob, and ye men of
Israel; I will help thee, saith the Lord, and thy redeemer, the Holy
One of Israel.   — Isaiah 41:10, 13, 14

It is both interesting and profitable to note the number and variety
of occasions when men heard the Divine Voice saying "Fear Not"
(41:10, 13, 14; 44:2, 8). What a mighty God this remarkable chapter
presents! To Isaiah He was no "middling God," as George Macdonald
put it. God is greater than all our needs and fears. When we produce
our cause (41:21) may grace be ours to trust Him to undertake for
us, no matter how pressing the load.

Prayer and Practice

(Isaiah 55)

Seek ye the Lord while he may be found, call ye upon him while he
is near: Let the wicked forsake his way, and the unrighteous man
his thoughts: and let him return unto the Lord, and he will have
mercy upon him; and to our God, for he will abundantly pardon.
                                                — Isaiah 55:6, 7

In the majority of previous chapters we have the Lord speaking
loudly and lovingly to me. What pathos and passion characterizes
many of His utterances! Of the prophecy that Jesus was to intercede
for His enemies (53:12), we shall have more to say when we come
to the Gospels.

While many of the Bible prayers are clear and direct, others are
there by implication. We read the prayers between the lines as here,
for example, when Isaiah calls upon the people to "seek the Lord"

(55:6). What is prayer? Is it not seeking God and calling upon Him? Prayer, however, must always be accompanied by practice. Wickedness must be forsaken (55:7). God's abundant pardon cannot be experienced unless all that has estranged the soul from Him is willingly yielded (58:4).

How blessed is any church when it is in reality "an house of prayer for all people" (56:7), where God is approached as the thrice Holy One (57:15)! Then all who are friends of God must be the friends of the poor and needy (58:9).

Prayer Unpopular to Many
(Isaiah 59)

Behold, the Lord's hand is not shortened, that it cannot save; neither his ear heavy, that it cannot hear: But your iniquities have separated between you and your God, and your sins have hid his face from you, that he will not hear. . . .
For our transgressions are multiplied before thee, and our sins testify against us: for our transgressions are with us; and as for our iniquities, we know them: In transgressing and lying against the Lord, and departing away from our God, speaking oppression and revolt, conceiving and uttering from the heart words of falsehood. And judgment is turned away backward, and justice standeth afar off: for truth is fallen in the street, and equity cannot enter. Yea, truth faileth: and he that departeth from evil maketh himself a prey: and the Lord saw it, and it displeased him that there was no judgment.
— Isaiah 59:1, 2, 12-15

Many thoughts about prayer are imbedded in this chapter. First of all, social injustice and iniquities separate people from God, causing Him to turn a deaf ear to their prayers (59:1, 2, 12-15; Psalm 66:18; Proverbs 15:29). Other causes of unanswered prayer are crossing the divine will (I John 3:21), entertainment of heart idols (Ezekiel 14:3), lack of gratitude (Philippians 4:6, 7), selfishness of spirit (Proverbs 21:13), unforgiving spirit (Mark 11:25), wrong motives in requests (James 4:3).

Can we not hear the sob in God's voice as He expresses His wonder over the lack of intercessors (59:16; 63:5)? Satan strives in every possible way to make such a necessary and powerful ministry unpopular or unessential. May we be among the Spirit-anointed ones who, with God's words in our mouth, cry unto Him day and night (59:19, 21)!

Prayer-Watcher
(Isaiah 62)

I have set watchmen upon thy walls, O Jerusalem, which shall never hold their peace day nor night: ye that make mention of the Lord, keep not silence, and give him no rest, till he establish, and till he make Jerusalem a praise in the earth.   — Isaiah 62: 6, 7

Watch-men in the East were alert as they went their rounds. Alarms were given with a loud cry. Isaiah uses the illustration of the watch-men in respect to prayer (62:6, 7). All who believe in instructing and warning people should recognize the importance of prayer — ardent, humble, holy prayer! Watching upon the high tower is a sacrificial task, but "praying-breath" is never in vain. Can we say that we are among the prayer-watchers who keep not silence (62:6)?

Prayer for Display of Divine Power

(Isaiah 63, 64)

For the day of vengeance is in mine heart, and the year of my redeemed is come. And I looked, and there was none to help; and I wondered that there was none to uphold: therefore mine own arm brought salvation unto me; and my fury, it upheld me. . . .

As a beast goeth down into the valley, the Spirit of the Lord caused him to rest: so didst thou lead thy people, to make thyself a glorious name.

Look down from heaven, and behold from the habitation of thy holiness and of thy glory: where is thy zeal and thy strength, the sounding of thy bowels and of thy mercies toward me? are they restrained? Doubtless thou art our father, though Abraham be ignorant of us, and Israel acknowledge us not: thou, O Lord, art our father, our redeemer; thy name is from everlasting. . . .

Oh that thou wouldest rend the heavens, that thou wouldest come down, that the mountains might flow down at thy presence. As when the melting fire burneth, the fire causeth the waters to boil, to make thy name known to thine adversaries, that the nations may tremble at thy presence! When thou didst terrible things which we looked not for, thou camest down, the mountains flowed down at thy presence. For since the beginning of the world men have not heard, nor perceived by the ear, neither hath the eye seen, O God, beside thee, what he hath prepared for him that waiteth for him. Thou meetest him that rejoiceth and worketh righteousness, those that remember thee in thy ways: behold, thou art wroth; for we have sinned: in those is continuance, and we shall be saved. But we are all as an unclean thing, and all our righteousnesses are as filthy rags; and we all do fade as a leaf; and our iniquities, like the wind, have taken us away. And there is none that calleth upon thy name, that stirreth up himself to take hold of thee: for thou hast hid thy face from us, and hast consumed us, because of our iniquities. But now, O Lord, thou art our father; we are the clay, and thou our potter; and we all are the work of thy hand.

Be not wroth very sore, O Lord, neither remember iniquity for ever: behold, see, we beseech thee, we are all thy people. Thy holy cities are a wilderness, Zion is a wilderness, Jerusalem a desolation. Our holy and our beautiful house, where our fathers praised thee, is burned up with fire: and all our pleasant things are laid waste. Wilt thou refrain thyself for these things, O Lord? wilt thou hold thy peace, and afflict us very sore?   — Isaiah 63:4, 5, 14-16; 64

These two chapters have one continuing thought, namely, vengeance upon the foes of God and His people (63:4). The prayer gives us a glimpse of the Temple trodden under an adversary's foot and burned with fire. Thus the people poured out their hearts for judgment (64:10-12). It was natural for them to address God as their Father (63:16; 64:8). In the cry of Israel for the punishment of her enemies there was the confession of their own sin (65:1-16). "As the grace of God was most typically manifested in the deliverance of Israel from Egypt, so the sins of that early period are typical of the sins of Israel's subsequent career: obstinacy, disobedience, rebellion, ingratitude, incredulity, forgetfulness, indifference, idolatry."

As we take leave of Isaiah, the praying-prophet, there are a few prayer-gems we can gather together. We are given an illustration of the poetical outpouring of the heart to God (63:14; 64:1-3). Passionate prayers blossom into arrestive figurative language. Scripture is extensively quoted in some prayers (63:14; 64:8). The mightiest prayers are often those drenched with the Word of God. The name of Jehovah is the ground of powerful appeal (64:12; 43:7). Some prayers are answered before they are offered (65:24). By way of contrast look at 66:4.

Jeremiah

Here is a prophet conspicuous for his sobs and supplications, for Jeremiah knew how to pray as well as weep. As with the Lord, whom the prophet pre-figures, his prayers were often saturated with tears (Hebrews 5:7). Jeremiah and Jesus are alike in many particulars. "No Old Testament figure is so prophetic of Jesus as Jeremiah." Both suffered rejection by their own (11:21; Mark 6:1-3). Both were threatened with death by the priests of Jerusalem (26:8). Both were led as lambs to slaughter (11:9; Isaiah 53:7). Both were men of sorrow and acquainted with grief, yet found consolation in prayer. Both were mystified over the ways of God (12:1; 15:18; Matthew 27:46). Jesus, however, experienced an agony incomparably deeper than Jeremiah's.

Prayer As Confession of Inability
(Jeremiah 1)
Then said I, Ah, Lord God! behold, I cannot speak: for I am a child.
— Jeremiah 1:6

The recorded prayers of the most human intercessor among the prophets deserve a fuller exposition than our space allows. Divinely called and impelled to undertake a mission of great import, youth and inexperience tempted him to recoil from such a God-given task. Yet the One calling him was at hand to empower. "Be not afraid, for I am with thee" (1:8). Resting in the Lord, Jeremiah went out to challenge a sinful nation, fanatical priests, and prophets who thirsted for his blood (26:15). The wonderful dialogue between God and the prophet is most precious. Jeremiah's ear was sensitive to the Divine Voice. Both God and Jeremiah knew how to listen as well as speak.

Prayer As Mourning for Backsliding
(Jeremiah 2, 3)

The priests said not, Where is the Lord? and they that handle the law knew me not: the pastors also transgressed against me, and the prophets prophesied by Baal, and walked after things that do not profit. . . .

For though thou wash thee with nitre, and take thee much soap, yet thine iniquity is marked before me, saith the Lord God. How canst thou say, I am not polluted, I have not gone after Baalim? see thy way in the valley, know what thou hast done: thou art a swift dromedary traversing her ways; A wild ass used to the wilderness, that snuffeth up the wind at her pleasure; in her occasion who can turn her away? all they that seek her will not weary themselves; in her month they shall find her. Withhold thy foot from being unshod, and thy throat from thirst: but thou saidst, There is no hope: no; for I have loved strangers, and after them will I go. As the thief is ashamed when he is found, so is the house of Israel ashamed; they, their kings, their princes, and their priests, and their prophets. Saying to a stock, Thou art my father; and to a stone, Thou hast brought me forth: for they have turned their back unto me, and not their face: but in the time of their trouble they will say, Arise, and save us. But where are thy gods that thou hast made thee? let them arise, if they can save thee in the time of thy trouble: for according to the number of thy cities are thy gods, O Judah. Wherefore will ye plead with me? ye all have transgressed against me, saith the Lord. In vain have I smitten your children; they received no correction: your own sword hath devoured your prophets, like a destroying lion. O generation, see ye the word of the Lord. Have I been a wilderness unto Israel? a land of darkness? wherefore say my people, We are lords; we will come no more unto thee? . . .

Lift up thine eyes unto the high places, and see where thou hast not been lien with. In the ways hast thou sat for them, as the Arabian in the wilderness; and thou hast polluted the land with thy whoredoms and with thy wickedness. Therefore the showers have been withholden, and there hath been no latter rain; and thou hadst a whore's forehead, thou refusedst to be ashamed. Wilt thou not from this time cry unto me, My father, thou art the guide of my youth? Will he reserve his anger for ever? will he keep it to the end? Behold, thou hast spoken and done evil things as thou couldest. . . .

Surely as a wife treacherously departeth from her husband, so have ye dealt treacherously with me, O house of Israel, saith the Lord. A voice was heard upon the high places, weeping and supplications of the children of Israel: for they have perverted their way, and they have forgotten the Lord their God. Return, ye backsliding children, and I will heal your backslidings. Behold, we come unto thee; for thou art the Lord our God. Truly in vain is salvation hoped for from the hills, and from the multitude of mountains: truly in the Lord our God is the salvation of Israel. — Jeremiah 2:8, 22-31; 3:2-5, 20-23

Many of Jeremiah's prayers were wrung from him by the treachery and heartlessness of his own people. In many ways he stands out as the most religious spirit in the Old Testament, and consequently understood the enormity of sin as few could. Coming before God on behalf of others, the prophet manifested the passion and fearlessness of a man speaking to his friend.

Professor MacFadyen remarks that Jeremiah's "temperament, his tragic experience, his sensitive religious nature, all combining to inspire his prayers with a passion and familiarity which have no parallel anywhere." This was why he could reproach his countrymen for their blatant idolatry and rejection of God (2:27). The sinning people were still God's children and Divine Fatherhood was the basis of appeal (3:4).

There are far too many in our day who handle the truth yet know not the Lord (2:8). The redeeming blood can alone cleanse from sin (2:22). How gracious God is in the restoration of the backslider (3:22, 23)!

Prayer As Complaint

(Jeremiah 4:10-31)

Then said I, Ah, Lord God! surely thou hast greatly deceived this people and Jerusalem, saying, Ye shall have peace; whereas the sword reacheth unto the soul. . . .
For I have heard a voice as of a woman in travail, and the anguish as of her that bringeth forth her first child, the voice of the daughter of Zion, that bewaileth herself, that spreadeth her hands, saying, Woe is me now! for my soul is wearied because of murderers.

— Jeremiah 4:10, 31

The prophet breaks in upon his solemn call to the people to return to God, to plead with God to declare His purpose. Jeremiah wants to know whether God is to send peace or a sword (4:10; Matthew 10:34). What a Calvary heart he had (4:19)! Such language is common to the heart-cries of Paul for those for whose sanctification he yearned (Philippians 1:8; 2:1; Colossians 3:12). God is never guilty of deception and cannot be deceived (4:10; Galatians 6:3).

Prayer of Lament over Rebellion

(Jeremiah 5)

How shall I pardon thee for this? thy children have forsaken me, and sworn by them that are no gods: when I had fed them to the full, they then committed adultery, and assembled themselves by troops in the harlots' houses. They were as fed horses in the morning: every one neighed after his neighbour's wife. Shall I not visit for

these things? saith the Lord: and shall not my soul be avenged on
such a nation as this?
Go ye up upon her walls, and destroy; but make not a full end:
take away her battlements; for they are not the Lord's. . . .
A wonderful and horrible thing is committed in the land; The
prophets prophesy falsely, and the priests bear rule by their means;
and my people love to have it so: and what will ye do in the end
thereof?   — Jeremiah 5:7-10, 30, 31

One cannot read this heart-sob without recalling our Lord's lament
over Jerusalem (Matthew 23:37, 38). Both Jeremiah and Jesus wept
and prayed over the so-called Holy City. The Church has built
battlements which are not of the Lord (5:10). How applicable is the
"horrible thing" Jeremiah speaks of (5:31), to a present day priest-
ridden and modernistic church!

Prayer from a Prison

(Jeremiah 6)

Prepare ye war against her; arise, and let us go up at noon. Woe unto
us! for the day goeth away, for the shadows of the evening are
stretched out. Arise, and let us go by night, and let us destroy her
palaces.
For thus hath the Lord of hosts said, Hew ye down trees, and cast a
mount against Jerusalem: this is the city to be visited; she is wholly
oppression in the midst of her. As a fountain casteth out her waters,
so she casteth out her wickedness: violence and spoil is heard in her;
before me continually is grief and wounds. Be thou instructed, O
Jerusalem, lest my soul depart from thee; lest I make thee desolate,
a land not inhabited.
Thus saith the Lord of hosts, They shall thoroughly glean the remnant of Israel as a vine: turn back thine hand as a grapegatherer
into the baskets. To whom shall I speak, and give warning, that they
may hear? behold, their ear is uncircumcised, and they cannot
hearken: behold, the word of the Lord is unto them a reproach;
they have no delight in it. Therefore I am full of the fury of the
Lord; I am weary with holding in: I will pour it out upon the
children abroad, and upon the assembly of young men together: for
even the husband with the wife shall be taken, the aged with him
that is full of days.   — Jeremiah 6:4-11

The full story of Jeremiah's imprisonment in Jerusalem is told in
a later chapter (37). Arrested for spreading "alarms and despond-
ency," Jeremiah was far from being an alarmist. He simply declared
that the city was doomed to destruction and that the people would
suffer captivity (6:11). But God would not utterly desert His people.

A great prayer like this reveals Jeremiah to be an anxious man
who cannot see clearly, but at the same time a believing man who is
ready to act on faith (6:4, 5). He is convinced about what is ultimately right and also that with God all things are possible.

Prayer Forbidden

(Jeremiah 7:16)

Therefore pray not thou for this people, neither lift up cry nor prayer for them, neither make intercession to me: for I will not hear thee.   — Jeremiah 7:16

There are times when even good men are forbidden to pray. Jeremiah habitually prayed for his own people (11:14; 14:11), and would have deemed it a sin not to intercede on their behalf. But here is an express command from God that Jeremiah is not to pray for the people. If the prophet persisted in prayer, God said that He would not listen. How doomed is any nation when God has to say to those who have its spiritual welfare at heart, "Pray not for it, for I will not hear you!" When all that alienates nations or individuals from God is abandoned, then He delights to hear and answer prayer (29:12-14).

Prayer for Justice

(Jeremiah 10:23-25)

O Lord, I know that the way of man is not in himself: it is not in man that walketh to direct his steps. O Lord, correct me, but with judgment; not in thine anger, lest thou bring me to nothing. Pour out thy fury upon the heathen that know thee not, and upon the families that call not on thy name: for they have eaten up Jacob, and devoured him, and consumed him, and have made his habitation desolate.   — Jeremiah 10:23-25

Again and again, the torn heart of Jeremiah utters itself in passionate appeals to God to destroy the enemies of truth and righteousness (11:20; 15:15; 17:18). Such prayers are an echo of many of the Imprecatory Psalms (Psalm 77:5-7). Some of the most appalling prayers in the Bible were those offered by Jeremiah that righteous judgment would overtake base and treacherous men (12:3; 17:18; 18:21; 20:12). The temper of such prayers suggests that if the foes of goodness succeeded then the character of God and His government of the world would be discredited. Because "His name is great in might" (10:6), God must arise and defend the right.

Prayer of Perplexity

(Jeremiah 12:1-4)

Righteous art thou, O Lord, when I plead with thee: yet let me talk with thee of thy judgments: Wherefore doth the way of the wicked prosper? wherefore are all they happy that deal very treacherously? Thou hast planted them, yea, they have taken root: they grow, yea, they bring forth fruit: thou art near in their mouth, and far from their reins. But thou, O Lord, knowest me: thou hast seen me, and tried mine heart toward thee: pull them out like sheep from the slaughter, and prepare them for the day of slaughter. How long shall the land mourn, and the herbs of every field wither, for the wickedness of them that dwell therein? the beasts are consumed, and the birds; because they said, He shall not see our last end.

— Jeremiah 12:1-4

Amid the din and confusion of battle Jeremiah listens for an answer to the age-long question, "Why do the wicked prosper?" (Psalm 37:1) The prophet does not doubt the justice of God, but he wants to know what principles govern the world. Perplexed and confounded by what he sees as a God-searched man (11:20; 12:3), Jeremiah pleads for a manifestation of divine wrath upon the wicked. It will be noted that although he prays with all the energy of perplexity and disappointment, the prophet only twice uses the term "O Jehovah."

Sometimes answers to prayers come in a form very different from those entreated by those who pray. Jeremiah prayed for deliverance from one distress, and for the answer learned that he had to face another. Wearied with footmen, he had to contend with horses (12:5).

Prayer for Relief from Sin and Drought

(Jeremiah 14:7-22)

O Lord, though our iniquities testify against us, do thou it for thy name's sake: for our backslidings are many; we have sinned against thee. O the hope of Israel, the saviour thereof in time of trouble, why shouldest thou be as a stranger in the land, and as a wayfaring man that turneth aside to tarry for a night? Why shouldest thou be as a man astonied, as a mighty man that cannot save? yet thou, O Lord, art in the midst of us, and we are called by thy name; leave us not. . . .

We acknowledge, O Lord, our wickedness, and the iniquity of our fathers: for we have sinned against thee. Do not abhor us, for thy name's sake, do not disgrace the throne of thy glory: remember, break not thy covenant with us. Are there any among the vanities of the Gentiles that can cause rain? or can the heavens give showers? art not thou he, O Lord our God? therefore we will wait upon thee: for thou hast made all these things.   — Jeremiah 14:7-9, 20-22

The prophet identified himself with the sins of the nation of which he formed part (14:7, 9). The ages are linked to each other by a chain of sin, "Our wickedness . . . our fathers" (14:20). How bold was Jeremiah, addressing God as one, behaving like a man who had lost his head and was powerless to save (14:9). Later on, he dared to compare God in his prayer to a deceitful brook and to failing waters (15:18).

Prayer for Divine Vengeance

(Jeremiah 15:15-21)

O Lord, thou knowest: remember me, and visit me, and revenge me of my persecutors; take me not away in thy longsuffering: know that for thy sake I have suffered rebuke. Thy words were found, and I did eat them; and thy word was unto me the joy and rejoicing of mine heart: for I am called by thy name, O Lord God of hosts. I sat not in the assembly of the mockers, nor rejoiced; I sat alone because of thy hand: for thou hast filled me with indignation. Why is my pain perpetual, and my wound incurable, which refuseth to be healed? wilt thou be altogether unto me as a liar and as waters that fail?

Therefore thus saith the Lord, If thou return, then will I bring thee again, and thou shalt stand before me: and if thou take forth the precious from the vile, thou shalt be as my mouth: let them return unto thee; but return not thou unto them. And I will make thee unto this people a fenced brasen wall: and they shall fight against thee, but they shall not prevail against thee: for I am with thee to save thee and to deliver thee, saith the Lord. And I will deliver thee out of the hand of the wicked, and I will redeem thee out of the hand of the terrible.   — Jeremiah 15:15-21

Here we have another of those dialogues between God and His servant, so common to the Old Testament. Jeremiah desired his intercession to be as efficacious as former prophets (15:1). The frequent and terrible prayers for vengeance (17:18; 18:21, 23) seem contrary to the Master's teaching about loving our enemies. Jeremiah, however, deals more upon the justice of God than upon His love. He himself had no fellowship with mockers who made merry and rejoiced. God was real to his heart, and His words were the rejoicing of his heart (15:16, 17).

Prayer for Confusion of Enemies

(Jeremiah 16:19-21; 17:13-18)

O Lord, my strength, and my fortress, and my refuge in the day of affliction, the Gentiles shall come unto thee from the ends of the earth, and shall say, Surely our fathers have inherited lies, vanity, and things wherein there is no profit. Shall a man make gods unto himself, and they are no gods? Therefore, behold, I will this once cause them to know, I will cause them to know mine hand and my might; and they shall know that my name is The Lord. . . .

O Lord, the hope of Israel, all that forsake thee shall be ashamed, and they that depart from me shall be written in the earth, because they have forsaken the Lord, the fountain of living waters. Heal me, O Lord, and I shall be healed; save me, and I shall be saved: for thou art my praise.

Behold, they say unto me, Where is the word of the Lord? let it come now. As for me, I have not hastened from being a pastor to follow thee· neither have I desired the woeful day; thou knowest: that which came out of my lips was right before thee. Be not a terror unto me: thou art my hope in the day of evil. Let them be confounded that persecute me, but let not me be confounded: let them be dismayed, but let not me be dismayed: bring upon them the day of evil, and destroy them with double destruction.

                                    — Jeremiah 16:19-21; 17:13-18

Taunted with the challenge, "Where is the Word of the Lord? let it come now (17:15), Jeremiah had no recourse but prayer. And how passionately he prayed for God to vindicate Himself. Such a challenge drove him to his knees. On the whole, Biblical praying is simple, and Jeremiah's prayers are unsurpassed for their simplicity (17:14). God was real to the prophet. If it be true that "religious individualism" was born with Jeremiah, then we can appreciate his conception of God as his refuge (16:19). Often in the course of his checkered and heart-breaking career, Jeremiah had to turn to God as his "rock in a weary land" (17:7). Alone, without any of the human joys consoling a man (16:2), the prophet knew what it was to be lost in God (16:21) .

Prayer for Overthrow of Evil Counsel
(Jeremiah 18:18-23)

Then said they, Come, and let us devise devices against Jeremiah; for the law shall not perish from the priest, nor counsel from the wise, nor the word from the prophet. Come, and let us smite him with the tongue, and let us not give heed to any of his words. Give heed to me, O Lord, and hearken to the voice of them that contend with me. Shall evil be recompensed for good? for they have digged a pit for my soul. Remember that I stood before thee to speak good for them, and to turn away thy wrath from them. Therefore deliver up their children to the famine and pour out their blood by the force of the sword; and let their wives be bereaved of their children, and be widows; and let their men be put to death; let their young men be slain by the sword in battle. Let a cry be heard from their houses, when thou shalt bring a troop suddenly upon them: for they have digged a pit to take me, and hid snares for my feet. Yet, Lord, thou knowest all their counsel against me to slay me: forgive not their iniquity, neither blot out their sin from thy sight, but let them be overthrown before thee; deal thus with them in the time of thine anger.   — Jeremiah 18:18-23

Jeremiah *stood* as he prayed for the defeat of treacherous devices conceived for the end of his mission (18:18, 20). To pray as the weeping prophet could pray, there had to be the foundation of integrity of life. It is, therefore, as one wholly separated unto the Lord that he now pleads for preservation against the murderous intentions of his foes. He wanted no weapon formed against him to prosper. How able the Lord is to defend His own against the evil machinations of Satan and men (Psalm 16:1) !

Prayer of a Despairing Heart
(Jeremiah 20:7-13)

O Lord, thou hast deceived me, and I was deceived: thou art stronger than I, and hast prevailed: I am in derision daily, every one mocketh me. For since I spake, I cried out, I cried violence and spoil; because the word of the Lord was made a reproach unto me, and a derision, daily. Then I said, I will not make mention of him, nor speak any more in his name. But his word was in mine heart as a burning fire shut up in my bones, and I was weary with forbearing, and I could not stay.

For I heard the defaming of many, fear on every side. Report, say they, and we will report it. All my familiars watched for my halting, saying, Peradventure he will be enticed, and we shall prevail against him, and we shall take our revenge on him. But the Lord is with me as a mighty terrible one: therefore my persecutors shall stumble, and they shall not prevail: they shall be greatly ashamed; for they shall not prosper: their everlasting confusion shall never be forgotten. But, O Lord of hosts, that triest the righteous, and seest the reins and the heart, let me see thy vengeance on them: for unto thee have I opened my cause. Sing unto the Lord, praise ye the Lord: for he hath delivered the soul of the poor from the hand of evildoers.

— Jeremiah 20:7-13

This prayer seems to carry a contradictory note. Jeremiah blames the Lord (20:7) yet praises Him (20:13). He appeals to God's knowledge of his heart (20:12; 12:3). What he cannot understand is why God had thrust upon him a mission in which he had become a laughing stock (20:7). Yet even though his message was rejected, Jeremiah's habitual and earnest intercessions left a tremendous impression upon the people (18:20; 21:1; 28:6; 37:3; 42:2). What a God-consumed man the prophet was (20:9)! Can we say that His word is as a burning fire in our bones, and that without fear or favor we must declare it? It is not enough to honor God with our lips, our hearts must cry unto Him (29:13; Hosea 7:14; Matthew 15:8). May the good Lord deliver us from becoming mere professionals or time-servers (23:9; I Kings 22:6). The fear of God drives out all fear of man (1:7; 30:10). Hunt up the variety of "Fear nots" in the Bible.

Prayer of Gratitude for Divine Goodness
(Jeremiah 32:16-25)

Now when I had delivered the evidence of the purchase unto Baruch the son of Neriah, I prayed unto the Lord, saying, Ah Lord God! behold thou hast made the heaven and the earth by thy great power and stretched out arm, and there is nothing too hard for thee: Thou shewest lovingkindness unto thousands, and recompensest the iniquity of the fathers into the bosom of their children after them: the Great, the Mighty God, the Lord of hosts, is his name, Great in counsel, and mighty in work: for thine eyes are open upon all the ways of the sons of men: to give every one according to his ways, and according to the fruit of his doings: Which hast set signs and wonders in the land of Egypt, even unto this day, and in Israel, and among other men; and hast made thee a name, as at this day: And hast brought forth thy people Israel out of the land of Egypt with signs, and with wonders, and with a strong hand, and with a stretched out arm, and with great terror; And hast given them this land, which thou didst swear to their fathers to give them, a land flowing with milk and honey; And they came in, and possessed it; but they obeyed not thy voice, neither walked in thy law; they have done nothing of all that thou commandest them to do: therefore thou hast caused all this evil to come upon them: Behold the mounts, they are come unto the city to take it; and the city is given into the hand of the Chaldeans, that fight against it, because of the sword, and of the famine, and of the pestilence: and what thou hast spoken is come to pass; and, behold, thou seest it. And thou hast said unto me, O Lord God, Buy thee the field for money, and take witnesses; for the city is given into the hand of the Chaldeans.

— Jeremiah 32:16-25

In this further dialogue it is interesting to observe God's answer to Jeremiah's declaration, "Nothing is too hard for thee" (32:17) — "Is there anything too hard for Me?" (32:27). Although he was in prison, nothing and no one could bind the spirit of Jeremiah. With a burning desire to see people turn to God, Jeremiah had to possess his soul in patience. We are so impatient. We do not know how to watch and wait (32:6-8). The prophet prayed on although imprisoned in the court of the guard (32:1; 33:3).

What a glorious description of God's transcendent attributes Jeremiah gives us (32:18, 19)! How disappointed God must be over the lack of appreciation on our part for all His grace and goodness (32:22, 23)! How grieved He must be when those blessed of Him turn the back and not the face to Him (32:33; 37:3).

If we would discover the secret of true revival we must lay hold of the promise God gave to Jeremiah (33:3) and make it our very own. Mighty spiritual upheavals always have their rise in prayer.

Prayer for a Believing Remnant

(Jeremiah 42)

And said unto Jeremiah the prophet, Let, we beseech thee, our supplication be accepted before thee, and pray for us unto the Lord thy God, even for all this remnant; (for we are left but a few of many, as thine eyes do behold us:) That the Lord thy God may shew us the way wherein we may walk, and the thing that we may do. Then Jeremiah the prophet said unto them, I have heard you; behold, I will pray unto the Lord your God according to your words; and it shall come to pass, that whatsoever thing the Lord shall answer you, I will declare it unto you; I will keep nothing back from you.   — Jeremiah 42:2-4

Jeremiah sought in prayer the guarantee of the hope of Israel's ultimate restoration (32:16; 50:5). Overwhelmed by a sense of their own unworthiness, men felt they needed a prophet to intercede for them. Because of their sin, they deemed themselves unworthy to approach God. If they came directly their prayer would be unavailing. Thus Jeremiah's prayers were sought, an acknowledgment surely of their peculiar efficacy (42:2, 3).

Lack of sincerity weakens the effect of prayer. The people promised

Jeremiah that they would obey the will of God as soon as he made it clear unto them (42:3). Their promise, however, was easier to make than to keep (42:20, 21).

God's will and purpose are ultimately accomplished. His mills may seem to grind slowly, but they grind exceeding sure (Habakkuk 2:3). His way becomes fully known (42:3). As we leave Jeremiah, the intercessor with a bleeding heart, how important it is to heed his warning — "Seekest thou great things for thyself? seek them not" (42:5). The greatest gifts come when we seek first the kingdom and glory of God (Matthew 6:33).

Lamentations

This dirge of desolation can be treated as a *postscript* to the Book of Jeremiah. The five Lamentations forming the book are actually five heart-cries, or, seeing that in their original form there were no chapter and verse divisions, one long prayer of pathos. Dr. C. I. Scofield says of Lamentations, "The touching significance of this book lies in the fact that it is the disclosure of the love and sorrow of Jehovah for the very people whom He is chastening — a sorrow wrought by the Spirit in the heart of Jeremiah (Jeremiah 13:17; Matthew 23:36, 38; Romans 9:1-5)."

Dr. Alexander Whyte had a profound admiration for the book. "There is nothing like the Lamentations of Jeremiah in the whole world. There has been plenty of sorrow in every age, and in every land, but such another preacher and author, with such a heart for sorrow has never again been born. Dante comes next to Jeremiah and we know that Jeremiah was that great exile's favorite prophet."

Attention must be drawn to the unique construction of this book filled with tears, the key verses of which (1:8, 10) remind us of Christ's heart-anguish over Jerusalem (Matthew 23:36; Isaiah 63:9). The literary form of the original presents an acrostic dirge. Each chapter is an elegy constructed as an acrostic in the order of the Hebrew alphabet. The lines were arranged in couplets or triplets, each of which began with a letter of the alphabet. The Third Lamentation is made up of sixty-six verses, and these are divided into groups each with three verses, with each group beginning with one of the twenty-two letters of the Hebrew alphabet. Thus verses 1-3 of our version form but three lines of the original, each line beginning with A, etc. The last chapter is not arranged acrostically.

Prayer of Pain
(Lamentations 1:20-22)

Behold, O Lord; for I am in distress: my bowels are troubled; mine heart is turned within me; for I have grievously rebelled: abroad the sword bereaveth, at home there is as death. They have heard that I sigh: there is none to comfort me: all mine enemies have heard of my trouble; they are glad that thou hast done it: thou wilt bring the day that thou hast called, and they shall be like unto me. Let all their wickedness come before thee; and do unto them, as thou hast done unto me for all my transgressions: for my sighs are many, and my heart is faint.   — Lamentations 1:20-22

The book as a whole can be looked upon as "the wailing wall of the Bible." Here we have a paean or prayer of pain. As Jeremiah thought of the sins of his people and of the just judgment they deserved, his sighs were many and his heart was faint (1:22). Separate as he was, from the sins he mourned, he yet classes himself among the offenders. What do we know about the distress of soul Jeremiah reveals in this prayer? Do the sins of those around us move our hearts to tears? The prophet knew a great deal about the tragedy of travail. Do we (Galatians 4:17)?

Prayer for Pity

(Lamentations 2:19-22)

Behold, O Lord, and consider to whom thou hast done this. Shall the women eat their fruit, and children of a span long? shall the priest and the prophet be slain in the sanctuary of the Lord? The young and the old lie on the ground in the streets: my virgins and my young men are fallen by the sword; thou hast slain them in the day of thine anger; thou hast killed, and not pitied. Thou hast called as in a solemn day my terrors round about, so that in the day of the Lord's anger none escaped nor remained: those that I have swaddled and brought up hath mine enemy consumed. — Lamentations 2:19-22

This symphony of sorrow commences in the same way as the previous one — "Behold, O Lord" (1:20). What a fearful prayer this is! It contains a vivid catalogue of the horrors of the Jerusalem siege and of the prophet's appeal for pity. Distress drives men to God. Grievously afflicted, they are constrained to pour out their heart before Him. Earnest, private prayer is naturally enough often associated with the night (2:19; Psalm 119:62).

Prayer As Complaint

(Lamentations 3)

Also when I cry and shout, he shutteth out my prayer. . . .
Who is he that saith, and it cometh to pass, when the Lord commandeth it not? Out of the mouth of the most High proceedeth not evil and good? Wherefore doth a living man complain, a man for the punishment of his sins? Let us search and try our ways, and turn again to the Lord. Let us lift up our heart with our hands unto God in the heavens. We have transgressed and have rebelled: thou hast not pardoned. Thou hast covered with anger, and persecuted us: thou hast slain, thou hast not pitied. Thou hast covered thyself with a cloud, that our prayer should not pass through. Thou hast made us

as the offscouring and refuse in the midst of the people. All our enemies have opened their mouths against us. Fear and a snare is come upon us, desolation and destruction. Mine eye runneth down with rivers of water for the destruction of the daughter of my people. Mine eye trickleth down, and ceaseth not, without any intermission, Till the Lord look down, and behold from heaven. Mine eye affecteth mine heart because of all the daughters of my city. Mine enemies chased me sore, like a bird, without cause. They have cut off my life in the dungeon, and cast a stone upon me. Waters flowed over mine head; then I said, I am cut off.

I called upon thy name, O Lord, out of the low dungeon. Thou hast heard my voice: hide not thine ear at my breathing, at my cry. Thou drewest near in the day that I called upon thee: thou saidst, Fear not. O Lord, thou hast pleaded the causes of my soul; thou hast redeemed my life. O Lord, thou hast seen my wrong: judge thou my cause. Thou hast seen all their vengeance and all their imaginations against me. Thou hast heard their reproach, O Lord, and all their imaginations against me; The lips of those that rose up against me, and their device against me all the day. Behold their sitting down, and their rising up; I am their musick.

Render unto them a recompence, O Lord, according to the work of their hands. Give them sorrow of heart, thy curse unto them. Persecute and destroy them in anger from under the heavens of the Lord.   — Lamentations 3:8, 37-66

In this Third Lamentation we have two or three impressive aspects of prayer. First of all, there are some prayers that never reach the ear of God. "He shutteth out my prayer . . . Prayer should not pass through" (3:8, 44). Satan endeavors to create a barricade between ourselves and God so that our prayers cannot get through to Him (Daniel 10:11-13).

Hearts as well as hands must be lifted up toward heaven (3:41). Then Jeremiah gives us another "Fear not" of prayer (3:57). The prayer for judgment upon wrongdoers is most expressive (3:58-66). Jeremiah wants them smitten with "sorrow of heart" such as they had caused him (3:65 with 2:11).

Prayer for the Oppressed

(Lamentations 5)

Remember, O Lord, what is come upon us: consider, and behold our reproach. Our inheritance is turned to strangers, our houses to aliens. We are orphans and fatherless, our mothers are as widows. . . . They took the young men to grind, and the children fell under the wood. The elders have ceased from the gate, the young men from their musick. The joy of our heart is ceased; our dance is turned into mourning. The crown is fallen from our head: woe unto us, that we have sinned! For this our heart is faint; for these things our eyes are dim. Because of the mountain of Zion, which is desolate, the foxes walk upon it. Thou, O Lord, remainest for ever; thy throne from generation to generation.   — Lamentations 5:1-3, 13-19

While the Fourth Lamentation is without prayer, this Fifth Lamentation is one whole prayer, with an appeal to Him who sits above the centuries (5:19). As a prayer, the dirge is an elaboration of the distress of those ravaged by war and banishment. The last World War broke loose because a servant, a one-time corporal, tried to rule the world. Amid all changes it is encouraging to know that God remains the same. "Thou remainest." Let us keep the Judgment Seat of Christ in view, lest our crown should fall from our head (5:16).

Ezekiel

Ezekiel, the mystic prophet, occupies an honorable place among the intercessors of the Old Testament. As the voice of Jehovah to "the whole house of Israel," Ezekiel lived in full fellowship with the One he represented. It is from him that we learn that promised blessings must be sought after and appropriated (36:37).

Temporal and spiritual blessings are before Ezekiel as he writes for God's own people. The consummation of the promises of God are to come as the result, among other blessings, of prayer. By prayer, we are prepared for the promises, and by prayer the promises become real to us.

It is also from Ezekiel that we discover that men do not pray enough. There is a wrestling which amounts to agony — a profitable yet painful agony —
"Which none but he that feels it knows."
The longing of a soul, which admits of no denial, ever receives the overflowing blessing of an opened heaven.

Comparing Ezekiel with Jeremiah, it would seem as if the former had a more profound reverence than the latter. Ezekiel may lack Jeremiah's bold daring approach to God, and he certainly is not characterized by Jeremiah's tense passion and his overwhelming sense of the need of God as his Refuge and Friend. Yet to Ezekiel God was very real and "girt about with a mysterious glory which renders Him all but inaccessible." It is significant of this remoteness of God that dialogue and prayer are rare in the book of Ezekiel. The dialogue in 4:14 turns upon ceremonial cleanness, and though "the hand of Jehovah was often upon him, there are very few prayers in the book." Ezekiel's must have been a prayerful heart to have discerned visions of God through the opened heavens (1:1).

Ezekiel fell on his face when he saw the glory of God on the plain (3:23), and in this attitude he offered his brief intercessory prayers (9:8; 11:13).

Prayer As Protest
(Ezekiel 4:14)

Then said I, Ah, Lord God! behold, my soul hath not been polluted: for from my youth up even till now have I not eaten of that which dieth of itself, or is torn in pieces; neither came there abominable flesh into my mouth. — Ezekiel 4:14

Ezekiel's usual address was "The Lord Jehovah" (4:14; 9:8; 11:13). He was always overwhelmed by the greatness of God as he approached Him. How his whole being revolted against what God asked him to do! God graciously made a distasteful task more congenial, and out the prophet went as a symbol of the famine the people were to endure (24:27).

When prevailing, intercessory prayer is ours we know what it is to be lifted up by the Spirit between the earth and the heaven (8:3; 11:1, 21).

Prayer for Preservation of Residue

(Ezekiel 9:8-11)

And it came to pass, while they were slaying them, and I was left, that I fell upon my face, and cried, and said, Ah Lord God! wilt thou destroy all the residue of Israel in thy pouring out of thy fury upon Jerusalem? — Ezekiel 9:8

Although Ezekiel knew that God's judgments were just he was yet moved to plead for the remnant of Israel. Like previous intercessors, the prophet tells God that His reputation is at stake. Because of His promises to His people, He cannot destroy all the residue of Israel. But the sternness of the divine answer left no room for any mitigation of the judgment. God, however, ever tempers judgment with mercy.

Prayer Sanctuary

(Ezekiel 11:13-16)

Then fell I down upon my face, and cried with a loud voice, and said, Ah Lord God! wilt thou make a full end of the remnant of Israel? . . .
Therefore say, Thus saith the Lord God; Although I have cast them far off among the heathen, and although I have scattered them among the countries, yet will I be to them as a little sanctuary in the countries where they shall come. — Ezekiel 11:13b, 16

God not only invites us into His sanctuary to pray. He is Himself as "a little sanctuary" to His exiled people (11:16). E. May Grimes has taught us to sing —

"A little Sanctuary" art Thou to me!
O Jesus, best beloved! I live with Thee:
My heart is stilled beneath love's canopy,
Its sure abiding place where'er I roam.

"A little Sanctuary" art Thou to me!
My heart has found its everlasting home,
The "Holiest of All" is opened wide,
And I may enter and be satisfied.

"A little Sanctuary" art Thou to me!
No fabled shrine, but deep reality!
Thou saidst it should be so when at Thy call
I rose and followed gladly, leaving all.

"A little Sanctuary" art Thou to me!
All joyfully I pitch my tent with Thee;
Or ready still to journey at Thy word —
"In Thee" I "live and move," most blessed Lord.

"A little Sanctuary" art Thou to me!
I always am "at home" on land or sea;
Alone, yet never lonely now, I prove
The "Hundredfold," Lord Jesus, in Thy love.

The precious phrase "I will be to thee as a little sanctuary" can be expressed "as a sanctuary for a little." During the captivity of His people, God's presence with them spiritually would be instead of the outward symbolical presence in His Temple. God had already declared that He would abandon the material sanctuary and give it up to destruction. Now He offers Himself as a sanctuary to His people scattered among enemies. It is blessed to know that when shut out from God's House, we can be shut in with Him.

Ezekiel deemed it a sin not to pray for those God had permitted to be led into captivity. As an intercessor, the prophet is akin to Abraham pleading for Sodom (14:14, 16, 18, 20). God has always just cause for His actions (14:23; 16:22, 27, 49; 18:25; 42:1-9). The normal function of prayer is to make intercession with God for others (22:30).

It was Ezekiel's sad mission to convey to Israel God's judgment upon the nation for its gross sins (22:23-31), but the message of the sighing prophet seemed as an idle tale and his heart-sob was —

"Ah Lord God! they say of me, Doth he not
speak parables" (20:49)?

Such a prayer echoes the hopelessness of Ezekiel's task. Yet he had the *imprimatur* of a true spokesman for God (33:33).

God never forgets His people, even although He may have occasion to afflict them. His "lovingkindness will He not utterly take from them." Thus when sin is thoroughly dealt with and hearts are fully restored, prayer-fellowship is a blessed reality once more (36:37).

Is not the life-giving wind the Holy Spirit (John 3:8), and are we not justified in praying to the Spirit (37:9, 10)? The Holy Spirit is also the River issuing from the sanctuary (47:1-12; John 7:37-39). While the priests exercised judicial functions and taught the people ritual distinctions (40-47), New Testament priests are conspicuous for their intercessory ministry (I Peter 2:5, 9; Revelation 1:6; 5:10; 20.6; I Timothy 2:8).

Daniel

Both Daniel and Ezekiel were Jewish captives in Babylon who knew how to rise above their adversity through prayer. Because he was of princely descent (1:3), Daniel's rank and comeliness equipped him for palace service, where in spite of the polluted atmosphere of an oriental court he lived a life of prayer and purity.

Daniel's prayers form a profitable study. Outstanding among the prayer-episodes of the book is the determination of Daniel, when prime minister to a proud and idolatrous monarch, to maintain an altar of prayer to which he could daily repair (6:10). Above and beyond all else, Daniel was a man of prayer (2:19, 23). Along with his godly companions (1:7) Daniel relied upon God for necessary wisdom and grace. As the result of their prayers, their heathen ruler came to know that there was a God in Heaven able to reveal all secrets. When it came to the interpretation of dreams, what prostration there was before God —

> Such as earth
> Saw never; such as Heaven stoops to see.

The prayers of the Hebrew captives were of the prevailing kind, bringing the desired unlocking of secrets and honor to the intercessors themselves.

Prayer for Interpretation

(Daniel 2:17, 18)

Then Daniel went to his house, and made the thing known to Hananiah, Mishael, and Azariah, his companions: That they would desire mercies of the God of heaven concerning this secret; that Daniel and his fellows should not perish with the rest of the wise men of Babylon.   — Daniel 2:17, 18

Along with the purpose of the captives not to defile themselves with the king's meat (1:8), there must have been earnest prayer that they might be kept from anything that would hinder them from becoming the media of revelation.

With their lives in peril, Daniel and his friends appealed to the God of heaven and were heard in that they feared. God gave them the ability to interpret Nebuchadnezzar's dream (2:18). Daniel did not forget to thank God for such a revelation (2:20-23).

Daniel knew the power of united prayer and so sought the fellowship of his companions (2:17). The prophet also believed in being definite in prayer. He knew exactly how to pray and what to pray for (2:18, 19). Daniel likewise mingled praises with his prayers (2:20-23). The continuity of national history is recognized in the prayer-phrase "God of our Fathers" (2:23). What sweet fellowship the Hebrew youths must have had with their Divine Companion in the fiery furnace (3:25)! While we have no spoken prayer of theirs, they had every confidence that God would vindicate their faith in Him (4:34).

Prayer in Defiance of Decree

(Daniel 6:10-15)

Now when Daniel knew that the writing was signed, he went into his house; and his windows being open in his chamber toward Jerusalem, he kneeled upon his knees three times a day, and prayed, and gave thanks before his God, as he did aforetime. — Daniel 6:10

In defiance of the decree of Darius, Daniel kept his window opened toward Jerusalem and prayed unto his God (6:10, 11; Psalm 5:7). Three times a day he prayed (Psalm 119:64).

Any home is blessed of God when its window is daily opened toward Jerusalem. The context of Daniel's prayer at this point is worthy of note. His re-modeling of the government was not favorably received by the princes who hated Daniel. Envious of his position, they attacked his reputation, but could find nothing against him. The only possible point of successful attack was Daniel's religion. Thrice daily he prayed. Now the decree of Darius forbade his recognition of God. What should he do? What did he do? Why, he continued to keep his prayer-watch, even though his action meant the den of lions. Prayer prevailed for Daniel, like his companions, was preserved, and doom intended for the praying one overtook his foes. If we keep the channel to heaven open, God will care for all concerning us.

Prayer of Confession

(Daniel 9)

And I prayed unto the Lord my God, and made my confession, and said, O Lord, the great and dreadful God, keeping the covenant and mercy to them that love him, and to them that keep his commandments; We have sinned, and have committed iniquity, and have done wickedly, and have rebelled, even by departing from thy precepts and from thy judgments: Neither have we hearkened unto thy servants the prophets, which spake in thy name to our kings, our princes, and our fathers, and to all the people of the land. O Lord, righteousness belongeth unto thee, but unto us confusion of faces, as at this day; to the men of Judah, and to the inhabitants of Jerusalem, and unto all Israel, that are near, and that are far off, through all the countries whither thou hast driven them, because of their trespass that they have trespassed against thee. O Lord, to us belongeth confusion of face, to our kings, to our princes, and to our fathers, because we have sinned against thee. To the Lord our God belong mercies and forgivenesses, though we have rebelled against him; Neither have we obeyed the voice of the Lord our God, to walk in his laws, which he set before us by his servants the prophets. Yea, all Israel have transgressed thy law, even by departing, that they might not obey thy voice; therefore the curse is poured upon us, and the oath that is written in the law of Moses the servant of God, because we have sinned against him. And he hath confirmed his words, which he spake against us, and against our judges that judged us, by bringing upon us a great evil: for under the whole heaven hath not been done as hath been done upon Jerusalem. As it is written in the law of Moses, all this evil is come upon us: yet made we not our prayer before the Lord our God, that we might turn from our iniquities, and understand thy truth. Therefore hath the Lord watched upon the evil, and brought it upon us: for the Lord our God is righteous in all his works which he doeth: for we obeyed not his voice. And now, O Lord our God, that hast brought thy people forth out of the land of Egypt with a mighty hand, and hast gotten thee renown, as at this day; we have sinned, we have done wickedly.

O Lord, according to all thy righteousness, I beseech thee, let thine anger and thy fury be turned away from thy city Jerusalem, thy holy mountain: because for our sins, and for the iniquities of our fathers, Jerusalem and thy people are become a reproach to all that are about us. Now therefore, O our God, hear the prayer of thy servant, and his supplications, and cause thy face to shine upon thy sanctuary that is desolate, for the Lord's sake. O my God, incline thine ear, and hear; open thine eyes, and behold our desolations, and the city which is called by thy name: for we do not present our supplications before thee for our righteousnesses, but for thy great mercies. O Lord, hear; O Lord, forgive; O Lord, hearken and do; defer not, for thine own sake, O my God: for thy city and thy people are called by thy name.   — Daniel 9:4-19

What a searching chapter this is! It should be read upon one's knees. Daniel made a full acknowledgment of his people's sins, linking himself to them. He relied upon God's justice, patience, and mercy (9:5, 9). A speedy answer was given (9:23). Answer to prayer begins with the assurance in the heart that God hears and answers prayer. Such faith was Daniel's (9:17-19). Summarizing this model prayer we can note these features Burgess and Proudlove deal with, fully and helpfully in their volume already mentioned —

1. Place of Prayer — "he went into his house"
2. Courage in Prayer — "his windows being open"
3. Direction in Prayer — "toward Jerusalem"
4. Attitude for Prayer — "he kneeled upon his knees"
5. Regularity in Prayer — "three times a day"
6. Thanksgiving in Prayer — "gave thanks before his God"
7. Continuance in Prayer — "as he did aforetime."

The conclusion of Daniel's prayer — one of the loveliest prayers in the Bible — is couched in terms that sound more like the New Testament than the Old (9:17-19).

Daniel's prayer was to the *God* of Israel, "My God" — "Our God" (9:8, 17, 18); a God who sits above the centuries (6:26); a God of Forgiveness (9:9, 18, 19); a God whose past word is never forgotten (9:11, 13); a God who delivers those called by His Name (9:19); a God who uses angels (9:21; Zechariah 1; Luke 1:19, 26).

Prayer and Its Spiritual Results
(Daniel 10)

And in the four and twentieth day of the first month, as I was by the side of the great river, which is Hiddekel; Then I lifted up mine eyes, and looked, and behold a certain man clothed in linen, whose loins were girded with fine gold of Uphaz: His body also was like the beryl, and his face as the appearance of lightning, and his eyes as lamps of fire, and his arms and his feet like in colour to polished brass, and the voice of his words like the voice of a multitude. And I Daniel alone saw the vision: for the men that were with me saw not the vision; but a great quaking fell upon them, so that they fled to hide themselves. Therefore I was left alone, and saw this great vision, and there remained no strength in me: for my comeliness was turned in me into corruption, and I retained no strength. Yet heard I the voice of his words: and when I heard the voice of his words, then was I in a deep sleep on my face, and my face toward the ground.

And, behold, an hand touched me, which set me upon my knees and upon the palms of my hands. And he said unto me, O Daniel, a man greatly beloved, understand the words that I speak unto thee, and stand upright: for unto thee am I now sent. And when he had spoken this word unto me, I stood trembling. Then said he unto me, Fear not, Daniel: for from the first day that thou didst set thine heart to understand, and to chasten thyself before thy God, thy words were heard, and I am come for thy words. But the prince of the kingdom of Persia withstood me one and twenty days: but, lo, Michael, one of the chief princes, came to help me; and I remained there with the kings of Persia. Now I am come to make thee understand what shall befall thy people in the latter days: for yet the vision is for many days. And when he had spoken such words unto me, I set my face toward the ground, and I became dumb. And, behold, one like the similitude of the sons of men touched my lips: then I opened my mouth, and spake, and said unto him that stood before me, O my lord, by the vision my sorrows are turned upon me, and I have retained no strength. For how can the servant of this my lord talk with this my lord? for as for me, straightway there remained no strength in me, neither is there breath left in me. Then there came again and touched me one like the appearance of a man, and he strengthened me, And said, O man greatly beloved, fear not: peace be unto thee, be strong, yea, be strong. And when he had spoken unto me, I was strengthened, and said, Let my lord speak; for thou hast strengthened me. Then said he, Knowest thou wherefore I come unto thee? and now will I return to fight with the prince of Persia: and when I am gone forth, lo, the prince of Grecia shall come. But I will shew thee that which is noted in the scripture of truth: and there is none that holdeth with me in these things, but Michael your prince.   — Daniel 10:4-21

In this great chapter with its soul-absorbing vision of the glory of God we are privileged to witness "the heavenly side of prayer."

1. Prayer results in inspired vision (10:7-11). Such a vision humbles us (9:8), yet assures us of God's unchanging love (9:11).

2. Prayer secures an instant audience with God (10:12). While answers may be delayed, the *hearing* is always assured.

3. Prayer results in inspired wisdom (10:14). Apart from unbroken communion with God, spiritual insight into His Word and ways is not possible.

4. Prayer provides us with necessary strength (10:18, 19). Waiting upon God we renew, or exchange, our strength (Isaiah 40:31). Compare 10:12 with Luke 11:24; John 11:41.

5. Prayer drives away all fear (10:12, 19). Faith and fear cannot exist together. The one destroys the other (Psalm 46:1, 2).

Prayer for Light on One's End
(Daniel 12:8-13)

And I heard, but I understood not: then said I, O my Lord, what shall be the end of these things?   — Daniel 12:8

Daniel's heart was troubled for a full revelation of the Church Age and the Rapture of the Church was not granted unto him (9:28). He was among the prophets who only discerned the sufferings of Christ and the glory that should follow (I Peter 1:10). Daniel believed in heaven and in hell (12:2); and that as the end draws near good men will become better, and bad men worse (12:10); and that a glorious resurrection would be his (12:13).

Hosea

In a style, somewhat abrupt and figurative, Hosea writes that Israel is not only apostate and sinful, but that her sin takes its character from her exalted relationship. The higher we climb, the deeper we fall. Israel had been Jehovah's wife. Becoming adulterous, she was repudiated. Hosea's message of hope is that when fully purified, she will be restored (3:5).

While no prayers, as such, are recorded in Hosea, yet many sidelights on "prayer" are touched upon by the prophet.

Prayers to idols go unanswered and grieve God (4:12).

Prayer, out of affliction, finds God ready to help (5:15).

Prayer is useless without penitence for sin (6:1-3).

Prayer must be sincere — out of the heart (7:14; 10:12).

Prayer can be brief and swift. Hosea, in a moment of intense emotion as he contemplates the depravity of Israel and its inevitable end, sent up to God the swift wild prayer: "Give them, O Jehovah — what wilt Thou give them? give them a miscarrying womb and dry breasts" (9:14).

Prayer has its roots in the past. Seeking to kindle in a wayward people a sense of the divine goodness, Hosea pointed them to history (11:1-4; Amos 2:9, 10).

Prayer, when accompanied by penitence, is expressive. "Take with you words . . . So will we render the calves of our lips" (14:2). The prayer-worth of true repentance which we take with us shall be our offerings in the place of calves (Psalm 51:17; 66:3; Isaiah 48:20; Hebrews 13:15).

Joel

Ellicott, in his commentary on Joel, says that this minor prophet "has a peculiar claim upon the attention of the Christian reader, inasmuch as he foretells the advent of the Comforter, who would hereafter carry on and complete the work of the Saviour. Joel is as emphatically the prophet of the Holy Spirit as Isaiah is emphatically of the Messiah."

Prayer in Emergency

(Joel 1:19, 20)

O Lord, to thee will I cry: for the fire hath devoured the pastures of the wilderness, and the flame hath burned all the trees of the field. The beasts of the field cry also unto thee: for the rivers of waters are dried up, and the fire hath devoured the pastures of the wilderness.
— Joel 1:19, 20

Too many people wait for a crisis to overtake them before they pray. An habitually prayerful attitude would have prepared them for the crisis. Here we have another of those Bible "emergency" prayers.

Ellicott further remarks: "There is further teaching in the words of this inspired prophet of extreme importance at all times, and especially in these latter days — the teaching that God heareth prayer in respect of those events which are due, as it is said to the laws of nature. We are sometimes met with the argument that it is even an impertinence to endeavor to interfere with such laws by our prayers. But we have a wiser teacher in Joel. When our land is threatened with famine through excessive drought (or through excessive rain) and the natural impulse of our hearts is to offer up prayers and intercessions to Almighty God, we may turn to the striking precedent which God has given us in this prophet, for who knoweth whether (even in *our* emergency) He will turn and repent and leave a blessing behind Him?"

Prayer and Weeping

(Joel 2:17)

Let the priests, the ministers of the Lord, weep between the porch and the altar, and let them say, Spare thy people, O Lord, and give not thine heritage to reproach, that the heathen should rule over them: wherefore should they say among the people, Where is their God?
— Joel 2:17

The distress occasioned by the destructive locusts caused the tears and prayers of the priests. What a strong appeal to God to consider His reputation! If He fails to help His people, what will the nations think of Him? They would think He was more unable than unwilling to rescue His own. To save His reputation then, He is bound to interpose. So in a day of dire calamity, as Joel describes, the priests are urged to plead with God to spare His people. And they are given another of those blessed "Fear nots" (2:21).

To the Jew, the Temple was, in an altogether unique sense, "the house of prayer" (Ezra 10:1; Matthew 21:13). The priests wept and prayed "between the porch and the altar" of "the beautiful house where our fathers praised thee" (Isaiah 64:11). Under grace it does not matter where we pray for whosoever calls upon the name of the Lord shall be delivered (2:32; Romans 10:13). Our Lord was more concerned about the *spirit* than the *sphere* of worship (John 4:20-24).

Amos

Although Amos looked upon himself as a layman rather than a prophet (7:14), yet the word of the Lord came unto him as he meditated among the lonely hills and out he went to prophesy and pray. "It is noteworthy that in Amos we have the first clear indication of the enlarging sweep of the prophet's gaze. His eye ranges over the surrounding kingdom. Israel is no longer thought of exclusively, its destiny is no longer contemplated apart from that of the surrounding empires with which it was closely connected. Jehovah is the God of the world, and not of His peculiar people the Hebrew race only."

Prayer for Respite and Forgiveness

(Amos 7:1-9)

And it came to pass, that when they had made an end of eating the grass of the land, then I said, O Lord God, forgive, I beseech thee: by whom shall Jacob arise? for he is small.
Then said I, O Lord God, cease, I beseech thee: by whom shall Jacob arise? for he is small.   — Amos 7:2, 5

This solitary prayer of the book is significant. Amos saw the first wave of disaster in the destruction of the food of the people and interceded for respite from the grasshopper plague and for forgiveness. The prophet's plea takes the form, "Who is Jacob that he should stand for he is small?" Amos the stern, from whom one would expect little pity, pleaded twice that the blow should not fall upon Israel (7:2, 5).

The Divine Voice can be detected in many ways, even in the measured westward tramp of the Assyrian hosts, and to the prophet that Voice was the most real of all realities (3:9). So deeply have its notes sunk into the soul that it is not so much the prophet who speaks as the Voice speaking through him. The fearlessness of Amos seen in his brave answer to the insinuation of the courtier-priest, Amaziah (7:12-17), issued from his fear of God. As with other prophets, Amos points to history (2:9, 10).

Seeking God is equivalent to seeking good (5:15), and the good is "the establishing of justice in the gate" (Micah 3:3, 4). Five times over, Amos uses the word "seek" (5:4-6, 8, 14). The One we seek in prayer is the God of creation and of grace, and able therefore to bless us with life.

Obadiah

No prayer is found in this shortest book of the Old Testament. Although Obadiah speaks exultingly of the destined overthrow of an enemy so bitter, there is the undercurrent of respectful tenderness in his message (5). Short though this prophecy is, it yet bears the stamp of Obadiah's personality. His style is vigorous and his images startlingly bold (4). Interrogations abound through the twenty-one verses of the book. Without prayer, Obadiah could not have received such a vision.

We are warned against forgetting our guilty past (11 with Isaiah 51:1) and urged to possess our possessions (17). As we think of every aspect of our life, can we say that the kingdom is the Lord's (21)?

Jonah

Different types of prayer are to be found in this small book, with its story of a runaway prophet. Indignant over the wickedness of Nineveh, God commissioned Jonah to cry against it, but the prophet turned coward and flew to Joppa. For an analysis of the book we have Jonah in a fix (chapter 1) — in a fish (chapter 2) — in a revival (chapter 3) — in a rage (chapter 4).

Prayer of Heathen Sailors

(Jonah 1:14-16)

Wherefore they cried unto the Lord, and said, We beseech thee, O Lord, we beseech thee, let us not perish for this man's life, and lay not upon us innocent blood: for thou, O Lord, hast done as it pleased thee.   — Jonah 1:14

Although Jonah could sleep in a storm (1:5, 6), he was wide awake enough in the fish's belly. Disobedience had closed the prophet's lips (1:6), but despair opened them (2:1; Psalm 51:14, 15). What a strong contrast this chapter presents between the readiness of the heathen to receive religious impressions and to pray, and the stubbornness and obstinacy of Israel. The raging storm, casting by lot, and the request of the prophet himself reveal that the sailors were but instruments in carrying out the divine purpose. God always uses the best at hand. The foreign sailors, in their distress, started praying to their heathen gods but ended by praying to the God Jonah had disobeyed (1:5, 14). By way of contrast look at Acts 27:24, where no prayer was prayed during a storm. That faith does not supercede effort can be seen by the way the sailors prayed but helped themselves (1:5; Nehemiah 4:9).

Prayer Out of Hell

(Jonah 2)

Then Jonah prayed unto the Lord his God out of the fish's belly. And said, I cried by reason of mine affliction unto the Lord, and he heard me; out of the belly of hell cried I, and thou heardest my voice. For thou hadst cast me into the deep, in the midst of the seas; and the floods compassed me about: all thy billows and thy waves passed over me. Then I said, I am cast out of thy sight; yet I will look again toward thy holy temple. The waters compassed me about, even to the soul: the depth closed me round about, the weeds were wrapped about my head. I went down to the bottoms of the mountains; the earth with her bars was about me for ever: yet hast thou brought up my life from corruption, O Lord my God. When my soul fainted within me I remembered the Lord: and my prayer came in unto thee, into thine holy temple. They that observe lying vanities forsake their own mercy. But I will sacrifice unto thee with the voice of thanksgiving; I will pay that that I have vowed. Salvation is of the Lord.   — Jonah 2:1-9

The key-phrase of this dramatic chapter is the opening one, "*Then* Jonah prayed" (2:1). Then! When? While in the belly of the great fish God had prepared to swallow Jonah (1:17). What a queer prayer-chamber, "Out of the belly of hell cried I." But it does not matter where we are, God can hear us. It was Jonah's dire need that drove him to pray. "When my soul fainted within me I remembered the Lord" (2:7). Had he remembered and obeyed the Lord before going down to Tarshish, Jonah would not have fainted. His "belly" prayer is remarkable for the fact that it was saturated with Scripture, especially with quotations from the Psalms (18:4-6; 22:24; 42:7; 88:6, etc.).

The sea was God's sea, and Jonah was God's prophet, and a prayer-stool was found in the heart of the raging waters. Prayer was answered and with a renewed consecration and commission Jonah arose and went to Ninevah. How grateful we should be that in our deepest trouble we can pour out our heart before the Lord and experience His power to deliver us from a sea of distress!

Further, this fervent prayer of thanksgiving teaches us a number of necessary lessons.

1. God can hear and help no matter who we may be (2:2).
2. There is no chance. Everything happens from God (2:3).

3. Fleeing from God is one thing, being cast away is quite another (2:4).
4. The deeper the despair, the greater the deliverance (2:5).
5. There is nothing like trouble to arouse us to our need (2:7).
6. Stubborn refusal to obey God does not pay (2:8).
7. Gratitude must be practical. Pay as well as pray (2:9).

Prayer of a Repentant City

(Jonah 3)

So the people of Nineveh believed God, and proclaimed a fast, and put on sackcloth, from the greatest of them even to the least of them. For word came unto the king of Nineveh, and he arose from his throne, and he laid his robe from him, and covered him with sackcloth, and sat in ashes. And he caused it to be proclaimed and published through Nineveh by the decree of the king and his nobles, saying, Let neither man nor beast, herd nor flock, taste any thing: let them not feed, nor drink water: But let man and beast be covered with sackcloth, and cry mightily unto God: yea, let them turn every one from his evil way, and from the violence that is in their hands. Who can tell if God will turn and repent, and turn away from his fierce anger, that we perish not?   — Jonah 3:5-9

What a sight it must have been to see an exceeding great city on its knees in prayer and penitence (3:8)! Man and beast were clothed with sackcloth and cried mightily unto God. History records how animals and human beings were associated in public mourning. Joel describes the mute appeal of animals against suffering as being audible to God (1:20). The sudden recognition of *one* God by the heathen king of Nineveh met with a gracious response from God (3:10). Would that we could see all our cities in the sackcloth of repentance because of their sins!

Prayer of a Displeased Prophet

(Jonah 4)

And he prayed unto the Lord, and said, I pray thee, O Lord, was not this my saying, when I was yet in my country? Therefore I fled before unto Tarshish: for I know that thou art a gracious God, and merciful, slow to anger, and of great kindness, and repentest thee of the evil. Therefore now, O Lord, take, I beseech thee, my life from me; for it is better for me to die than to live.   — Jonah 4:2, 3

The grieved prophet did not know what manner of spirit he was of, when he desired some desolating calamity to overtake the Ninevites for repenting under his message of warning. Instead of having a song of praise for the mighty revival he witnessed, Jonah was displeased with God. The word for "displeased" is a strong one, meaning vexed and irritated. Anger burned within him. An old writer has expressed it, "In all the book of God, we scarcely find a servant of the Lord so much out of temper, as he is here — so peevish and provoking to God." What are we like when our prayers are not answered according to our wishes?

Other prophets in their petulance beseeched God to kill them (4:3; Numbers 11:11-15; I Kings 19:4). In the dialogue of the gourd God reasons with the narrow-hearted prophet and appeals to his common sense. "*You* care for a little plant, on which you have spent no thought or effort, and am *I* not to care for the great city of Nineveh" (4:9-11)? In the petulance of disappointment, Jonah prays a somewhat foolish and impudent prayer. He asked God to kill him (4:2, 3). But he was not in the mood to pray when displeased and angry. Those who pray thus have not an adequate vision of God.

How infinitely kind and gracious God is! With a mother's sweet gentleness He asked: "Doest thou well to be angry?" Then with exquisite kindness God took special loving care of His tired servant. God did not chide Jonah, but comforted him. The booth Jonah made (4:5) let the heat through; not so the *Palma Christi*, so famed for its thick, wide foliage, which God spread over him. When the worm-eaten gourd failed Jonah, the gentle challenge came — "Doest thou well to be angry for the gourd?" Proud, blind Jonah resented the destruction of the gourd but was willing to greet with equanimity the destruction of Nineveh. Jonah was condemned out of his own mouth. How he profited by his interview with God we are not told. The story breaks off suddenly, with God having the last word and the best.

Micah

Micah the Morasthite must have had a vivid personality. Evidently he was a man of profound affection for his nation and fatherland and was raised up to warn rulers and people alike of sure judgment for their gross wickedness. His style of writing is similar to Isaiah (4:1-3; Isaiah 2:2-4). Conspicuous among the prophets for the boldness and thoroughness of his denunciations and for the rapidity of his contrasts, we do not have a record of any prayers he offered. Yet his predictions could only have come to him as he tarried in the presence of the Lord he so fully describes (1:2, 3). As an interpreter of the divine will, Micah denounces those prophets who uttered false messages (3:5). Micah knew God as One who pardoneth iniquity (6:8; 7:18).

Apart from prayer, we cannot be full of power by the Spirit of the Lord (3:8), neither can we stand and feed in the strength of the Lord (5:4). Looking unto the Lord and waiting for Him are surely aspects of prayer, making real light about us in our darkness (7:8).

Nahum

Under the preaching of Jonah, Nineveh turned to God, but a century later it became wholly apostatized from God, and ripe for divine judgment (1:9; 3:10). So Nahum has but one subject — the destruction of Nineveh. Here is another prayerless book. Prayer, of course, is implied in the performance of our vows (1:15).

Habakkuk

Habakkuk was raised up to announce God's intention of punishing the iniquities which prevailed among his compatriots. Catastrophe of strange and incredible extent was to overtake them (1:5). It is profitable to trace how the prophet expostulated with God.

Prayer of Complaint and Vindication

(Habakkuk 1:1-4, 12-17)

O Lord, how long shall I cry, and thou wilt not hear! even cry out unto thee of violence, and thou wilt not save! Why dost thou shew me iniquity, and cause me to behold grievance? for spoiling and violence are before me: and there are that raise up strife and contention. Therefore the law is slacked, and judgment doth never go forth: for the wicked doth compass about the righteous; therefore wrong judgment proceedeth. . . .

Art thou not from everlasting, O Lord my God, mine Holy One? we shall not die. O Lord, thou hast ordained them for judgment; and, O mighty God, thou hast established them for correction. Thou art of purer eyes than to behold evil, and canst not look on iniquity: wherefore lookest thou upon them that deal treacherously, and holdest thy tongue when the wicked devoureth the man that is more righteous than he? And makest men as the fishes of the sea, as the creeping things, that have no ruler over them? They take up all of them with the angle, they catch them in their net, and gather them in their drag; therefore they rejoice and are glad. Therefore they sacrifice unto their net, and burn incense unto their drag; because by them their portion is fat, and their meat plenteous. Shall they therefore empty their net, and not spare continually to slay the nations?   — Habakkuk 1:2-4; 12-17

We are here given another example of the interpolated prayers of the Bible. The prophet prays to God about Israel's distressed condition, then God answers (1:5-11), following which Habakkuk takes up his prayer again and vindicates God's actions (1:12-17 to 2:1). Professor MacFadyen remarks that "Habakkuk thought he had found an answer in his own day to his prayer for Divine intervention (1:5); but, after fear of disappointment he begins to learn that the purpose of God, though sure, may be slow. The will of God is ultimately done in history, but not as and when we will; therefore 'though it tarry, wait for it' (2:3). But if it is slow, it is sure. It has its appointed time. It will not lag behind (2:3)."

Greatly perplexed and disturbed, as he surveys the sin of his time, Habakkuk stands upon his watch-tower, there to listen-in to God (2:1; Psalm 85:8). He had to pause to hear God speak. As a prayer-watcher he received God's message for a sinning people. What a golden verse he gave to the world (2:3)! Another precious verse is the last one of chapter 2, in which the reality of the invisible God is set against the mockery of the image. In the presence of God silence is wisdom (2:20; Zechariah 2:13).

Prayer of Faith

(Habakkuk 3)

A prayer of Habakkuk the prophet upon Shigionoth. O Lord, I have heard thy speech, and was afraid: O Lord, revive thy work in the midst of the years, in the midst of the years make known; in wrath remember mercy. God came from Teman, and the Holy One from mount Paran. Selah. His glory covered the heavens, and the earth was full of his praise. And his brightness was as the light; he had horns coming out of his hand: and there was the hiding of his power. Before him went the pestilence, and burning coals went forth at his feet. He stood, and measured the earth: he beheld, and drove asunder the nations; and the everlasting mountains were scattered, the perpetual hills did bow: his ways are everlasting. I saw the tents of Cushan in affliction: and the curtains of the land of Midian did tremble. Was the Lord displeased against the rivers? was thine anger against the rivers? was thy wrath against the sea, that thou didst ride upon thine horses and thy chariots of salvation? Thy bow was made quite naked, according to the oaths of the tribes, even thy word. Selah. Thou didst cleave the earth with rivers. The mountains saw thee, and they trembled: the overflowing of the water passed by: the deep uttered his voice, and lifted up his hands on high. The sun and moon stood still in their habitation: at the light of thine arrows they went, and at the shining of thy glittering spear. Thou didst march through the land in indignation, thou didst thresh the heathen in anger. Thou wentest forth for the salvation of thy people, even for salvation with thine anointed; thou woundedst the head out of the house of the wicked, by discovering the foundation unto the neck. Selah. Thou didst strike through with his staves the head of his villages: they came out as a whirlwind to scatter me: their rejoicing was as to devour the poor secretly. Thou didst walk through the sea with thine horses, through the heap of great waters. When I heard, my belly trembled; my lips quivered at the voice: rottenness entered into my bones, and I trembled in myself, that I might rest in the day of trouble: when he cometh up unto the people, he will invade them with his troops.

Although the fig tree shall not blossom, neither shall fruit be in the vines; the labour of the olive shall fail, and the fields shall yield no meat; the flock shall be cut off from the fold, and there shall be no herd in the stalls: Yet I will rejoice in the Lord, I will joy in the

God of my salvation. The Lord God is my strength, and he will make my feet like hinds' feet, and he will make me to walk upon mine high places. To the chief singer on my stringed instruments.

— Habakkuk 3

When the prophet entered upon his work, the Jewish nation was apostate. Threatened judgments had been announced. Then came this remarkable prayer of Habakkuk's (3:1), a prayer which for sublimity of thought and beauty of diction has never been surpassed. As the patriotic prophet prays, he reminds God of past providential interventions on behalf of Israel and then pleads for God to do it again (3:2). It is a remarkable prayer, expressing confidence in God and in His power to do great and mighty things. Nations can do nothing else but tremble as they witness the forces of nature acknowledging God's awful presence.

Habakkuk rises to sublime heights in his prayer when he affirms that no matter how many calamities may overtake him, he will cling confidently and cheerfully to God, the all-powerful One (3:16-19). Persevering, patient faith is the practical lesson of the book before us.

> To learn from self to cease,
> Leave all things to a Father's will,
> And taste before Him lying still,
> E'er in affliction, peace.

One quaint writer advises us to strum away on "Habakkuk's fiddle," when troublesome days are ours. The last part of the prophet's prayer is said to be very beautiful in the Hebrew rhythm, being written in short lines of three words each and set to music.

Zephaniah

This ancestor of Hezekiah had a mission of mingled reproof and consolation. "In the foreground of the prophetic portraiture stands the Chaldean invasion, with its fearful consequences — the sack of Jerusalem and deportation of God's chosen people." Zephaniah, however, paints a bright horizon for a purged people.

Because a day of great wrath is depicted (1:14, 15), prayer is absent from the book. Those who had turned from the Lord must hold their peace at His presence (1:6, 7). When His judgments are abroad, He will hide the meek who seek His face (2:3).

Searching Jerusalem with candles (1:12), speaks of thoroughness in the exposure of evil and contradicts the estimation of God that would do neither one thing or the other. "He will not do good, neither will He do evil." God does not leave the world to run itself, never intervening in its affairs. A "Fear not" assures us of all God is able and willing to do (3:16, 17). "Morning by morning He brings justice to light: He faileth not" (3:5). Every day is a fresh reminder of our need and of God's ability to meet the need. Throughout the day His goodness is the portion of the prayerful, trustful heart, and through the night He unslumberingly watches over His own. While Zephaniah contains no prayers, the exhortation to wait upon the Lord is present (3:8).

Haggai

"The *theme* of Haggai is the unfinished temple," says Dr. C. I. Scofield, "and his mission to admonish and encourage the builders" (1:4). Apathy towards the rebuilding of the temple comes in for rebuke. The prophet also emphasized the ritual distinction between the clean and the unclean (2:11-13) — a separation so necessary in these days when a good mixer seems to be popular.

While no prayers of Haggai are recorded, he must have been a man of prayer to have functioned as the Lord's messenger (1:13) and to have received a vision of God's ultimate plan and purpose (2:5-9). With prevalent dearth springing from religious apathy, and no sign of better times visible, Haggai had the assurance of a brighter day — "From this day will I bless you" (2:19). Are we as the *signet* of the Lord (2:23; Song of Solomon 8:6; Jeremiah 22:24)?

Zechariah

Zechariah is another of the prophets who gave witness to Christ (Acts 10:43), and who testified beforehand His suffering and glory (3:8; 9:9; 11:12, etc.; I Peter 1:11). The universal worship of the Lord is one of the themes the prophet describes (8:22). Divine messages are mediated to men by angels (1:12; 2:3, etc). The prayers of cruel men guilty of social injustice God does not hear (7:9-13). While Zechariah is not found praying to God, we do find him speaking to the angels God sent to the prophet (4:4; 6:1). Mention is made of some who prayed before the Lord (7:3, 4). In the Millennial Reign of our Lord, the inhabitants of the center of earth's worship will go speedily to pray before the Lord (8:21). Encouragement is given to pray for the latter rain (10:1), by which we understand rain — natural and spiritual. "Rain as of old will be restored to Palestine, but, also there will be a mighty effusion of the Spirit upon restored Israel."

The Holy Spirit who inspires true prayer (Romans 8:26, 27) is the Spirit of supplication, as well as of grace (12:10). The ministry of the Spirit in showing Zechariah "things to come" is clearly evident throughout the book. All who love the Lord and who diligently obey His voice (6:15), are "prisoners of hope" (9:12). Ere long, He will return and cry, "Turn you to the stronghold," and up we shall ascend, to walk up and down on high forever (10:12).

Malachi

A European expositor of note has given us a thought worthy of citation, "Malachi is like a late evening which closes a long day, but he is at the same time the morning twilight, which bears in its womb a glorious day."

Malachi's prophecy is one continual, scathing rebuke from beginning to end. His style is clearly evident. He prefers an accusation against Israel in which he shows the deepest insight into the inmost thoughts of the nation. He then supposes an objection on the part of those rebuked. Under the oft-repeated "Wherein," Malachi exhibits in the most telling manner the moral degradation of the people and their indifference to their spiritual condition. Last of all, the prophet confutes their objections or protests which are actually prayers, in forcible, trenchant terms (1:2-5; 2:14-17; 3:7-13).

Six times over we have the key-word, "Wherein" (1:1, 2, 3; 2:17; 3:7, 8), used as a challenge to God in response to His rebukes through Malachi. It has been pointed out that these prayer-protests bear a marked similarity to the messages sent to the Seven Churches (Revelation 2:3).

The "Wherein" of a *despised love* (1:2) is placed alongside of Ephesus, leaving her first love (Revelation 2:4).

The "Wherein" of a *despised name* (1:4) is compared with those in Smyrna who say they are Jews, but are not Judaism before "the name" (Revelation 2:9).

The "Wherein" of a *despised order* (1:7) appears again in Pergamos where man's order was preferred to God's order (Revelation 2:14).

The "Wherein" of a *despised patience* (2:17) is seen in Thyatira who had space to repent but did not (Revelation 2:21).

The "Wherein" of a *despised welcome* (3:7) is akin to those who in Sardis who had a name that they lived but were dead (Revelation 3:1-3).

The "Wherein" of a *despised portion* (3:8) foreshadows those in Laodicea who deemed themselves rich and in need of nothing (Revelation 3:15).

Prayer-Protest One

(Malachi 1:2)

I have loved you, saith the Lord. Yet ye say, Wherein hast thou loved us? Was not Esau Jacob's brother? saith the Lord: yet I loved Jacob.   — Malachi 1:2

What an impudent approach to God it was to be told that He had not loved His people! They seem surprised to be reminded that He did love them. Evidently they had forgotten past assurances of His love (Deuteronomy 7:8; 33:2; Jeremiah 31:3; Hosea 11:4). When sorrow surges around our lives and we are mystified over what God permits, Satan is active, instilling doubt into the mind concerning God's love and we are tempted to cry, "How can You love me?" Yet His love never wanes nor changes.

Too often the heart's affection is dissipated and divine love is not fully appreciated.

> Hast thou many "loves" within
> That there is scant room for Him?
> In His place within thy heart
> But a small and grudging part?

Prayer-Protest Two

(Malachi 1:6)

A son honoureth his father, and a servant his master: if then I be a father, where is mine honour? and if I be a master, where is my fear? saith the Lord of hosts unto you, O priests, that despise my name. And ye say, Wherein have we despised thy name?   — Malachi 1:6

God expresses another grievance, this time against the priests who had set His Name at nought. Simple similes are used to describe the lack of honor. Yet with audacity they replied to God, "Wherein have we despised Thy name?" The priests had lightly esteemed the Great Name of Jehovah, so much so that *Ichabod* came to be written over the portals of the Temple.

We have life through His name (John 20:31) and gather in His name (Matthew 18:20). May we never be guilty of despising nor of disgracing such a peerless name (II Timothy 2:19)! A despised Name follows quickly on the heels of a despised Love.

Prayer-Protest Three

(Malachi 1:7, 13)

Ye offer polluted bread upon mine altar; and ye say, Wherein have we polluted thee? In that ye say, The table of the Lord is contemptible.
Ye said also, Behold, what a weariness is it! and ye have snuffed at it, saith the Lord of hosts; and ye brought that which was torn, and the lame, and the sick; thus ye brought an offering: should I accept this of your hand? saith the Lord.   — Malachi 1:7, 13

Explicit commands in regards to sacrifices presented to God upon prescribed altars had been disobeyed. God demanded the first and the best, and He had every right to same. But the divine altar was treated with contempt. The priests insulted God by giving Him their cast-offs (1:8-14).

In their protest, the priests pleaded ignorance. It was so with Balaam (Revelation 2:14). As the Church Age progressed there came a departure from God's order of worship and of Church polity. May we ever shun to offer God less than the best!

Prayer-Protest Four

(Malachi 2:17)

Ye have wearied the Lord with your words. Yet ye say, Wherein
have we wearied him? When ye say, Every one that doeth evil is
good in the sight of the Lord, and he delighteth in them; or,
Where is the God of judgment?   — Malachi 2:17

Dr. C. I. Scofield describes this protest as "a sin of insincere religious profusion." Divine patience has been sorely tried through the
ages (Genesis 6:6). Yet God ever acts in mercy. Otherwise the sons of
Jacob would have been consumed. The people had wearied God with
words — unchaste, untrue, unbecoming words as those who professed
to be His. Yet again in their prayer-protest they assume the role of
innocents, "Wherein have we wearied Thee?" How glibly the people
could repudiate every challenge of God.

Thyatira tolerated the wicked and evil Jezebel, yet God did not
wreak His vengeance upon the lying, idolatrous woman at once (I
Kings 21). How long-suffering and patient He is! But the day is
coming when His patience will be tried to the limit and His wrath
descend upon a guilty world (Revelation 15:7). May we be saved
from wearying the Lord!

Prayer-Protest Five

(Malachi 3:7)

Even from the days of your fathers ye are gone away from mine
ordinances, and have not kept them. Return unto me, and I will
return unto you, saith the Lord of hosts. But ye said, Wherein shall
we return?   — Malachi 3:7

With full knowledge of all past disobedience, self-will and backsliding, God yet calls His people to return, seeing there is forgiveness
with Him that He might be feared (Psalm 103:4). Alas, God's gracious
proposal was met by an attitude of disdain and antipathy. "Wherein
shall we return?" Here we have a divine invitation and welcome
despised. The sinners in Sardis were exhorted to "Remember . . .
Return . . . Repent." Countless numbers today are guilty of rejecting
divine overtures of mercy (Matthew 11:28-30). They will not come to
God that they might have life (John 10:10).

Prayer-Protest Six

(Malachi 3:8)

Will a man rob God? Yet ye have robbed me. But ye say, Wherein
have we robbed thee? In tithes and offerings.   — Malachi 3:8

The last rebuke of God met a like response. What hypocritical
innocence is in the prayer-protest, "Wherein have we robbed *Thee?*"
(3:8). What an indictment! The people had robbed God of tithes and
offerings, yet when condemned for such a sin they insolently pro-

tested such a rebuke. Turning to Laodicea we find her going off "the gold-standard and operating a currency secured from the filthy rags of her own self-righteousness."

How prone are we to rob God of many things — of our love and life, service and substance! We are all thieves, plundering God of what is His by right and redemption. The Bible says, "Pay that thou owest" (Matthew 26:28). Malachi would have us know that contemptible offerings hinder blessing. Tithes, fully paid, result in the open windows of heaven (1:13; 3:10).

We are further reminded by the prophet that God records all who live in fellowship with Him in a book (3:16). Sometimes disconsolate we may cry, "Where is the God of justice?" (2:11), but Malachi assures us of a judgment day when the righteous will be rewarded and the wicked consumed (3:18).

Our fruitful task of recording and expounding all the prayers of the Old Testament is ended. Prayers, covering thousands of years and coming from all classes and offered for widely differing reasons, have been considered. Summarizing the prayers of Old Testament saints, we would say that they are —

1. Generally *short* and *simple* — a good pattern to follow.
2. *Particular and direct* — particular as to object, directed toward that object.
3. *Expressed* with great *earnestness*. Delay increased *importunity*.
4. Offered with *expectation* of *identical blessing* sought.
5. Presented as *requests,* not as *demands*.
6. In *conformity* with *life* of *intercessors*. Prayer and life were one.
7. Presented with all due *reverence* and *humility*.

Prayers and Prayer in the
New Testament

II

Prayers and Prayer in the
New Testament

As we approach the still richer treasure of prayer the New Testament contains, what else can we say but, "Lord, it is good for us to be here"? At the outset of our meditation, let it be clearly understood that while we find further confirmation, we do not have any higher evidence than the Old Testament presents of the fact that God hears and answers prayer.

From Genesis to Malachi we have ample proof of prayer being fully answered by God. No sincere saint was sent away empty. No petition in submission to the divine will failed of an appropriate answer. As the Bible, however, contains a progressive revelation of the mind and will of God, we have aspects concerning the duty and privilege of prayer of new and intense interest.

That a later and richer revelation should present added prayer-secrets is in keeping with the purpose of God to cause a brighter light to shine upon those redeemed by the blood of His Son. The advantage in respect to prayer believers enjoy in this Church Age over Old Testament saints are manifold as we shall see. How solemn a thing it is to live up to these superior advantages!

Prayers of the two Testaments are different in several ways. First of all, Old Testament saints were taken up in the majority of cases, with secular or temporal blessings. Their prayers were, more or less, of an *earthly* nature. One exception is David, whose Psalm-Prayers were of a *heavenly* nature. Spiritual communion was his desire as he panted after God (Psalm 42:1).

The New Testament abounds with directions to pray for and seek after spiritual blessings (Ephesians 1:3). Under grace, believers are on vantage-ground. Theirs is a fuller revelation than that enjoyed by saints of old. They have been given specific directions on how to desire spiritual gifts and graces, with promises and assurances inspiring confidence to possess their possessions.

Another decided advantage the Christian enjoys over saints of the earlier revelation is that of using the name of Jesus in petitions to God. We hope to deal more fully with this New Testament aspect

173

of prayer when we reach the subject of required attitudes. Old Testament believers came direct to God and were accepted through the future propitiatory sacrifice of Christ. Abraham, who saw Christ's day, was mighty as an intercessor on this behalf. Hitherto, he had not asked anything in Christ's name, nor had any prophet or disciple, for that matter. "Ye have asked nothing in My name" (John 16:24).

The full merit of the Cross could not be pleaded until Christ's atonement was complete. Now in all confidence we can rely upon His declaration, "Verily, verily, I say unto you, Whatsoever ye shall ask the Father in my name, he will give it you" (John 16:23).

Another prayer-advantage under grace is the pledge of Christ to act on our behalf as a personal Intercessor. "I will pray the Father for you" (John 14:16; Hebrews 7:25). Here is a revelation and an assurance Old Testament saints never had. Such a power and a resource were denied them. How it would have imparted strength and animation to their mighty prayers if such a Mediator had been theirs. Now our prayers ascend to God, mingled and blended with the ascending incense of the Saviour's merit. Our voices before they reach the ear of God fall in and blend with the voice of Him whom the Father heareth always.

> Great Advocate! Almighty Friend!
> On Thee our humble hopes depend;
> Our cause can never, never fail
> For Thou dost plead and must prevail.

A further advantage Christians enjoy is the fact that Christ assures them that He Himself will answer their supplication. "Whatsoever ye ask . . . that will *I* do." Not only are we authorized to use the peerless name of Jesus, we have His word that He will hear and answer our prayers.

Ere we approach the New Testament aspect of our theme, one other advantage can be mentioned, namely, that of the ministry of the Holy Spirit in the realm of prayer. Old Testament saints only realized a limited measure of such a gift. As the result of the finished work of Christ, the full bestowment of this Gift is ours. What the coming of the Holy Spirit meant to praying saints is seen in *The Acts of the Apostles*. It was the Spirit who led them and waits to lead us into "A broad land of wealth unknown."

CHRIST'S PRECEPTS AND PRACTICE OF PRAYER

Before we apply the method we followed in the Old Testament to the New Testament (examining the books in their given order to discover their prayer-content), it may prove helpful to summarize the precepts and practice of prayer in the life and labors of our Lord.

The Master never discussed any difficulties about prayer. He took it for granted that men ought always to pray. He did, of course, enumerate practical reasons for our obvious failures in prayer and clearly defined those principles affecting prevailing prayer.

Specific instructions gathered from the four Gospels prove that Jesus believed prayer to be a working force, a dynamic, rather than a doctrine, in the life of a believer. To Him, prayer was not sentiment or theory or presumption to the soul owning its reality. To Christ, prayer persists because of the proof of its efficiency. The unmistakable witness of Jesus to prayer agrees with the sentiment of William Gladstone that, "Prayer is the highest exercise of the human intellect," or with the words of William Law, "Prayer is the divinest exercise the heart of man can engage in."

A. PRAYER IN THE PRECEPTS OF CHRIST

To be efficacious, prayer must be offered according to the divine order. So many prayers remain unanswered simply because the pray-er failed to observe clearly defined conditions. Let us try, then, to analyze what Christ taught regarding the laws of true prayer.

Sincerity

The Pharisees did not pray from the heart. They made prayer a mockery (Matthew 6:5, 15). Their lives contradicted the prayer-language they used (Matthew 15:8). The expressive lines of Tennyson could not be applied to the hypocrites Christ exposed —

> Thrice blest, whose *lives* are faithful prayers,
> Whose lives in higher love endure!
> What souls possess themselves so pure! —
> Or is there blessedness like theirs.

Sincerity, it would seem, is the first requisite of successful prayer. God *must* be approached in spirit and in truth (John 4:24).

The Psalms reveal the urgency and earnestness men felt as they approached God. Their souls panted for Him as the hart for the water-brooks (Psalm 42:1). Such sincerity presupposes the soul's sense of need, then puts the whole weight of being behind the request. Inner desire and urgency of petitions are before us in the parable of the importunate friend (Luke 11:5-13) and in the plea of the Syrophenician woman (Mark 7:24-30).

Humility

As prayer is a privilege, ours must ever be the attitude of a subject coming into the presence of a Sovereign. Deep humility is taught and expected (II Chronicles 7:14; 34:27). Is this not the lesson to be learned from the parable of the Pharisee and the Publican (Luke 18:9-14)?

> Two went to pray; oh, rather say,
> One went to brag, and one to pray;
> One stood up close, and trod on high;
> The other dared not lift up his eye;
> One nearer to God's altar trod,
> The other to the altar's God!

Our Lord was ever the enemy of fleshly ambition. Pride He abhorred (Matthew 26:20-23). Meek and lowly in heart Himself, He constantly rebuked the proud arrogant Pharisees. Humility is the twin virtue of repentance.

> Still to the lowly soul,
> He doth Himself impart
> And for His dwelling and His throne
> Chooseth the poor in heart.

Repentance

Here is another requisite to effectual prayer. The prodigal, although his part was so unworthy, found acceptance with his father when truly repentant (Luke 15:18, 21). Sin causes separation from God. Repentance for sin is a turning back to God, a step so necessary to restored communion (II Kings 8:33, 34; Jeremiah 36:7; Acts 8:22).

Bound up with repentance is confession to God (Nehemiah 1:4-7; Daniel 9:4-11; Luke 18:13). When necessary, there must be confession to one another if prayer is to be answered (James 5:16). Public confession of past sin God has forgiven, and which does not concern the public, is unnecessary and can be harmful. Confession of sin should never be any more public than the sin committed.

Obedience

Our whole personality must move in the direction of our prayers. It is —

> Not what you say in what you pray;
> It's what you are and fain would be.
> God knows the intent of the heart;
> And feels your importunity.

Obedience to the requirements of the divine will must be from the heart (Deuteronomy 11:13; Romans 6:17). This essential to true prayer is also a test of Lordship (Romans 6:16). God answers the prayers of those who know, obey and keep His commands. "If ye ask . . . keep my commandments" (John 14:14, 15; I John 3:22). We have our Lord's example in this matter (John 8:29).

Faith

Without faith it is not only impossible to please God, but also to gain anything from Him. There must be unshaken faith in His love, wisdom and power (Mark 11:22-24; Hebrews 11:6; James 1:6, 7). All things are possible to those who *believe*. Faith claims what it asks for. Our Lord's illustration, enforcing the value of believing prayer (Mark 11:23), would appeal to the Eastern mind. The seeming paradox must be taken along with this and understood in the light of Christ's general teaching.

The need of faith is further illustrated by Christ's attitude to those seeking His aid (Matthew 8:13; 9:28; Mark 5:36; 9:23; Luke 8:48).

Forgiveness

Our Lord was very emphatic about a personal heart-condition as necessary to acceptable communion with God. He warned against expecting forgiveness from God, if we harbored an unforgiving spirit toward others (Matthew 6:14, 15). Unless we forgive, how can we expect to be forgiven?

Forgiveness of others is often the crucial test in our spiritual experience. Such a text exposes the weakness of humanity. "To forgive is divine," we often remark. It is also the climax of our Christian obligation to forgive, even our enemies. As we forgive, we show ourselves to be the children of our heavenly Father (Matthew 5:22-26, 44, 45; 6:14; 18:21, 35; Mark 11:35). Forgiveness of others is the four-fold repeated phrase in the Sermon on the Mount. We reach the pinnacle of Christlikeness when we forgive (Matthew 5:44; 6:12, 14). Further, we are enjoined, not only to forgive our enemies, but to love them. Without love all other virtues are valueless (I Corinthians 13).

Fasting

Being appropriate for times of solicitude and sorrow, fasting naturally became associated with prayer (Psalm 35:13; Nehemiah 1:4; Daniel 9:23). Our Lord emphasized the combination of prayer and fasting as an avenue of power (Matthew 9:15; 17:21; Mark 9:29). While Jesus did not lay stress upon fasting, He did not discountenance it, but regarded it as "legitimate so long as it was the spontaneous and unostentatious expression of the religious mood." Saints of God have proved the virtue of abstinence from food, when prayer-burdens have been theirs (Luke 2:37; Acts 10:30; 13:3; 14:23; I Corinthians 7:5). A season of fasting, not only from food but from any bodily pleasure that may ensnare us, is a helpful regimen. Tennyson marries fasting to praying in the lines —

> Fast and pray!
> That so perchance the Vision may be seen
> By thee and those, and all the world be heal'd.

Persistence

Jesus taught that God hears importunate prayer. The whole point of the parable of the friend coming at midnight begging bread is that of persistency (Luke 11:5-10). Our Lord did not imply that God is an unwilling Friend to give us the loaves we need. Did He not teach His disciples to pray to God for their daily bread (Matthew 6:11)? God is more willing to bless than we are to be blessed. The same thought of persistency dominates the parable of the unjust judge (Luke 18:1-8).

Praying that prevails is the praying-through attitude, the Jacob-spirit of not letting God go until prayer is answered. The word Jesus used for *importunity* carries the primary meaning of "shamelessness," that is, a persistent determination in prayer that will not be put to shame by any apparent refusal on God's part to grant the good thing we ask for. How He delights in that holy boldness refusing to take "No" for an answer (Matthew 15:21-28)!

We need more perseverance in prayer (Ephesians 6:18). We must ask until seventy times seven. How often have we prayed and then said to our heart, "What's the use of praying? There's no sign of change in the wayward life so dear to me; no deliverance from my own failure, or perplexities!" But we must pray on, wrestling like Jacob, panting like David, hoping like Elijah, persistent like Bartimaeas and the Syrophenician woman, crying with tears like our blessed Lord Himself.

We can only prove the energies of prayer as it is of the right sort — humble, believing, expectant and very persevering. Well might we plead, "Lord, teach us to pray!" Yet we are not to plead as though success at heaven's court depended *in chief* upon the petitioner's persistence and self-willed resolve to urge his own preference. Answered prayer, like everything else from God, is all of grace. The consciousness that the persistent prayer we pray is in harmony with the will of God feeds the importunity Jesus commended.

Further, the conscious avoidance of all known sin (Psalm 66:18; Matthew 5:8) gives virtue to the unceasing flow of stedfast prayer (Acts 12:5; I Thessalonians 5:17, 23, 25). Old George Herbert gave us the quaint couplet —

> Who goes to bed and doth not pray,
> Maketh two nights of every day.

Privacy

Christ recommended privacy in prayer when He spoke of the shut door (Matthew 6:6). Ostentatious praying at street corners or elsewhere was discouraged by Him (Matthew 6:5). Mere mechanical prayer, such as heathen incantations, or of pretense was strongly condemned (Mark 12:40). Our Lord has left us an example of solitude in prayer (Luke 6:12).

Accordance with Divine Will

When we ask according to God's will confidence is ours that He hears and that He will grant our request (I John 5:14, 15). When His will is our will we may ask whatsoever we desire. If we would have His will we must continue in living union with Him (John 15:7).

In the Divine Name

In the progressive revelation of prayer Christ declared the necessity of presenting our petitions in His own name and in the Father's name. To whom exactly are we to pray?

1. To God the Father, who hears and answers prayer (Matthew 6:6, 9; John 15:16).

2. To God the Son, as the One co-equal with the Father (Acts 7:59; 9:13-17; Romans 10:12, etc.).
3. To God the Spirit. While we have no recorded instance of prayers addressed to the Spirit, surely it is apropos to talk to Him about our service, sorrow and sanctification, seeing He is associated with all three. Our prayer-life must be under the control of the Spirit so that He can pray through us (Romans 8:26, 27).

The prescribed way to pray is in the Spirit, through the Son, to the Father.

Praying in the Divine Name means pleading the merit, power, work, the Name represents. "In the *Name* (singular form, indicating the unity of the Godhead) of the Father, and of the Son, and of the Holy Spirit" (Matthew 28:19). Trace the use of the Name in the following passages — Matthew 7:22; 18:19, 20; John 14:13, 14; 15:7, 16; 16:23, 24, 26; Acts 3:6; Ephesians 5:20. The use of the Divine Name implies a frame of mind rather than a form of speech (Matthew 10:26; 18:5; Acts 3:16).

But what exactly does it mean to pray in the all-prevailing Name? It is certain that it does not imply the repetition of a phrase, with no more relationship to the prayer offered, as a label has to the parcel it is tied to. "In His Name" loosely appended to a prayer does not convert an unholy desire into a worthy one. The phrase is not a cheap sesame to open a door in heaven for those who use it.

"For Christ's sake," or "In His Name" indicate the key to the true motive in prayer. The phrases mean that Christ is Lord of our prayer-life (I Corinthians 12:3) and that our prayers must have His sanction ere He can endorse them for payment by God. The use of the words implies that we are praying as He would pray if in our place. "In His Name" signifies, *In His nature*, that is, according to all He is in Himself, and all He has accomplished.

Prayer truly offered for Christ's sake, or in His stead, cannot fail. If unChristlike, as we use the phrase, prayer will be unavailing. We must have His mind (Philippians 2:5) and correspondence with His will and harmony with His wishes (Acts 19:13-16). As we give Him the right of way in our life, our prayers find the right of way in God's program. Dr. R. A. Torrey writes —

> To pray in the Name of Jesus Christ is to recognize that we have no claims on God whatever, that God owes us nothing whatever, that we deserve nothing of God; but, believing what God Himself tells us about Jesus Christ's claim upon Him, we ask God for things on the ground of Jesus Christ's claim upon God.

The disciples knew the power of praying in the Divine Name (Romans 10:12; I Corinthians 1:2; II Corinthians 12:8, 9). They never raised any objection to speaking to God in another's name. Some have argued that Old Testament saints prayed directly to God and that prayer is made poorer if we now have to come to God indirectly through a mediator. But as M. P. Falling points out in his most valuable book on *Extempore Prayer:* "The whole beauty of our Saviour's place and aid in the economy of prayer is misunderstood and misrepresented. Through Christ the world has discovered its kinship to God. By the way in which God has made Himself known to man, man can best come to God" (John 14:6).

All we seek in prayer must be for the glory of the Divine Name. If our prayers are self-weighted, they will never rise very high. All selfish or unworthy desires must be shunned. The spirit of any prayer must be, "Thine is the glory" (Matthew 6:13).

In the Spirit

Another important instruction regarding successful prayer is that of knowing how to pray in the Holy Spirit (Ephesians 6:18; Jude 20). He must pray in and through us. He it is who helps our weakness in prayer and makes intercession to the will of God (Romans 8:9, 26, 27). It is God the Spirit who indites true prayer in the heart. We pray in the Spirit, through the merits of Christ, to the Father. To pray in the Spirit means consciously to place ourselves under the Holy Spirit's influence. He, it is, who makes our conscience sensitive to sin and inspires prayers God delights to listen to. Andrew Murray has given us the pregnant thought —

> The Spirit breathing, the Son's intercession,
> the Father's will — these three become one in us.

B. PRAYER AS PRACTICED BY CHRIST

That Jesus taught the necessity of prayer by personal example is a striking feature of the Gospels. Dr. S. D. Gordon in his penetrating book, *Quiet Talks on Prayer,* tells us that "there are two ways of receiving instruction; one, by being told; the other, by watching someone else. The latter is the simpler and surer way. How better can we learn how to pray than by watching how Jesus prayed, and then try to imitate Him . . . He Himself prayed when down here surrounded by our same circumstances and temptations."

Jesus loved to pray. Prayer was a part of His life and was as involuntary as His breathing. Prayer was His regular habit and His resort in every emergency. In a most impressive paragraph Dr. Gordon says that if we turn to the the Gospels we find —

> The picture of a praying Jesus like an etching, a sketch in black and white, the fewest possible strokes of the pen, a scratch here, a line there, frequently a single word added by one writer to the narrative of the other, which gradually bring to view the outline of a lone figure with upturned face.

We are told that in the days of His flesh Jesus offered up prayers and supplications (Hebrews 5:7), yet apart from one full prayer (John 17), only a few fragments of all the prayers He prayed through His sojourn of 33 years among men are recorded. During the so-called

30 silent years, He must have prayed often and long, yet no prayers of this period have been preserved for our edification.

If we gather together all the prayers of Christ as set forth in the Gospels, we could repeat them all inside of ten minutes, yet what extended prayer-periods must have been His especially when He spent whole nights in prayer. At all times He practiced the principles of true prayer which He enumerated in His precepts and parables. Dr. Gordon informs us that, "Of the 15 mentions of His praying found in the Four Gospels, it is interesting to note that while Matthew gives 3, and Mark and John each 4, it is Luke, Paul's companion and mirror-like friend, who, in all such allusions, supplies most of the picture . . . The Holy Spirit makes it plain throughout Luke's narrative that the Man Christ Jesus prayed; prayed much; needed to pray; loved to pray."

A brief reference to the prayers of Christ might suffice at this point. Fuller notice will be taken of them as we reach them in the narratives in which they are mentioned.

Prayer at His Baptism

(Luke 3:21, 22)

Now when all the people were baptized, it came to pass, that Jesus also being baptized, and praying, the heaven was opened, And the Holy Ghost descended in a bodily shape like a dove upon him, and a voice came from heaven, which said, Thou art my beloved Son; in thee I am well pleased.   — Luke 3:21, 22

This is the first mention out of Luke's records of our Lord's prayers. While the first three Gospels tell of Jesus' double baptism — by water and the Spirit — only Luke adds "and praying." While waiting in prayer, the Gift, without which Christ could not commence His ministry, was bestowed upon Him (Acts 10:38). "Standing in Jordan, He waits and prays until the blue above is burst through by the gleams of the glory-like from the upper side and the dove-like Spirit wings down and abides upon Him."

Prayer after a Crowded Day

(Luke 4:42; Mark 1:35)

And when it was day, he departed and went into a desert place: and the people sought him, and came unto him, and stayed him, that he should not depart from them.   — Luke 4:42
And in the morning, rising up a great while before day, he went out, and departed into a solitary place, and there prayed.   — Mark 1:35

What Luke hints at Mark elaborates upon. Jesus, after a crowded day before, arose early and went out into a solitary place to pray. Those, who labor hard in the Lord's work on His Day, feel like an extra hour's sleep on the Monday. But Jesus had another way of resting in addition to sleep. Sometimes praying was His way of resting. So before He went out to meet the old crowds of yesterday, prayer re-invigorated Him, sweetened and strengthened His spirit.

Prayer As an Escape from Popularity
(Luke 5:15, 16)

But so much the more went there a fame abroad of him: and great multitudes came together to hear, and to be healed by him of their infirmities. And he withdrew himself into the wilderness, and prayed.
— Luke 5:15, 16

Christ could see Satan coming with the crowds. His fame was quickly spreading and there was the danger of becoming a popular idol. But Jesus had no inclinations toward self-honor or self-glory. In the wilderness, Christ had gained the victory over all satanic temptation in the direction of popularity. If one is privileged to face crowds for Christ, receiving an unusual amount of fame and public acclaim thereby, prayer is the only avenue of escape from the perils of popularity.

Prayer after a Trying Day
(Mark 6:30, 31)

And the apostles gathered themselves together unto Jesus, and told him all things, both what they had done, and what they had taught. And he said unto them, Come ye yourselves apart into a desert place, and rest a while: for there were many coming and going, and they had no leisure so much as to eat.   — Mark 6:30, 31

After the news of John Baptist's tragic death, Jesus climbed the hill of prayer. In such a sorrow, coupled with the exhausting service of caring for great throngs, coming and going, Jesus had need of mental and physical rest and knew where to find it for Himself and His weary disciples.

Prayer with His Own
(Luke 9:18-31)

And it came to pass, as he was alone praying, his disciples were with him: and he asked them saying, Whom say the people that I am?
— Luke 9:18

Jesus was alone, so far as the crowds were concerned, but He is found drawing the twelve nearer to His inner life as His death approaches and inviting them to follow Him in death and glory (Luke 9:22-26). Many followers were to forsake Him, so the conditions of discipleship are more sharply put.

Prayer on the Mount
(Luke 9:29)

And as he prayed, the fashion of his countenance was altered, and his raiment was white and glistering.   — Luke 9:29

While praying on the Mount, Jesus was transfigured. What do we know of the transfigured life born of prayer? While Matthew and

Mark also record the Transfiguration scene it is only Luke who records this third night of prayer, and that as Christ prayed the fashion of His countenance was altered. "Look to Him, and be radiant" (Psalm 34:5 R.V.). Transfigured while praying! A shining face caused by contact with God (II Corinthians 3:18)!

Prayer after Success
(Luke 10:21)

In that hour Jesus rejoiced in spirit, and said, I thank thee, O Father, Lord of heaven and earth, that thou hast hid these things from the wise and prudent, and hast revealed them unto babes: even so, Father; for so it seemed good in thy sight.   — Luke 10:21

With the return of the Seventy after their fruitful service, Jesus gave thanks for the revelation of God made possible to, and through, humble men. The group Jesus had selected and sent out, two by two, came back with a joyful report, causing His heart to overflow with joy — a joy coming from the Holy Spirit whose fruit is joy (Galatians 5:22).

Christ seemed always to be conscious of His Father's presence, and it was the most natural thing to speak to Him, whether in joy or sorrow. Father and Son were ever on speaking terms. The line of communication between them was always open. Perfect unity between Father and Son is another aspect Luke notices (Luke 10:22; John 10:30) .

Prayer As a Habit
(Luke 11:1)

And it came to pass, that, as he was praying in a certain place, when he ceased, one of his disciples said unto him, Lord, teach us to pray, as John also taught his disciples.   — Luke 11:1

This reference is full of significance. It reveals Christ's *habit* of prayer. How dear that "certain place" was to Him! If He had need of such a retreat, how deep must be our need of one. Such a prayer-habit greatly impressed the disciples, who, without doubt, were praying men. But they could not live for three years with Jesus, without observing that He was a master in the fine art of prayer. They knew that prayer was His life and that when He prayed there were marvelous results. And who but the praying Christ can teach His own to pray? Who can teach like Him (Job 36:22)?

Jesus then went on to give His disciples the model prayer, called "The Lord's Prayer," and also the parable of prayer found in the friend begging bread for another friend (Luke 11:2-10).

Prayer at a Grave
(John 11:41, 42)

Then they took away the stone from the place where the dead was laid. And Jesus lifted up his eyes, and said, Father, I thank thee that thou hast heard me. And I knew that thou hearest me always:

but because of the people which stand by I said it, that they may
believe that thou hast sent me.   — John 11:41, 42

Doubtless Jesus had been much in prayer since hearing of the sickness of one He loved, but the great miracle of resurrection demanded
the manifestation of the power of God. Here we have one of the
ejaculatory prayers Jesus prayed. How brief a prayer it was, yet how
effective! Christ's certainty of faith in God as the Hearer and Answerer of prayer is in the note of thanksgiving, "I thank thee that
thou heardest me." Such faith believed that God could and would
raise the dead.

Prayer on a Mountain

(Mark 6:46)

And when he had sent them away, he departed into a mountain to
pray.   — Mark 6:46

Here is another mountain prayer of Jesus. While it was a night
of tranquillity for Him, what a night of trouble it was for His disciples. Yet seeing their fight against boisterous winds, He left the
mountain and walked upon the sea, much to the amazement of the
troubled toilers. It was easier to walk upon a stormy sea after having
walked with God upon the mountain.

Prayer of Anguish

(John 12:27, 28)

Now is my soul troubled; and what shall I say? Father, save me from
this hour: but for this cause came I unto this hour. Father, glorify
thy name. Then came there a voice from heaven, saying, I have both
glorified it, and will glorify it again.   — John 12:27, 28

The request of the Greeks (12:21) stirred Jesus to the depths. They
were part of the great outside world needing what He alone could
give. But the only way to meet such a need must have caused the
humanity in Him to shrink in horror. "Father, save me from this
hour." He knew, however, that there was no other way by which He
could draw all men unto Himself. Thus, "the intense conflict of
soul merges into the complete victory of a wholly surrendered will."

Prayer for a Backsliding Disciple

(Luke 22:31, 32)

And the Lord said, Simon, Simon, behold, Satan hath desired to have
you, that he may sift you as wheat: But I have prayed for thee, that
thy faith fail not: and when thou art converted, strengthen thy
brethren.   — Luke 22:31, 32

Jesus had tried to forewarn Peter of his coming test. Peter, however, was not fully aware of the power of Satan. But what can Satan
do against the prayers of Christ? Peter was prayed for by name, and
this prayer-habit of Christ's has never ceased. Is it not comforting

to know that each of us are on His prayer-list? Does He not live to make intercession for us, every one of us, no matter how insignificant in the eyes of the world we may appear?

Prayer of the Great High Priest

(John 17)

These words spake Jesus, and lifted up his eyes to heaven, and said, Father, the hour is come; glorify thy Son, that thy Son also may glorify thee: As thou hast given him power over all flesh, that he should give eternal life to as many as thou hast given him. And this is life eternal, that they might know thee the only true God, and Jesus Christ whom thou hast sent. I have glorified thee on the earth: I have finished the work which thou gavest me to do. And now, O Father, glorify thou me with thine own self with the glory which I had with thee before the world was. I have manifested thy name unto the men which thou gavest me out of the world: thine they were, and thou gavest them me; and they have kept thy word. Now they have known that all things whatsoever thou hast given me are of thee. For I have given unto them the words which thou gavest me; and they have received them, and have known surely that I came out from thee, and they have believed that thou didst send me. I pray for them: I pray not for the world, but for them which thou hast given me; for they are thine. And all mine are thine, and thine are mine; and I am glorified in them. And now I am no more in the world, but these are in the world, and I come to thee. Holy Father, keep through thine own name those whom thou hast given me, that they may be one, as we are. While I was with them in the world, I kept them in thy name: those that thou gavest me I have kept, and none of them is lost, but the son of perdition; that the scripture might be fulfilled. And now come I to thee; and these things I speak in the world, that they might have my joy fulfilled in themselves. I have given them thy word; and the world hath hated them, because they are not of the world, even as I am not of the world. I pray not that thou shouldest take them out of the world, but that thou shouldest keep them from the evil. They are not of the world, even as I am not of the world. Sanctify them through thy truth: thy word is truth. As thou hast sent me into the world, even so have I also sent them into the world. And for their sakes I sanctify myself, that they also might be sanctified through the truth. Neither pray I for these alone, but for them also which shall believe on me through their word; That they all may be one; as thou, Father, art in me, and I in thee, that they also may be one in us: that the world may believe that thou hast sent me. And the glory which thou gavest me I have given them; that they may be one, even as we are one: I in them, and thou in me, that they may be made perfect in one; and that the world may know that thou hast sent me, and hast loved them, as thou hast loved me. Father, I will that they also, whom thou hast given me, be with me where I am; that they may behold my glory, which thou hast given me: for thou lovedst me before the foundation of the world. O righteous Father, the world hath not known thee: but I have known thee, and these have known that thou hast sent me. And I have declared unto them thy name, and will declare it: that the love wherewith thou hast loved me may be in them, and I in them.   — John 17

With the complete prayer Jesus prayed, we come to the Holy of Holies in the New Testament. This intercessory prayer was offered beneath the shadow of the Cross. As He prays, Jesus thinks of His work as accomplished. "I have finished the work thou gavest me to do" (17:4). It would seem as if the high-priestly prayer moves in three circles —

Jesus speaks to God about His own life and labors (1-8).

Jesus prays for His own — those given Him by God (9-18).

Jesus prays for the multitudes who down through the ages listen to His word and believe (19-26).

Prayer in Gethsemane

(Luke 22:39-46; Matthew 26:36-46; John 18:1)

And he was withdrawn from them about a stone's cast, and kneeled down, and prayed, Saying, Father, if thou be willing, remove this cup from me: nevertheless not my will, but thine, be done. And there appeared an angel unto him from heaven, strengthening him. And being in an agony he prayed more earnestly: and his sweat was as it were great drops of blood falling down to the ground.
                                               — Luke 22:41-44

And he went a little farther, and fell on his face, and prayed, saying, O my Father, if it be possible, let this cup pass from me: nevertheless not as I will, but as thou wilt. And he cometh unto the disciples, and findeth them asleep, and saith unto Peter, What, could ye not watch with me one hour? Watch and pray, that ye enter not into temptation: the spirit indeed is willing, but the flesh is weak. He went away again the second time, and prayed, saying, O my Father, if this cup may not pass away from me, except I drink it, thy will be done. And he came and found them asleep again: for their eyes were heavy. And he left them, and went away again, and prayed the third time, saying the same words.   — Matthew 26:39-44

What a lifetime of temptation and anguish were crowded into that Gethsemane hour, as Jesus trod the winepress alone! Gethsemane was the trysting place of prayer which Judas betrayed. This treacherous friend "knew the place," but its sanctity had made no impression upon his disloyal heart.

Our finite minds cannot understand Christ's anguish of soul as He faced the reality of Calvary. The blood He was about to shed for "sinners lost and ruined by the fall," oozed from His brow as He prayed for the bitter cup to be kept from Him. But He rose from that season of conflict and communion, calm and victorious. "If this cup *cannot* pass away except I drink it, Thy will be done." Matthew tells us that He prayed three times using the same words (26:38-46). The crisis was over and out He went to die, not as a victim but as a mighty victor. None of the ransomed, however, will ever know how dark a night that was, or how deep were the waters through which He waded.

Prayer from the Cross

(Luke 23:34-46)

Then said Jesus, Father, forgive them; for they know not what they do. . . .   — Luke 23:34
And about the ninth hour Jesus cried with a loud voice, saying, Eli, Eli, lama sabachthani? that is to say, My God, my God, why hast thou forsaken me?   — Matthew 27:46
And when Jesus had cried with a loud voice, he said, Father into thy hands I commend my spirit: and having said thus, he gave up the ghost.   — Luke 23:46

Three times Christ prayed as He died upon the Cross.
  "Father, forgive them for they know not what they do."
  "My God, My God, why hast thou forsaken me?"
  "Father, into thy hands I commend my Spirit."
His closing breath was used to pray. Each of these prayers hold oceans of truth for our hearts as those redeemed by His blood. He prayed for His enemies: do we? He had a dread moment of loneliness as He bore our sin, yet in the darkness He could still pray, "*My* God." Dying, He committed Himself to God. May our end be as His!

> He prayed upon the mountain,
>   He prayed for you and me,
> He prayed in humble dwellings,
>   He prayed beside the sea.
>
> He prayed in early morning,
>   Prayed with all His might,
> He prayed at noonday and at dusk,
>   He prayed all thro' the night.
>
> He prayed for those who scorned Him,
>   For those who killed Him, too,
> He prayed, "Father forgive them:
>   They know not what they do."
>
> He prayed when He was lonely,
>   He prayed when He was sad,
> He prayed when He was weary,
>   He prayed when He was glad.
>
> He prayed for those in sorrow,
>   He prayed for those in sin,
> He prayed for those in trouble
>   That they might come to *Him*.
>   — D. W. L.

As there are one or two further particular features of our Lord's prayer-life worthy of note, it may prove helpful to summarize them at this juncture.

His Seasons of Prayer

While our Lord must have lived in unbroken fellowship with His Father, it would seem as if it was His regular habit to devote the early hours of the day to prayer for guidance and grace (Mark 1:35; John 7:16-18; 8:29; 12:49; Isaiah 30:4-6). In addition to set times for prayer, Christ sought opportunity for secret prayer as special needs arose. He prayed late at night after others had retired. He prayed at irregular intervals between times. He prayed before and after important events. It was His custom, always, to steal away and pray when the noises of earth were hushed.

Time does not matter, however, because God's ear is ever open to our cry. David prayed all day (Psalm 55:17; Acts 3:1). Daniel prayed at noon (Daniel 6:10). Paul and Silas prayed at midnight (Acts 16:25). Christ sometimes prayed all night (Mark 1:35). At all times, we have access into the presence of Him who awaits our sincere petitions.

His Spheres for Prayer

Jesus, who had nowhere to lay His head, had no fixed inner-chamber during His public career. His was no prayer-closet to which He could retire to make easier and habitual His fellowship with God. He loved Nature and often His prayer-chambers were the deserts, mountains and solitary places which He sought for their freedom from the discordant voices of earth. How Jesus liked to retreat to Bethany for prayer and fellowship with the three kindred souls there for whom He had a peculiar affection (John 11:5). No matter where we may be God can hear us. He heard Hagar in the wilderness, Jonah in the deep, Hezekiah in his bed, David in a cave, Peter on a ship, the thief on the cross.

While the place of prayer makes little difference we are not to forsake the assembling of ourselves for prayer and worship in places of prescribed worship (Hebrews 10:25). For us, there are the shut-doors and the sanctuary as spheres of contact with heaven.

His Spirit in Prayer

Beyond all matters relating to the place, period, posture and plan of prayer, is the spirit in which we approach God. There is the three-fold solitude of time, place and spirit, and Christ experienced all three phases. He lived in the spirit of prayer. He could be alone with God in a dense crowd, lost to all around save His inner thought. There was never a cloud between Father and Son. As has already been briefly noted, the greatest blessings of Christ's life came as the result of unbroken fellowship with God. Prayer was His life, His regular habit, His resort in every emergency, and consequently brought Him unmeasured power.

His Scope in Prayer

How varied were the prayers of Christ! He prayed for all kinds of people, and over everything.

He prayed in the great moments of life (Luke 3:21; 6:12, 13; 9:16; 9:29; 22:39-46).

He prayed for the little children, who were His concern (Matthew 19:13).

He prayed for others by name (Luke 22:32).

There are three things an intercessor must remember if his prayers for others are to prevail —

1. He must have a sincere desire for the highest interests of those for whom he prays (spiritual as well as material).
2. He must have the utmost confidence in divine promise and sufficiency to meet the need.
3. He must hold himself in readiness to cooperate in action as an outcome of his intercession. Christ certainly fulfilled all three requirements as He prayed, and still prays, so effectively for others (John 17; Hebrews 7:25).

He prayed with others, which is a habit we should cultivate. Mutual prayer at home or church, solves problems, cements friendship, sweetens the spirit, gladdens the heart of God (Malachi 3:16). How expressive are the following lines of Trench —

> Lord, what a change within us one short hour
> Spent in Thy presence will prevail to make —
> What heavy burdens from our bosoms take,
> What parched grounds refresh as with a shower!
> We kneel and all around us seems to lower;
> We rise, and all, the distant and the near,
> Stands forth in sunny outline, brave and clear;
> We kneel how weak, we rise how full of power!
> Why, therefore, should we do ourselves this wrong,
> Or others — that we are not always strong;
> That we are ever overborne with care;
> That we should ever weak or heartless be,
> Anxious or troubled, when with us in prayer,
> And joy and strength and courage are with Thee?

As we come to analyze the great prayers of the New Testament, especially those of the Gospels, it must be borne in mind that some of the incidents in the life of our Lord we mention as prayers were actually pleas offered to Him by needy hearts as they met Him going about doing good. If, as the lad replied in response to the teacher's question, "What is prayer?" — "Prayer is talking to Jesus," then many of the requests of the disciples come under the category of "Prayer."

We are only listing, however, the definite pleas presented to God by Christ, and the pleas presented to Christ by men and women in need of His power, pardon and peace.

Matthew

From the precepts, parables and practice of Jesus, much can be learned about such a holy art as prayer. While the general theme of the first Gospel is "The King and His Kingdom," Christ is also portrayed as One humble enough to bend a sympathetic ear to the cries of those in distress. We cannot fail to see Him in this Gospel as "The Sympathizing Jesus."

Prayer and the Necessity of Forgiveness

(Matthew 5:22-26; 6:12, 14, 15)

But I say unto you, That whosoever is angry with his brother without a cause shall be in danger of the judgment: and whosoever shall say to his brother, Raca, shall be in danger of the council: but whosoever shall say, Thou fool, shall be in danger of hell fire. Therefore if thou bring thy gift to the altar, and there rememberest that thy brother hath ought against thee; Leave there thy gift before the altar, and go thy way; first be reconciled to thy brother, and then come and offer thy gift. Agree with thine adversary quickly, whiles thou art in the way with him; lest at any time the adversary deliver thee to the judge, and the judge deliver thee to the officer, and thou be cast into prison. Verily I say unto thee, Thou shalt by no means come out thence, till thou hast paid the uttermost farthing.

— Matthew 5:22-26

And forgive us our debts, as we forgive our debtors. . . .
For if ye forgive men their trespasses, your heavenly Father will also forgive you: But if ye forgive not men their trespasses, neither will your Father forgive your trespasses.   — Matthew 6:12, 14, 15

Prayer for the forgiveness of those who abuse and persecute us is the highest form and the hardest, and includes all the lesser intercessions. Jesus, enforcing such a spirit, practiced it upon the Cross at a time when prayers for forgiveness of His crucifiers was nothing less than a miracle. Those who intercede for their enemies are not likely to forget their friends. The prayer, "Forgive us our debts," excludes all possibility of self-righteousness.

Nothing is more Godlike than a spirit of forgiveness. Nothing is more Christlike than prayer for enemies. An old divine wrote, "Love for love is but justice and gratitude: love for no love is favor and kindness; but love for **hatred** is a most divine temper." Christ taught that we are to pray for, and forgive, those who treat us unworthily. How can we expect God to forgive us our sins as we plead with Him to do so, if we are not willing to forgive those who offend us and pray for their well-being? The unforgiving remains unforgiven.

Prayer and Hypocrisy
(Matthew 6:5-7; Luke 11:1-4)

And when thou prayest, thou shalt not be as the hypocrites are: for they love to pray standing in the synagogues and in the corners of the streets, that they may be seen of men. Verily I say unto you, They have their reward. But thou, when thou prayest, enter into thy closet, and when thou hast shut thy door, pray to thy Father which is in secret; and thy Father which seeth in secret shall reward thee openly. But when ye pray, use not vain repetitions, as the heathen do: for they think that they shall be heard for their much speaking. Be not ye therefore like unto them: — Matthew 6:5-7

He who sees in secret (6:6) knows whether our approach to Him is true or false. The hypocrites, although they stood at prayer, earned Christ's condemnation (6:5), who is here found teaching the necessity of reality and naturalness in prayer. When people pose as they pray, or fashion prayers simply for the sake of effect, all the glory and strength and power of prayer vanishes. Hypocrites never pray in secret. Prayers that are a pretense require an audience. What use are prayers beautiful in sentiment and phrasing if they have no life in them? We must guard ourselves against mechanical and repetitious praying.

We are not heard for our much speaking (6:7). "We may pray most when we say least, and we may pray least when we say most." Prayer is a prodigious farce if it "goeth out of feigned lips" (Psalm 17:1), but a powerful force when it comes from a heart right with God (I John 3:22). The prayers of a hypocrite find a deaf ear (Job 27:9; 35:13).

While Christ does not fix the *length* of our prayers, He forbids the repetition of a need, as if God does not hear. "It is not improbable," observes Barnes, "that Christ intended to condemn the practice of long prayers. His own supplications were remarkably short."

Secret prayer is also urged by Christ in this dissertation of His (6:6). "Closet" prayer, He calls it. He Himself had no door to shut. Homeless and ceaselessly on the move, He yet sought out an undisturbed place of retreat, whether a garden or desert place. The shut door for us conveys the same idea of a place where we find ourselves shut off from the world and shut in with God. At times the shut door is more spiritual than local. Some there are who live in restricted quarters, but who yet experience quiet of heart while surroundings are anything but tranquil. Quietude of spirit to pray, even when distractions surround us, can be ours, even as it was the Master's.

Prayer As Taught by Christ
(Matthew 6:9-13)

After this manner therefore pray ye: Our Father which art in heaven, Hallowed be thy name. Thy kingdom come, Thy will be done in

earth, as it is in heaven. Give us this day our daily bread. And forgive us our debts, as we forgive our debtors. And lead us not into
temptation, but deliver us from evil: For thine is the kingdom, and
the power, and the glory, for ever. Amen.   — Matthew 6:9-13

While this section is commonly known as "The Lord's Prayer,"
actually it was not a prayer He Himself prayed. There are some
aspects of the prayer Jesus could not use as the sinless Son of God.
It was a model prayer which He taught His own to use. Being made
up of invocation, petition and doxology, in this prayer He taught
the necessity of method even in our prayers.

"When ye pray." This exhortation settles once for all man's instinct and capacity for prayer. Here is Christ's warrant that man is
"a praying animal." Haysman says in *En Route*, "The rich, the
healthy, the happy seldom pray." But here is one prayer which saints
and sinners alike are fond of using. Burgess and Proudlove inform
us that "the Jewish Rabbis were in the habit of teaching the people
outline prayers which were known as 'Index Prayers.' They would
gather together a number of short sentences each of which suggested
an item for prayer. They would recite one sentence and then, before
proceeding with the next, would enlarge upon it, drawing out some of
its implications and applications. So, when Christ's disciples sought
instruction in prayer, He gave them an 'Index Prayer' (6:9) ."

We likewise gather from this pearl of prayers that prayer is not
giving God information about ourselves (6:8, 32). We do not pray
to acquaint God of our needs nor to persuade Him to hear us. His
love needs neither to be induced or coaxed (7:7, 8). Professor Mc-
Fadyen reminds us that Christ, "both by precept and example, taught
the duty of brevity in prayer, and grounded it upon God's knowledge
of our needs (6:7, 8)."

In this most complete and connected expression of Christ's conception of prayer, we can discern seven voices —
1.   The Voice of the Son — "Our Father which is in heaven"
2.   The Voice of the Saint — "Hallowed be Thy Name"
3.   The Voice of the Subject — "Thy kingdom come"
4.   The Voice of the Servant — "Thy will be done"
5.   The Voice of the Suppliant — "Give us our daily bread"
6.   The Voice of the Sinner — "Forgive us our debts"
7.   The Voice of the Sojourner — "Lead us," etc.

Prayer As Specified by Christ

(Matthew 7:7-11)

Ask, and it shall be given you; seek, and ye shall find; knock, and it
shall be opened unto you: For every one that asketh receiveth; and
he that seeketh findeth; and to him that knocketh it shall be opened.
Or what man is there of you, whom if his son ask bread, will he
give him a stone? Or if he ask a fish, will he give him a serpent?
If ye then, being evil, know how to give good gifts unto your chil-

dren, how much more shall your Father which is in heaven give good
things to them that ask him?   — Matthew 7:7-11

Each generation has to learn anew the secret and credibility of
prayer. Bishop Winnington Ingram in his helpful volume, *Banners
of the Christian Faith*, illustrates the truth our Lord is here expounding with spiritual insight and clarity:

> When Queen Victoria was opening the Town Hall of Sheffield,
> she had put into her hand a little golden key, and she was told as
> she sat in her carriage that she only had to turn the golden key
> and in a moment the Town Hall gates of Sheffield would fly open.
> In obedience to the authority of experts who gave her the di-
> rections, she turned the golden key, and in a moment, by the
> action of electric wires, the Town Hall gates of Sheffield flew
> open. Exactly in the same way Jesus Christ must know one thing,
> if he knows anything, and that is, what opens heaven's gates. He
> must know that; he must know what golden key it is that opens
> heaven's gates; and in his teaching he reiterated over and over
> again, as if he thought that this was one of the things we should
> find it hardest to believe: "Ask, and it shall be given; seek, and
> ye shall find; knock, and it shall be opened unto you." And I say
> that if we are justified in believing in the divinity of Christ, then
> we are justified in going a step further and saying that His
> authority is good enough to make us believe that the golden key
> of prayer, if we use it, will open the gates of heaven.

If our knees are "heaven's knockers," then may we keep them
supple enough to knock long and hard. "Knock— keep on knocking
— and it shall be opened unto you" (7:7). The three laws governing
our prayer-life, three steps into the very heart of God are, *Ask, Seek,
Knock*. As prayer is "making request with earnestness and zeal, as
for something desired; making entreaty or supplication," the word
ASK, made up of the first letter of these fixed laws, Ask, Seek,
Knock, epitomizes the elements making up true prayer.

Some there are who affirm that they have asked and sought for
certain desired blessings but prayer was not answered. The "asking,"
of course, is conditioned by sympathy with God's will and purpose
(James 4:3; John 15:7; Psalm 37:4). *Asking* implies dependence
upon God, the coming to Him as beggars. *Seeking* speaks of endeavor, an urgency constraining us to search until we find. *Knocking*
carries the idea of importunity, the unwillingness to let God go until
He blesses us. Our difficulty is the lack of simplicity of approach to
God, of intense and purposeful praying, the lack of expectant waiting
upon God. Dr. Adoniram Judson as he lay dying heard of the remarkable answer to his prayer for the Jews when he was a missionary
in Burma, and he uttered this testimony: "I never prayed sincerely
and earnestly for anything but it came; at some time — no matter how
distant the day — somehow, in some shape, probably the last I should
have devised, it came."

We gather from our Lord's teaching that good things are given to men whether they ask God or not. He causes His sun to shine and His rain to fall no less upon the unjust than upon the just (7:11). Alas, no prayer of gratitude arises from the hearts of the godless blessed by God (Psalm 107:8). As the kindest of fathers, God is ever willing to bestow gifts upon His needy children (7:11). "Good things" are changed into "The Holy Spirit" (Matthew 7:11 with Luke 11:13). *Goodness* is His fruit (Galatians 5:22).

Prayer of a Leper
(Matthew 8:1-4; Mark 1:40-45; Luke 5:12-14)

And, behold, there came a leper and worshipped him, saying, Lord, if thou wilt, thou canst make me clean.   —Matthew 8:2

As our Lord is described coming down from the mountain (8:1), it is most likely that He had been engaged in a season of communion with God (Mark 1:35; 6:46). How poignant was the prayer of this diseased man, "Lord, if Thou wilt, thou canst make me clean"! How swift was the answer of Christ, "Immediately his leprosy was cleansed."

Christ imposed silence upon the cleansed leper but he blazed abroad the matter and all unconsciously hindered the work of the Master (Luke 5:14, 15).

Prayer of the Centurion
(Matthew 8:5-13; Luke 7:1-10)

And when Jesus was entered into Capernaum, there came unto him a centurion, beseeching him, And saying, Lord, my servant lieth at home sick of the palsy, grievously tormented. And Jesus saith unto him, I will come and heal him. The centurion answered and said, Lord, I am not worthy that thou shouldest come under my roof: but speak the word only, and my servant shall be healed. For I am a man under authority, having soldiers under me: and I say to this man, Go, and he goeth; and to another, Come, and he cometh; and to my servant, Do this, and he doeth it.   — Matthew 8:5-9

The humility, faith and request of this man of authority greatly impressed Christ, leading Him to declare that He had not encountered such faith in prayer, no, not in Israel (8:10). Such believing prayer was graciously answered (8:13). Recovery from sickness was often acknowledged by gratitude, expressed either personally or publicly.

Prayer in Peril
(Matthew 8:23-27; Mark 4:36-41; Luke 8:22-25)

And, behold, there arose a great tempest in the sea, insomuch that the ship was covered with the waves: but he was asleep. And his disciples came to him, and awoke him, saying, Lord, save us: we perish.   — Matthew 8:24, 25

Among the sea-prayers of the Bible this one was brief yet heartfelt, "Lord, save us: we perish." Here is another of those ejaculatory-prayers we have already mentioned and of which Dr. Alexander

Whyte says they are the perfection and the finish of all these kinds of prayers in which we make haste. "When ejaculatory prayer has once taken possession of any man's heart and habits, that man is not very far off from his Father's house. For —

> Each moment by ejaculated prayer,
> He takes possession of his mansion there."

Jaculum means "a dart." Ejaculatory prayer! A prayer shot up like a spear out of a soldier's hand; shot up like an arrow sped off an archer's sudden string . . . "Every time the clock strikes, call, ejaculate and call." The disciples "made haste" to pray as shipwreck faced them. Their recognition of the Master's *Lordship* assured them that He would be able to relieve their distress. As the "Lord," He is adequate for all the crises and circumstances of life. Because He is the Creator, the elements He created obey Him.

> The wild waves hushed, the angry deep
> Sank, like a little child, to sleep.

Prayer of Maniacs

(Matthew 8:28-34; Mark 1:1-20; Luke 8:26-37)

And when he was come to the other side into the country of the Gergesenes, there met him two possessed with devils, coming out of the tombs, exceeding fierce, so that no man might pass by that way. And, behold, they cried out, saying, What have we to do with thee, Jesus, thou Son of God? art thou come hither to torment us before the time? And there was a good way off from them an herd of many swine feeding. So the devils besought him, saying, If thou cast us out, suffer us to go away into the herd of swine. — Matthew 8:28-31

Here we have the spectacle, not only of the demon-possessed pleading for emancipation, the demons themselves recognizing Christ's deity and beseeching Him not to interfere with them. But all hell must obey Him who defeated the devil both in the wilderness and at Calvary. As we plead the efficacious blood of Jesus we become jubilant overcomers. Satanic forces have to yield to the all-victorious Saviour (Revelation 12:7-12). Do we know how to pray prevailingly for the demon-possessed around us today? The owner of the swine prayed Jesus to depart (Matthew 5:17) and the delivered ones prayed that they might remain with their wonderful Deliverer (Mark 5:18).

Prayer of Jairus

(Matthew 9:18, 19, 23-26; Mark 5:22-24, 35-43; Luke 8:40-42, 49-56)

While he spake these things unto them, behold, there came a certain ruler, and worshipped him, saying, My daughter is even now dead: but come and lay thy hand upon her, and she shall live.
— Matthew 9:18

How immediately Jesus responded to need (9:19)! Here, however, we have a miracle dove-tailing a miracle, for on the way to revive the dead girl, a diseased woman was healed. How unbelieving men are, even in the presence of the mighty Lord of life — "They laughed Him to scorn" (9:24)! Ridicule was soon silenced. The dead girl arose and the fame of the miracle spread abroad (9:26).

Prayer of the Diseased Woman

(Matthew 9:20-22; Mark 5:25-34; Luke 8:43-48)

And, behold, a woman, which was diseased with an issue of blood twelve years, came behind him, and touched the hem of his garment: For she said within herself, If I may but touch his garment, I shall be whole. — Matthew 9:20, 21

Jairus' daughter was twelve years old, and the period of this woman's sufferings coincided with the age of the ruler's daughter (9:20). As "the issue of blood" brought with it ceremonial uncleanness (Leviticus 15:26), the woman shrank from applying to the Healer openly and from confessing afterward what she had done. Ellicott remarks, "Jairus' sorrow was sudden after twelve years of joyful hope; hers had brought with it, through twelve long years, the sickness of hope deferred." Prayer, however, in both cases prevailed. Weak though her faith may have been, it was accepted and she became the recipient of Christ's healing virtue. He is the Healer of the souls and bodies of men.

Prayer of Two Blind Men

(Matthew 9:27-31)

And when Jesus departed thence, two blind men followed him, crying, and saying, Thou son of David, have mercy on us.
— Matthew 9:27

In their request to Christ, the blind addressed Him as "the Son of David," an indication that they accepted Him as the promised, expected Christ (see also 15:22; 20:30, 31; Mark 10:47; Luke 18:38, 39). What a touching prayer they offered in "Have mercy on us"! Such a request implies that Christ could restore their sight. "Faith was the antecedent condition of the miracle." We must pray believingly. As blind men they could not see Jesus as the other afflicted souls we have considered. They were encouraged to seek Him by the sympathy of His look. This absence was supplied by acts, naturally connected with the purpose to heal them. "Then touched He their eyes." It is to be regretted that these men, blessed with sight, did not realize that "to obey is better than sacrifice." They disobeyed the vehement command of Jesus not to publish the miracle abroad.

Prayer for Laborers

(Matthew 9:37-39; Luke 10:2)

Then saith he unto his disciples, The harvest truly is plenteous, but the labourers are few; Pray ye therefore the Lord of the harvest, that he will send forth labourers into his harvest. — Matthew 9:37, 38

A study of Christ's teaching on prayer, and also His own prayers and those He exhorted others to offer, shows they were predominantly spiritual. Pre-eminently the Kingdom of God had to be sought (Matthew 6:33). "One of the chief prayers of those who love the Lord of the harvest is that labourers be sent into His harvest. The prayers of the early Church for boldness in preaching the Gospel shew that she had learned the lesson of Jesus well (Acts 4:29)." Are we as earnest as we should be in this matter? Do we pray with intensity that more laborers might be sent forth into fields white unto harvest?

All whom the Lord sends forth are given all necessary grace to witness for Him (10:18, 19), especially if their witness involves persecution. "Be not anxious," is one of the great watchwords of Jesus (Matthew 6:25, 34; 10:19). Opening the City Council meeting with prayer, Councilman Carl Stillwell expressed himself thus: "Our Heavenly Father, fill our mouths with what we should say, and nudge us when we've said enough." All of us have need to say *Amen!* to a prayer like that.

Prayer of Christ's Gratitude to God

(Matthew 11:25-27)

At that time Jesus answered and said, I thank thee, O Father, Lord ɔf heaven and earth, because thou hast hid these things from the wise and prudent, and hast revealed them unto babes. Even so, Father: for so it seemed good in thy sight. All things are delivered unto me of my Father: and no man knoweth the Son, but the Father; neither knoweth any man the Father, save the Son, and he to whomsoever the Son will reveal him.   — Matthew 11:25-27

Luke connects this prayer with the return of the Seventy (10:17-24). However, it may be associated with the return of the Twelve, whose report greatly cheered the Master's heart (Mark 6:30; Luke 9:10). Thanksgiving occupied a large place in the prayers of Christ. The phrase, "I thank Thee," means, "I acknowledge with praise and thanksgiving." He knew God to be the One who *heard* prayer (11:25; Mark 7:34; John 11:41). His was the glad consciousness that His Father's ear was ever open to His cry and so His prayer was a happy one (Luke 10:21). Christ based His prayer on the consciousness of His own unique relation to His Father and to men. It was thus He prayed for the glory of God and Himself (John 17:1). We, too, have received the spirit of adoption whereby we cry *Abba, Father* (Galatians 4:6). Doubting souls need to be re-assured by a sign (Judges 6:36). "The best need no sign, and the bad need look for none" (Matthew 12:39).

Prayer on a Mountain

(Matthew 14:23)

And when he had sent the multitudes away, he went up into a mountain apart to pray: and when the evening was come, he was there alone.   — Matthew 14:23

Christ was not ashamed publicly to say grace for His meals (14:19).
It is amazing how many professing Christians sit down to eat without
giving God thanks. Jesus never forgot gratitude for material blessings
(Matthew 15:36; Mark 6:41; 8:6, 7, etc.). How He loved "the great
spacious silence of the night, when He could be alone (14:23). The
mountain, the evening, the loneliness — these things are the earthly
background of the strength of Christ."

> Cold mountains, and the midnight air
> Witness'd the fervour of His prayer.

Devotional solitude is commended by the high example and commanded by the high authority of Christ. To Him, solitude was
essential. Daniel Heitmeyer in his poem, "He Prayed Alone," beautifully expressed the glimpse Matthew gives us of Jesus outstaying
the night on the mountain in prayer —

> The care-filled day in Galilee seemed long;
>   Now, golden on the sea, the low sun shone,
> And, each on his own way intent, the throng
>   Trudged homeward, while the Nazarene, alone
>   With His vast vision of a kingdom fair,
>   Among the darkling hills remained in prayer.

> In street and dusty lane the people walked
>   In drowsy silence; fishers on the shore
> Worked late with nets and gear, and idly talked
>   Of prices and of wives and weather lore;
>   A starveling, supperless, crept in a shed,
>   And thought on things the Lord that day had said.

> In Rome great Caesar made a night's carouse;
>   Kept priests at altars watched a dying flame,
> Philosophers rehearsed old whys and hows,
>   And wastrels dallied late in dens of shame: —
>   And on a clouded Galilean height
>   The Nazarene, alone, outstay'd the night.

Prayer of Peter in Distress

(Matthew 14:28-30)

And Peter answered him and said, Lord, if it be thou, bid me come
unto thee on the water. And he said, Come. And when Peter was
come down out of the ship, he walked on the water, to go to Jesus.
But when he saw the wind boisterous, he was afraid; and beginning
to sink, he cried, saying, Lord, save me.   — Matthew 14:28-30

Here is the shortest prayer one could pray, "Lord save me." Peter
has been given the assurance that the One walking on the storm-
tossed sea was the One who made it (Psalm 95:5), and eager to obey
Christ as He called him to walk on the water, Peter's faith seems to
sustain him for a little. The conflict between faith and sight, however, was too much for Peter, for when he turned his eyes from Christ

to the boisterous waves, sight triumphed and faith was worsted. Supernatural strength left Peter and, beginning to sink, he cried out in his agony. How gracious it was of the Master to help "little faith" with His powerful, sustaining grasp!

Prayer of the Syro-Phoenician Woman
(Matthew 15:21-28; Mark 7:24-30)

Then Jesus went thence, and departed into the coasts of Tyre and Sidon. And, behold, a woman of Canaan came out of the same coasts, and cried unto him, saying, Have mercy on me, O Lord, thou son of David; my daughter is grievously vexed with a devil. But he answered her not a word. And his disciples came and besought him, saying, Send her away; for she crieth after us. But he answered and said, I am not sent but unto the lost sheep of the house of Israel. Then came she and worshipped him, saying, Lord, help me. But he answered and said, It is not meet to take the children's bread, and to cast it to dogs. And she said, Truth, Lord: yet the dogs eat of the crumbs which fall from their masters' table. Then Jesus answered and said unto her, O woman, great is thy faith: be it unto thee even as thou wilt. And her daughter was made whole from that very hour.
— Matthew 15:21-28

Before dealing with this woman's prayer of distress, we must draw attention to the wrong and right approach to God. Those condemned by Christ did not "pray in their prayers" (15:8). Christ Himself lived His prayers. They were part of Him (15:36). A true heart is necessary when we draw nigh to God (Hebrews 10:2). The prayer of the upright is ever His delight (Proverbs 15:8).

Mark identifies the woman of Canaan as "a Greek." Her prayer proves that the fame of Jesus had spread beyond the limits of Galilee and that He was recognized as the Messiah. At first, Jesus paid no attention to the woman's cry for help (15:23). Did He want to test her faith? Ellicott suggests that we here see "the prevailing power of prayer working on the sympathy of Christ, leading Him to pass beyond the ordinary limits of His appointed work." The disciples urged Christ to grant her request and dismiss her. Christ's somewhat harsh statement was met by the woman in all humility and taking her place among "the dogs" she begged for "crumbs" of Him who came as the Saviour of the World. Her faith was rewarded and commended, and reaching home she found her child calm and peaceful. Restless frenzy had vanished.

Prayer for a Lunatic Son
(Matthew 17:14-21; Mark 9:14-29; Luke 9:37-43)

And when they were come to the multitude, there came to him a certain man, kneeling down to him, and saying, Lord, have mercy on my son: for he is a lunatick, and sore vexed: for ofttimes he falleth into the fire, and oft into the water. And I brought him to thy disciples, and they could not cure him.   — Matthew 17:14-16

The disciples were unable to relieve this mentally deficient boy because of their little faith (17:19, 20). The distressed father recognized Christ's *Lordship*, "Lord," he prayed, "have mercy on my son." Somewhat despairing, he appealed to our Lord's pity. Then came the cry of faith, struggling with his despair: "Lord, I believe; help Thou my unbelief," and faith, although weak, was accepted as sufficient. For it is not faith that saves, whether weak or strong, but the Object of our faith.

Scribes and disciples were rebuked by Christ (17:14), for they were alike in their want of the faith which utters itself in prayer to the Father. Their lack of faith was the cause of powerlessness in the work of healing.

Prayer in Unity
(Matthew 18:19, 20)

Again I say unto you, That if two of you shall agree on earth as touching anything that they shall ask, it shall be done for them of my Father which is in heaven. For where two or three are gathered together in my name, there am I in the midst of them.

— Matthew 18:19, 20

The promise of Christ to answer the prayers of gathered saints is dependent on implied conditions. Believers who meet to pray must be gathered together in the Name of Christ (18:20). Surely this means that we are to plead His merit and ask in entire submission to the will of God. It was the failure of these conditions that prevented the answer to the prayer of the sons of Zebedee, who asked they knew not what (20:20).

While Christ taught the need of private prayer, He also instructs His own in the need and nature of united prayer. The latter form of prayer is most powerful, seeing it recognizes our common membership in God's family, as well as our common membership of Christ's Body. "Where three are there, there is a church." Then it is the presence of the Unseen Christ Himself that makes united prayer so mighty. "There am I." Here is one of the greatest of all prayer secrets. "No simpler words could be found in all the dictionary; no profounder truth could be found in all the language." As we meet in His Name, *He* is in the midst, not as a mere spiritual influence, but as the One gloriously alive forevermore.

Did Christ know that prayer-meetings would not be popular when He spoke of "two or three" gathering in His Name for prayer (18:16, 20)? How much the church owes to "the little flock" carrying a burden for its spiritual welfare the church itself will never know!

Prayer in a Parable
(Matthew 18:23-35)

Therefore is the kingdom of heaven likened unto a certain king, which would take account of his servants. And when he had begun to reckon, one was brought unto him, which owed him ten thousand talents. But forasmuch as he had not to pay, his lord commanded him to be sold, and his wife, and children, and all that he had, and payment to be made. The servant therefore fell down, and worshipped him, saying, Lord, have patience with me, and I will pay thee all. Then the lord of that servant was moved with compassion, and loosed him, and forgave him the debt. But the same servant went out, and found one of his fellowservants, which owed him an hundred pence: and he laid hands on him, and took him by the throat, saying, Pay me that thou owest. And his fellowservant fell down at his feet, and besought him, saying, Have patience with me, and I will pay thee all. And he would not: but went and cast him into prison, till he should pay the debt. So when his fellowservants saw what was done, they were very sorry, and came and told unto their lord all that was done. Then his lord, after that he had called him, said unto him, O thou wicked servant, I forgave thee all that debt, because thou desiredst me: Shouldest not thou also have had compassion on thy fellowservant, even as I had pity on thee? And his lord was wroth, and delivered him to the tormentors, till he should pay all that was due unto him. So likewise shall my heavenly Father do also unto you, if ye from your hearts forgive not every one his brother their trespasses.   — Matthew 18:23-35

Associated with this parable of debts is Christ's favorite theme of forgiveness. He was so insistent upon the importance of forgiveness and the condition upon which it depends (6:14; Mark 11:25). The attitude of the servant who could not pay his debt is worthy of note. As an inferior in the presence of a superior, "he fell down and prostrated himself and said: 'Have patience with me and I will pay thee all.'" We were deep in debt to God and had nothing whatever to meet the bill, but "Jesus paid it all." The lord of the servant in debt "forgave him the debt," but forgiven he was not willing to forgive. Well might we ask the question, "Can a man who has really been justified and pardoned become thus merciless?" Experience teaches that a person justified, but not sanctified, can treat fellow-believers in a most harsh, loveless and ungodly fashion. The faith of such is not one which "worketh by love" (Galatians 5:6).

Prayer for a Privileged Position

(Matthew 20:20-28; Mark 10:35-45)

Then came to him the mother of Zebedee's children with her sons, worshipping him, and desiring a certain thing of him. And he said unto her, What wilt thou? She saith unto him, Grant that these my two sons may sit, the one on thy right hand, and the other on the left, in thy kingdom.   — Matthew 20:20, 21

The request of Salome, the mother of James and John, was one that Christ could not answer and which also produced indignation among the other ten disciples. Many of our prayers are not answered simply because we know not what we ask (20:22), even although we come before the Lord "worshipping Him" (20:20). If He is truly *Lord* of our life, the Spirit will guard us from offering prayers He cannot answer.

Doubtless Salome felt she had some warrant for her petition. One of her sons, John, was known emphatically as "the disciple whom Jesus loved" (John 13:23; 19:26; 20:3), and had the honor of nearness to Christ (John 13:23). Her other son, James, was one of the three who had witnessed the Transfiguration of Christ (Matthew 17:1). Both James and John had been marked for special honor (Mark 3:17), but in infinite tenderness and sadness Jesus answered Salome, "ye know not what ye ask" (20:22). The cost of position near to Him in glory could not be obtained by identification with Him in suffering. That both James and John drank of the bitter cup is proved by the baptism of blood James experienced (Acts 12:2), and the baptism of persecution and loneliness in Patmos John endured (Revelation 1:9). Let us be careful how we pray. Some answers to our petitions may be costly. A. Procter has given us the lines —

> Pray! though the gift you ask for
> May never comfort your fears,
> May never repay your pleading,
> Yet pray, and with hopeful tears!
> An answer — not that you long for,
> But diviner — will come some day;
> Your eyes are too dim to see it,
> Yet strive and wait and pray!

Prayer for Healing of Blindness

(Matthew 20:29-34; Mark 10:46-52; see Luke 18:35-43)

And, behold, two blind men sitting by the way side, when they heard that Jesus passed by, cried out saying, Have mercy on us, O Lord, thou son of David. And the multitude rebuked them, because they should hold their peace: but they cried the more, saying, Have mercy on us, O Lord, thou son of David. And Jesus stood still, and called them, and said, What will ye that I shall do unto you? They say unto him, Lord that our eyes may be opened.

— Matthew 20:30-33

A difficulty arises over whether there was one or two blind men, seeing Mark mentions only one blind man and gives his name as Bartimaeus. One explanation given is that of the two the one Mark names was the more conspicuous and better known. It is, of course, possible that a different miracle is recorded. The feature of the incident before us, however, is the prayer of the blind beggars as they appealed to the pity of the King. In their double plea, they echoed the whispered murmurs of the crowd as to the Messiah-ship of Jesus. Three times, the blind men called Him, "Lord," and compassion drew from Him the work of power, establishing His claims to deity.

Prayer of Faith

(Matthew 21:18-22; Mark 11:22-26)

And all things, whatsoever ye shall ask in prayer, believing, ye
shall receive.   — Matthew 21:22

Jesus recognized the fact that God had a temple for His people to
worship in (21:13). Under grace, He has a redeemed people as His
Temple (Ephesians 1:22, 23; 2:20-22).

Faith and prayer are bound together. Their inter-relation is suggested by Christ's phrase, "in prayer believing" (21:22). Faith is the
inspiration of prayer, as prayer is our expression of faith. We hope
to deal more fully with this aspect of prayer when we come to Mark's
narrative of our Lord's precept. Our only observation at this point is
that here again is the implied condition about praying in harmony
with the laws and will of God (7:7). If it was not so it would not be
asked in faith, and every true prayer involves the submission of what
it asks to the divine judgment.

Prayer of Pretense

(Matthew 23:14, 25; see Mark 12:40; Luke 20:47)

Woe unto you, scribes and Pharisees, hypocrites! for ye devour
widows' houses, and for a pretence make long prayer: therefore ye
shall receive the greater damnation.   — Matthew 23:14

Christ taught His disciples to pray *briefly*. The scribes, however,
loved to make "long prayers." Professor McFadyen comments: "It is
as if Jesus said: 'A true prayer must be brief; ye shall not be heard
for your much speaking.' The publican's prayer, which is approved,
is little more than a cry; the Pharisee's, which is condemned, is relatively much longer." The Pharisees and Scribes were proud of their
prayers. They prayed for effect. A reporter describing a religious
meeting held in Boston, Mass., said of the opening prayer that "it was
the best ever offered to a Boston audience." The prayers Christ condemned were those dependent upon an audience for effect.

Two other references to prayer are indicated by Matthew. Christ
encouraged prayer for deliverance from distress (24:20). Then there
are some cries He cannot answer (24:11, 12).

Prayer of Accountability

(Matthew 25:20, 22, 24)

And so he that had received five talents came and brought other
five talents, saying, Lord, thou deliveredst unto me five talents:
behold, I have gained beside them five talents more. . . .
He also that had received two talents came and said, Lord, thou
deliveredst unto me two talents: behold, I have gained two other
talents beside them. . . .
Then he which had received the one talent came and said, Lord, I
knew thee that thou art an hard man, reaping where thou hast not

sown, and gathering where thou hast not strawed: And I was afraid, and went and hid thy talent in the earth: lo, there thou hast that is thine.   — Matthew 25:20, 22, 24, 25

In this further parable, the servants are found addressing their master as "Lord," which, although a common designation of God, was also applied to man. Applied to Christ, the term carries a profounder religious sense. He is Lord, as God is Lord. Beyond the framework of the parable, we have its application to the Judgment Seat of Christ, where service will be rewarded or condemned as the case may be. The language used is hardly what a human master would employ in addressing his slaves (25:23). The reality breaks through the symbol, and we hear the voice of the divine Master speaking to His servants, bidding them delight in a joy springing from loyal, faithful service (John 15:10, 11; II Corinthians 5:9, 10).

Prayer of a Resigned Will
(Mathew 26:26, 36-46; Mark 14:32-42; Luke 22:39-46)

And he went a little farther, and fell on his face, and prayed, saying, O my Father, if it be possible, let this cup pass from me: nevertheless not as I will, but as thou wilt. And he cometh unto the disciples, and findeth them asleep, and saith unto Peter, What, could ye not watch with me one hour? Watch and pray, that ye enter not into temptation: the spirit indeed is willing, but the flesh is weak. He went away again the second time, and prayed, saying, O my Father, if this cup may not pass away from me, except I drink it, thy will be done. And he came and found them asleep again: for their eyes were heavy. And he left them, and went away again, and prayed the third time, saying the same words.   — Matthew 26:39-44

Jesus had a grateful heart for all the bounties of heaven (26:26). How impressed onlookers must have been over His uplifted eyes. Do we pray before meat? Christ's prayers were addressed to God as Father (26: 39, 42). What holy intimacy existed between Father and Son! The prayer for the removal of the cup was not answered. It had to be drained to the dregs. The will of God is the ultimate and only real longing of the devout soul, and as Jesus prayed for the accomplishment of the divine will, His prayer was answered (Hebrews 5:7). A. Procter speaks of —

Prayers, which God in pity
Refused to grant or hear!

But the thrice-repeated prayer in Gethsemane was heard and answered but in a word with the Father's will.

Prostration was not above the Son of God, who fell on His face in the Garden (26:39). Having taught the duty of persistency in prayer, Jesus here practices it. "He prayed the third time, saying the same words" (26:44). Prayer He compared to knocking until the knock is heard. Repeated prayers are never cold and mechanical when offered by a burdened, trusting heart. Some have seen in the phrase, "the same words," an argument for a fixed form in prayer.

Into the mystery and agony of Gethsemane we cannot intrude. It was not the Father's will that the cup should pass. An angel strengthened Christ during the bitter ordeal. Here is a conflict beyond our sharing, for He trod the winepress alone. The first prayer was: "If it be possible, let this cup pass away from me; nevertheless not as I will, but as thou wilt" (26:29). Such a prayer offered with strong crying and blood-like sweat was terrible in its reality. As the struggle continued that prayer was merged into another, "If this cup cannot pass away except I drink it, thy will be done" (26:42). The first cry was "Save me from this hour" (John 12:27); but the second was, "Father, glorify thy name" (John 12:28).

Professor McFadyen's most impressive summary can fittingly conclude this prayer-agony of Christ's in the garden.

> From the beginning, the deepest desire of Jesus was that the will of God be done, but the human will prayed vehemently that the cup should pass. But through the deadly earnestness of His prayer, He reached the absolute harmony of His will with God's; and He came forth from the Garden, calm and triumphant, to face the treachery of a disciple, the fanaticism of the mob, and the jealous cruelty of the priests.

For ourselves, we can learn the lesson of submission to the good and perfect will of God and also the necessity of watching and praying (26:41). We should watch before we pray — watch as we pray — watch after we pray (Nehemiah 4:9).

Prayer at Calvary
(Matthew 27:46, 50; Luke 23:34, 46)

And about the ninth hour Jesus cried with a loud voice, saying, Eli, Eli, lama sabachthani? that is to say, My God, my God, why hast thou forsaken me?   — Matthew 27:46
Jesus, when he had cried again with a loud voice, yielded up the ghost.   — Matthew 27:50
Then said Jesus, Father, forgive them; for they know not what they do. And they parted his raiment, and cast lots.   — Luke 23:34
And when Jesus had cried with a loud voice, he said, Father, into thy hands I commend my spirit: and having said thus, he gave up the ghost.   — Luke 23:46

Three prayers were offered by Jesus as He died upon the Cross for our sins — and what prayers they were!

"Father, forgive them for they know not what they do."

Grace was His to pray for His murderers (Isaiah 53:12).

"My God, My God, why hast Thou forsaken Me?"

Here, as Martin Luther expressed it, is God forsaken of God. As Jesus bore the load of our sin, His sustaining consciousness of fellowship with the Father was momentarily clouded (Psalm 22:1, 2). This was a prayer out of the deepest depths that sorrow has ever sounded. Yet the Saviour knew He was not utterly forsaken. He could still pray, "My God."

"Father, into thy hands I commend my spirit."

The ancient Word sustained our Lord in His dying hour (Psalm 31:5). He returned to God *as Father* and died with triumphant confidence.

The prayer of the penitent thief was answered beyond expectation (Luke 23:40-43). He was the first trophy of the blood of Jesus to enter Paradise. Now in heaven all power is Christ's (28:17) — a power enabling us to pray and witness in His Name.

Mark

The servant-character of Jesus Christ is manifest throughout this vivid account of His life and work. Mark depicts the Master as the mighty Worker rather than as the unique Teacher. This is why the second gospel is one of *works* rather than of *words*.

Throughout the gospel we have the characteristic and ever-recurring "immediately," "anon," "presently," "forthwith," "by-and-by," "straightway" — all representing the self-same Greek word, occurring no less than 41 times. It was a word Mark constantly used of his own work. He believed the king's business required haste (I Samuel 21:8). And realizing that Christ's work exhibited the perfect fulfilment of the law, it was a work that must be immediately accomplished without haste and without pause. Here, as elsewhere, Christ is portrayed as "The Praying One."

Prayer of a Demon
(Mark 1:23-28, 32-34; Luke 4:31-37)

And there was in their synagogue a man with an unclean spirit; and he cried out, Saying, Let us alone; what have we to do with thee, thou Jesus of Nazareth? art thou come to destroy us? I know thee who thou art, the Holy One of God.   — Mark 1:23, 24

The prayer of this "unclean spirit" is identical with that of the Gadarene demoniacs (Matthew 8:29). What a wonderful preternatural intuition of our Lord's greatness the demon had! *The Holy One of God.* It was a recognition of the Messianic prophecy of Psalm 16:10. The strict meaning of the term is, "The Holy One whom God owns as such" — the One who has attained the highest form of holiness. How pathetic it is that some religious leaders deny the deity of Christ. Hell has no doubt about it!

Prayer-Habits of Christ
(Mark 1:35; 6:41, 46)

And in the morning, rising up a great while before day, he went out, and departed into a solitary place, and there prayed.   — Mark 1:35

And when he had taken the five loaves and the two fishes, he looked
up to heaven, and blessed, and brake the loaves, and gave them to
his disciples to set before them: and the two fishes divided he
among them all.
And when he had sent them away, he departed into a mountain to
pray.   — Mark 6:41, 46

Night was Christ's favorite time for prayer. He had need of
eloquent silence after the noisy din of the crowd. The original means,
"while there was yet much appearance of night," which is true of
day-break to which Luke refers. The stars which He made were
witnesses of those long uninterrupted prayer-hours.

How strangely impressive the upturned face of Jesus must have
been as He gave thanks (Mark 8:6)! We wonder whether the grace
He offered was the one offered by the head of a Jewish household?
From the Emmaus story we know that there was a peculiar solemnity
about the way Jesus gave thanks to God and broke bread (Luke
24:30).

Prayer for the Deaf and Dumb

(Mark 7:31-37; see Matthew 15:29-31)

And they bring unto him one that was deaf, and had an impediment
in his speech; and they beseech him to put his hand upon him.
And he took him aside from the multitude, and put his fingers into
his ears, and he spit, and touched his tongue; And looking up to
heaven, he sighed, and saith unto him, Ephphatha, that is, Be
opened.   — Mark 7:32-34

It is the custom for us to close our eyes in prayer — an effort to
exclude the world. Often prayer in the Bible was offered with eyes
open, but turned heavenward (Luke 18:13). Christ is here found
looking towards heaven as He healed the deaf and dumb man. It
would seem to be a silent prayer Jesus prayed, yet He said, "Because
of the multitude that standeth around I *said* it." It was a prayer not
only for heaven's vindication, but one calculated to impress the people
with His deity. Prayer accompanied His miraculous acts of healing.

President Eisenhower, addressing a large crowd of college students,
ended his 40-minute speech by saying: "Prayer is still the mightiest
force in the world and, when used by dedicated men and women,
nothing in this world remains impossible." Well, Jesus found it so.
May we prove it so!

Mark goes on to tell us that "Jesus sighed deeply in His spirit"
(8:12). Was this an unspoken wordless prayer?

"Prayer is the burden of a sigh."

Prayer and Fasting

(Mark 2:18; 9:29)

And the disciples of John and of the Pharisees used to fast: and
they come and say unto him, Why do the disciples of John and of
the Pharisees fast, but thy disciples fast not?   — Mark 2:18

> And he said unto them, This kind can come forth by nothing, but by prayer and fasting.
>
> — Mark 9:29

Reference has already been made to "Fasting" as one of the associations of true prayer. The Apocrypha has it: "Prayer is good, with fasting and alms and righteousness" (Tobit 12:8). It is mentioned as a frequent accompaniment of prayer (I Samuel 7:6; Ezra 8:21; Nehemiah 1:4; Daniel 9:3; Luke 5:33; Acts 13:3; 14:23).

For the prayer of blind Bartimaeus (10:46-52) the reader is referred back to the incident of the two blind men (Matthew 20:29-34). The cheering words of the disciples, given by Mark only (10:49), as well as the eager action of Bartimaeus in throwing away his outer garment and leaping up, prove the impressiveness of the miracle. This we know, "he followed Jesus in the way" and used his new-found gift of sight as a witness of Christ's miraculous power.

Prayer of the Young Ruler

(Mark 10:17-22; Matthew 19:16-30; Luke 10:25; 18:18-30)

> And when he was gone forth into the way, there came one running, and kneeled to him, and asked him, Good Master, what shall I do that I may inherit eternal life?
>
> — Mark 10:17

Mark gives us one or two vivid descriptive touches of this young man who came praying, "Good Master, what shall I do to inherit eternal life?" He came "running and kneeling." Then he had Christ's look of love (10:21), a fact noticed by Mark only. Then there was the glance and gesture in "He looked around" (10:23). The answer the seeker received to his prayer saddened him (10:22), but gave Jesus the opportunity of addressing His disciples on the lure of riches and the cost of true discipleship.

As we leave the Gospel of Mark there are one or two aspects and axioms of prayer we have previously mentioned which deserve a further word as they reappear in Mark. We are reminded, for example, of the two-fold requirement of prayer:

1. *Faith* (11:22-24).

Faith is fundamental to any success in prayer. Unless we believe that God is the Rewarder of those who diligently seek Him, what is the use of praying? Guy H. King reminds us that —

1. Faith is the vessel that fetches the blessing. "Believe . . . and ye shall have."
2. Faith is a vessel that fetches from such a fount of blessing. "Have faith in God."
3. Faith is a vessel that can grow big enough to fetch the biggest blessing. "What things soever ye desire."

Faith, then, is the vehicle through which all God had, reaches His children.

2. *Forgiveness* (Mark 11:25, 26).

Both faith and forgiveness are required if we are to live a right relationship with God. His forgiveness of us is not based upon our forgiveness of others, but upon the finished work of Christ (Ephesians 4:32). Divinely forgiven, however, we must forgive others. "When ye stand praying, forgive." How we shrink from this most necessary axiom of prayer! If we are harboring an unforgiving spirit then our prayer power is atrophied.

This forgiving spirit in prayer works both ways — "If ye have ought against any" (11:25). "If . . . thy brother hath ought against thee" (Matthew 5:23). What a dynamic force prayer is when it is based upon harmony with God, and harmony with our fellows! Because our lives are so full of injuries — real and supposed — there is no theme our Lord returns to so often as the forgiveness of injuries.

Further, two glimpses of prayer are before us in Christ's description of the end-time period of the Gentile Age (Mark 13:18-33). As we await His return, all of His risen power is behind us as we continue in prayer and service (Mark 16:17-20).

Luke

Luke, physician-like (Colossians 4:14), was meticulous in the gathering and setting forth of facts (1:1-4; Acts 1:1-3). Because of his noble profession he was also in close contact with humanity, having a sympathizing heart earning him the title of "beloved physician." This is one reason why the gospel he has given us provides us with fascinating human touches in our Lord's life, such as cannot be found in the other gospels.

"Luke relates those things concerning Jesus which demonstrate how entirely human Christ was," says Dr. C. I. Scofield. "The parables peculiar to Luke have distinctively the human and the seeking role."

It is also to Luke's gospel, "the most beautiful book ever written," that we are indebted for profitable mentions of our Lord's prayer messages and ministry. Dr. C. J. Vaughan speaks of Luke as "the special Evangelist of the prayers of Christ." Luke gives pre-eminence to this particular department of revelation — the record of the prayers of Jesus. It was left to Luke to enumerate, more fully, the examples of our Lord's prayer-life. Out of the treasure of his manifold reminiscences of the Master he revered, Luke tells us of the Man who needed and loved to pray.

Prayer of Zacharias

(Luke 1:8, 13, 67-80)

And it came to pass, that while he executed the priest's office before God in the order of his course. . . .
But the angel said unto him, Fear Not, Zacharias: for thy prayer is heard; and thy wife Elisabeth shall bear thee a son, and thou shalt call his name John. . . .

And his father Zacharias was filled with the Holy Ghost, and prophesied, saying, Blessed be the Lord God of Israel; for he hath visited and redeemed his people, And hath raised up an horn of salvation for us in the house of his servant David; As he spake by the mouth of his holy prophets, which have been since the world began: That we should be saved from our enemies, and from the hand of all that hate us; To perform the mercy promised to our fathers, and to remember his holy covenant; The oath which he sware to our father Abraham, That he would grant unto us, that we being delivered out of the hand of our enemies might serve him without fear, In holiness and righteousness before him, all the days of our life. And thou, child, shalt be called the prophet of the Highest: for thou shalt go before the face of the Lord to prepare his ways; To give knowledge of salvation unto his people by the remission of their sins, Through the tender mercy of our God; whereby the dayspring from on high hath visited us, To give light to them that sit in darkness and in the shadow of death, to guide our feet into the way of peace. And the child grew, and waxed strong in spirit, and was in the deserts till the day of his shewing unto Israel.   — Luke 1:8, 13, 67-80

As a priest, Zacharias was accustomed to the prayers and service of the Temple (1:8-10). When the angel, Gabriel, came to him with one of the "Fear nots" of the Bible (Luke 1:13, 30; 2:10; 5:10; 12:4, 7, 32) and told him that his prayer had been heard (1:13), we can take it for granted that his prayers, both in the Temple and at home, for a son, were implied. How he must have prayed incessantly and earnestly through Elisabeth's barren years! Now in extreme old age, after long and weary expectation, prayers are answered and he is blessed with sudden happiness beyond all hope. Zacharias came to prove that —

"Praying breath is never spent in vain."

The association of incense with prayer is worthy of note (1:10). *Prayer* often connected with *incense* and compared to it (Psalm 141:2; Malachi 1:11; Revelation 8:3, 4). The reason for ordaining *incense* might be to intimate the acceptance of those pious *prayers* which were to accompany it. Matthew Henry has the quaint but forcible comment: "Prayers of faith are filed in heaven; and, although not presently answered are not *forgotten*. Prayer made when we are young, and coming into the world, may be answered when we are old, and going out of the world." It was so with old Zacharias.

In his salutation and benediction, Zacharias overwhelmed with ecstasy and filled with the Holy Spirit, sees the Old Testament covenant fulfilled and the dawning of the glorious day of freedom and righteousness, and of his child's part in ushering in the kingdom for which loyal hearts had sighed and prayed. What a preacher of repentance John the Baptist, miraculously born (1:18, 36), became!

Prayer As a Magnificat

(Luke 1:46-55; see I Samuel 2:1-10)

And Mary said, My soul doth magnify the Lord, And my spirit hath rejoiced in God my Saviour. For he hath regarded the low estate of his handmaiden: for, behold, from henceforth all generations shall call me blessed. For he that is mighty hath done to me great things; and holy is his name. And his mercy is on them that fear him from generation to generation. He hath shewed strength with his arm; he hath scattered the proud in the imagination of their hearts. He hath put down the mighty from their seats, and exalted them of low degree. He hath filled the hungry with good things; and the rich he hath sent empty away. He hath holpen his servant Israel, in remembrance of his mercy; As he spake to our fathers, to Abraham, and to his seed for ever. — Luke 1:46-55

The Song of Mary, the mother of our Lord, was a prayer — a prayer of praise and penitence. Even Mary recognized her need of a Saviour (1:47). The majority of the church's songs are prayers. If only we realized this fact, we would be more careful in our congregational singing, when we take solemn vows and covenants upon our lips in our song-prayers. All of us are liars when it comes to hymn-singing, for we have little intention of fulfilling all we express to God in the church's spiritual songs.

A marked feature of the majority of Bible prayers is the confession of sin they contain. A prayer like David's, for example, is stained with his penitential tears (Psalm 51). Even in the Magnificats of Zacharias and Mary, and also in Gabriel's announcement, the recognition of sin and the need of a Saviour are present (Luke 1:16, 17; Matthew 1:21 with Luke 1:31, 47, 50, 77; 2:20).

Shortcomings, sin, and sanctification form the topics of our prayers. Our inherent sinfulness is the goad driving us, willing or unwilling, to the throne of Grace. But such a topic is wanting in the prayers of Christ. This is one reason why He could not pray the prayer He taught His disciples to use. As the One, "holy, harmless, undefiled and separate from sinners" (Hebrews 7:26), He could not pray, "Forgive Me My Trespasses." He never sinned against God or man (John 8:46). Whenever or wherever Jesus knelt in prayer He had no sins of His own to confess. When He prayed for forgiveness it was never for Himself — always for others. No "conscience of sins" was His when He knelt to pray. Yet His prayers, devoid of any confession of sin, were real prayers, just as His temptations were real ones. He really prayed — *prayed* in His prayers.

Prayer As Adoration

(Luke 2:10-20, 25-38)

And suddenly there was with the angel a multitude of the heavenly host praising God, and saying, Glory to God in the highest, and on earth peace, good will toward men. — Luke 2:13, 14

And the shepherds returned, glorifying and praising God for all the things that they had heard and seen, as it was told unto them.
— Luke 2:20

And, behold, there was a man in Jerusalem, whose name was Simeon. . . . Then took he him up in his arms, and blessed God, and said, Lord now lettest thou thy servant depart in peace, according to thy word: For mine eyes have seen thy salvation, Which thou hast prepared before the face of all people; A light to lighten the Gentiles, and the glory of thy people Israel.   — Luke 2:25a, 28-32

And there was one Anna. . . . And she coming in that instant gave thanks likewise unto the Lord, and spake of him to all them that looked for redemption in Jerusalem.   — Luke 2:36a, 38

The Angels, the Shepherds, Simeon, and Anna all combine to magnify God for the gift of His beloved Son as the Saviour of the world. The earliest prayers in Luke are prayers of thanksgiving to God for Christ and reflect faithfully the spirit of the Early Church (Acts 4:25). To Simeon, the One born of Mary was the *Despotēs*, from which "despot" is derived (2:29). How grateful Anna was for the coming of Jesus. Had she not prayed night and day for the redemption of Jerusalem (2:37)?

Although we have no record of Christ's prayers during the thirty years He spent in Nazareth, He must have lived near to the heart of God otherwise He would never have increased in wisdom and in favor with God and man (2:52).

Prayer at the Portal of Service

(Luke 3:21, 22)

Now when all the people were baptized, it came to pass, that Jesus also being baptized, and praying, the heaven was opened, And the Holy Ghost descended in a bodily shape like a dove upon him, and a voice came from heaven, which said, Thou art my beloved Son; in thee I am well pleased.   — Luke 3:21, 22

We have previously indicated that the great crises of our Lord's ministry were accompanied by prayer. Do you never wonder what kind of a prayer Jesus prayed between His thirty years' seclusion and the three years' of public ministry? This first mention of Him at prayer found Him facing the forty days and forty nights' fast in the wilderness among wild beasts and His encounter with "the roaring lion," with his subtle temptations to secure an empire bought without blood. Perhaps His prayer after the baptism was taken up with a plea for strength to face a dread ordeal. It might have been His act of "putting on the whole armor of God" for the conflict "in the evil day." This we do know, His prayer had an instant answer, for the heavens opened and the Holy Spirit came upon Him, and with the Spirit's empowerment, the benediction of His Father (3:22; 5:8).

For the implication of prayer in Luke 4:25 see James 5:17.

Prayer As Escape from Popularity

(Luke 5:16)

And he withdrew himself into the wilderness, and prayed.

— Luke 5:16

The narrative makes it clear that Jesus was caught up in the wave of great popularity. People came to treat Him as a desired hero, but He saw Satan coming with the crowds, and knowing that later on He would have to warn His disciples, "Woe unto you when all men speak well of you," He here escapes the perils of popularity by withdrawing to pray.

Characteristically, Christ shrank from mere notoriety, from the gaze of crowds drawn together to delight in signs and wonders, and ready to acclaim the Wonder-Worker a king (Matthew 12:16-21). "He felt the need of fortifying His soul against the false Messianic hopes of the people who would gladly have made Him King" (John 6:15; Luke 5:15, 16). The withdrawal Luke mentions suggests not a single act, but rather a habit of action, "He was retiring in the deserts and praying." As Dr. C. J. Vaughan expresses it, "The withdrawals were repeated, the wildernesses were more than one, the prayers were habitual."

If Christ had need of constant withdrawals from the gaze and glamor of the world, how deep must our need be of the "desecularizing, decarnalizing process of which the desert seclusions of Jesus are the perpetual parable!" All of us know that God often creates wildernesses for His children — the wilderness of bereavement; the wilderness of difficult decision; the still more desert wilderness of self-accusation and of self-shame. These wildernesses are not to be refused, for they are of grace. If we go apart with Him, the desert will blossom as the rose.

If, because of our prestige, position, money, success, or fame, the snare of popularity besets us, our only escape from the pride of life and of the flesh is the desert with its prayer-watch. It is only in God's presence that we are able to rightly assess our value and victories. Earthly fame can prove to be disastrous. If the Master praises, what of man's praise?

Prayer and the Twelve

(Luke 6:12, 13, 20, 28)

And it came to pass in those days, that he went out into a mountain to pray, and continued all night in prayer to God. And when it was day, he called unto him his disciples: and of them he chose twelve, whom also he named apostles. . . .

And he lifted up his eyes on his disciples, and said, Blessed be ye poor: for yours in the kingdom of God. . . .

Bless them that curse you, and pray for them which despitefully use you.   — Luke 6:12, 13, 20, 28

Because of the importance of the time intervening between the discipleship and the apostleship of the Twelve, Jesus spent the night in prayer. The crisis was one of supreme importance. It is not surprising, therefore, to read that He prayed not only earnestly, but all night. In such an all-night prayer-period our Lord doubtless asked for infallible directions in the solemn choice He was about to make. Would He not pray that there might not be one unworthy one in His selection? Why, then, does the list end with "Judas Iscariot, which also was a traitor"?

Later on, Jesus could say, "I know whom I have chosen," (John 13:8), why then was Judas chosen? Must it not have introduced a sorrowful ingredient into the prayer of that night to know that close to Him through three years would be the treacherous presence of Judas? It is beyond our finite wisdom to fathom the choice of Judas. A deeper mystery is the fact that He chose *us* to be His followers.

From the prayerful choice that night sprang — apart from Judas — a little company, supplanted by Matthias (Acts 1:23-26) and later on, the Apostle Paul, instrumental in the first spiritual Reformation, the real Christianity of Christendom. Because of Christ's all-night vigil there will come a great multitude which no man can number (Revelation 7:9). For our hearts the lesson is clear. Because we never know the ultimate effect of decisions we make, much prayer should be ours before the die is cast.

Luke goes on to tell us that Jesus "lifted up His eyes" upon those He had chosen (6:21). They were poor men as far as this world's resources are concerned, but if "poor in spirit," theirs would be the kingdom of heaven. Then Jesus went on to exhort His disciples to pray for those who would abuse and persecute them (6:28; Matthew 5:44). Such form of prayer is hard, yet blessedly possible as the witness of Stephen proves (Acts 7:60). Intercessions are to be made for all men, especially for our foes. Who exactly are we to pray for?

1. Our Enemies (Luke 6:28)
2. Our Friends (James 5:16)
3. Our Families (II Samuel 7:17)
4. Ourselves (Psalm 50:1)
5. Our fellow-men (I Timothy 2:1)
6. Our fellow-workers in Christ (II Thessalonians 3:1)
7. Our fellow-members in the Church (Ephesians 6:18)

Prayer and Transfiguration

(Luke 9:28, 29)

And it came to pass about eight days after these sayings, he took Peter and John and James, and went up into a mountain to pray. And as he prayed, the fashion of his countenance was altered, and his raiment was white and glistering.   — Luke 9:28, 29

Christ prayed not only to maintain His communion with God, and to obtain guidance and power from God, but also to perfect His Manhood. Thus, the Transfiguration was not only the outflashing of our Lord's inherent glory and majesty, but the witness of the perfection of His humanity. He was perfect in creation, perfect in probation, and was now ready to be perfected in glory. "As He prayed the fashion of His countenance was altered." Transfigured while praying! What a truth to ponder! Prayer can transfigure a person's countenance and character.

As to the nature of that transfiguring prayer Jesus prayed, Dr. C. J. Vaughan asks —

> Was it a prayer for such a sign of His Sonship as should write once for all upon the hearts of those witnesses the conviction of the good confession?
> Was it for the presence of those holy men of old time who might receive the interpretation of their own life's work and carry back with them into Paradise of their rest and their preparation?
> Was it that He Himself might be refreshed and comforted by some visible and audible proof of the Father's love and the Father's presence, such as might send Him back into His toilsome life and speed Him toward His suffering death, the stronger and the braver and the more resolute?

Before leaving this great chapter we can note the habit Jesus had of going apart to pray (9:10, 18) as well as His prayer toward the end of the confession of His Messiahship (9:18). Then we have His regular grace before meals (9:16). James and John prayed for judgment upon Christ's foes (9:53-56). Last of all, we have His rebuke of a man who prayed that he might follow Jesus wherever He went (9:57-62). Like so many of us, this man was unconscious of his own inability to follow the Master all the way.

Prayer in Parable Form

(Luke 11:5-13)

And he said unto them, Which of you shall have a friend, and shall go unto him at midnight, and say unto him, Friend, lend me three loaves; For a friend of mine in his journey is come to me, and I have nothing to set before him? And he from within shall answer and say, Trouble me not: the door is now shut, and my children are with me in bed; I cannot rise and give thee. I say unto you, Though he will not rise and give him, because he is his friend, yet because of his importunity he will rise and give him as many as he needeth. And I say unto you, Ask, and it shall be given you; seek, and ye shall find; knock, and it shall be opened unto you. For every one that asketh receiveth; and he that seeketh findeth; and to him that knocketh it shall be opened. If a son shall ask bread of any of you that is a father, will he give him a stone? or if he ask a fish, will he for a fish give him a serpent? Or if he shall ask an egg, will he offer him a scorpion? If ye then, being evil, know how to give good gifts unto your children: how much more shall your heavenly Father give the Holy Spirit to them that ask him?   — Luke 11:5-13

Having briefly dealt with this prayer-parable, let us now seek to examine it more thoroughly. In a most dramatic fashion Dr. Alexander Whyte, in *The Man Who Knocked at Midnight*, describes the friend who came begging loaves.

> "Friend!" he cries, till the dogs bark at him. He puts his ear to the door. There is a sound inside, and then the light of a candle shines through the hole of the door. The bars of the door are drawn back, and he gets not three loaves only but as many as he needs . . . Our Lord Himself was often like that importunate man, out at midnight, knocking for bread. When He was a child, He had lain, full of fear and heard all that knocking at midnight at Joseph's door. And, when He became a man, He remembered that sleepless midnight, and spiritualized it and put it into this parable.

Christ's invitation to ask, seek and knock does not imply that prayer is a forcing of ourselves into God's presence nor the wringing of something from a reluctant God. He is more ready to hear than we are to pray. Persistence in prayer, both on our own behalf and on behalf of others, is the lesson in prayer our Lord is teaching in the parable. Archbishop Trench observes: "If a bad man will yield to the mere force of an importunity which he hates, how much more certainly will a righteous God be prevailed on by the powerful prayer which He loves?" Endurance in prayer is hard but fruitful.

In the opening part of this chapter we have the request of the disciples about the art of praying (11:1) and the pattern prayer He gave them. While they had prayed, somehow the prayers of Jesus were different. He knew how to *pray* in His prayers. Praying in a certain place, His disciples asked, "Lord, teach us to pray." In His prayers there was the incomparable union of simplicity and depth, serenity and earnestness — features of prayer emulated by John (11:1). What a difference Jesus had made to the prayers of the saints both by precept and example! Answering the disciples' request, Jesus gave them the most complete and connected expression of prayer ever to be uttered. Well might C. J. Vaughan ask, "Might He not be praying, in that prayer of preface and prelude, that the spirit of Prayer He was about to prescribe might be indeed the spirit in all future ages of His disciples and of His Church? That the filial heart might be the religion of His people — the filial and the brotherly. That sinners might be enabled to view aright their own standing; as sinners, yet sons; sons still, however sinful."

As prayer was the fountain of power in our Lord's ministry, so is it in the service of His followers. The teaching of the chapter confirms the remark of a French writer that "the ideal of the Christian life is a perpetual communion with God, sustained by prayer as frequent as possible." But although Christ has taught us to pray, prayer remains a mysterious force, for no one knows why God should need our prayers. That He does is not only a part of our faith, but partly explains the inborn propensity of the human heart; which, as a *Collect* of the Church of England Prayer Book expresses it, has "an hearty desire to pray."

Prayer of the Prodigal

(Luke 15:11-24, 29, 30)

And he said, A certain man had two sons: And the younger of them said to his father, Father, give me the portion of goods that falleth to me. And he divided unto them his living. . . .
And when he came to himself, he said, How many hired servants of my father's have bread enough and to spare, and I perish with hunger! I will arise and go to my father, and will say unto him, Father, I have sinned against heaven, and before thee, And am no more worthy to be called thy son: make me as one of thy hired servants.   — Luke 15:11, 12, 17-19

It is not our intention to expound the Parables of this chapter, but to show that confession of sin is usually solemn and brief (Daniel 9:15; Luke 15:21). Penitents pour out their hearts in a series of sobs, giving their prayers for pardon a resistless appeal. There are two striking phrases in the Prodigal's prayer to his father — *"Give me . . . Make me"* (Luke 15:13, 19). The young man got what he wanted and with it leanness of body and soul (Psalm 106:15). Claiming, what he felt was his right, he wanted to be *someone*, but when destitute and homeless he was willing to become *no-one* — a hired slave.

The elder brother was no less a prodigal. Self-righteousness is as abhorrent in the sight of our heavenly Father as the conspicuous wickedness of a notorious sinner. How gracious the generous father was, "Son, thou art ever with me, and all that I have is thine" (Luke 15:31). What a godly attitude to assume!

Prayer Out of Hell

(Luke 16:22-31)

And it came to pass, that the beggar died, and was carried by the angels into Abraham's bosom: the rich man also died, and was buried; And in hell he lift up his eyes, being in torments, and seeth Abraham afar off, and Lazarus in his bosom. And he cried and said, Father Abraham, have mercy on me, and send Lazarus, that he may dip the tip of his finger in water, and cool my tongue; for I am tormented in this flame. But Abraham said, Son, remember that thou in thy lifetime receivedst thy good things, and likewise Lazarus evil things: but now he is comforted, and thou art tormented. And beside all this, between us and you there is a great gulf fixed: so that they which would pass from hence to you cannot; neither can they pass to us, that would come from thence. Then he said, I pray thee therefore, father, that thou wouldest send him to my father's house: For I have five brethren; that he may testify unto them, lest they also come into this place of torment. Abraham saith unto him, They have Moses and the prophets: let them hear them. And he said, Nay, father Abraham: but if one went unto them from the dead, they will repent. And he said unto him, If they hear not Moses and the prophets, neither will they be persuaded, though one rose from the dead.   — Luke 16:22-31

What a dreadfully solemn narrative this is! Hell, as a place of torment, was real to Christ. The gospels reveal Him as the most powerful Preacher of hell the world has ever known (Mark 9:44, 45). While the rich man in this parable cried to Abraham to have mercy upon him (16:24, 27, 30), an evidence that men believed angels could intercede for men (Job 5:1; see Tobiah 12:15, "I am Raphael, one of the seven holy angels who present the prayers of saints,") in hell the lost still cry in vain for relief. In a graphic way our Lord proves that prayers from hell and messengers from hell have no effect whatever.

Prayers for the departed, whether in heaven or hell, are likewise useless and have no Scriptural warrant. Do you remember the words of Longfellow?

> Why pray for the dead, who are at rest!
> Pray for the living! — in whose breast
> The struggle between right and wrong
> Is raging terrible and strong —
> As when good Angels were with Devils.

Prayer of Ten Lepers

(Luke 17:12-19)

And as he entered into a certain village, there met him ten men that were lepers, which stood afar off: And they lifted up their voice, and said, Jesus, Master, have mercy on us.
And one of them, when he saw that he was healed, turned back, and with a loud voice glorified God, And fell down on his face at his feet, giving him thanks: and he was a Samaritan.
                                                    — Luke 17:12, 13, 15, 16

It is more than likely that these diseased creatures had heard of an earlier instance of leprosy being cleansed (Matthew 8:2; 11:5) and thus threw themselves upon the mercy of the Master. All ten were cleansed but only one turned back to give thanks for the gift of healing received. How disappointed was the healing Christ! What a tone of mingled surprise, and grief, and indignation there is in the question asked: "Were there not ten cleansed? but where are the nine?" (17:17). Our blessed Lord was vexed that the natural obligatory duty of gratitude was forgotten. The healed leper "glorified God with a loud voice" (17:15). May we be loud in our praises for the unfailing goodness of God!

Prayer in Parable Form

(Luke 18:1-8)

And he spake a parable unto them to this end, that men ought always to pray, and not to faint; Saying, There was in a city a judge,

which feared not God, neither regarded man: And there was a widow
in that city; and she came unto him, saying, Avenge me of mine
adversary. And he would not for a while: but afterward he said
within himself, Though I fear not God, nor regard man; Yet because
this widow troubleth me, I will avenge her, lest by her continual
coming she weary me. And the Lord said, Hear what the unjust
judge saith. And shall not God avenge his own elect, which cry day
and night unto him, though he bear long with them? I tell you
that he will avenge them speedily. Nevertheless when the Son of man
cometh, shall he find faith on the earth?   — Luke 18:1-8

The key to the parable of the Unjust Judge is "hanging on the
front door," as an ancient writer speaks of the opening verse. The
two parables suggesting the duty of persistence and importunity in
prayer are those of the friend coming at midnight (10:5-8), and the
one before us of the unjust judge. What a striking contrast there is
between this judge and "the righteous judge of all the earth" (Genesis
18:25)! The special function of a judge was to hear the cause of the
poor and the oppressed, and then redress their wrongs and relieve
their wants (Deuteronomy 16:18-20; II Chronicles 19:5-7; Psalm
82:2-4). But the judge in the parable "feared not God, neither regarded man." He turned a deaf ear to the entreaties of the distressed
widow. The judge felt that she was too poor to bribe him and too
weak to compel him, so why bother about her?

At last, however, her importunity prevailed and the judge granted
her request, "lest she wear me out by her continual coming" (18:5
R.V.). How different it is with the Almighty who never perverts
justice (Job 8:3; 34:10, 12)! The poor and oppressed are His special
care (Psalm 10:14, 18; 68:5). He is never weary with our oft coming.
He urges us to give Him no rest (Isaiah 43:24, 26; 62:6, 7 R.V.). The
design of the parable is to inculcate perseverance in prayer, though
it should long appear to be unanswered.

The widow had no promises to plead. At no time had the judge
intimated that he would willingly attend to her case. But we have
the promises of God to plead, and they feed our fervency and importunity.

The widow could not plead any ties of affinity, for the judge was
in no wise related to the woman. How different it is with those of
us "born by a new celestial birth" — adopted into the family of God
(Psalm 103:13)!

The widow had no friend at hand to aid her in pleading her cause.
But we have an "Advocate *with* the Father" — resident at Court — to
attend to our cause. He is at the Judge's right hand, "Great Advocate! Almighty Friend!" So let us not faint but pray on until "the
muscles of Omnipotence" move on our behalf. May grace be ours to
rest in "the philanthropy of our Saviour God."

>Then earnest let us cry,
>And never faint in prayer;
>God loves our importunity,
>And makes our cause His care.

Prayer of the Pharisee and the Publican
(Luke 18:9-14)

The Pharisee stood and prayed thus with himself, God, I thank thee, that I am not as other men are, extortioners, unjust, adulterers, or even as this publican. I fast twice in the week, I give tithes of all that I possess. And the publican, standing afar off, would not lift up so much as his eyes unto heaven, but smote upon his breast, saying, God be merciful to me a sinner.   — Luke 18:11-13

Without the overwhelming and humbling vision of divine holiness (Job 42:5), one might pray, like the Pharisee, a prayer of gratitude, but not cry, like the Publican, for mercy. The confession of obedience to the Law was not backed up by an obedient heart and thus found rejection (18:12; Deuteronomy 26:13). Position will be noted in these prayers. The Pharisee offered his heartless prayer of gratitude standing; so did the Publican as he cried for mercy (Matthew 6:5; Mark 11:25; Luke 18:11, 13). Both went up to the Temple, the house of prayer to pray (Luke 18:10; 19:46).

When Jesus instructed His disciples, "After this manner pray ye," He meant prayers to be brief and real. He thus approved the seven-word prayer of the Publican, but condemned the longer prayer of the Pharisee (Matthew 20:47; Luke 18:11, 13; Mark 12:46). His further parable on prayer teaches us the true spirit which should animate us as we approach God in prayer. Here are two men in the same place, at the same time, in the same posture, but what a striking contrast between their prayers.

The Pharisee took his stand by himself, for so the words imply, in the spirit of the boaster Isaiah describes (65:5, see Matthew 6:5). He spoke of himself five times but his prayer lacked adoration (unless of himself), confession, petition, thanksgiving (except of himself as not being like "the rest of men" — 18:11. R.V.). Such a bumptious prayer received no answer. He asked for nothing and got it (18:14). Augustine says: "He was like the sufferer on the table of a physician, who would show his sound limbs and cover his hurts." May the Lord save us from the vain-glory and offensive ostentation of the Pharisee.

The Publican asking for mercy received justification. He "stood afar off, and would not lift up so much as his eyes to heaven" (Ezra 9:8; Psalm 40:12). "The foundation of prayer," Paley observes, "in cases, is a sense of want. No man prays in earnest, or to any purpose, for what he does not feel that he wants." Consciousness of his need and guilt prevented the Publican from raising his eyes, but his heart ascended in godly sorrow. Sighs and groans swallowed up his words, but what he did say was to purpose. He beat upon his breast (18:2). Groaning is an evidence of need (Romans 8:26). The Pharisee felt he had no sin to confess, hence he had no occasion to cry for mercy. But the Publican pleading for mercy was answered on the ground of propitiation (18:13 R.V. margin). His is the prayer God ever hearkens to —

O God of mercy, hear my call!
My load of guilt remove;
Break down this separating wall,
That bars me from Thy love.

Prayer for Peter's Preservation

(Luke 22:31, 32)

And the Lord said, Simon, Simon, behold, Satan hath desired to have you, that he may sift you as wheat: But I have prayed for thee, that thy faith fail not: and when thou art converted, strengthen thy brethren.   — Luke 22:31, 32

There are some prayers even disciples would like to quench but which the Master encourages (19:37, 38). What a difference it would have made if Peter had kept in mind the warning of the Master: "Watch ye therefore, and pray always" (21:26). Intercessory prayers in the Old Testament were usually offered for forfeited or imperilled lives. In the New Testament the object of intercessory prayer is usually related to the spiritual welfare of those prayed for. It was thus that Christ prayed for Peter's protection in the hour of satanic assault, and as He prayed for him, He prays for all His own (John 17:6-19).

Robert Murray M'Cheyne said: "If I could hear Jesus praying for me in the next room, I should not fear a thousand devils." Christ *is* praying for us, just as He prayed for Peter, which should be a comfort when fierce temptations arise. The "next room" is not far away, for space has nothing to do with the life of the unseen world. "He ever liveth to make intercession for us."

Prayer of Agony

(Luke 22:39-46)

And he was withdrawn from them about a stone's cast, and kneeled down, and prayed, Saying, Father, if thou be willing, remove this cup from me: nevertheless not my will, but thine, be done. And there appeared an angel unto him from heaven, strengthening him. And being in an agony he prayed more earnestly: and his sweat was as it were great drops of blood falling down to the ground.
                                    — Luke 22:41-44

Having given thanks for the cup, filled to the brim with our "death and curse" (22:19, 20), Jesus comes to Gethsemane to an agony of prayer (22:44). Truly there is no intensity in prayer comparable to our Saviour's strong crying and tears (Hebrews 5:7). We will never understand what is meant by His sweat appearing as great drops of blood. While Luke is not alone in describing Christ's agony, he is alone nevertheless in some of Gethsemane's most touching details. When in the *Litany* people pray — "By Thine Agony and bloody sweat . . . Good Lord, deliver us," they use a word found only in Luke. It is to Luke that we owe mention of the drops of blood and the presence of the ministering Angel to strengthen Jesus for a yet more intense and fervent supplication.

Christ's agony came as He thought upon, not that He was to die, but that, in dying, He was to be made sin for us. This was why He had to tread the wine-press alone.

> Gethsemane can I forget?
> Or there Thy conflict see,
> Thine agony and bloody sweat —
> And not remember Thee?

The three disciples Jesus took with Him that they might pray with, and for, Him, failed Him (Luke 22:45). Not only had they failed Him, but they needed to learn how to pray with intensity for themselves in preparation for their own hour of anguish (22:46).

Prayer and the Risen Lord

(Luke 24:30, 50-53)

And it came to pass, as he sat at meat with them, he took bread, and blessed it, and brake, and gave to them.
And he led them out as far as to Bethany, and he lifted up his hands, and blessed them. And it came to pass, while he blessed them, he was parted from them, and carried up into heaven. And they worshipped him, and returned to Jerusalem with great joy: And were continually in the temple, praising and blessing God. Amen.

— Luke 24:30, 50-53

The prayer-habits of Jesus continue into His risen life. Accepting the hospitality of the saints He met on the Emmaus Road, He gave thanks for the evening meal (24:30). Was it this characteristic feature that revealed the true identity of the One saying grace to the disciples (24:31; John 6:11)?

As Christ left His own, He lifted up His hands in priestly fashion and blessed them, and was carried up into heaven with uplifted hands. Was this attitude not symbolic of the ministry He was about to enter upon, namely, the Advocate on high? When the hands of Moses were uplifted on the mountain-top, Israel prevailed in the valley below (Exodus 17:11, 12).

> The holy hands uplifted
> In suffering's longest hour
> Are truly Spirit-gifted
> With intercessive power.

The true Church of Jesus Christ cannot fail for behind her is His prevailing intercession, as He pleads for her that her faith fail not. What else can we do but praise and bless God for such an Intercessor (24:53)! Dr. David H. Macintyre reminds us of the fruits of Christ's present-intercession:

1. It secures to us peace of conscience and the assurance of our Father's free and unalterable forgiving (Romans 8:34).

2. It provides for our complete sanctification. He is now able to save *from* the uttermost to the uttermost.

John

The fourth gospel is in a category all its own, in that it emphasizes the deity of Jesus Christ as the Son of God (1:34). That there was a peculiar affection between Jesus and John is attested to by the fact that the latter is always designated as "the disciple whom Jesus loved." It was also John who is spoken of as leaning on the bosom of Jesus (13:23). John, above the other disciples, seemed to have understood his Lord's secrets, even the secret of prayer.

Prayer for the Spirit

(John 4:9, 15, 19, 28; 7:37-39; 14:16)

The woman saith unto him, Sir, give me this water, that I thirst not, neither come hither to draw.   — John 4:15
In the last day, that great day of the feast, Jesus stood and cried, saying, If any man thirst, let him come unto me, and drink. He that believeth on me, as the scripture hath said, out of his belly shall flow rivers of living water. (But this spake he of the Spirit, which they that believe on him should receive: for the Holy Ghost was not yet given; because that Jesus was not yet glorified.)   — John 7:37-39
And I will pray the Father, and he shall give you another Comforter, that he may abide with you for ever.   — John 14:16

The woman of Samaria came with her waterpot to draw water but finding a Well, she had no further need of her waterpot (4:28). The believer's work of intercession has a wide sweep (John 4:35), and his Source of power as He witnesses for the Master are "the rivers of living water" (7:37-39), even the Holy Spirit, Jesus prayed might be given to His own (John 14:16).

Prayer of a Nobleman

(John 4:46-54)

So Jesus came again into Cana of Galilee, where he made the water wine. And there was a certain nobleman, whose son was sick at Capernaum. When he heard that Jesus was come out of Judaea into Galilee, he went unto him, and besought him that he would come down, and heal his son: for he was at the point of death. Then said Jesus unto him, Except ye see signs and wonders, ye will not believe. The nobleman saith unto him, Sir, come down ere my child die. Jesus saith unto him, Go thy way; thy son liveth. And the man believed the word that Jesus had spoken unto him, and he went his way.   — John 4:46-50

That God does hear sinners (9:31) is borne out by Christ's response to the prayers of the Capernaum nobleman. How else can sinners come to Him (5:40) but by prayer and faith? Human sorrow is the birth-pang of prayer. The distressed father's sense of utter powerlessness drove him to Christ. His presence, however, was not necessary for the child's healing. "Go thy way, thy son liveth." Believing the spoken word of Christ, the nobleman returned home and was met by his servants with the good news. He had no doubt about the Lord's word — he knew there was power in it (Ecclesiastes 8:4). With the performance of the miracle there came a yet higher faith — *himself believed* (4:53). He believed when he went to Cana, he believed the word of Christ when he was told to go his way, but here we have a fuller faith, faith's development (2:11; 4:41, 42).

Prayer for the Bread of Life

(John 6:34)

Then said they unto him, Lord, evermore give us this bread.

— John 6:34

This "Bread Chapter" reveals Christ giving thanks for bread to eat (6:11, 23), and also His prayer-escape when the throngs would have made Him a king before His time (6:15; Revelation 11:15; 19:16). Prayer as a confession of faith concludes the chapter (6:68, 69). What interests us most in the chapter is the prayer, "Lord, evermore give us this bread." As the woman at the well understood the words of Jesus about water in a physical sense (4:15), so here the people thought only of the satisfaction of a physical need. They did not realize that man cannot live by bread alone. Jesus spoke of the bread of God coming in the same way as the manna fell from heaven, giving life to the Israelites, and the people wanted an unfailing supply of bread. Yesterday they ate the bread He blessed, but they were hungry again today and so prayed, "Lord, give us evermore this bread."

Jesus went on to describe how He Himself is the Bread giving life: that He is the One sustaining the spiritual life in strength and refreshing it in weariness. And as we eat and drink of Him, hunger and thirst are removed (6:51-58; Matthew 5:6). Well might we pray, "Lord, give us evermore of Thyself."

> Thou bruised and broken Bread,
> My life-long wants supply,
> As living souls are fed,
> O feed me, or I die.

Prayer for Confirmation

(John 11:40-42)

And Jesus lifted up his eyes, and said, Father, I thank thee that thou hast heard me. And I knew that thou hearest me always: but because of the people which stand by I said it, that they may believe that thou hast sent me.   — John 11:41, 42

When Jesus went to the Mount to pray (8:1), He always went alone. Thus we have no record of any position He adopted. Here, with others around, He lifted up His eyes impressively to heaven. The raising of Lazarus would be a miracle demanding all the power of God manifested through His Son. What favor Christ had with His Father — "Thou hearest me always" (11:42). He was heard always, for He always did those things pleasing to the Father (John 8:29). Is ours the glad and confident consciousness that God hears and favors our prayers?

Prayer with a Double Aspect

(John 12:27, 28)

Now is my soul troubled; and what shall I say? Father, save me from this hour: but for this cause came I unto this hour. Father, glorify thy name. Then came there a voice from heaven, saying, I have both glorified it, and will glorify it again.   — John 12:27, 28

No wonder Jesus had a troubled soul (12:27; 13:21), He was about to die as a felon on a wooden gibbet (12:32), and suffer the onslaughts of hell. Yet He was the One who could also speak to His disciples about the secret of the untroubled heart (14:1). The significance of the two clauses of Christ's must be noted —

"Father, save me from this hour."
"Father, glorify thy name."

John does not pass over the agony of the garden of Gethsemane — it is all compressed in these lines. The first line indicates that the moment of agony is the moment of victory. The second line proves the Son's will to be one with that of the Father's; the Son's glory is in the glorifying of the Father's Name. The deepest desire of Jesus was that the will of God be done, but His human will prayed vehemently that the cup should pass.

Prayer as an acknowledgment of Christ's Lordship and of His revelation of the Father, also finds mention in this fourth gospel (13:13-17; 14:8; see 5:23).

Prayer As a Privilege

(John 14:13-15; 15:16; 16:23-26)

And whatsoever ye shall ask in my name, that will I do, that the Father may be glorified in the Son. If ye shall ask any thing in my name, I will do it.   — John 14:13, 14

Ye have not chosen me, but I have chosen you, and ordained you, that ye should go and bring forth fruit, and that your fruit should remain: that whatsoever ye shall ask of the Father in my name, he may give it you.   — John 15:16

And in that day ye shall ask me nothing. Verily, verily, I say unto you, Whatsoever ye shall ask the Father in my name, he will give it you. Hitherto have ye asked nothing in my name: ask, and ye shall receive, that your joy may be full. These things have I spoken unto you in proverbs: but the time cometh, when I shall no more speak unto you in proverbs, but I shall shew you plainly of the Father. At that day ye shall ask in my name: and I say not unto you, that I will pray the Father for you: For the Father himself loveth you, because ye have loved me, and have believed that I came out from God. — John 16:23-27

Is it not the greatest of all privileges to pray, and to know that, if obedient to the divine will, prayer is always answered? The "greater works" Jesus refers to (14:12) are spiritual works. He probably had in mind the physical miracles He performed by the power of the Spirit (Matthew 12:28). In this age, the self-same Spirit enables us to perform spiritual miracles. Raising the dead was indeed wonderful, but all the persons Jesus raised died again. Those whom we are the means of raising from a grave of sin and lust are robed with life eternal.

Already we have discussed our warrant for prayer, namely, prayer in Christ's Name (14:13, 14; 15:16; 16:23). In the prayer of Manasseh, God is addressed as the One who has "shut up the deep and sealed it by thy terrible and glorious name." The power of His name is written large over the Word. "The higher the being, the more powerful the name." Prayers in His name are the ones answered either by God or Christ (14:13, 14; 15:16). In urging His disciples to ask in His name, Christ seems to be deliberately avoiding prayer being offered to Himself. He explicitly urges them to ask the Father (14:13, 14; 15:16; 16:23).

The prime motive at the back of all our praying should be the glory of God. "Ask . . . that the Father may be glorified (14:13)." This is the supreme prayer secret. This is the highest purpose we must aspire to in all our prayers, and which can be realized as we ask, as He would ask, and abide in Him (14:13, 14; 15:7). How we need to lay to heart these parting directions regarding the exercise of the most powerful force in the world! If we would be fruitful branches of the vine, our wills must be in unison with Christ's as we pray in His name (15:16).

Prayer of All Prayers

(John 17)

These words spake Jesus, and lifted up his eyes to heaven, and said, Father, the hour is come; glorify thy Son, that thy Son also may glorify thee: As thou hast given him power over all flesh, that he should give eternal life to as many as thou hast given him. And this is life eternal, that they might know thee the only true God, and Jesus Christ, whom thou hast sent. I have glorified thee on the earth: I have finished the work which thou gavest me to do. And now, O Father, glorify thou me with thine own self with the glory which I had with thee before the world was. I have manifested thy name unto the men which thou gavest me out of the world: thine they were, and thou gavest them me; and they have kept thy word. Now they have known that all things whatsoever thou hast given me are of thee. For I have given unto them the words which thou gavest me; and they have received them, and have known surely that I came out from thee, and they have believed that thou didst send me. I pray for them: I pray not for the world, but for them which thou hast given me; for they are thine. And all mine are thine, and thine are mine; and I am glorified in them. And now I am no more in the world, but these are in the world, and I come to thee. Holy Father, keep through thine own name those whom thou hast given me, that they may be one, as we are. While I was with them in the world, I kept them in thy name: those that thou gavest me I have kept, and none of them is lost, but the son of perdition; that the scripture might be fulfilled. And now come I to thee; and these things I speak in the world, that they might have my joy fulfilled in themselves. I have given them thy word; and the world hath hated them, because they are not of the world, even as I am not of the world. I pray not that thou shouldest take them out of the world, but that thou shouldest keep them from the evil. They are not of the world, even as I am not of the world. Sanctify them through thy truth: thy word is truth. As thou hast sent me into the world, even so have I also sent them into the world. And for their sakes I sanctify myself, that they also might be sanctified through the truth. Neither pray I for these alone, but for them also which shall believe on me through their word; That they all may be one; as thou, Father, art in me, and I in thee, that they also may be one in us: that the world may believe that thou hast sent me. And the glory which thou gavest me I have given them; that they may be one, even as we are one: I in them, and thou in me, that they may be made perfect in one; and that the world may know that thou hast sent me, and hast loved them, as thou hast loved me. Father, I will that they also, whom thou hast given me, be with me where I am; that they may behold my glory, which thou hast given me: for thou lovedst me before the foundation of the world. O righteous Father, the world hath not known thee: but I have known thee, and these have known that thou hast sent me. And I have declared unto them thy name, and will declare it: that the love wherewith thou hast loved me may be in them, and I in them.   — John 17

We have now come to the Holy of Holies in the New Testament. Here Christ is revealed as the mighty Intercessor. This great chapter in which John Knox cast his anchor, contains the longest recorded and only prolonged prayer of Christ — the unexampled outpouring of His heart to the Father He ever glorified.

This High-Priestly Prayer of Christ's was the prayer of the night in which He was betrayed and preceded by an hour or two the terrible agony itself. We conclude our meditation of the Prayers of Christ with this continuous prayer, seeing that it lights up all the other recorded prayers of His. Not only so, we consider it last because although it was prayed on earth, it is an anticipation of the Saviour's heavenly intercession. "It belongs, as it were," says Vaughan, "to the two lives and the two worlds — 'the days of His flesh' and the years of His glory — earth and heaven."

Here we have the true "Lord's Prayer," the one He actually prayed. We are accustomed to speak of the prayer He taught His disciples to use as the "Lord's Prayer," but as the Sinless One, He could not offer the prayer Himself. The prayer before us, however, abundantly poured out for His own, begins and ends with the glory of God, and is, as Mrs. A. T. Robertson beautifully expresses it, "Like a rose, half drowning us with its sweetness, like some lovely falling melody that comes again and again, the reiterated love and longing of the chapter are almost more than we can bear."

It would seem as if our Lord's prayer moved in three distinct circles — He prayed for Himself, for His own, for the world.

1. He Prayed for Himself (1-8)

The Fatherhood of God permeates most of the New Testament prayers. Here Jesus calls Him Father (1-5), Holy Father (11), Righteous Father (25). The prayer has all the atmosphere of Christ's last days and contains the characteristic truths He taught. Note His four "I haves" in this section

"I have glorified thee on earth" (4)

"I have finished the work thou gavest me to do" (4)

"I have manifested thy name" (6)

"I have given unto them the words thou gavest me" (8)

It is impressive that this great intercessory prayer begins with a petition for the glory of the Father *and* the Son, each through the other.

2. He Prayed for His Own (9-19)

For His Church, He prayed, and still prays, that she may be preserved from the evil one and sanctified through the truth. Preservation and Sanctification! How deep our need is in both directions.

3. He Prayed for the World (20-26)

In this concluding section of His prayer, Christ looks down the corridor of time and prays for all those who are to listen to His preached word and intercedes that "the world may believe." Commenting on this sentence, Vaughan remarks: "What if by face and name some of us had place in that prayer? What if in all our afflictions He was afflicted, and was then bespeaking the Angel of the Presence on behalf of definite trials, personal sorrows, now gradually evolving and realizing themselves in us?"

As attention has been drawn to the betrayal by Judas of Christ's prayer-trysting place (18:1, 2), there is no need to linger over his dastardly act.

The prayer or confession of Thomas, "My Lord and my God" (20:28), suggests His right to worship because of His Sovereignty and Deity. John concludes his intimate Gospel with a lament that he had not the opportunity of recording all the things Jesus did (21:25). If only we could have had all the prayers Jesus prayed from His earliest days until His Ascension, what a spiritual classic they would have made. We can only re-echo the sentiment of Professor McFadyen:

"Thrice happy those who were privileged to hear Jesus pray! His manner can never be recalled or repeated, because He stands alone among the sons of men, but the prayers themselves are for us and for all men." Following the spotless One in His earthly prayer-ministry, what else can we do but cry, "Lord, teach us to pray"?

Acts

This fifth book of the New Testament, which has been called "The Acts of the Holy Spirit through the Apostles," is saturated with prayer. The Early Church was the Church Militant, seeing she was a Church living on her knees. Her witness was dynamic for behind it there was that prevailing prayer, conquering even the proud legions of Rome. The early Apostolic prayers were radiant with hope. After Christ's Ascension, the disciples returned to Jerusalem to await the coming of the promised Spirit with a three-fold joy, for Jesus had given them a Promise, a Person and a Plan.

Prayer in the Upper Chamber

(Acts 1:13, 14)

These all continued with one accord in prayer and supplication, with the women, and Mary the mother of Jesus, and with his brethren.   — Acts 1:14

Here we have the first prayer meeting of the Church. Historically, the Church of Jesus Christ was born in a prayer meeting and her life can only be maintained in the same atmosphere. What a time of blessed fellowship those 120 believers must have had! Why were they gathered together there? Not to pray for the coming Holy Spirit. It was not necessary to pray for Someone who had been promised (John 14:26; 1:4). In prayer, they were preparing themselves for the reception of and fellowship with the Spirit in the outworking of Christ's redemptive plan. Those ten days of prayer prefaced the great task of evangelization (Acts 1:8). Would that prayer meetings were as popular and powerful today as they were in the life of the early Church!

How essential it is for us to "tarry in Jerusalem," not in indolence or mere passiveness, but in expectation and yearning — in silence and meditation and prayer and desire. If we are to be fit for service, we must be very familiar with the secret place of the Most High, where He will whisper in our ears the message to be sounded from the housetop.

Prayer for a Successor

(Acts 1:15-26)

And they prayed, and said, Thou, Lord, which knowest the hearts of all men, shew whether of these two thou hast chosen, That he may take part of this ministry and apostleship, from which Judas by transgression fell, that he might go to his own place. — Acts 1:24, 25

Luke gives us the last reference of the casting of lots in the Bible, as he records the appointment of a successor to Judas. Prayer accompanied the lot (1:26). Doubtless the apostles felt that such a method of seeking direction was no longer worthy or compatible with absolute reliance upon the Holy Spirit who had come to lead them into all truth. With two suitable candidates to fill the vacancy in the apostleship sincere prayer was offered to the Searcher of hearts (1:24). Wherever there is doubt regarding a decision the heart should turn instinctively to God.

Whether the apostles' prayer for a successor to Judas was addressed to God or to Christ is not easy to affirm. As the epithet "Who knowest the heart" was used, it suggests that the prayer was addressed to God, as it is later on (15:8). Prayers, however, were offered to Christ (9:17).

Prayer and Worship
(Acts 2:42-47)

And they continued stedfastly in the apostles' doctrine and fellowship, and in breaking of bread, and in prayers.   — Acts 2:42

The Church has drifted far from the simplicity of worship of the Early Church. Did not the Spirit inspire those first disciples to set forth a pattern of worship for all ages? Teaching of doctrine, fellowship around the Word, the breaking of bread, intercession — these were powerfully influential in the lives of the early saints. And their "togetherness" made an impact upon the world around.

When "prayers" were offered, it is reasonable to assume that men and *women* participated. Among those who "continued stedfastly in prayer" in the upper room were the women, among whom was Mary the mother of Jesus. The mark of a true widow is continuance in supplications and prayers (I Timothy 5:5). Evidently, women in the Corinthian Church prayed publicly, as well as prophesied (I Corinthians 11:5).

Prayer As an Observance
(Acts 3:1)

Now Peter and John went up together into the temple at the hour of prayer, being the ninth hour.   — Acts 3:1

In the book before us, the three recognized hours of prayer — the third hour (2:15), the sixth hour (10:9), the ninth hour (3:1; 10:36), are expressly mentioned, and were periods observed by Jews and Christians (2:15; 10:30; 3:1; 10:9). The early Christians as well as Jews thought of the Temple as "the house of prayer" (3:1; 22:17; Luke 24:53).

Praying Peter and John were given power to heal the lame beggar (3:6), a miracle resulting in the gratitude of the man himself, who twice over is spoken of as "praising God" (3:8, 9). Healing of infirmity was often acknowledged by prayer, the praise being offered by the person cured, or by those witnessing the cure (Matthew 9:8; Mark 2:12). The power of Christ's Name is prominent throughout Acts (3:6, 16; 4:30).

Prayer for Boldness of Witness

(Acts 4:23-31)

And when they heard that, they lifted up their voice to God with one accord, and said, Lord, thou art God, which hast made heaven, and earth, and the sea, and all that in them is: Who by the mouth of thy servant David hast said, Why did the heathen rage, and the people imagine vain things? The kings of the earth stood up, and the rulers were gathered together against the Lord, and against his Christ. For of a truth against thy holy child Jesus, whom thou hast anointed, both Herod, and Pontius Pilate, with the Gentiles, and the people of Israel, were gathered together. For to do whatsoever thy hand and thy counsel determined before to be done. And now, Lord, behold their threatenings: and grant unto thy servants, that with all boldness they may speak thy word. By stretching forth thine hand to heal; and that signs and wonders may be done by the name of thy holy child Jesus.   — Acts 4:24-30

Peter proved that prayer could banish all fear and impart a holy audacity for Christ (4:13). Such boldness is not mere fleshly courage, it is an utter disregard for all cost of witness born in the presence of our fearless Lord. "They had been with Jesus." Certain epithets, it would seem, became favorite expressions in the vocabulary of prayer and preaching (4:24; 14:15; Philippians 1:3). This prayer of Peter and John liberated from prison is saturated with Old Testament Scripture (4:24-26 with Psalm 2:1, 2). The Messiah they now preached was indeed the One "by prophet-bards foretold."

Prayer inspired the apostolic church for offensive action against Pagan Rome, with its puppet Herod, as well as against Jewish and Gentile animosity. The apostles were well aware of the strength of the opposition, but they believed that God not only ruled but over-ruled (4:24, 28, 29). Their heart-felt prayers had a three-fold result.

1. Conspicuous boldness of utterance was given (4:33).

2. Unity of purpose and of prayer characterized their efforts (4:24, 32). "They lifted up their voice to God with one accord . . . they were of one heart and of one soul." It is interesting to note that our word *symphony* is from the oft-repeated "accord" we have in Acts.

3. Beauty of character became theirs. "Great grace was upon them all" (4:33). Lives were in full harmony with their lips.

As the apostles prayed, immediate evidence was theirs that God had heard them (4:31). How the prayer-room was shaken, we are not told. We do read that there was an exhibition of great power carrying conviction to those who prayed that God was their Protector.

Sometimes the supernatural voice was that of an angel's, as in the case when one appeared to the apostles in prison commanding them to go and preach in the Temple (5:20). Supernatural power is delegated to angels (5:19).

Prayer and the Ministry of the Word

(Acts 6:4-7)

But we will give ourselves continually to prayer, and to the ministry
of the word.   — Acts 6:4

"Prayer is the fountain of the ministry, co-ordinate in importance
with preaching and the source of its power." Prayer was given the
first place. If only we could restore the apostolic order, apostolic
results would be experienced. Those who felt they were called to
minister the word of God (6:2) gave themselves *continually* to prayer.
No wonder their preaching of the Word was dynamic. It is tragic how
little time present-day preachers and teachers of the Word devote
to prayer.

Prayer of the First Martyr

(Acts 7:55-60)

And they stoned Stephen, calling upon God, and saying, Lord Jesus,
receive my spirit. And he kneeled down, and cried with a loud voice,
Lord, lay not this sin to their charge. And when he had said this, he
fell asleep.   — Acts 7:59, 60

Like the Master before him, Stephen experienced the transfiguring
power of prayer (6:8, 10, 15). "His eyes were beautiful, because you
saw that they saw Christ." Dying, Stephen reflected the spirit of Jesus
who prayed for His murderers (Isaiah 53:12; Luke 23:34). Kneeling
down, Stephen prayed with a loud voice for those stoning him to
death. Like Jesus, this first martyr of the Church died as a victor,
not a victim. Praying to the Lord Jesus to receive his spirit (7:59), he
re-echoed the Master's last prayer on the Cross (Luke 23:46).

> Like Him with pardon on His tongue,
> In midst of mortal pain,
> He prayed for them that did the wrong:
> Who follows in His train?

How different was the dying prayer of vengeance Samson prayed
(Judges 16:28).

It is remarkable that Stephen saw Jesus *standing* on the right hand
of God (7:55, 56). At His Ascension, Christ "sat down on the right
hand of the Majesty on high" (Hebrews 1:3), a posture indicating a
finished work. But here He stands. Why? Was it to honor the entrance
into heaven of such a Spirit-filled saint, willing to shed his blood for
the Christ who had shed His?

Prayer for Samaritans and a Sorcerer

(Acts 8:9-25)

Now when the apostles which were at Jerusalem heard that Samaria
had received the word of God, they sent unto them Peter and John:
Who, when they were come down, prayed for them, that they might
receive the Holy Ghost. . . .

And when Simon saw that through laying on of the apostles' hands the Holy Ghost was given, he offered them money, Saying, Give me also this power, that on whomsoever I lay hands, he may receive the Holy Ghost. But Peter said unto him, Thy money perish with thee, because thou hast thought that the gift of God may be purchased with money. Thou hast neither part nor lot in this matter: for thy heart is not right in the sight of God. Repent therefore of this thy wickedness, and pray God, if perhaps the thought of thine heart may be forgiven thee. For I perceive that thou art in the gall of bitterness, and in the bond of iniquity. Then answered Simon, and said, Pray ye to the Lord for me, that none of these things which ye have spoken come upon me.   — Acts 8:14, 15, 18-24

Persecution scattered the disciples, and the blood of a martyr became the seed of the Church (8:1, 4, 6-8). Praying Philip fulfilled his part of the commission (1:8) and in Samaria saw God work miracles (8:6). Through prayer the Samaritans came into the fulness of the blessing of the Gospel of Christ (8:15). Simon Magus, feeling that Spirit-produced miracles was good magic (8:13), became terrified over Peter's scathing rebuke and prayed for forgiveness for mistaking the nature of prayer and the gifts of God. It is not every revivalist who is willing to leave the heart of a revival (8:5-7) and go to the heart of the desert (8:26, 27) to speak to a solitary soul about the saving grace of Christ (8:25).

Prayer of a Convert

(Acts 9:5, 6, 11, see 22:8-18; 26:12-19)

And he said, Who art thou, Lord? And the Lord said, I am Jesus whom thou persecutest: it is hard for thee to kick against the pricks. And he trembling and astonished said, Lord, what wilt thou have me to do? And the Lord said unto him, Arise, and go into the city, and it shall be told thee what thou must do. . . .
And the Lord said unto him, Arise, and go into the street which is called Straight, and enquire in the house of Judas for one called Saul, of Tarsus: for, behold, he prayeth.   — Acts 9:5, 6, 11

God interprets prayer as a sign of all that happened to Saul of Tarsus at the noonday hour, on the Damascus road. "Behold, he prayeth." God seems to speak in terms of wonder at the remarkable, sudden change of the persecutor into a pleader. As an orthodox Jew, Paul had been a praying man all his life, but not until he was born anew by the Spirit did he know what it was to pray as God interprets prayer.

> I often say my prayers,
> Do I ever pray?

The biggest thing in God's universe is a person who prays in the Spirit. Prayer is the symbol and proof and gauge of Grace, and of growth in it. Young converts should be encouraged to pray, not only in private but in public, for prayer is a privilege more vital as it is used.

Prayer for Dorcas

(Acts 9:36-43)

But Peter put them all forth, and kneeled down, and prayed; and turning him to the body said, Tabitha, arise.   — Acts 9:40a

Bowing his knees, Peter prayed for dead Dorcas. His posture was a recognition of dependence upon God for the display of His power. Answered prayers for the restoration of the dead are naturally rare in Scripture (I Kings 17:12; II Kings 4:35; Acts 9:40). Delegated power to raise the dead was discontinued after the establishment of the Church as a divine institution.

Emulating the example of Christ at the resurrection of Jairus' daughter (Matthew 9:23, 24), Peter requested the mourners to leave him alone with the dead. The miracle could not be performed by his own power or holiness (3:12), but only by the power and prayer of faith and this called for the silence and solitude of communion with God, who alone can raise the dead.

Prayer of Cornelius

(Acts 10:2-4, 9, 31)

A devout man, and one that feared God with all his house, which gave much alms to the people, and prayed to God alway. He saw in a vision evidently about the ninth hour of the day an angel of God coming in to him, and saying unto him, Cornelius. And when he looked on him, he was afraid, and said, What is it, Lord? And he said unto him, Thy prayers and thine alms are come up for a memorial before God. . . .
On the morrow, as they went on their journey, and drew nigh unto the city, Peter went up upon the house top to pray about the sixth hour: . . .
And said, Cornelius, thy prayer is heard, and thine alms are had in remembrance in the sight of God.   — Acts 10: 2-4, 9, 31

Because of the universality of prayers, Jews and Gentiles alike have access to God. Thus the Roman Cornelius may pray to God as well as the Hebrew Peter (Zechariah 8:22). Peter acted under the direction of the Spirit (10:19). Prayers and alms are united (10:4). While Cornelius did not know how to plead the promises as a child of Abraham nor pray in the Name of Jesus Christ, nevertheless his prayers were accepted for their sincerity.

Little did Peter realize that when he went to the house top to pray, that he was to encounter one of the great moments of his life and labors. While in prayer, the vision of God's purpose to save Gentiles as well as Jews came to Peter, and thoroughly Jewish though he was, believing that salvation was for Jews only, he obeyed the vision. "God hath shewed me." How could he resist such a revelation? Out Peter went to preach to the Gentiles repentance unto life (11:18). The triumph of the Gospel among the Gentiles became a source of profoundest gratitude (Ephesians 3:8).

Prayer for Peter in Prison

(Acts 12:5, 12-17)

Peter therefore was kept in prison: but prayer was made without ceasing of the church unto God for him. . . .
And when he had considered the thing, he came to the house of Mary the mother of John, whose surname was Mark: where many were gathered together praying.   — Acts 12:5, 12

Early in its existence, the Church knew what it was to have fellowship with Christ in His baptism of death. James had been killed by the sword and Peter is under sentence. The Church went to her knees, yet the praying disciples would not believe it when the answer to their prayers was at the door. God is greater than our prayers. The prayer-watchers prayed without ceasing unto God for the release of Peter, but their prayer meeting was interrupted by a knock at the door. When told it was Peter they could not believe it and told Rhoda she was mad. "Too good to be true" — "It cannot be" — "Impossible" were the feelings of those who prayed, who failed to pray believingly. It is not sufficient to pray for great things from God. We must have faith to *expect* great things from Him. Peter's miraculous release while the saints were praying for it is a striking illustration of God hearing our cry as we cry (Isaiah 65:24).

Prayer of Ordination

(Acts 13:2, 3, 43)

As they ministered to the Lord, and fasted, the Holy Ghost said, Separate me Barnabas and Saul for the work whereunto I have called them. And when they had fasted and prayed, and laid their hands on them, they sent them away.   — Acts 13:2, 3

Chosen of the Spirit to work together in the expansion of the Church, Paul and Barnabas were prayerfully commissioned for such a task. "The end must be consecrated, as the beginning." The repetition of the words prayed and fasted (13:2, 3) implies that such a double act was prolonged until the ordination was completed. The Church as a whole did not set apart Paul and Barnabas for the work of the Lord, it simply attested its acceptance of the Spirit's choice and invoked divine blessing upon the chosen two.

Prayer with Fasting

(Acts 13:2, 3; 14:15, 23, 26)

And when they had fasted and prayed, and laid their hands on them, they sent them away.   — Acts 13:3
And when they had ordained them elders in every church, and had prayed with fasting, they commended them to the Lord, on whom they believed.   — Acts 14:23

The strenuous missionary work facing the apostles called for that intensity of spiritual life of which *fasting* was more or less the normal condition. Paul and Barnabas also recognized these two acts as necessary preparation for the solemn work of appointing others to spiritual functions. "Without prayer such an appointment was a mockery, and fasting served to intensify prayer." Confirmation of the double act of prayer and fasting quickly followed (15:8, 28, 40). Fasting, as an accompaniment of prayer, is common to Old and New Testaments alike (I Samuel 7:6; Ezra 8:21; Daniel 9:3; Luke 5:33).

A devout Englishman of a past century wrote: "I shall be spare of sleep, sparer of diet, and sparest of time, that when the days for eating, drinking, clothing, and sleeping shall be no more, I may eat of my Saviour's hidden manna, drink of the new wine in my Father's kingdom, and inherit that rest which remaineth for the people of my God for ever and ever."

Prayer at the Riverside

(Acts 16:13, 16)

And on the sabbath we went out of the city by a river side, where prayer was wont to be made; and we sat down, and spake unto the women which resorted thither. . . .
And it came to pass, as we went to prayer, a certain damsel possessed with a spirit of divination met us, which brought her masters much gain by soothsaying: . . .   — Acts 16:13, 16

What far-reaching results that Sabbath Day riverside prayer-meeting had! Lydia was converted and through her the Gospel found its way to Europe. Prayer can be offered in every place (I Timothy 2:8). At a riverside and seashore (16:13; 21:5), saints gathered for prayer and were blessed. On the way to another season of prayer at the same sacred spot, Paul and Silas were met by the demon-possessed girl, and had they not been men mighty in prayer, the miracle of her deliverance and salvation would not have been possible (Acts 16:16, 18).

Prayer in a Dungeon

(Acts 16:25, 34)

And at midnight Paul and Silas prayed, and sang praises unto God: and the prisoners heard them.   — Acts 16:25

That God is able to give songs in the night is evidenced by the way Paul and Silas triumphed over their adversity. Because of the effect of the demon-possessed girl's salvation, these two apostles found themselves in the foulness and darkness of a cavern-like cell, with the companionship of the vilest outcasts. With their feet in stocks they were left with little ease. But "The leg feels not the stocks when the mind is in heaven. Though the body is held fast, all things lie open to the spirit." The praying, praising hearts of Paul and Silas could not be bound. The present writer once heard General William Booth, founder of the Salvation Army, preach on the portion before us. Dealing with the prayers and praises of Paul and Silas, the General thundered forth — "And God said Amen! with a mighty earthquake." So He did, in an earthquake resulting in the conversion of the hard-hearted jailer. Paul and Silas proved that —

"Prayer is a creature's strength — his very breath and being."

Prayer of Committal

(Acts 20:36)

And when he had thus spoken, he kneeled down, and prayed with them all.   — Acts 20:36

What a sad farewell this was for Paul on the sands of Miletus! Those Church Elders at Ephesus had traveled some thirty miles to see and hear their beloved teacher once more. How he reminiscenced, charged and warned them! Then came the climax as they all knelt on the shore and Paul commended them to God and to the word of His grace. No wonder his friends wept and kissed Paul (20:36).

There are two touching and picturesque farewells in *Acts*. Here at Miletus and at Tyre, when after seven days' stay there, Paul was escorted to the shore by a large company where they knelt and prayed and bade each other goodbye (21:5). Praying saints never say "Goodbye" for the last time. Sorrowful separations are bound to come, but there is always the glorious prospect of reunion in the land where we never say, "Goodbye."

Prayer in a Shipwreck

(Acts 27:23-35)

For there stood by me this night the angel of God, whose I am, and whom I serve, Saying, Fear not, Paul; thou must be brought before Caesar: and lo, God hath given thee all them that sail with thee. . . .

And when he had thus spoken, he took bread, and gave thanks to God in presence of them all: and when he had broken it, he began to eat.   — Acts 27:23, 24, 35

We are not told that Paul prayed during the storm, yet he must have sent up many a "dart" prayer during those anxious hours. The fact that the Lord stood by him as he faced imminent peril is evidence enough that he was in vital touch with the Lord. What a master of the situation Paul was! He knew how to keep his head in a storm. Confidence in God enabled him to calm and cheer the shipwrecked men around him. The assurance the angel brought to Paul was communicated to others (27:24). "Throughout those dreary days and nights upon the sea and amid the impending terrors of shipwreck, Paul remains clear and calm," writes Professor McFadyen. "It was the man who had stayed his soul on God that was able to issue practical orders to his confused companions, and who succeeded in inspiring them with a calmness like his own."

Was it the observance of the Lord's Supper or an ordinary meal Paul gave thanks to God for (27:35)? This we do know, it must have been a heart-felt prayer of gratitude for God's vindication of his faith (27:25).

Prayer for the Fever-Stricken

(Acts 28:8, 15, 28)

And it came to pass, that the father of Publius lay sick of a fever and of a bloody flux: to whom Paul entered in, and prayed, and laid his hands on him, and healed him.   — Acts 28:8

The miraculous preservation of Paul from the poison of the viper (28:3-6), must have made a profound impression upon the Melitese and encouraged Publius, the chief man of Melita, to seek Paul's aid for his sick father. The apostle recognized he had no power of his own to heal, and so prayed. The double act of praying and the laying on of hands appears again in the rule James gives (5:14, 15).

The dramatic Book of Acts closes with the delightful visit of the brethren who had come from Rome to Appii Forum to meet Paul, whose ministry they deeply appreciated. When he saw them, the apostle thanked God and took courage, which courage he needed if, as legend has it, Paul was taken out to the Appian Way, where his noble head was severed from his frail body and he died for the Lord he dearly loved.

Romans

As we come to examine the Epistles for their prayer-content we shall not find an historical account of events that took place, as in the Book of Acts. This is why few prayers are recorded. We shall find, however, the outpouring of the hearts of the apostles and learn what were their desires for their fellow-believers, and, as these afford us happy instructions as to what may *now* be the character of the prayers of those who have the welfare of God's people at heart. Embracing, as these prayers did, the whole Church of God, we may believe that they were abundantly answered as regards many of whose lives we have no record, but whose record is on high.

The last book we considered gave us a deep insight into the prayer life of Paul. To him, prayer was more than a doctrine — it was a dynamic. We now approach a field of spiritual inquiry, rich in influence, namely, the Apostolic Prayers. In his *Glimpses of the Prayer-Life of the Apostle Paul*, E. W. Moore suggests that "in these days of multiplied manuals of devotion and directories for the spiritual life there is a real danger of overlooking the fact that we have in Paul's master-piece of intercession a guide to holy living, such as cannot be approached, far less excelled, in the devotional literature of any age or country. It is a remarkable feature of Paul's prayers that they are all conceived on the highest plane of spiritual living. Temporal matters, though most certainly they have their place in intercession, are not prominent — indeed, are scarcely contemplated here. These prayers breathe the Air of Heaven and conduct the suppliant thither."

Prayer for a Prosperous Journey

(Romans 1:8-15)

First, I thank my God through Jesus Christ for you all, that your faith is spoken of throughout the whole world. For God is my witness, whom I serve with my spirit in the gospel of his Son, that without ceasing I make mention of you always in my prayers; Making request, if by any means now at length I might have a prosperous journey by the will of God to come unto you.   — Romans 1:8-10

What a prayer-burden Paul had for the saints in Rome! How he longed to visit them and preach the Word for their encouragement and edification! The apostle was not only a great Thinker, Theologian, Missionary — he was also a great Intercessor. Without ceasing, he prayed for those receiving his letter — a people he had not seen. It is not as easy to pray for those we have never met, as it is for those we know. How warmly Paul praised those Roman Christians for their faith in God! Martin Luther spoke of Christianity as a "religion of possessive pronouns." Note Paul's appropriation of God in his prayers: "I thank *my* God." Thanksgiving is an integral part of prayer.

Paul must have had a remarkable prayer-list. Often he speaks of "making mention of you in my prayers" (Romans 1:9; Ephesians 1:16; I Thessalonians 1:2). The many incidental allusions to prayer in Paul's life and letters show what an enormous place it must have had in his life.

Prayer Inspired by the Spirit

(Romans 8:15, 23, 26, 27)

For ye have not received the spirit of bondage again to fear; but ye have received the Spirit of adoption, whereby we cry, Abba, Father. . . .
And not only they, but ourselves also, which have the firstfruits of the Spirit, even we ourselves groan within ourselves, waiting for the adoption, to wit, the redemption of our body. . . .
Likewise the Spirit also helpeth our infirmities: for we know not what we should pray for as we ought: but the Spirit itself maketh intercession for us with groanings which cannot be uttered. And he that searcheth the hearts knoweth what is the mind of the Spirit, because he maketh intercession for the saints according to the will of God.   — Romans 8:15, 23, 26, 27

All who are born of the Spirit are no longer bondservants unto fear, but sons, privileged to commune with their Heavenly Father (8:15; Galatians 4:6). What do we know, however, about the Gethsemane groans Paul mentions (8:26)? The apostle looked upon prayer as a grim struggle (15:20; Colossians 2:1).

The Holy Spirit is the Inspirer of true prayer and aids us in our infirmity to pray aright. We are inclined to ask for things that would be harmful instead of helpful, as Shakespeare reminds: "We, ignorant of ourselves, beg often our own harm." But knowing not what we should pray for as we ought, the interceding Spirit purifies the motives of our prayers.

The two-fold reference to the Spirit's intercession (8:26, 27) must be distinguished from Christ's intercession (8:34). How blessed we are having two powerful divine Intercessors!

> Hear me, for Thy Spirit pleads;
> Hear, for Jesus intercedes.

"The Spirit is in our hearts, prompting us to pray aright. The Saviour is in heaven, presenting our petitions."

W. C. Procter uses the following effective illustration:

"The Holy Spirit acts in spiritual matters as a solicitor does in our temporal affairs. He is a 'chamber Advocate,' who prepares our case. Christ is our 'Advocate with the Father' (I John 2:1), who 'appears in the presence of God for us' (Hebrews 9:24), 'Who also maketh intercession for us' (8:34)."

The Epistles make it clear that our need of the aid of the Spirit in prayer, on earth, is deep (Ephesians 6:18; Philippians 3:3 R.V.; Jude 20), just as the Saviour's representation in heaven is urgent. Between the two Intercessors there is unity of purpose and harmony of method. The two are One. Knowing the mind and will of Christ, the Spirit prompts us to pray accordingly.

> Nor prayer is made on earth alone —
> The Holy Spirit pleads;
> And Jesus, on the eternal Throne
> For sinners intercedes.

Prayer for Israel's Sake
(Romans 10:1; 11:26)

Brethren, my heart's desire and prayer to God for Israel is, that they might be saved. — Romans 10:1

What a prayer-burden Paul had for the nation of which he was part! Here he calls prayer his "heart's desire," which is equivalent to Montgomery's thought of prayer as "the soul's sincere desire." It is impossible to read Paul's writings without being impressed with his powerful intercessory ministry. Rejoicing over the salvation and progress of his converts, he never ceased to pray for them. Too often, preachers who bring souls into the light forget to continue in prayer for them that they might grow in grace (I Thessalonians 3:13). While Paul directed his prayer to God, he knew Christ existed in the form of God (14:6; Philippians 2:6-11) and could therefore have addressed either the Father or the Son.

A study of Paul's prayers also reveals that he often closed an argument with prayer (11:33-36). He was fond of beginning his epistles with thanksgiving and ending his arguments with doxology.

Prayer As a Continuing Ministry
(Romans 12:12)

Rejoicing in hope; patient in tribulation; continuing instant in prayer;   — Romans 12:12

Prayer is not mentioned among the gifts (12:6-8), yet no gift can be exercised without it. Paul was nothing if not practical. Those who continued stedfastly in prayer were not to forget to help needy saints (12:12) and to love impoverished enemies (12:20). Like his Master, Paul also believed in giving thanks for meat (14:6).

Prayer for Likemindedness
(Romans 15:5, 6, 30-33)

Now the God of patience and consolation grant you to be likeminded one toward another according to Christ Jesus: That ye may with one mind and one mouth glorify God, even the Father of our Lord Jesus Christ.
Now I beseech you, brethren, for the Lord Jesus Christ's sake, and for the love of the Spirit, that ye strive together with me in your prayers to God for me; That I may be delivered from them that do not believe in Judaea; and that my service which I have for Jerusalem may be accepted of the saints; That I may come unto you with joy by the will of God, and may with you be refreshed. Now the God of peace be with you all. Amen.   — Romans 15:5, 6, 30-33

With Paul, prayer-counsel-admonition-argument seem to flow in one silvery stream (15:1-13; II Thessalonians 2:13-16). With a true preacher's heart, Paul prays for his spiritual children that they may glorify the Master (15:5, 6; Philippians 1:11). Often he urged his friends to have fellowship with him in prayer for deliverance from evil men (15:30; II Thessalonians 3:1). What a grand conception of God Paul had! To him, He was One able to cope with any situation and need. The Apostle speaks of Him as the God of peace, of love, of hope, of consolation (15:33; 16:20; Philippians 4:9; I Thessalonians 5:23).

Prayer for Satan's Conquest
(Romans 16:20, 24, 25-27)

And the God of peace shall bruise Satan under your feet shortly. The grace of our Lord Jesus Christ be with you. Amen.
                                                            — Romans 16:20

Phebe, the highly-recommended succorer of many (16:1-3), and Appelles approved in Christ (16:10), as well as the other helpers of Paul must have been men and women of much prayer.

It is quite understandable that Paul, in the midst of "fightings without and fears within," should speak of God as the God of peace, and think of the time when all the bitterness of division the devil had caused, as well as the devil himself, would be conquered. Paul must have had the first promise of the overthrow of satanic powers in mind when he wrote this verse (16:20 with Genesis 3:15).

While we have the duplicated benediction (16:20, 24), the second one introduces one of the Apostle's masterly doxologies (16:25-27). What a fitting conclusion this doxology makes to an epistle extolling the power of the Gospel (1:16; 16:25)!

I Corinthians

The Church at Corinth, founded by Paul (Acts 18:1-18), provided the Apostle with many a heartache and headache. Yet in spite of the carnality of the Corinthian believers and the grief they caused Paul, he continues to instruct them in the deepest truths of the Christian faith. "Called to be saints," they must be shown how to become saintly.

While there are no actual prayers in this Epistle, it yet carries a few facets of prayer:

Prayer of Gratitude for the Church (I Corinthians 1:2-9). How different those fighting Corinthians would have been if only their standing and gifts in Christ had been translated into a holy state! What are the use of gifts unless there is grace to adorn them?

One of the ways of Paul (4:17) was certainly the way of prayer, a way the Corinthians had need to emulate.

Prayer and fasting form a safeguard against all the wiles of the devil (7:5). We can be made more than conquerors (10:12-14).

Prayer-order in Church is emphasized as the Apostle comes to deal with Church affairs (11:4, 5, 13). Corinthian Christian women apparently prayed in public. They prayed with their heads veiled, men with bare heads. It would seem as if there had been a movement among the sisters for emancipation from the custom of covered heads. His urging men to pray with uncovered heads, proves how Paul had completely overcome his old Jewish prejudice. It is still the custom for Jewish men to pray with covered heads.

While prayer is not mentioned among the gifts distinguishing the number of Christ's body from one another, it is nevertheless implied for no man can call Jesus *Lord*, in prayer, save by the Spirit (12:3).

Love. extolled in one of the noblest prose-poems ever written, was a truth the Corinthians, wrangling like children, sadly needed (13). For those who were so loveless, Paul wrote this hymn in praise of love.

Prayer, with understanding, finds a place in the counsel concerning "Prophecy" (14:14-17). As we are discovering, the Bible supplies us with ample guidance as to the most profitable method of praying with our understanding. Many prayers we offer are so thoughtless. If prayer is unintelligible, how can an unlearned person be expected to say *the* Amen (14:16)? Clumsy, confused or complicated prayers cannot edify a church. Thanksgiving dominates the prayers of Paul (14:18). The wife of Robert Louis Stevenson said of her renowned husband: "When he was happy, he felt impelled to offer thanks for that undeserved joy; when in sorrow or pain, to call for strength to bear what must be borne." It was so with Paul.

Public prayers should be simple, fervent and intelligible — which they are not if offered in Latin where English only is understood. Dr. John Hunter reminds us that, "The best prayers are those which express in simplest language the simplest needs, trusts and fidelities of the Christian soul." Orderly, intelligent prayers are never spoiled with verbosity or speculative theology. They express in simple and free language the deep needs, confessions and gratitudes of the soul. When Paul urged the saints to do all things decently and in order (14:40), he certainly included orderliness in prayer in such an exhortation.

Praise for final victory also found a place in Paul's prayers (15:28, 57). The Apostle's heart was kindled to rapture as he meditated upon the victory over sin and death, and the blessings received through Christ, especially for the subjugation of all things to the Father.

The benediction of Paul is somewhat unusual, being a mixture of love and judgment (16:21-24). An anathema is pronounced upon all who blatantly reject Christ, who, at His coming will punish them as they deserve (II Thessalonians 1:8, 9). For professed Christians who failed to bear the love-fruit of the Spirit, Paul has a final word about his undying love for them (II Corinthians 12:15).

II Corinthians

When Paul penned this Epistle he was enduring much physical weakness, weariness, pain and disappointment. Many spiritual burdens were also his yet he wrote courageously. What a prayer-agony he had for the sanctification of the unspiritual Corinthians (13:5-10)!

Prayer As a Benediction
(II Corinthians 1:2-4)

Grace be to you and peace from God our Father, and from the Lord Jesus Christ. Blessed be God, even the Father of our Lord Jesus Christ, the Father of mercies, and the God of all comfort; Who comforteth us in all our tribulation, that we may be able to comfort them which are in any trouble, by the comfort wherewith we ourselves are comforted of God.   — II Corinthians 1:2-4

Paul usually closes with a benediction. Here he opens his letter with one — and what a gracious benediction it was! God is addressed as the Father of Mercies and the God of all comfort (13:11). Mercy and comfort — both blessings are needed! Paul blesses God for the ministry of comfort he had been enabled to exercise.

Paul sought the prayers of others for success in his great task (1:11). What a source of encouragement it is to have prayer-partners! Without boasting, he refers to his watchings and fastings (6:5; 11:27). Many lonely vigils in intercession had been his for those less faithful than Titus (8:16). Paul also knew how to praise God from whom all blessings flow (9:11, 15).

What a sincere prayer Paul prayed for the sanctification of the Corinthians (13:5-7)! The greatest of all benedictions closes the Epistle (13:14).

Prayer for Removal of Thorn

(II Corinthians 12:7-10)

And lest I should be exalted above measure through the abundance of the revelations, there was given to me a thorn in the flesh, the messenger of Satan to buffet me, lest I should be exalted above measure. For this thing I besought the Lord thrice, that it might depart from me. And he said unto me, My grace is sufficient for thee: for my strength is made perfect in weakness. Most gladly therefore will I rather glory in my infirmities, that the power of Christ may rest upon me.　　　　　— II Corinthians 12:7-9

Paul was sustained in his tremendous task by words of divine cheer (12:8, 9). Although he besought the Lord three times about the removal of his thorn in the flesh, his desire was not granted. Assurance of the grace of Christ was given, and that was sufficient. Now he could glory in his weakness. While Paul prayed, day and night, for others, this is the only prayer he offered for himself — a prayer of a very modest and negative kind.

Paul's ungranted request brings us once again to the perplexing subject of unanswered prayer. Divine love permits pain and many prayers to go unanswered (John 11). Paul prayed once — twice — thrice, even as the Master he loved prayed thrice in the garden of Gethsemane, but his cry was apparently unheeded. But grace was his to bow in submission to God's will and joyfully resign himself to it.

> So weak is man
> So ignorant and blind, that did not God
> Sometimes withhold in mercy what we ask
> We should be ruined at our own request.

Dealing with the problem of prayers unanswered, Dr. F. B. Meyer asks: "What has become of so many thousands of our prayers? They were not deficient in earnestness; we uttered them with strong crying and tears. They were not deficient in perseverance; we offered them three times a day for years. They were not deficient in faith; for they have originated in hearts that have never for a moment doubted that God was, and that He was the rewarder of them that diligently sought Him. Still no answer has come. The argosies went forth to sea; but, like some ill-fated vessel, have never been heard of since. There was no voice, nor any to answer, nor, apparently, any to regard.

What is the history of these unanswered prayers? Some may say that they sought things which were not good — and this may explain some of the perplexity; but a better clue is given here: this was a prayer touchingly pathetic and earnest for something which was prompted by natural affection; for something which it was in the scope of God's love to give, for it was given; and yet the prayer was apparently unanswered. The answer was postponed and delayed.

When prayer is unanswered it may be that it has been mistaken in its object, and the mistake will be indicated by inability to continue praying and by the dying down of the desire in the soul. In other cases, especially when desire and faith remain buoyant and elastic, and still the answer comes not, God's intention is that in the delay the soul may be led to take up a position which it had never assumed before, but from which it will never be again dislodged. No praying breath is ever spent in vain. If you can believe for the blessings you ask, they are certainly yours. The goods are consigned, though not delivered; the blessing is labelled with your name, but not sent. The vision is yet for an appointed time; it will come and will not tarry. The black head may have become white, the bright eye dim, the loving heart impaired in its beating; but the answer must come at length. God will give the answer at the earliest moment consistent with the true well-being of the one He loves.

It may be hard to persevere in prayer when no response seems to come. The patience God makes possible, however, assures us that He has a wise and gracious reason for refusal, a refusal which will become plainer as the days go by, and which, once we know it, will arouse a song within our waiting, weary spirit. It has been said that "when our prayers make long voyages, they come back laden with richer cargoes of blessing"; and "when God keeps us waiting for an answer, He gives liberal interest for the interval!" Meantime, as we cry, "How long, O Lord, how long?" may grace be ours to sing with Lucy A. Bennett:

> As seemeth best to Thee, my God,
>   I ask no other thing;
> All care beside may be at rest,
>   For Thine is on the wing.
> If Thou, Eternal Lord, to-day
>   Should'st yield the choice to me,
> Then, most of all, my heart would pray,
>   "As seemeth best to Thee."

Galatians

In this argumentative book, in which Paul deals with a mutilated Gospel (1:7-9) and a compromising ministry (6:12, 13), we have no reference to prayer. He did, however, write to those Galatians who were tossed between two parties — those who represented the law, and others preaching liberty and license, about the beautiful fruits of the Spirit (5:22).

Paul knew what it was to go to a desert place apart (1:17), there to learn the secrets of his Lord (1:11, 12). The Apostle recognizes the Spirit's part in the adoption into sonship and our right to pray, "Abba, Father" (4:4-7). All that God was to Paul, He was through the Lord Jesus Christ (I Timothy 2:5). Paul's prayer-travail for their sanctification is expressed in delicate terms (4:19). While prayer is not mentioned among the fruits of the Spirit (5:22), it is nevertheless a very definite aspect of His fruits (Ephesians 6:18).

> The prayers I make will then be sweet indeed,
> If Thou the Spirit give by which I pray;
> My unassisted heart is barren clay
> That of its native self can nothing feed.

Galatians closes with the apostle's usual benediction (6:18).

Ephesians

This most impersonal of Paul's letters has been called "The Spiritual Alps of The New Testament." Because of its high spiritual order we would expect it to be rich in its prayer-content. The whole Epistle is fragrant with the prayer-ministry of Paul.

Prayer and the Believer's Position
(Ephesians 1:1-11)

Paul, an apostle of Jesus Christ by the will of God, to the saints which are at Ephesus, and to the faithful in Christ Jesus: Grace be to you, and peace, from God our Father, and from the Lord Jesus Christ. Blessed be the God and Father of our Lord Jesus Christ, who hath blessed us with all spiritual blessings in heavenly places in Christ: According as he hath chosen us in him before the foundation of the world, that we should be holy and without blame before him in love: Having predestinated us unto the adoption of children by Jesus Christ to himself, according to the good pleasure of his will, To the praise of the glory of his grace, wherein he hath made us accepted in the beloved. In whom we have redemption through his blood, the forgiveness of sins, according to the riches of his grace; Wherein he hath abounded toward us in all wisdom and prudence; Having made known unto us the mystery of his will, according to his good pleasure which he hath purposed in himself: That in the dispensation of the fulness of times he might gather together in one all things in Christ, both which are in heaven, and which are on earth; even in him: In whom also we have obtained an inheritance, being predestinated according to the purpose of him who worketh all things after the counsel of his own will: — Ephesians 1:1-11

Paul could say that Christ lived in him (Galatians 2:20). Is this not the reason why he possessed the spirit of Jesus and knew what it was to have the Master breathe new life into every phase of his ministry? Professor McFadyen points out one striking contrast between Jesus and Paul. "The direct reminiscences of the Master's teaching are not many; the intricate and impetuous prayers of Paul (1:16) are unlike the simple serenity of Jesus. But the contrast is so great because Paul is so completely overmastered and controlled by Jesus. He is at once His slave and freeman." Track down the manifold blessings of the Spirit in this benedictory-prayer. Its introduction, "Blessed be God" (1:3), is a phrase warm with the gratitude of Paul's heart for all the spiritual blessings of which God had made His saints the recipients. May we know what it is to join Paul in his breath-taking burst of praise!

Prayer for Perception and Power

(Ephesians 1:15-20)

Wherefore I also, after I heard of your faith in the Lord Jesus, and love unto all the saints, Cease not to give thanks for you, making mention of you in my prayers; That the God of our Lord Jesus Christ, the Father of glory, may give unto you the spirit of wisdom and revelation in the knowledge of him: The eyes of your understanding being enlightened; that ye may know what is the hope of his calling, and what the riches of the glory of his inheritance in the saints, And what is the exceeding greatness of his power to us-ward who believe, according to the working of his mighty power, Which he wrought in Christ, when he raised him from the dead, and set him at his own right hand in the heavenly places. . . .
                                                    — Ephesians 1:15-20

The acceptance of Christ as Saviour and fidelity to Him are the things that chiefly inspired Paul to thanksgiving (1:15). As the quality of the outward life depends entirely upon the inward spirit, Paul prays for the Ephesians that God would grant them a spirit of wisdom to realize all that was theirs in Christ, namely, the hope of His calling, the riches of His inheritance, the greatness of His power.

This great prayer has been called, "The Prayer of the Three *Whats*"

"What is the hope of His calling"

"What the riches of the glory . . ."

"What the exceeding greatness of His power . . ."

The many references to prayer in the life of Paul show what an enormous place it had in his life (1:16).

Paul's conception of Christ was so exalted that the worship of Him is certainly anything but inconceivable. What a privilege it is to belong to One who is far above all rule and authority, here and hereafter (1:20-23)! The Apostle's conception of God is also unique. Here he calls Him "The Father of Glory" (1:17).

Prayer As Access to God

(Ephesians 2:18; 3:12)

For through him we both have access by one Spirit unto the Father.
— Ephesians 2:18

In whom we have boldness and access with confidence by the faith of him.
— Ephesians 3:12

Each Person in the Trinity is concerned in the soul's approach to God. We have access to the Father, through the Son, by the Spirit. Separating the offices of the Blessed Three, we can say that —

God the Father is the Hearer and Answerer of Prayer (Matthew 7:11).

God the Son is the One who presents our imperfect prayers, perfumed with the incense of His perfect propitiation (Revelation 8:3, 4).

God the Spirit is the Sole Inspirer of true prayers, enabling us to approach the Throne of Grace with boldness (3:12).

Prayer for Inner Fulness

(Ephesians 3:13-21)

For this cause I bow my knees unto the Father of our Lord Jesus Christ, Of whom the whole family in heaven and earth is named, That he would grant you, according to the riches of his glory, to be strengthened with might by his Spirit in the inner man; That Christ may dwell in your hearts by faith; that ye, being rooted and grounded in love, May be able to comprehend with all saints what is the breadth, and length, and depth, and height; And to know the love of Christ, which passeth knowledge, that ye might be filled with all the fulness of God. Now unto him that is able to do exceeding abundantly above all that we ask or think, according to the power that worketh in us, Unto him be glory in the church by Christ Jesus throughout all ages, world without end. Amen. — Ephesians 3:14-21

Of this remarkable chapter as a whole, Mrs. A. T. Robertson writes: "There is a majestic prelude about the necessity of one Gospel for all men, and the glory of preaching that Gospel, then a prayer which is like the ocean breaking wave upon wave, on a quiet shore."

For a vivid exposition of this prayer of Paul's, the reader is directed to the chapter in Dr. Alexander Whyte's book dealing with it:

"If we do not learn to pray, it will not be for want of instruction and example. Look at Paul, as great in prayer as he is in preaching, or in writing Epistles . . . Kneeling on his prison floor (3:14), its dark roof becomes a canopy of light: and its walls of iron become crystal until Paul sees the whole family in Heaven and on earth gathered together in one, and all filled with the fulness of God. . . . The interceding Apostle concentrates and directs his prayer on one special kind of strength." Paul prayed that his Ephesian converts be strengthened with power in the inward man by the presence of the indwelling Christ (3:16).

The gracious presence of Christ within the heart is a privileged and pentecostal presence. It is the Spirit who forms Christ within us (Galatians 4:19). The phrase, "come to dwell," denotes "singleness of act" and points to an epoch in the soul's history. Once Christ enters, He enters to remain. The word *strengthen* is "endynamited" from which we have our modern term "dynamite." Who or what can resist the spiritual dynamite? No wonder the early saints had power to turn the world upside-down! May the apostle's prayer be answered on your behalf and mine!

Prayer and Inner Melody

(Ephesians 5:19, 20)

Speaking to yourselves in psalms and hymns and spiritual songs, singing and making melody in your heart to the Lord; Giving thanks always for all things unto God and the Father in the name of our Lord Jesus Christ.   — Ephesians 5:19, 20

The inner melody Paul writes about, expressing itself in gratitude to God, is dependent upon the experience of all the apostle writes about in the first part of the chapter, in which the walk and warfare of the believer are clearly set forth.

The Spirit-filled life knows how to give thanks for *all* things. Thanking Christ is equivalent to thanking God. The narrative indicates that Paul had in mind the giving of thanks *aloud* for the benefit of heaven. Is ours as a heart-melody revealing itself in outer songs of praise?

Prayer As a Warrior's Reserve

(Ephesians 6:18, 19)

Praying always with all prayer and supplication in the Spirit, and watching thereunto with all perseverance and supplication for all saints; And for me, that utterance may be given unto me, that I may open my mouth boldly, to make known the mystery of the gospel. . . .
                                                        — Ephesians 6:18, 19

While prayer is not specially mentioned as a part of the believer's armor, it is yet necessary for his protection. Armored knees cannot bend. Paul, urging the warrior to "pray always" practiced what he preached (Romans 1:9; I Thessalonians 2:13; II Thessalonians 1:11; Ephesians 1:6). Because prayer is an attitude as well as an act, we should constantly live in the spirit of devotion. While acts of prayer may be intermittent, the spiritual attitude should be incessant.

The cooperation and fellowship of the Spirit in prayer gives power to intercession. It is the Spirit who creates the conditions and atmosphere of prayer, assuring us of its acceptance on high. How we need to be taught about prayer in the Spirit! We cannot be men and women of prayer in the Biblical sense, until we are filled and controlled by the Spirit of supplication and grace. "All prayer" for "all saints" — what key phrases these are! Paul's benediction breathes his sincere desire for the saints (6:23, 24).

Philippians

What a joyful letter this is! Constant fellowship with God results in gladness of heart. Prayerless Christians are usually praiseless ones. To rejoice always (4:4) we must pray always (Ephesians 6:18).

Prayer As a Request for Joy
(Philippians 1:2-7)

Grace be unto you, and peace, from God our Father, and from the Lord Jesus Christ. I thank my God upon every remembrance of you, Always in every prayer of mine for you all making request with joy, For your fellowship in the gospel from the first day until now; Being confident of this very thing, that he which hath begun a good work in you will perform it until the day of Jesus Christ: Even as it is meet for me to think this of you all, because I have you in my heart; inasmuch as both in my bonds, and in the defence and confirmation of the gospel, ye all are partakers of my grace.　— Philippians 1:2-7

Paul prays that the Philippians may abound more and more in love (1:9). A loveless heart can never pray nor praise effectively. The apostle's frequent address appears to have been "My God" (1:3). He believed in the possessive pronoun. Is this spirit of blameless sincerity ours (1:10)? Paul prayed for men because he loved them. This was the secret of his passion in intercessory prayer. Many of his expressions are touching (1:7, 8). Because of the value of intercessory prayer, Paul solicited prayer on his own behalf (1:13; Ephesians 6:19; II Corinthians 1:11). Included in his prayer was a plea for a deeper understanding of the love of Christ (1:9-11). Love for as well as the love of Christ makes for the enlargement and enrichment of life. Because Paul's view of Christ was so exalted, his worship of Him was of the highest order (2:6-11).

Prayer and Peace of Mind
(Philippians 4:6, 7, 19-23)

Be careful for nothing; but in everything by prayer and supplication with thanksgiving let your requests be made known unto God. And the peace of God, which passeth understanding, shall keep your hearts and minds through Christ Jesus.　— Philippians 4:6, 7

Paul emulates the spirit of the Master when he urges the saints to be anxious in nothing (Matthew 6:8, 9). He also caught the Master's note of *thanksgiving*. To him, prayer and supplication should be blended with praise (4:6). This is why his Epistles begin with thanksgiving and end with doxology. Praise is not only a privilege, but a duty (4:4; I Thessalonians 5:18). Note the connection between "the peace of God" (4:7) and "the God of peace" (4:9). One of the blessed results of prayer is the flooding of the soul with an habitual peace and confidence, even in the midst of danger and difficult duty. Paul's three-fold cord is suggestive —

1. *Careful for nothing* (I Peter 5:7)
2. *Prayerful for everything* (Ephesians 6:18)
3. *Thankful for everything* (Psalm 50:23)

God has an amazing storehouse from which He is able to draw all that is necessary for the answering of our prayers. There are —

"The riches of His grace" (1:17) — an inexhaustible reservoir.

"The riches of His glory" (3:16) — such wealth is beyond us.

"The riches of His goodness" (Romans 2:4) — His goodness faileth never.

Colossians

Paul deemed it necessary to write to the Church at Colosse in order to combat two subtle forms of error, calculated to destroy the spirit of the fundamental Church there (1:3-8). Legality in the form of asceticism and a system of false mysticism were the perils Paul warned the Colossians against (2:14-23). Prayer, mighty Spirit-inspired prayer, can alone enable us to detect the wiles of Satan and preserve us from the perils of deflection from Christ, who, in this Epistle, is exalted as the Head of the Body, the Church (1:18).

Prayer As Praise for Loyalty

(Colossians 1:1-8)

We give thanks to God and the Father of our Lord Jesus Christ, praying always for you, Since we heard of your faith in Christ Jesus, and of the love which ye have to all the saints, For the hope which is laid up for you in heaven, whereof ye heard before in the word of the truth of the gospel; Which is come unto you, as it is in all the world; and bringeth forth fruit, as it doth also in you, since the day ye heard of it, and knew the grace of God in truth: As ye also learned of Epaphras our dear fellowservant, who is for you a faithful minister of Christ; Who also declared unto us your love in the Spirit.
— Colossians 1:3-8

Paul describes the Colossians as saints (1:2). All believers are saints, but some are more saintly than others. In this expressive salutation Paul rings the changes on the three Christian virtues of Faith, Hope and Love (1:4, 5, 8; I Corinthians 13:13). With the intercession of

Christ (John 17) before him, Paul prays that his converts might be kept from evil and perfected in the will of God (1:9). The chief causes of thanksgiving are the salvation of sinners (1:13) and for the fidelity of saints (1:3, 4, 9, 10). The reverence due to God, for all He is in Himself and in His works, pervades the prayers of Paul (1:15-18; 2:9). What unceasing prayer and praise we have in this chapter (1:9, 12).

Prayer for a Sevenfold Blessing

(Colossians 1:9-14)

For this cause we also, since the day we heard it, do not cease to pray for you, and to desire that ye might be filled with the knowledge of his will in all wisdom and spiritual understanding; That ye might walk worthy of the Lord unto all pleasing, being fruitful in every good work, and increasing in the knowledge of God; Strengthened with all might, according to his glorious power, unto all patience and longsuffering with joyfulness; Giving thanks unto the Father, which hath made us meet to be partakers of the inheritance of the saints in light: Who hath delivered us from the power of darkness, and hath translated us into the kingdom of his dear Son: In whom we have redemption through his blood, even the forgiveness of sins.

— Colossians 1:9-14

This further prayer serves to prove the value Paul attaches to intercessory prayer. How we have to confess our shortcoming in this respect! We pray plenty for our own needs, but the Church and the world have little place in our petition. We need large hearts, Calvary hearts, in order to pray for others.

1. The Occasion of Paul's Prayer (1:3)

Epaphras had been instrumental in founding the Colossian Church, and from him Paul heard the story of the progress of the converts. Now his joy leads him to renewed intercession on their behalf.

2. The Subject of Paul's Prayer (1:9)

The burden of his plea to God on the behalf of the Colossian converts was that "they might be filled with the knowledge of God's will." The word he used for "knowledge" implies "a thorough knowledge, excluding doubt and error." The reason why many of us are not filled with the knowledge of God's will is that we are so very much occupied with the knowledge of our own will.

3. The Purpose of Paul's Prayer (1:10)

Here is the lofty standard the apostle pleads. "That ye might walk worthy of the Lord unto all pleasing." Is it our aim to please God as Enoch did? Too often our walk and ways displease God, and consequently we are not fruitful in every good work. May Paul's prayer for Colosse be abundantly answered for you and me!

Paul suggests that prayer is a struggle (2:1). When we pray we battle against the foes of God and His truth. All the forces of hell are marshalled against Spirit-inspired prayer.

The combination of the peace of God and the word of Christ

(3:15, 16) is suggestive. When both rule within our hearts, then whatever we do is done in the name of the Lord Jesus (3:17). We can pray — daily live — suffer and toil, all in His name. Over life and death and eternity, we can engrave the ennobling and transfiguring inscription — "All in His Name."

For saints, who were tempted to split hairs over philosophy and rationalism, and who held their heads so high that they stumbled into sin, Paul's loving exhortation was most fitting (3:12).

Prayer Fellowship

(Colossians 4:2-4, 12, 17)

Continue in prayer, and watch in the same with thanksgiving;
Withal praying also for us, that God would open unto us a door
of utterance, to speak the mystery of Christ, for which I am also in
bonds: That I may make it manifest, as I ought to speak. . . .
Epaphras, who is one of you, a servant of Christ, saluteth you,
always labouring fervently for you in prayers, that ye may stand
perfect and complete in all the will of God. — Colossians 4:2-4, 12

A phase of the ministry we have received in the Lord (4:17) is that of prayer one for another. Epaphras prayed earnestly that the Colossians might stand perfect and fully assured in all the will of God (4:12). They were urged to continue stedfastly in prayer (2:7; 3:15, 17; 4:2). They were to pray that Paul might have boldness as he declared the Gospel (4:3).

What a commendable character Epaphras is! Although one of the lesser lights of the New Testament, he was a disciple and friend of the Apostle, and a noble Christian leader. He established the church in Colosse, his native place. He was a praying pastor who strove and labored in prayer. Paul says of him that he was *always* striving in prayer. What a gift of intercession was his! It is from "labouring fervently" (4:12) that the word "agony" comes, and is a term used for the extreme exertions of the wrestler. Horatius Bonar, in one of his hymns, has the arrestive phrase —

"With strong, great wrestlings souls are won."

What do we know of this type of prayer which Jacob experienced at Peniel (Genesis 32:26)? Such prayer is ever costly but always fruitful. As this Epistle, along with the three former ones, are known as "The Prison Epistles," the Prayers of Paul in all four books take on an added significance as we remember that his prayer-chamber was a foul-smelling prison cell.

I Thessalonians

It is to be expected in an Epistle prominently declaring the blessed truth of our Lord's return, that prayer has frequent mention. Paul in his exhortation to holiness of life, and consolation for sorrowing hearts, assures the Thessalonians of his unfailing intercession on their behalf.

Prayer of Remembrance

(I Thessalonians 1:1-3)

We give thanks to God always for you all, making mention of you in our prayers; Remembering without ceasing your work of faith, and labour of love, and patience of hope in our Lord Jesus Christ, in the sight of God and our Father.   — I Thessalonians 1:2, 3

It is not to be wondered at that Paul's converts grew spiritually. Behind them were his ceaseless intercessions for their growth in grace. Yet although the Thessalonians were Paul's "glory and crown" (I Thessalonians 2:19, 20), he administered some sharp admonitions as to common sense and steadiness. They had many admirable qualities but were somehow easily led astray in doctrine. Idlers were among them, for whom Satan found some mischief still, hence Paul's earnest prayers on their behalf. He interceded that their faith in Christ, devotion in His service, and love toward each other, might continue and abound. This chapter affords a fitting illustration of Scripture explaining Scripture (1:3 with 1:9, 10).

Prayer for a Return Visit

(I Thessalonians 3:9-13)

For what thanks can we render to God again for you, for all the joy wherewith we joy for your sakes before our God; Night and day praying exceedingly that we might see your face, and might perfect that which is lacking in your faith? Now God himself and our Father, and our Lord Jesus Christ, direct our way unto you. And the Lord make you to increase and abound in love one toward another, and toward all men, even as we do toward you: To the end he may stablish your hearts unblameable in holiness before God, even our Father, at the coming of our Lord Jesus Christ with all his saints.
     — I Thessalonians 3:9-13

How unique Paul was in his expression of gratitude for spiritual things! He thanked God for the salvation of the Thessalonians (2:13). He urged his converts to pray and praise unceasingly, pointing to his own example in this matter (5:17; 2:13; II Thessalonians 1:11).

In the portion before us he seeks prayer that he might return to Thessalonica for a season of ministry. During his first visit the Church was founded (Acts 20:2). Words seemed to fail Paul when he came to express his rapture at the thought of re-visiting the scene of revival.

Meantime, he prays that the saints may be sustained in the good life (3:13). Paul's unbounded interest in his converts is attested by the almost extravagant language in which he describes his intercessions for them. He felt that as their spiritual father, he was one of them, and prayed that he might become a more fit channel of blessing whenever he could visit them (3:11), under the guidance of God who would open up the way.

Paul's prayer that the Thessalonian Church might increase and abound in love, needs to be re-echoed today, when the greatest lack is that of love among ourselves. God grant His Church in these last days a baptism of divine love (John 13:35).

Prayer, Praise and Perfection

(I Thessalonians 5:17, 18, 23, 24, 28)

Pray without ceasing. In every thing give thanks: for this is the will of God in Christ Jesus concerning you. . . .
And the very God of peace sanctify you wholly; and I pray God your whole spirit and soul and body be preserved blameless unto the coming of our Lord Jesus Christ. Faithful is he that calleth you, who also will do it. . . .
The grace of our Lord Jesus Christ be with you. Amen.
— I Thessalonians 5:17, 18, 23, 24, 28

We shall find it helpful to gather together a few prayer-nuggets in this chapter. First of all, praise and prayer are paired together (5:16, 18).

What does it mean to "pray without ceasing," or "Be unceasing in prayer— praying perseveringly," as the Amplified translation has it? The phrase has to do with the habit rather than acts of prayer. Unceasing prayer for Peter's release (Acts 12:5), reads "prayer was made *earnestly* of the Church of God for him" (R.V.). The same thought is present in our Lord's Gethsemane prayer (Luke 22:44). The original words for "without ceasing" mean *stretched-out-edly*. The translators thought of prayer as stretched out a long time and represent the soul stretched out in the intensity of its earnestness toward God. Intense, earnest prayer then, is what Paul meant (Jeremiah 29:13; Romans 15:30). "Strive together with me in your prayers." *Agonizo,* is the word Paul used, and it implies the throwing of one's whole soul into their praying. Paul's last injunction was "Brethren, pray for us" (5:25). The apostle was always conscious of the duty and power of intercessory prayer. And his request for prayer was never selfish, but always for the progress of the Gospel. Such intercession is ever a test of sincerity and reality.

The prayer for the purity of the Thessalonians is one we need to pray for ourselves (5:23, 24). Paul prayed for the entire sanctification of those he had led to Christ. In spirit, soul and body, they had to be wholly sanctified. All they were, and possessed, had to be brought under divine control. The Apostle makes it clear, however, that what God commands, He graciously supplies. He calls us to holiness of life (I Peter 1:15, 16), and His "commands are His enablings." Augustine gave us the blessed prayer —

"Give what Thou commandest, then command what Thou wilt." It is thus that verse 24 follows verse 23, "Faithful is he that calleth you (to holiness), who also will do it." Holiness, then, like our salvation, is a gift and becomes ours by faith.

II Thessalonians

This further letter to the Thessalonian Church was necessary to correct false impressions arising from a letter as from Paul that the persecutions from which they were suffering were those of "the great and terrible day of the Lord," from which they had been taught to expect deliverance by "the day of Christ, and our gathering unto him" (2:1). Most prayerfully, Paul instructs the troubled Thessalonians in the distinction between "the day of Christ" and "the day of the Lord."

Prayer for Worthiness of Calling

(II Thessalonians 1:3, 11, 12)

We are bound to thank God always for you, brethren, as it is meet, because that your faith groweth exceedingly, and the charity of every one of you all toward each other aboundeth. . . .
Wherefore also we pray always for you, that our God would count you worthy of this calling, and fulfil all the good pleasure of his goodness, and the work of faith with power: That the name of our Lord Jesus Christ may be glorified in you, and ye in him, according to the grace of our God and the Lord Jesus Christ.
— II Thessalonians 1:3, 11, 12

We can call this a "multum in parvo" (much in little) prayer. In brief sentences Paul could press sublime truths. His words were never wasted. Faith and love among Christians was something to be thankful for (1:2, 3). Paul prayed that the Thessalonians might be fruitful believers, thereby glorifying the Saviour who had died for them (1:12). If we are to be among the number glorifying Him when He comes (1:10), He must be glorified in us *now* (1:12).

Prayer for Comfort and Stability

(II Thessalonians 2:13, 16, 17)

But we are bound to give thanks alway to God for you, brethren beloved of the Lord, because God hath from the beginning chosen you to salvation through sanctification of the Spirit and belief of the truth: . . .
Now our Lord Jesus Christ himself, and God, even our Father,

which hath loved us, and hath given us everlasting consolation and good hope through grace, Comfort your hearts, and stablish you in every good word and work.   — II Thessalonians 2:13, 16, 17

God and Christ are equal in the comfort, strength and guidance they make possible for the saints (2:16; I Thessalonians 3:11). Paul was a master at blending prayer and counsel in all his letters. Here we have his exhortation to "stand fast," sandwiched between a beautiful thanksgiving and a still more beautiful petition.

Prayer for the Word and Protection

(II Thessalonians 3:1-5)

Finally, brethren, pray for us, that the word of the Lord may have free course, and be glorified, even as it is with you: And that we may be delivered from unreasonable and wicked men: for all men have not faith. But the Lord is faithful, who shall stablish you, and keep you from evil. And we have confidence in the Lord touching you, that ye both do and will do the things which we command you. And the Lord direct your hearts into the love of God, and into the patient waiting for Christ.   — II Thessalonians 3:1-5

The benedictory prayers of Paul afford the reader a rich study (3:5, 16). As the shadows gather, inward strength is needed, which can only come from the indwelling Christ (Ephesians 3:16, 17). It is only thus that we are prepared to meet Christ at His coming, and experience an undisturbed peace as we await such a blissful event (3:5-16). The saints still need deliverance "from unreasonable and evil men" (3:1).

Paul prayed that the Thessalonians might have "peace always by all means." The prophet prayed that the saints might be kept in "perfect peace" or *peace, peace,* as it should read — a double peace: peace before the throne and a peace within the heart. E. H. Hopkins never tired of pointing out that there is a peace *connected with Christ's rule* as well as a peace *connected with Christ's work.* Is the prayer of both apostle and prophet being answered on our behalf? Have we experienced peace of conscience because of our acceptance of Christ as Saviour? Are we enjoying peace of heart because of His indwelling life? Peace is God's will for us, and Christ's gift to us. He, Himself, is our Peace (Ephesians 2:14).

I Timothy

With the expansion of the Church it became necessary to advise Churches as they were formed, on all matters relating to decorum, doctrine and discipline. Thus, the key-verse of this Epistle is the one where Paul urges the saints to behave themselves in the house of God (3:15). While there are no prayers here apart from one or two benedictory prayers, we have a few pertinent references to prayer.

We have, of course, Paul's usual salutation — a trinity in unity — Grace, Mercy, Peace (1:3).

Prayer as thanksgiving for salvation and service (1:12-16). Paul follows his acknowledgment of the power to save him, the chief of sinners, with a most remarkable doxology (1:17). With all humility, the Apostle marvels at the grace of God in putting him into the ministry.

Prayer for those in authority (2:1-4). National leaders, particularly in these critical days, need to be upheld by our prayers. Paul never forgot that he was a citizen of this world, and that citizenship, like every other privilege, imposed responsibilities. The scope of intercession is universal. References like Ezra 6:10 and Jeremiah 29:7 are associated with prayers for heathen rulers. How much more should we pray for nominal or actual Christian rulers.

Pulpit prayers for royalty, presidents, and ministers of state are formal, monotonous and meaningless rubric. Rulers are prayed for every Sunday, but no one is any better, because no one is in earnest. What a difference it would make, however, in the lives of national leaders, if only there were hundreds in the countries they represent praying with importunity for them, that they might reign and rule in righteousness. Coleridge wrote about —

> Praying for all in those appointed phrases,
>   Like a vast river, from a thousand fountains,
> Swoll'n with the waters of the lakes and mountains
>   The Pastor bears along the Prayers and Praises
> Of many souls in channel well-defined —
> Yet leaves no drop of Prayer or Praise behind.

Prayers are necessary for those in position of authority "that we may lead a tranquil and quiet life in all godliness and gravity."

Prayers are to be offered without wrong feelings (2:8). With uplifted hands, a recognized gesture of prayer, and "everywhere," prayer must ascend out of a clean heart. God will not place His gifts in dirty hands, neither will He answer prayers out of a doubting or spiteful heart.

Prayer's sanctifying influence (4:4, 5). Here again, prayer and praise are combined. "No healthy recognition in prayer of the natural basis of life can be unworthy." The whole earth is the Lord's, and the fulness thereof. Every creature is good, and may be sanctified through prayer (4:4). The God who loads our tables with His providential bounties surely deserves our thanks (I Corinthians 10:31; Colossians 3:17).

Prayer as a profitable ministry for widows (5:5). Widows occupy a prominent place in the lives of a few Bible saints. We will never know what the church owes to its lonely, godly, praying widows. The mark of a true widow, says Paul, is her continuance in supplications and prayers night and day. With what a marvelous description of the Lord, Paul closes (6:15, 16)!

II Timothy

This further letter to Paul's "dearly beloved son," is taken up with the walk and witness of the believer in a day of apostasy and declension. If I Timothy shows us the ideal church every pastor ought to have, this Second Epistle describes the ideal pastor every church should have.

Prayer for Timothy's Ministry

(II Timothy 1:2-7)

I thank God, whom I serve from my forefathers with pure conscience, that without ceasing I have remembrance of thee in my prayers night and day; Greatly desiring to see thee, being mindful of thy tears, that I may be filled with joy; When I call to remembrance the unfeigned faith that is in thee, which dwelt first in thy grandmother Lois, and thy mother Eunice; and I am persuaded that in thee also. Wherefore I put thee in remembrance that thou stir up the gift of God, which is in thee by the putting on of my hands. For God hath not given us the spirit of fear; but of power, and of love, and of a sound mind.   — II Timothy 1:3-7

Timothy learned from his godly mother, not only love for the Scriptures (3:14, 15), but also the value of prayer. How he must have appreciated the ceaseless prayers of Paul on his behalf! Having a somewhat timid and sensitive nature, he needed the apostle's heartening word about the mighty Holy Spirit (1:6-8).

If only elder Christians could pray for young believers, as Paul prayed for young Timothy, what spiritual progress they would make. The more we pray for young Christians, the better we shall understand them, share their outlook, sympathize with them, and influence them for God and His glorious work.

Prayer for the House of Onesiphorus

(II Timothy 1:6-18)

The Lord give mercy unto the house of Onesiphorus; for he oft refreshed me, and was not ashamed of my chain: — II Timothy 1:16

There are those who have wrongly surmised that we have here in Paul's prayer for the house of Onesiphorus, an argument for prayers for the dead. Such, however, is not the case. There is little doubt that when Paul wrote this Epistle Onesiphorus had recently died, and full of gratitude for the devotion of such a faithful friend, Paul prayed not for *Onesiphorus,* but for his *house.*

Onesiphorus often visited Paul in prison and cheered his heart by his open intimacy for Paul the prisoner, and what Paul prays for now that Onesiphorus is dead, is not for mercy or deliverance from purgatory on the other side, but that at the Judgment Seat of Christ, Onesiphorus might be rewarded for his kindness to Paul.

The Romish doctrine of praying for the dead, based upon this passage, is utterly false and contrary to a divine revelation as to our contact with the dead. Once those we have prayed for, and with, leave this earth, they pass beyond the influence of our prayers.

Prayer for False Friends
(II Timothy 4:14-18)

Alexander the coppersmith did me much evil: the Lord reward him according to his works: Of whom be thou ware also; for he hath greatly withstood our words. At my first answer no man stood with me, but all men forsook me: I pray God that it may not be laid to their charge. Notwithstanding the Lord stood with me, and strengthened me; that by me the preaching might be fully known, and that all the Gentiles might hear: and I was delivered out of the mouth of the lion. And the Lord shall deliver me from every evil work, and will preserve me unto his heavenly kingdom: to whom be glory for ever and ever. Amen. — II Timothy 4:14-18

Stephen's death Paul had witnessed, and which doubtless was used by the Spirit for Paul's conversion, left an indelible impression upon his mind. How could he forget that blood-stained face upturned to heaven as he prayed for the forgiveness of his murderers! Here Paul emulates such an example, as he prays that God will have compassion on those who had treated him so cruelly. He did not vindicate himself against the evil treatment of Alexander, nor pour out anathemas upon those who had forsaken him. Paul prayed that God would vindicate His servant. His heart was full of praise as he realized the abiding presence of Christ amid the cruel desertion of so-called friends. No wonder he closes with the precious benediction, "The Lord Jesus Christ be with thy spirit" (II Timothy 4:21, 22). He has promised never to leave us alone (Hebrews 13:5).

Titus

I Timothy, II Timothy, and Titus are known as "The Pastoral Epistles," seeing that all three are taken up with the divine and due order of the church. Of the three Epistles, Dr. C. I. Schofield says, "Their permanent use lies in this two-fold application. On the one hand to churches grown careless as to the *truth* of God — on the other, to churches careless as to the *order* of God's house."

Titus is another book with no recorded prayers. It has the usual salutation of Paul (1:4). In Timothy, Paul urges us to pray for those in authority (I Timothy 2:1, 2). Titus tells us to be subject to those who have the rule over us (3:1). The customary benediction closes the brief letter (3:15).

Philemon

In this matchless story of a runaway slave, who, like Titus and Timothy had also been brought to Christ through Paul's labors, we have no actual prayers. There are, however, one or two glimpses of the range of prayer's effectiveness.

Prayer of thanksgiving. Both Philemon and Onesimus were Paul's converts, and that was much for which to praise God. The faith and love of Philemon were also something else for which to be grateful. As the slave-owner had a warm place in Paul's affections, he likewise occupied a conspicuous place in his prayers. Can we not imagine the apostle pleading with God to graciously incline the heart of the master to receive his runaway slave, now a brother in the Lord (16)? We have no doubt whatever that the intercessions of Paul led to a reconciliation between Philemon and Onesimus.

Prayer is asked for a return from prison confinement (22). Knowing the power of intercessory prayer, Paul urges Philemon to do two things: pray for his, Paul's, release and prepare to house and care for him once out of prison.

The Epistle begins with the accustomed salutation (3) and ends with the apostolic benediction (25), of which there are some 26 in the New Testament.

Hebrews

This wonderful Epistle, every sentence of which bears the authorship of the Spirit, and with a message, not for one age but all ages, is the New Testament Commentary on its Old Testament counterpart, *Leviticus.* In the latter book we have "Shadow" — here is "Substance."

The Epistle was addressed to Jewish believers who were in danger of going back to Judaism. These persecuted and wavering Hebrews in a primitive age had started well (6:10; 10:33, 34), but exhibited a tendency to pause or journey back to a forfeited position (5:11, 12). We cannot remain static in the Christian life. We either progress or retreat. Those addressed had not striven after a deeper spiritual experience. They had remained in a state of spiritual immaturity (5:12-14) and were therefore in danger of being carried away by erroneous doctrines (13:9). Thus they are urged to go on to know the Lord in a richer measure in this "Epistle of Christian Progress" (6:1).

While volumes have been written over the authorship of Hebrews, we see no reason to doubt that it came from the mind of Paul, if not from his pen. Campbell Morgan said that in the book we have "Paul's thinking in Luke's language." While there are so many aspects we could consider, our main search in these studies is for its prayer-content.

Phrases like "come boldly" (4:6), "come unto God" (7:19, 25), "way into the holiest" (9:8; 10:9), "a new and living way" (10:20), "draw near" (10:22), "cometh to God" (11:6), "now come unto Mount Sion" (12:22), all speak of the privilege of union with God and of a privileged communion with Him. Such phrases remind us that —

> There is a place of quiet rest,
> Near to the heart of God.
> A place where sin cannot molest,
> Near to the heart of God.

Prayer As Praise for Creation

(Hebrews 1:10-12)

And, Thou, Lord, in the beginning hast laid the foundation of the earth; and the heavens are the works of thine hands: They shall perish; but thou remainest; and they all shall wax old as doth a garment; And as a vesture shalt thou fold them up, and they shall be changed: but thou art the same, and thy years shall not fail.

— Hebrews 1:10-12

Here the excellence, eternity and exaltation of Christ are eloquently emphasized! This outburst of praise also reveals how the writer was immersed in Old Testament Scriptures (compare Psalms 45:7; 102:25-27; 110:9).

Prayer for Mercy and Favor

(Hebrews 4:16)

Let us therefore come boldly unto the throne of grace, that we may obtain mercy, and find grace to help in time of need. — Hebrews 4:16

While there is need of grace, let us bless God that there is always grace for the need. Sincerity and boldness must characterize those who approach the throne of grace (4:16; 10:2-19). That God will hear prayers answering out of clean hearts is proven by the fact that this throne is one of *grace*. If it were any other kind of throne, we could not dare to approach.

Prayer and the Ministry of Christ

Did not Jesus Himself declare, "No man cometh unto the Father but by me" (John 14:6)? How this truth is written large over this Epistle!

Prayer in the days of His flesh (5:7, 8). While such a statement covers our Lord's entire sojourn among men, "strong crying and tears" suggest Gethsemane. We have the haunting refrain —

"The beautiful garden of prayer."

Beautiful! Those blood drops were far from beautiful, as Jesus prayed in agony. His prayer was saturated with tears. Are ours? It may be that many of our prayers never reach heaven because they are too dry. The writer is careful to add that Jesus *was heard* because of His godly fear (5:7).

Prayer continues in heaven (7:24, 25; 9:24). As intercession was one of the chief features of our Lord's earthly life, it is certainly the perpetual occupation of His heavenly life (Romans 8:34; I Timothy 2:5; I John 2:1). Thus it is Biblically correct to sing "I have a Saviour who's pleading in glory." His mighty heart still pours "a tide of ceaseless prayer." Prayer is central in heaven. Samuel Chadwick wrote, "That our Lord should need to pray in the days of His flesh is a mystery of humiliation; that He should need to make intercession in heaven is a mystery of glory." But how blessed it is to know that our ascended Lord is the Priest-King at the right hand of God.

The two great essentials in prayer are — faith in the fact of God ("He that cometh to God must believe that He *is*"): and faith that He is the God who hears and answers diligent prayer ("He is the Rewarder of them that diligently seek Him" — 11:6).

Since His ascension over nineteen hundred years ago, Christ has been in continual intercession for them who have been in intercession for themselves and for other men on earth. He slumbers not nor sleeps. How we should praise Him for His unceasing, importunate intercession in the Glory!

> He Who, for men, their Surety stood,
> And poured on earth His precious blood,
> Pursues in Heaven His mighty plan,
> The Saviour and the Friend of Man.

Prayer for the Outworking of God's Will

Venturing nigh, through the blood of Jesus, prayer must have a practical result in our lives. Hands must be uplifted in intercession (12:12). It is only thus that we can be in subjection to God and live (12:9). Having boldness to enter the holiest of all, a similar boldness is ours in confession (13:6). Christ takes the prayers of the earthly altar and adds to them the fires of the heavenly, and they become acceptable and effective through His name (13:15; Revelation 5:8; 8:3). The request, "Pray for us," is definitely Pauline (13:18; I Thessalonians 5:25). Paul prayed for his converts and sought their prayers on his behalf.

> I pray for you, and yet I cannot frame
> In words the thousand wishes of my heart.
> It is a prayer only to speak your name
> And think of you when we are far apart.
> God has not need of words. He knows our love,
> And though my lips are mute, I bow my head
> And know He leans to listen from above,
> And understand the things that are not said.
> For love is prayer — and so prayers for you
> Mount upward unto Him eternally —

They are not many, and they are not few,
All are as one that ever seems to be
Thus do I pray for you, and cannot say
When I begin, or when I cease, to pray.

Prayer for Perfectness

(Hebrews 13:20, 21)

Now the God of peace, that brought again from the dead our Lord Jesus, that great shepherd of the sheep, through the blood of the everlasting covenant, Make you perfect in every good work to do his will, working in you that which is wellpleasing in his sight, through Jesus Christ; to whom be glory for ever and ever. Amen.

— Hebrews 13:20, 21

What an inspiration and a benediction this prayer for perfection contains! All Paul's wishes for the Hebrew Christians are swallowed up in this consuming passion — to do His will. This is the simple yet sublime end he emphasizes. The apostle prayed thus because the glory of God demands it, and our own happiness depends upon conformity to the will of God; and because obedience to His will is essential to our holiness and usefulness. It is sadly possible to be doing God's *work* and yet not be doing His *will*.

Let us not be afraid of the word "perfect" used here. Many of us are more afraid of the doctrine of perfection than we are of the practice of imperfection. The word is translated "fitted" (Romans 9:22), "prepared" (Hebrews 10:5), "framed" (Hebrews 11:3), "restore" (Galatians 6:1), "mend" (Mark 1:19). At the heart of the term there is the idea of being "fit." This is what the apostle prays for here. He wanted those Hebrew converts to be "fit," ready to do God's will or to suffer for it. He had in mind "not a perfection of doing, but a *perfection to do*."

"There are four pillars of strength on which this temple of Paul's prayer rests," says E. W. Moore:

1. The covenant of grace provides it.

Progress, power and perfection can only be ours "through the blood of the everlasting covenant." We cannot get out of our sin apart from the blood (12:14) — we cannot get anything out of heaven except through the blood (13:20) — we cannot get into heaven when we come to leave this earth without the blood (13:12, 14).

2. The Resurrection of Christ exemplifies it.

The power that raised Jesus from the dead is at our disposal, and pledged to work in us to will and to do of God's good pleasure.

3. The indwelling of Christ insures it.

By His Spirit, He is working *in* us. Without this inner impulse and force we cannot accomplish His plan and purpose.

4. The God of peace undertakes it.

Among the divine titles, this is one of the most blessed. Dwelling in peace, God wants His children to be like Himself. *Peace* means "to join," and this is what God is working for, to harmonize all discordant elements in, and among, His people, bringing them into oneness with Himself and with each other.

The benediction closing the Epistle is a striking evidence of its Pauline authorship (13:25; II Thessalonians 3:18). "The salutation of Paul with my own hand, which is the token in every Epistle: so I write —

The grace of our Lord Jesus Christ be with you all
Amen."

James

Scholars may be divided about the value of this book; Martin Luther had little use for it. He called it "a strawy epistle." We hold it contains the simple, unspoiled teaching of Jesus. In it, we have the belief that behaves. The aspect of the Epistle concerning us is that of the real importance of prayer it stresses. While there are no actual prayers in the book, we have a good deal of instruction regarding the privilege and power of prayer.

James, the brother of our Lord, and the writer of this Epistle, was known as "Camel-knees" by the early Church. "When they came to coffin him," says Alexander Whyte, "it was like coffining the knees of a camel rather than the knees of a man, so hard, so worn, so stiff were they with prayer, and so unlike any other dead man's knees they had ever coffined." Because "Camel-knees" knew how to "pray in his prayers," let us humbly meditate upon what James has to say about such a holy art.

Prayer for Wisdom
(James 1:5-8, 17)

If any of you lack wisdom, let him ask of God, that giveth to all men liberally, and upbraideth not; and it shall be given him. But let him ask in faith, nothing wavering. For he that wavereth is like a wave of the sea driven with the wind and tossed. For let not that man think that he shall receive any thing of the Lord. A double minded man is unstable in all his ways. . . .
Every good gift and every perfect gift is from above, and cometh down from the Father of lights, with whom is no variableness, neither shadow of turning.   — James 1:5-8, 17

Whether simple or educated, we can approach God without fear or timidity and ask for the divine wisdom God alone can bestow (1:17) and which is so distinct from the acquired wisdom of the world (3:15, 17).

Prayer for wisdom must be accompanied by faith, nothing doubting (1:6-8). The double-minded man is unstable in all his ways. With doubts surging to and fro like a storm-tossed sea, how can he expect to receive anything from the Lord? Faith is a requisite condition of prayer. James has a poor opinion of a "faith" that does not work itself out in practice. The faith the Apostle calls for is no mere intellectual assent to certain propositions (the demons have this kind of faith — 2:19) — but the out and going of the whole personality in prayer. Intellectual assent merely, cannot save a person, nor merit anything from God (2:14-17).

First of all then, we must *ask* (John 16:23, 24), and secondly ask in *faith*. Faith sets the sails and settles the way we go. What we are to ask for is *wisdom*, which all of us lack. The noble prayer of Solomon for heavenly wisdom was answered, just as our prayer will be (I Kings 3:11). God is the Source of answered prayer. Behind all we seek is the Giver Himself (1:17).

The praying-tongue is the bridled tongue (1:26; 3:8, 9). "The taming of the untamable tongue is no small part of a man's religion." Prayer, however, can keep the tongue from harmful uses. James also believed that "he prayed best who loveth best" (2:14-20).

Prayer That Misses the Target
(James 4:2, 3)

Ye lust, and have not: ye kill, and desire to have, and cannot obtain: ye fight and war, yet ye have not, because ye ask not. Ye ask, and receive not, because ye ask amiss, that ye may consume it upon your lusts.   — James 4:2, 3

When we pray in the Spirit all supplications are purified of selfishness and worldliness. The only true prayers are those that can live in the white, searching light of His presence (4:3). Two thoughts are present in this rebuke of James. We receive not because we ask *not,* and because we ask *amiss.* If we expect God to answer us, we must ask aright. He takes into account, not only *what* we want but *why* we want it. Many things make answered prayer impossible.

Sin shuts us out of His presence (Psalm 66:18)

Unbelief meets with a deaf ear (Hebrews 3:19; 11:6)

Unforgiveness hinders answers to prayer (Matthew 5:23, 24)

Unstable minds cannot receive anything from God (James 1:7)

A condemning conscience cuts the line of communication
(I John 3:19-22)

Self-seeking motives prevent answered prayer (James 4:3)

Have we been guilty of praying with a wrong motive? The word "amiss" means, "with wrong intent." We can ask for good things with the wrong motive. What folly it is to make God the instrument of *our* desires, rather than subjecting all our desires to *Him*.

Among other hindrances to prayer James names *pugnacity*. Wars and fightings come from passions let loose, from covetousness and cupidity, from unfulfilled desire (4:1, 2). Men try to get what they need by force. But what they truly need can only come from God.

Pride is perhaps the greatest hindrance to answered prayer (4:6).

If we would have God hear and answer prayer, we must be subject to Him (4:7; Proverbs 3:34). Arrogant vaunting of one's own abilities nullifies praying. We must draw nigh to God in all humility (4:8). The only way up (4:10) is down.

Prayer That Prevails

(James 5:13-18)

Is any among you afflicted? let him pray. Is any merry? let him sing psalms. Is any sick among you? let him call for the elders of the church; and let them pray over him, anointing him with oil in the name of the Lord: And the prayer of faith shall save the sick, and the Lord shall raise him up; and if he have committed sins, they shall be forgiven him. Confess your faults one to another, and pray one for another, that ye may be healed. The effectual fervent prayer of a righteous man availeth much. Elias was a man subject to like passions as we are, and he prayed earnestly that it might not rain: and it rained not on the earth by the space of three years and six months. And he prayed again, and the heaven gave rain, and the earth brought forth her fruit.   — James 5:13-18

What a revelation this portion affords of the power of prayer! Prayer operates in any realm. Distress drives men to God and He graciously undertakes (5:13). James was never guilty of false mysticism. His was the practical approach, even to things spiritual. We are to draw nigh to God, not merely for our own sakes but also for others. "Pray one for another" (5:16). Prayer must be offered for the sick and afflicted (5:14, 15). Life, whether glad or sad, should be conspicuous for praise (5:13). The use of means is not contradictory to insistence upon faith. The prayer of faith to save the sick was accompanied by an anointing with oil (5:14). Belief in the power of the Name must accompany prayer (5:14).

What a lot there is in the narrative at this point to encourage our faith in the efficacy of earnest prayer! Let us examine the arrestive phrase James uses about the effectual fervent prayer of a righteous man availeth much (5:16). *Effectual* means "to labor hard" or "energize," implying that the energetic prayer of a godly man has great efficacy. Here are various translations of this verse —

"The supplications of a righteous man availeth much in its working" (R.V.).

"The prayer of a righteous man has great power in its effects" (R.S.V.).

"The prayer of a righteous man is of great force when it is energized" (Rendel Harris).

"The earnest (heartfelt, continued) prayer of a righteous man makes tremendous power available — dynamic in its working" (The Amplified New Testament).

Applied to Elijah, as the verse is, we are reminded of the supernatural power of prayer. The prophet of old, whose prayers were miracles of power, never discussed natural laws, for he knew that God's power could transcend the known laws of His world. In Elijah, prayer was the greatest force on earth and his prayers prevailed seeing they were energized prayers. "The prayer of faith," says Bishop Porteus, "moves the Hand of Him that moveth all things." Of James' word about the efficacy of prayer, Dean Scott comments, "This is a special zeal, a special emotion and fervour of heart, an agony of prayer such as takes heaven by storm."

What do we know of such urgency in prayer? "He prayed earnestly" (5:17) means, "he prayed in his prayer." He did not *say* a prayer — his soul went out in prayer. Too often, our prayers are shot like arrows into the wide and vague expanse of air; there is no mark set before them to which they are winged. We ask for nothing definite or practical. We ask for nothing — and get what we ask for. We do not have particular petitions to plead before the King.

> Pray, pray, pray — no help but prayer,
> A breath that fleets beyond this iron world,
> And touches Him who made it.

Let it not be forgotten that righteousness is certainly a prime condition for the man who prays. It is the prayer of the *righteous* man that is powerful in its working. Our own self-righteousness or confident self-approval are of little avail. Cleanness of hands, heart, and action must accompany prayer (5:1-6). Saying without doing (1:22), or favoritism (2:1, 9), weakens prayer's effectiveness. Prayer must begin with the yearning of the heart, express itself in noble speech, and inevitably issue in unselfish activity for others. This is the prayer that can heal the sick, open the heavens, win back the erring child of God (5:19, 20). The legacy of such prayer is of priceless worth.

That James practiced what he preached is proved by the reputation he had of being a man of prayer. His knees, the Early Church declared, were worn as hard as a camel's, through his frequent kneeling. When he died a martyr's death in Jerusalem at the hands of cruel persecutors, the bystanders said, "The just James is praying for you."

So it has always been. It is impossible to over-estimate the effect of a righteous man's prayers. The saintly and strong servants of the Lord knew how to pray without ceasing.

Martin Luther's ejaculation helped him to witness his good confession before Kaiser and Pope.

John Welsh spent eight hours out of the twenty-four in communion with God, and therefore was equipped and armed to dare and to suffer.

David Brainerd rode through the endless American woods praying, and so he fulfilled a long time in a short time, and all the trumpets sounded for him on the other side.

John Wesley came out from his seclusion to change the face of England by his prayers and preaching.

In response to the mighty prayers of prophets and saints of old, they received a mandate from heaven. To them, prayer had all the purchase upon the throne which is accorded to it in the Word of God, so they exercised "the slender nerve" of prayer "that moveth the muscles of Omnipotence."

I Peter

That the distinctive note of this Epistle is preparation for victory over suffering is evident from the fact that "suffering," the key-word of the book, occurs some fifteen times. Peter had proved prayer to be a wonderful avenue of consolation amid his manifold trials.

Prayer of Gratitude for an Inheritance

(I Peter 1:3, 4)

Blessed be the God and Father of our Lord Jesus Christ, which according to his abundant mercy hath begotten us again unto a lively hope by the resurrection of Jesus Christ from the dead, To an inheritance incorruptible, and that fadeth not away, reserved in heaven for you. . . .   — I Peter 1:3, 4

Peter gives thanks for the hope of immortality which is inspired by the resurrection of Jesus. Here on earth, people are sometimes made rich by an inheritance left them by relatives. Every saint has a glorious, abiding inheritance reserved in heaven. The Hand that bled to provide such a heritage is keeping it for us.

Prayer is included in the spiritual sacrifice, acceptable to God through Christ (2:5, 9). Peter confirms the teaching of our Lord and also of Paul (2:13-15; with Matthew 22:21; Romans 13:1, 2).

Prayer in the Married State

(I Peter 3:7-12)

Likewise, ye husbands, dwell with them according to knowledge, giving honour unto the wife, as unto the weaker vessel, and as being heirs together of the grace of life; that your prayers be not hindered.
                                        — I Peter 3:7

Unless husband and wife are heirs together of the grace of life, and treat each other as becometh saints, how can they expect their prayers to have any weight with God? Many family prayers are hindered, that is, of no avail, because of the lack of consideration, sympathy, unselfishness on the part of one toward another. Is there anything in your home life clogging your prayers? God's ears are ever open to hear these prayers (3:12), ascending from sanctified hearts. Alexander Whyte says: "God cannot resist a parent's prayer when it is sufficiently backed up with a parent's sanctification."

Prayer-Watch

(I Peter 4:7)

But the end of all things is at hand: be ye therefore sober, and
watch unto prayer. — I Peter 4:7

As the end draws near, we should be found, not only praying at
set seasons, but creating fresh opportunities for prayer. We must
learn how to watch before we pray — watch as we pray — watch after
we pray. We should ever be on the outlook for motives and occasions
to pray, and for helps in prayer. Sir Thomas Browne, the eminent
surgeon, confessed: "I cannot go to cure the body of my patient, but
I forget my profession and call unto God for his soul." Our prayers
will not ramble nor be haphazard if they set out from a fixed and
definite mark and journey toward a fixed and definite goal.

Prayer for Christian Stability

(I Peter 5:10, 11)

But the God of all grace, who hath called us unto his eternal glory
by Christ Jesus, after that ye have suffered a while, make you
perfect, stablish, strengthen, settle you. To him be glory and dominion for ever and ever. Amen. — I Peter 5:10, 11

The exhortation to wrap around ourselves the apron of humility
(5:5, 6) must be followed if we would experience the strength and
stability God can bestow. The phrase, "make you perfect," actually
means, "mend your nets." Jesus found His first disciples "mending
their nets" (Matthew 4:21). We cannot very well fish with a torn net.
The devil is out to destroy our usefulness, this is why we must be
vigilant (5:8). If we realize that our net is torn, and in need of repair,
is it not heartening to know that "the God of all *grace*" is the
Repairer? Whole nets mean peace now (5:14) and a reward hereafter (5:4).

II Peter

Although the Church was not so very old when Peter penned the
Second Epistle of his, apostasy was beginning to make itself felt.
Suffering for the truth's sake was the lot of almost all of the apostles,
but prayer and the praises of God (1:4) were the unfailing resources
of the faithful. Peter's martyrdom was near when he wrote his
heartening book (1:13, 14).

Prayer was offered for the multiplication of grace and peace (1:2).
While the Epistle contains no record of offered prayers, the closing
benediction addressed to Christ (3:18). Peter asks that those who are
rightly taught (3:17) might grow *in* grace. We must be *in* it before
we can grow *in* it. We cannot grow *into* grace. Grace is the unmerited
favor we receive when Christ is received as Saviour. He is Grace

(Titus 2:11; John 1:14). Once He is accepted, we grow *in* Him. It is only in the school of prayer that we can grow both in grace and knowledge. Are we growing Christians?

I John

In his Gospel, John shows us the way into the family of God (3:7; 14:6). In his Epistles, the Apostle emphasizes life in the family (1:9; 2:1). Love for God, love for each other, love for the world permeates this most intimate of the inspired writings. While no repeated prayers are to be found in this book, prayer is everywhere implied.

Prayer is fellowship with the Trinity (1:3, 6 with II Corinthians 13:14).

Prayer is confession of sin (1:8-10; 2:1). As there are one or two religious groups strongly advocating public confession of sin as a means of grace, this may be the place to deal with such a matter. Confessing publicly unsavory sins is most unhealthy and certainly unwarranted. Confession should never be more public than the sin committed. Why drag *private* sins into *public* prayer and confession? Says Alexander Whyte: "You cannot do it. You dare not do it. And when you do it, under some unbearable load of guilt, or under some overpowering pain of heart — you do yourself no good, and you do all who hear you real evil — you offend them."

If we have sins to confess, let us humbly turn to Him who is our Advocate on high (2:1, 2), whose blood can make the vilest clean. Then, as He not only forgives our sins, but forgets them (Hebrews 8:12; 10:17), let us not be foolish enough to drag them out and gloat over them in public.

Prayer is efficacious when offered by an obedient heart (3:20-24). Condemned hearts can never approach God with boldness (3:21 with Hebrews 10:19). Loveless hearts cannot offer warm prayers (3:17). Two things are necessary to answered prayer — obedience and pleasing God (3:22).

Prayer according to the divine Will (5:14-16).

We cannot have boldness and confidence as we come to God unless there is unquestioned obedience to His will (Hebrews 10:19). The sequence here is a simple one: "Ask according to his will, and God will hear" (5:16). "When God hears, he will answer our prayers" (5:15). There is no need to be in doubt as to the nature of God's will. His Word reveals His will. Then we have the inner ministry of the Holy Spirit, who, when there is an obedient heart, makes clear the desire and purpose of God.

There is no limit as to what we can pray for. "Whatsoever." The only limit is "anything according to His will." Whatever is not of that "sweet beloved will of God" is not worth praying about and is certainly not good for us. The whole purpose of prayer is the accomplishment of His known will (Colossians 1:9).

II John

An aged apostle, could, in all humility, call himself "The Elder" (v. 1.). John must have been around 90 years of age when he sent this letter either to a Christian lady and her family, or to a known church and its members.

The theme of this precious gem of a letter expresses John's joy at the true faith exhibited by those he had met. He lovingly entreats them to continue in Christian love and to resist to the end all false teachers coming their way.

Apart from the expressive salutation (v. 3.), so apostolic in nature, the letter carries no aspect of prayer. Full joy would be experienced when John met his friends "face to face" (v. 12; III John 4). Moses was privileged to meet God "face to face" (Genesis 32:30; Exodus 33:11). Ere long it will be our joy to see our blessed Lord "face to face" (I Corinthians 13:12), and when we do what rapture will be ours. Meantime, as we linger amid the shadows, we can experience the sweet intimacy of fellowship with Him, who although unseen, is not unknown (John 20:29).

III John

This Third Epistle, from the pen of the writer of the first two Epistles and written about the same time, was addressed to godly Gaius, possibly a pastor of a small church in Asia Minor. It is a letter of commendation and condemnation. Both Gaius and Demetrius are commended for their virtues, and Diotrephes condemned for his vices. Conceited, proud men like Diotrephes are not praying men. The word "pre-eminence" appears twice in the New Testament. Here, applied to Diotrephes, who loved to have pre-eminence among men (v. 9.), and then in Colossians, where we read that Christ has pre-eminence in all things (Colossians 1:18). The one pre-eminence destroys the other. If Christ is pre-eminent in all things, then the spirit of Diotrephes cannot live.

Gaius' spiritual prosperity, and the good report of all Demetrius enjoyed, suggest that there was a life of unbroken fellowship with God. Malicious words do not come out of praying lips (v. 10). Praying men must live in constancy with their supplications.

Jude

In dramatic terms Jude describes the cause, course and cure of apostasy. We are delivered from all contentiousness as we contend for the Faith (v. 3.), if we pray in the Spirit (v. 20). The seven-fold duty characterizing true believers (20-23), must be taken together: Building, Praying, Keeping, Looking, Pitying, Saving, Hating. Building ourselves up in the most holy faith does not exempt us from praying in the Spirit, or from any of the other obligations.

When we pray in the Spirit, the Spirit makes intercession for us. The Spirit in my spirit prays. We are never men or women of prayer in the best sense, until we are filled with the Spirit (Ephesians 5:18, 19).

> The praying Spirit breathe,
> The watching power impart,
> From all entanglements beneath,
> Call off my anxious heart.

Praying in the Spirit is profitable at all times —
1. It provides a live contact with divine forces (Daniel 9:23)
2. It acquaints God with all our needs (Philippians 4:4, 7)
3. It calls God to our immediate aid (I Kings 8:36-39)
4. It enables God to remove all obstacles (Matthew 17:19-21)
5. It is always crowned with heaven's success (Acts 4:31; John 14:13; Daniel 10:10-21)
6. It causes the forces of hell to tremble (Ephesians 6:10-20; James 4:7)
7. It frees men from the shackles of sin (Luke 22:40)

In this we rest, no prayer inspired by the Spirit and prayed in the Spirit ever goes unanswered. If we do not live to see the answer, nevertheless, in God's good time the answer will be given.

Prayer in the Spirit is effective no matter where, or by whom, it is offered. Such praying is never bound by any language barrier. One of the wonders of our wonderful God is His ability to hear and understand the mighty volume of Spirit-inspired prayer ascending to Him from all over the world. Think of the millions who are offering prayer at this moment in their own native tongue. There are thousands upon thousands of languages, dialects and accents, yet God, the marvelous Linguist, can listen to a thousand and one languages at the same time, understand each native cry, and answer every praying heart in their own tongue.

The God who created man's ability to speak, and gave our first parents an original language, then at Babel broke up that one tongue into many (Genesis 11:1-7), and who at Pentecost made it possible for foreigners, far and near, to hear the Gospel in their own language (Acts 2:6), has no difficulty in listening to the cries of men in their native tongues. When the redeemed out of all nations are in heaven, one new tongue will be theirs, to magnify the Lamb throughout eternity.

Revelation

What a dramatic unfolding of God's final program this climatic book of the Bible presents! Here, as nowhere else, do we find God's blue print of the future. Certainly the book is highly symbolic, but it contains no symbol that is not explained for us in other parts of the Bible. As it is the only book to which there is attached a blessing if we will read it (1:3), let us pursue it with our main theme of prayer in mind.

In this dramatic book of last things we have two unusual salutations (1:3, 4-6). Adoration is a form of prayer and *Revelation* abounds in adorations (1:7; 4:8; 5:11, 12, etc.). The book is jubilant with songs of praise to God and to the Lamb. God, as the Lord God Almighty, is magnified (4:8; 16:7). Praises are offered with voices that can be heard (5:12; 7:10).

Prayer As Praise to the Lamb for Redemption

(Revelation 5:9)

And they sung a new song, saying, Thou art worthy to take the book, and to open the seals thereof: for thou wast slain, and hast redeemed us to God by thy blood out of every kindred, and tongue, and people, and nation;   — Revelation 5:9

This jubilant song of the glorified has three notes in it —
1. The note of redemption — "Thou didst purchase us unto God with thy blood."
2. The Note of Royalty — "Thou madest us to be unto our God a kingdom."
3. The Note of Consecration — "And priests."

Prayer As Golden Incense

(Revelation 5:8; 8:3)

And when he had taken the book, the four beasts and four and twenty elders fell down before the Lamb, having every one of them harps, and golden vials full of odours, which are the prayers of the saints.   — Revelation 5:8
And another angel came and stood at the altar, having a golden censer; and there was given unto him much incense, that he should offer it with the prayers of all saints upon the golden altar which was before the throne.   — Revelation 8:3

The smoke of incense ascends with the prayers of the redeemed unto God. What a different smoke is associated with those who worship the Beast (14:11)! Harps and vials are related (5:8). Harps represent *praises,* and vials, our *prayers.*

The comparison of prayer with incense is common in the Old Testament. "Let my prayer be set forth before thee as incense" (Psalm 141:2). The greatest care was taken in the composition of the incense because of its spiritual significance. "The true odours are the heart-prayers of God's children . . . Every prayer which broke out in a sob from an agonizing heart, every sigh of the solitary and struggling Christian, every groan of those groping Godward, mingles here with the songs of the happy and triumphant."

In that golden censer (8:3) are many of the prayers of saints awaiting an answer. Matthew Henry has the forcible remark: "Prayers of faith are *filed* in Heaven; and, though not presently answered, are not *forgotten*."

Prayer of the Martyred Host

(Revelation 6:10; Psalm 13:1, 2)

And they cried with a loud voice, saying, How long, O Lord, holy and true, dost thou not judge and avenge our blood on them that dwell on the earth?   — Revelation 6:10

The martyred souls beneath the altar cry aloud for vengeance on those who had tortured and slain them, and as the One, "true and righteous" in His judgments (16:7), He will repay (Romans 12:19). The thoroughness and terribleness of divine judgment upon Satan and the gigantic forces of evil and cruelty, stirred the heart of John (6:10).

Prayer of the Gentile Host

(Revelation 7:9-12)

After this I beheld, and, lo, a great multitude, which no man could number, of all nations, and kindreds, and people, and tongues, stood before the throne, and before the Lamb, clothed with white robes, and palms in their hands; And cried with a loud voice, saying, Salvation to our God which sitteth upon the throne, and unto the Lamb. And all the angels stood round about the throne, and about the elders and the four beasts, and fell before the throne on their faces, and worshipped God, Saying, Amen: Blessing, and glory, and wisdom, and thanksgiving, and honour, and power, and might, be unto our God for ever and ever. Amen.   — Revelation 7:9-12

Out of "The Great Tribulation" (7:14), a multitude no man could number are to come, washed in the blood of the Lamb. There is no salvation apart from His blood. As the Church will be complete at the return of the Lord for her (I Thessalonians 4:17), this unnumbered redeemed host will not be a part of that mystic fabric — the Church of the living God. Nevertheless, they will be in the presence of the Lamb singing their eternal praises.

Prayer of the Elders

(Revelation 11:15-19)

And the four and twenty elders, which sat before God on their seats, fell upon their faces, and worshipped God, Saying, We give thee thanks, O Lord God Almighty, which art, and wast, and art to come; because thou hast taken to thee thy great power, and hast reigned. And the nations were angry, and thy wrath is come, and the time of the dead, that they should be judged, and that thou shouldest give reward unto thy servants the prophets, and to the saints, and them that fear thy name, small and great; and shouldest destroy them which destroy the earth.   — Revelation 11:16-18

Prostration, falling upon faces (11:16), is the position of worship. Gratitude from worshiping hearts is ever acceptable to God (Hebrews 13:15). By the four-and-twenty elders we can understand the Church of God in all ages. The twelve tribes represent the redeemed out of Israel — the twelve Apostles represent the New Testament Church Jesus bought with His blood.

Prayer of Moses

(Revelation 15:3, 4)

And they sing the song of Moses the servant of God, and the song of the Lamb, saying, Great and marvellous are thy works, Lord God Almighty; just and true are thy ways, thou King of Saints. Who shall not fear thee, O Lord, and glorify thy name? for thou only art holy: for all nations shall come and worship before thee; for thy judgments are made manifest.   — Revelation 15:3, 4

The Old Testament provides the background of this triumphant song (Exodus 15:1). But such a song is also, "the song of the Lamb." Along with Moses, He is to extol God as the One "Great and marvelous" in all His works, "just and true" in all His ways, and as "the King of the Ages" (15:3). What a difference there is in what mouths give utterance to (14:5 with 13:6; 16:11)!

Prayer of the Glorified Saints

(Revelation 19:1-10)

And after these things I heard a great voice of much people in heaven, saying, Alleluia; Salvation, and glory, and honour, and power, unto the Lord our God: For true and righteous are his judgments: for he hath judged the great whore, which did corrupt the earth with her fornication, and hath avenged the blood of his servants at her hand. And again they said, Alleluia. And her smoke rose up for ever and ever. And the four and twenty elders and the four beasts fell down and worshipped God that sat on the throne, saying, Amen; Alleluia. And a voice came out of the throne, saying, Praise our God, all ye his servants, and ye that fear him, both small and great. And I heard as it were the voice of a great multitude, and as the voice of many waters, and as the voice of mighty thunderings, saying Alleluia: for the Lord God omnipotent reigneth. Let us be glad and rejoice, and give honour to him: for the marriage of the Lamb is come, and his wife hath made herself ready. And to her was granted that she should be arrayed in fine linen, clean and white: for the fine linen is the righteousness of saints.

— Revelation 19:1-10

In this graphic prayer of praise with its four Hallelujahs, "the writer sees, if only with the eye of faith, what Jeremiah had longed to see, and was perplexed and grieved because he could not see — the manifest vindication of the moral order, the indisputable triumph of the Kingdom of God." What a paean of triumph these verses contain!

> Glory, honor, praise and power,
> Be unto the Lamb for ever;
> Jesus Christ is our Redeemer.
> Hallelujah! Hallelujah!
> Hallelujah! Praise the Lord.

Prayers Ending the Bible

(Revelation 22:17, 20)

And the Spirit and the bride say, Come. And let him that heareth say, Come. And let him that is athirst come. And whosoever will, let him take the water of life freely. . . .
He which testifieth these things saith, Surely I come quickly. Amen.
Even so, come, Lord Jesus.   — Revelation 22:17, 20

The only recorded prayer of the Holy Spirit is in the cry, "The Spirit . . . say, Come thou" (22:17). Even then His prayer is united with the Church, for Whose completion He is responsible. The united prayer is addressed to Jesus, who three times over is found saying: "I come quickly" (22:7, 12, 20). The prayer of the Spirit through the Bride is for Jesus to redeem His promise and come. We have already seen that the Spirit is engaged in a ministry of intercession (Romans 8:25). As the Spirit Divine, He attends our prayers.

The last prayer in the Bible is the one John prayed, "Even so, come, Lord Jesus" (22:20), and which has echoed throughout the ages. This verse is one of the most remarkable in Holy Writ, seeing that in such small compass it has —

> The last Promise of the Bible —
> "Surely, I come quickly"
> The last Prayer of the Bible —
> "Even so, come, Lord Jesus."

Thus the last promise and the last prayer are taken up with "the blessed hope" (Titus 2:13). What a glorious end to a glorious revelation! May we crave —

> Faith's patience imperturbable in Thee
> Hope's patience till the long-drawn shadows flee.

As we await the passing of the shadows, the sufficiency of His grace will be ours (22:21). Then, when we see His face (22:4), no need will be ours to express. Prayers, as we now know them, will be no longer necessary. Nothing but praise will escape our glorified lips. Till His name is in our foreheads (22:4), however, we will have need to sing —

> Come, my soul, thy suit prepare,
> Jesus loves to answer prayer;
> He Himself has bid thee pray.
> Therefore will not say thee nay.

Bibliography

Bibliography

Burgess, F. J., and Proudlove, D. B., *Watching unto Prayer* (London: Lutterworth Press), 1944.

Chadwick, Samuel, *The Path of Prayer* (London: Hodder and Stoughton), 1931.

Ellicott, Charles John, *Ellicott's Commentary on the Whole Bible* (Grand Rapids: Zondervan Publishing House), 1954.

Goodrich, C. A., *Bible History of Prayer* (London: Case, Tiffany, Hartford), 1850.

Gordon, S. D., *A Miscellany of Quiet Talks* (London: Pickering and Inglis), 1940.

Hastings, James, *Dictionary of the Bible* (London: T. and T. Clark), 1909.

King, Guy H., *Prayer Secrets* (London: Marshall, Morgan and Scott), 1940.

Macintyre, David M., *The Prayer Life of Our Lord* (London: Marshall, Morgan and Scott), 1920.

McFadyen, J. E., *The Prayers of the Bible* (London: Hodder and Stoughton), 1906.

Moore, E. W., *The Pattern Prayer Book* (London: Marshall, Morgan and Scott), 1900.

Procter, W. C., *The Principles and Practice of Prayer* (London: Oliphants, Ltd.), 1927.

Rixon, Mary E., and Gordon, Mary C., *Prayers Recorded in the Bible* (New York: Loizeaux Brothers), 1930.

Robertson, A. T., *Along the Highway of Prayer* (Grand Rapids: Zondervan Publishing House), 1951.

Talling, M. P., *Effective Prayer* (New York: Fleming Revell), 1902.

Thomas, Alfred, *Prayers of the Old Testament* (London: Allenson and Co.), 1945.

Torrey, R. A., *The Power of Prayer and the Prayer of Power* (Grand Rapids: Zondervan Publishing House), 1955.

Vaughan, C. J., *The Prayers of Jesus Christ* (London: Macmillan and Co.), 1891.

Whyte, Alexander, *Lord, Teach Us to Pray* (London: Oliphants. Ltd.), 1935.

Scripture Index

Scripture Index

294